Understanding
Green Revolutions

Understanding Green Revolutions

Agrarian change and development planning in South Asia

Essays in honour of B.H. Farmer
edited by
Tim P. Bayliss-Smith and Sudhir Wanmali

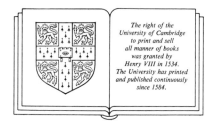

Cambridge University Press

Cambridge
London   New York   New Rochelle
Melbourne   Sydney

Published by the Press Syndicate of the University of Cambridge
The Pitt Building, Trumpington Street, Cambridge CB2 1RP
32 East 57th Street, New York, NY 10022, USA
296 Beaconsfield Parade, Middle Park, Melbourne 3206, Australia

© Cambridge University Press 1984

First published 1984

Printed in Great Britain at the University Press, Cambridge

Library of Congress catalogue card number: 83–14434

British Library cataloguing in publication data
Understanding Green Revolutions.
1. Agriculture – South Asia – Addresses, essays, lectures
I. Bayliss-Smith, Timothy P.
II. Wanmali, Sudhir III. Farmer, B.H.
338.1'0954   HD2065.3

ISBN 0 521 24942 2

Contents

List of contributors	*page*	viii
Preface *Sir Joseph Hutchinson*		ix

I Understanding Green Revolutions: an overview

1 The agricultural revolution in Western Europe 1
  David B. Grigg

2 Land reform as a pre-condition for Green Revolution in Latin America 18
  Clifford T. Smith

3 Frogs and farmers: the Green Revolution in India, and its murky past 37
  Christopher J. Baker

4 Agrarian change and the Merchant State in Tamil Nadu 53
  Barbara Harriss

II Agrarian change at village level

5 Agrarian policy and agrarian change in tribal India 87
  Stuart Corbridge

6 Migration and agrarian change in Garhwal District, Uttar Pradesh 109
  William Whittaker

7 Agricultural development in Tamil Nadu: two decades of land use change at village level 136
  Robert W. Bradnock

8 Energy flows and agrarian change in Karnataka: the Green Revolution at micro-scale 153
  Tim P. Bayliss-Smith

9 Income and wealth disparities in a land settlement of the Sri Lanka Dry Zone 173
  Vidyamali Samarasinghe and S.W.R. de A. Samarasinghe

10 Agrarian structure and agricultural innovation in Bangladesh: Panimara village, Dhaka district 194
  Steve Jones

11	A structural analysis of two farms in Bangladesh *Graham P. Chapman*	212

III Development planning and agrarian change

12	Rural-based models for rural development: the Indian experience *Sudhir Wanmali*	253
13	Planning and agrarian change in East Africa: appropriate and inappropriate models for land settlement schemes *Deryke G.R. Belshaw*	270
14	Metropolitan expansion in India: spatial dynamics and rural transformation *K.V. Sundaram and V.L.S. Prakasa Rao*	280
15	Green Revolution and water demand: irrigation and ground water in Sri Lanka and Tamil Nadu *C.M. Madduma Bandara*	296
16	Social organisation and irrigation: ideology, planning and practice in Sri Lanka's settlement schemes *John C. Harriss*	315
17	Environmental hazard and coastal reclamation: problems and prospects in Bangladesh *David R. Stoddart and John S. Pethick*	339
18	Beyond the Green Revolution: a selective essay *Robert Chambers*	362
	Index	381

Contributors

Christopher J. Baker,
55 Soi Patanaves,
Sukumwit 71,
Bangkok,
Thailand

Tim P. Bayliss-Smith,
Department of Geography,
University of Cambridge,
Cambridge CB2 3EN,
England

Deryke G.R. Belshaw,
School of Development Studies,
University of East Anglia,
Norwich NR4 7TJ,
England

Robert W. Bradnock,
Department of Geography,
School of Oriental and African Studies,
Malet Street,
London WC1E 7HP,
England

Robert Chambers,
The Ford Foundation,
55 Lodi Estate,
New Delhi 110003,
India

Graham P. Chapman,
Department of Geography,
University of Cambridge,
Cambridge CB2 3EN,
England

Stuart Corbridge,
Department of Geography and
    Geology,
The Polytechnic,
Queensgate,
Huddersfield HD1 3DH,
England

David B. Grigg,
Department of Geography,
University of Sheffield,
Sheffield S10 2TN,
England

Barbara Harriss,
Nutrition Unit,
London School of Hygiene and
    Tropical Medicine,
Gower Street,
London WC1E 7HT,
England

John C. Harriss,
School of Development Studies,
University of East Anglia,
Norwich NR4 7TJ,
England

Sir Joseph B. Hutchinson,
St John's College,
Cambridge,
England

Steve Jones,
Department of Geography,
University of Cambridge,
Cambridge CB2 3EN,
England

CONTRIBUTORS

C.M. Madduma Bandara,
Department of Geography,
University of Peradeniya,
Peradeniya,
Sri Lanka

John S. Pethick,
Department of Geography,
University of Hull,
Cottingham Road,
Hull HU6 7RX,
England

V.L.S. Prakasa Rao,
Centre of Economic and Social Studies,
Hyderabad 50004,
Andhra Pradesh,
India

S.W.R. de A. Samarasinghe,
Department of Economics,
University of Peradeniya,
Peradeniya,
Sri Lanka

Vidyamali Samarasinghe,
Department of Geography,
University of Peradeniya,
Peradeniya,
Sri Lanka

Clifford T. Smith,
Centre for Latin American Studies,
University of Liverpool,
86–88 Bedford Street South,
Liverpool L69 3BX,
England

David R. Stoddart,
Department of Geography,
University of Cambridge,
Cambridge CB2 3EN,
England

K.V. Sundaram,
Planning Commission,
Government of India,
Parliament Street,
New Delhi 110002,
India

Sudhir Wanmali,
International Food Policy Research
   Institute,
1776 Massachusetts Avenue NW,
Washington DC 20036,
USA

William Whittaker,
Department of Geography,
University of Cambridge,
Cambridge CB2 3EN, England

The editors would like to thank Michael Young and Dennis Blackburn of the Geography Department, University of Cambridge, for their assistance with maps, diagrams and photographs.

Preface

SIR JOSEPH HUTCHINSON

This volume is a tribute by his students and colleagues, to B.H. Farmer on his retirement as Reader in South Asian Geography and Director of the Centre of South Asian Studies in the University of Cambridge. The essays it contains are evidence of the esteem and affection in which he is held. Moreover their content bears the stamp of his critical and encouraging guidance. It is not the function of a preface to enlarge upon them. They speak for themselves.

This is, however, an opportunity to record something of Farmer's influence on geographical studies in Cambridge. My first experience of his work came when I was asked to review his *Pioneer Peasant Colonisation in Ceylon*. Coming from East Africa where the term 'dry zone' would be interpreted as an area with an uncertain rainfall averaging perhaps 400 mm a year, I was immediately struck by his use of 'dry zone' to embrace areas with a very high (though seasonal) rainfall. It was an indication of his powers as a writer and a teacher that I found his exposition conclusive, and thereby widened my concept of the relations between climate, season and soil.

I regarded Farmer at that time as a specialist on Sri Lanka. The opportunity for him to widen his horizons, and to develop research and teaching interests throughout the subcontinent of India, came in 1961 with the allocation to Cambridge University of resources to develop modern studies of some of the major cultural regions of the world. To Ben Farmer fell the task of establishing the Centre of South Asian Studies. The resources available were not large, and had to be carefully husbanded. There was no definition of the range and scope of 'modern studies' so Farmer had to draw one up. Those in the University who were interested in South Asia were scattered in several Faculties, and had no meeting place. Indeed in many cases they did not know each other. Farmer set out first to make the Centre a meeting ground. He then organised lectures and seminars that brought together, not only those working in Cambridge, but also South Asian specialists in London and the southeast, and visiting scholars from overseas. He built up a library, so planned as to complement the South Asian holdings in the University Library and in Faculty libraries. And he was himself constantly available to scholars, graduate students, and above all visitors from abroad.

All human studies are rooted in the past, and the wise scholar takes history fully into account. Modern studies have the advantage over ancient history that much of the basic data on their roots is still extant, though scattered and often unknown or inaccessible. Farmer established an archive. With an enterprising and devoted assistant, and with support from grant-giving bodies, he acquired much valuable material that would otherwise have been lost. The South Asian archive is now a research resource of great value.

A Study Centre is more than a focus for academics pursuing their individual research interests, and Farmer set about planning a research project that would be sponsored by the Centre, and would be carried out by a team brought together by the Centre. He chose a study of the agricultural changes that have become known as the 'Green Revolution', and he decided to compare their impact in two areas, North Arcot in Tamil Nadu in India and Hambantota and Monergala Districts in Sri Lanka. Farmer had been increasingly concerned about the lack of intimate, practical experience of agricultural change that characterised the debate then raging on the nature and the significance of the Green Revolution. He felt that there was a great need for study in the villages and in the fields of the impact of changing technology on peasant communities. So he invited men and women from among his old students and colleagues to join him in studying these changes by means of detailed fieldwork in the two areas.

He solicited financial support from a wide range of grant-giving bodies, and he himself coordinated the work from Cambridge, with an occasional visit to the field. It was characteristic of him that he brought his team together (in December 1974) to discuss their findings and plan the outline of a publication, when the fieldwork was still incomplete. This short conference gave form and substance to the research findings, and enabled the team members to see what each still needed to do to complement the work of colleagues. The book which resulted from this meeting was published in 1977; it remains one of the few integrated studies at village scale of the various social, economic and environmental changes that are taking place in rural South Asia.

Ben Farmer has contributed widely to the discipline of Geography – as writer, reviewer, editor and teacher. In research the authority of his leadership is clear from the extent to which his team project in Tamil Nadu and Sri Lanka is reflected in the essays that follow. For this wide-ranging scholarship we honour him.

J.B. Hutchinson

St John's College,
Cambridge
October 1982

PART I
Understanding Green Revolutions: an overview

1 The agricultural revolution in Western Europe

DAVID B. GRIGG

Much of the literature that has described the agriculture of the less developed countries has emphasised the backwardness of their farming methods. But it is worth noting that both their food and total agricultural output has increased rapidly since 1950; indeed it has not only increased as rapidly as output in the developed countries in this period, but more rapidly than in Europe at any time before 1950. In Europe agricultural output has also grown at a high rate since 1950, and many have described this as an agricultural revolution. The achievements of Afro-Asia and Latin America, in contrast, have been damned with faint praise. The first reason for this is that population has grown nearly as rapidly as food output in this period so that there have not been dramatic improvements in per caput food supplies, although a smaller proportion of the population have inadequate diets than in 1950 (Grigg, 1981, 1982a). A second reason is that the Green Revolution, which many regard as the principal cause of increased output, is alleged to have also caused landlessness and increasing income inequality in rural Asia. A third reason for confusion is the lack of any agreed methodology for measuring the nature and pace of agricultural change in these regions. This problem is not new. The agricultural revolution in Western Europe has also been the subject of much controversy. The aim of this chapter is to show why the past has been so variously interpreted.

Use of the term agricultural revolution

The term agricultural revolution has been used to describe events in many parts of the world and at different times (Ross & Tontz, 1942). It has, for example, been applied to changes in English agriculture in the period since 1945 (Slater, 1961; Duckham, 1959). But its use goes further back. L.T. White believed the years between the sixth and the ninth centuries saw an agricultural revolution in Western Europe (White, 1962). Georges Duby (1954) put a similar change between the late eighth and the twelfth centuries, and believed there were no further improvements in farming methods before the mid-eighteenth century. Lord Ernle thought the agricultural revolution in England began in 1760 (Ernle, 1968) and was completed by 1820; his views influenced three generations of historians. In the 1960s an alternative view was put forward by Eric Kerridge (1967) who argued that new methods were adopted in the late sixteenth century that transformed English agriculture; this revolution was complete by 1767 and there was no comparable progress thereafter. Although it is now widely agreed that new farming methods were introduced in England in the mid-seventeenth century, there are few who believe that there was little progress after 1767 (E.L. Jones, 1967). F.M.L. Thompson (1968) has argued that the English agricultural revolution had four stages. Beginning in the sixteenth century there was a shift from subsistence to commercial farming; then the agricultural revolution proper involved the extinction of the open fields and the introduction of new rotations and livestock improvements and was largely complete by 1815.

The period between 1820 and 1880, the third stage, was characterised by the purchase by farmers of cattle-feeds and artificial fertilisers, and investment in new buildings and underdrainage. The last stage, after 1914, saw the introduction of the tractor and of labour-saving machinery. Thus the English agricultural revolution, once thought to be a short, sharp break in the history of English farming, largely achieved between 1760 and 1820, has now been stretched to cover some three hundred years. French historians, in contrast, have brought the agricultural revolution even nearer the present. Early writers believed the French agricultural revolution began, like the English, in the mid-eighteenth century (Bloch, 1966; Faucher, 1956). But recent work has cast doubt upon this, and has suggested that the 1820s or 1840s were a more likely time for its commencement (Morineau, 1968; Newell, 1973).

One of the problems in discussing the agricultural revolution in Europe is that it is rarely defined; one rare such instance is by J.D. Chambers and G.E. Mingay, who define it as the transition from traditional husbandry practices to modern scientific agriculture and high farming (Chambers & Mingay, 1966). But this could be said to cover a period of several centuries; yet the term revolution implies a short period of radical change after a period of little change. But how long is an agricultural revolution, how radical must the changes be, and what exactly is changing?

Approaches to the study of the agricultural revolution

Enclosure

Few historians have specified what they mean by an agricultural revolution; nonetheless three contrasting approaches have been adopted. First are those who have seen changes in landownership, farm size and labour supply as critical. Such work derives from Marx's interpretation of English agricultural history and it is noteworthy that he referred to 'an agrarian revolution' (Marx, 1977). His approach has been followed widely by later writers, not by any means all of them neo-Marxists. Marx thought England in the fifteenth century was a nation of small peasant farmers, who held approximately equal areas of land, farmed the land with their own labour and owned their livestock and farm implements. Over the next four hundred years this was radically changed. First, the ownership of land was concentrated in relatively few hands; these *rentier* landlords did not farm the land themselves but rented it to tenants with capital. Second, farms became much larger than in the fifteenth century and were worked by landless labourers who owned no livestock or implements, and were paid wages. Marx believed that the peasant was deprived of his land by force and later legally by enclosure. It is not clear when this happened although he and later writers have emphasised two periods, the sixteenth century and the period after 1750. In the latter era Parliamentary enclosure not only led to the final expropriation of the peasant, and the creation of large farms, but drove the expropriated to the towns where they formed the labour supply for the new factories of the industrial revolution (Saville, 1969; Dobb, 1963; Hammond & Hammond, 1911). Such a view has been subject to much criticism, but the absence of any comprehensive records of land ownership until 1873–74, of farm size until 1885, and of the labour supply until 1851, has made confirmation or refutation of this thesis difficult. The lack of reliable records of enclosure before the era of Parliamentary acts and awards, and the difficulty of interpreting the acreages listed in the latter all add to the problem (Turner, 1980).

Technology

A second approach has been to emphasise the importance of changing farm technology; historians have used farm records, estate archives, contemporary descriptions of farming, and works on agronomy to trace the adoption of improved farming methods, and hence by implication, increased output and productivity. The most common method of measuring improved productivity has been to trace changes in crop yields. But there are few national records of these before 1840; the first French agricultural census was published in that year. Before then crop yields covering more than a few farms for a few years are rare. The only accurate long-run series are for manors in the south of England in the thirteenth and fourteenth centuries (Titow, 1972). There are of course data for individual farms for single years at different times in profusion, but they are rarely part of a series. Thus the main means of tracing changes in land productivity has been by using written descriptions of methods and implements and assuming that the adoption of new methods implies increased productivity. There are several difficulties in such an approach.

First, it is too often assumed that the first recorded instance of a new method was followed by widespread and rapid adoption of the innovation, and hence a sharp increase in productivity. Yet modern studies of innovation adoption amongst farmers shows that there is invariably a considerable lag between the first adoption by the more enterprising farmers and majority adoption (G.E. Jones, 1967). This lag could be considerable. Thus in a sample of farms in Norfolk and Suffolk the turnip was first recorded in the 1640s, and may have been introduced some decades earlier; by the 1730s less than half the farms in the sample were growing the crop (Overton, 1979). The first practical milking machine was exhibited in Scotland in 1895. On the eve of the Second World War only 8% of the dairy farmers in Britain were using a machine, and it was not until the 1960s that it had become generally adopted. We can reasonably suppose that before the seventeenth century the rate of adoption was even slower.

Second, innovations introduced in one region were slow to spread to other areas; farmers learned mainly from observing their neighbours, and so innovations spread slowly outwards from farmer to farmer, taking time to reach the remoter areas. Thomas Coke, the celebrated improving landlord of Holkham in Norfolk, believed his improvements spread at about a mile a year in the eighteenth century, about the same speed at which, one archaeologist has estimated, the domestication of wheat and barley spread into Europe from the Near East some five or six thousand years ago (Clark, 1965; Ernle, 1968, p. 220). Neither estimate can be taken too seriously, but it can be assumed that new ideas were slow to travel from one region to another. It follows from this that even if one region in a country can be shown to have adopted an innovation at a given date, it does not follow that all other regions progressed at the same rate. This point has been well made for the north and south of France in the nineteenth century (Newell, 1973).

Third, without adequate figures on crop yields it is difficult to estimate just how important the adoption of a new method would be. What increase in crop yields did the use of a new rotation give, or an improved plough or harrow? Did the selection of seed from better crops give yield increases? How far did underdrainage increase yields? The same questions could be asked of improvements in livestock breeding, and are equally difficult to answer. Crop yields are a function of a great variety of factors, and the importance of one technical change is hard to disentangle from others (Fig. 1.1). Even in modern times it is difficult to assess the quantitative role of new factor inputs. However, in experimental plots in the north-eastern United States the same fertiliser and other inputs have been applied to wheat varieties grown in the 1920s as to later improved varieties. From this it can be argued that the introduction of the new variety accounted for nearly half the increase in wheat yield between 1935 and 1975 (Jensen, 1978). No such calculation can be made for the past. However, attempts to trace the flow of the nitrogen cycle suggest the great importance of the adoption of fodder legumes in Western Europe after 1770; they accounted for one third of the increase in crop yields between 1770 and 1880 (Chorley, 1981).

Green Revolutions: an overview

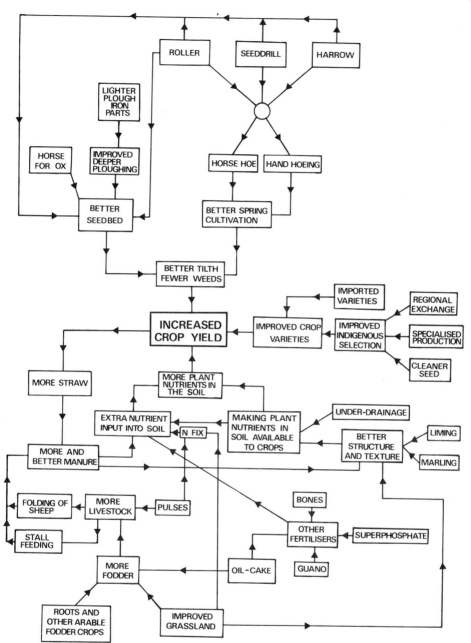

Fig. 1.1. The interrelationships of changes in cultivation practices and the effect upon crop yields.

Fourth, not all farming methods were necessarily suitable for all regions. Lord Ernle and later historians emphasised the importance of the turnip. If sown with the drill upon the fallow it allowed weeding during growth, which was not possible with cereals. Fed to livestock it helped them put on weight and increased milk and meat output per animal. Their dung, mixed with the straw from cereal crops, was thought to have increased cereal yields, although it may be that clover was more important in maintaining soil nutrient status. But the turnip was not grown in all parts of England – there were difficulties in growing and lifting it in heavy clay soils (Grigg, 1966) – and was not widely grown in continental Europe, where sugar-beet and potatoes served a similar function. In the south maize was the major new crop, but it could not be grown successfully in Northern Europe (Hohenburg, 1977). Indeed much of the discussion of the agricultural revolution has emphasised improvements in arable farming; yet even as early as 1750 a considerable proportion of the value of West European farm output came from livestock products.

Economics

A third approach to the study of the agricultural revolution not widely applied as yet, is to follow the procedures adopted by economists in analysing changes in modern agriculture. Provided data are available for production and prices, it is possible to measure changes in the rate at which agricultural and food output is increasing. Many developed nations publish such estimates, whilst the Food and Agricultural Organisation of the United Nations has published indices of output for most individual countries since the early 1960s, and for major regions of the world since the 1950s. If data are also available for inputs then it is possible to measure productivity changes. Four such indices have been used. First, changes in output can be related to *total factor input*, measuring the efficiency with which all inputs are processed into outputs. Although such indices have been published for a few western countries since the 1950s, the lack of data makes it difficult to construct them before the mid-nineteenth century. Thus *partial productivity indices* have been more commonly used. The most widely used index is *labour productivity growth*, which relates changes in total output to changes in total labour input: this requires consistent figures on the labour input, not easy to obtain in an industry which uses a great deal of family, seasonal and casual labour: consequently the adult male labour force is often used as a measure. A second partial productivity index is *land productivity growth*, or changes in total output per hectare of agricultural land (Hayami & Ruttan, 1971); land productivity changes are more commonly measured by using yields of the major food crop. A final index widely used in the post-war era is to relate total food output to total population. The reason for this of course is the concern over food supplies in the developing countries since 1950. However, it is equally applicable to Western Europe in the past. Paul Bairoch has argued that prior to the agricultural revolution, variability in crop yields meant that harvest failure was frequent and food supplies periodically inadequate; further the surplus above the needs of the agricultural population was insufficient to maintain a manufacturing population (Bairoch, 1973). Thus an agricultural revolution was a necessary prerequisite for an industrial revolution; others would argue that it was the improved nutrition made possible by the agricultural revolution that led to population increase after 1750 (McKeown, 1976).

Thus there are clearly a variety of possible meanings of the term 'agricultural revolution'. It could be, first, a radical change in the tenurial and structural character of agriculture. Second, it could be the accelerated adoption of new farming methods. Third, it could be an accelerated rate of growth of total output or food output. Fourth, it could be an increase in the rate of productivity growth in agriculture, measured either by total factor productivity growth, the growth of total output per hectare, or total food output per head of the total population. It is these measures which are considered here.

The measurement of input and output during the agricultural revolution

It should be said straight away that the measurement of agricultural output and productivity changes even today is hampered by methodological differences about the construction of such indices and also by lack of reliable data. Prior to the commencement of agricultural censuses – few of which exist before the 1840s – the estimates of output, arable acreages, changes in labour supply or crop yields are based upon contemporary estimates which are at the best of doubtful provenance, at worst, wishful thinking. Further there are few if any estimates for any country before 1700, yet the period between 1600 and 1700 in the Low Countries and England is regarded as critical by many historians (Kerridge, 1967; Slicher van Bath, 1960).

Output

There are few estimates of the growth of agricultural output for the eighteenth century: in England and France output is thought to have grown little faster than total population (Slicher van Bath, 1977; Ladurie, 1975). In both countries output accelerated in the first half of the nineteenth century, but the rate of increase declined in the later nineteenth century, rising later to much higher rates after the 1930s (Fig. 1.2). In other West European countries the rate of increase in output in the later nineteenth century was higher than in England and France (Eddie, 1968; Dovring, 1969; Bairoch, 1965), but, as in England and France, reached the highest rates after the

1930s. The record is thus one of steady growth in the rate of increase, without any sudden spurts, except possibly in the early nineteenth century. It is sadly impossible to compare this with changes before 1700.

Land

Most historians have emphasised the importance of the adoption of new farming methods in the eighteenth and nineteenth centuries, and thus implied that increased crop yields were the major reason for increased output. But there is no doubt that between 1700 and the 1880s there was a substantial increase in the arable area of Western Europe (Fig. 1.3). Even where estimates of the area in cultivation are not available, contemporary descriptions support this view. In addition the proportion of the arable area in bare fallow declined quite dramatically; in France for example, from one third in 1701–10 to 13% in 1892 (Toutain, 1961), and in Sweden from about 50% in 1750 to only 7% in 1900 (Osvald, 1952; Thomas, 1941). This was used not only to increase the area in cereals but also to grow fodder legumes and roots, sugar-beet and potatoes. Hence a considerable part of the increased output of West European agriculture in this period came from increases in area rather than yields. In England the increase in output due to the rise in the sown area between 1700 and 1850 has been put at nearly two thirds (Mingay, 1977; Grigg, 1982b). However, in England and France the arable area had reached its peak by the 1870s, elsewhere by the 1920s. Since then there have been fluctuations in the area in crops, but no further increase. Indeed the general trend has been downwards, particularly since the 1950s. Hence crop yield increases have become of increasing importance in raising total output (Dovring, 1965b).

Labour

It is notoriously difficult to measure the labour input in agriculture, and there are few accurate occupational statistics in national censuses before the mid-nineteenth century. These may neglect family labour and seasonal labour. Yet there is little doubt that the numbers employed in agriculture increased in the eighteenth century and continued its increase in the first half of the nineteenth century (Fig. 1.4). In the 1850s there began a long decline in the labour force in Britain and Ireland; somewhat later a decline began in Belgium and Switzerland, although very slowly, and at the turn of the century France and Germany followed suit and later Scandinavia and the Netherlands (Grigg, 1974). Thus the agricultural revolution before 1850 did not see a decline in the labour force. Indeed many of the new techniques and crops required greater labour inputs (Timmer, 1969). The slow reduction of the fallow increased labour needs; the widespread cultivation of the potato in

Green Revolutions: an overview

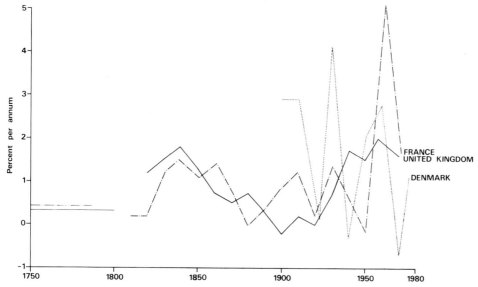

Fig. 1.2. The rate of increase in agricultural output 1750–1976 (per cent per annum). Source: Toutain (1961); Deane & Cole (1962); Hayami & Ruttan (1971); F.A.O. (1963, 1980).

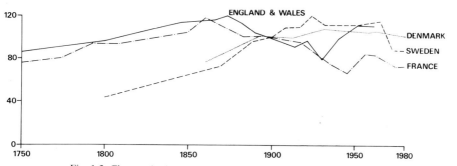

Fig. 1.3. Changes in the arable area, 1750–1980. Source: Toutain (1961); Grigg (1980); Thomas (1941); F.A.O. (1958, 1980); Jensen (1937).

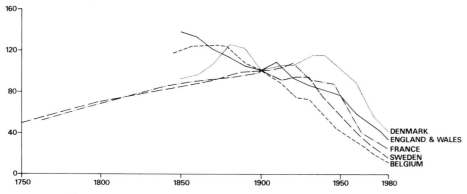

Fig. 1.4. Changes in the agricultural labour force, 1750–1980. Source: Bairoch (1969); F.A.O. (1963, 1980).

Ireland, Belgium and Norway necessitated extra labour, as did the turnip in England and the sugar-beet in northern France; the greater application of farmyard manure and, later, artificial fertilisers, increased labour needs as did the greater attention given to livestock. During this period few specifically labour-saving methods or implements were adopted except the threshing machine in parts of England, the winnowing machine and the horse drill, yet it is certain that output per head rose in this period. This was largely achieved by the more widespread adoption of techniques already known: the scythe was substituted for the sickle (Collins, 1969), the horse for the ox, and lighter ploughs for the heavy plough. A very crude estimate suggests that the output of cereals per head doubled in England between 1700 and 1850 (Grigg, 1982b). But the major advances in labour productivity have come in this century with the invention and later adoption of a wide variety of labour-saving machines and the substitution of the tractor for the horse, and, in a few areas, for the ox. For most of this century emigration from the countryside to the towns has exceeded natural increase, and the agricultural labour supply has diminished slowly until 1945, and since then very rapidly. Thus whilst labour productivity was increasing in the late nineteenth and early twentieth centuries, it never approached the levels of 4–5% p.a. achieved in parts of Western Europe since 1950 (F.A.O., 1977).

Land productivity

Greater output per hectare can be obtained in a variety of ways. A shift to more valuable crops such as vegetables or fruits is one method, or the substitution of dairying for extensive cereal production. The later nineteenth and twentieth centuries have seen an almost universal shift toward livestock production in response to demand for these goods but made possible by the import of grain for flour and a variety of crops for cattle-feed. But in the eighteenth and nineteenth centuries the principal means of increasing the productivity of land were the adoption of new higher yielding crops and increasing the yield of the existing crops.

Some authorities believe that the introduction of the potato and maize from the Americas made possible the upswing of population after 1750 (Langer, 1963). It is certainly true that the potato gave a much higher calorific yield than cereals in the eighteenth century; the superiority of maize was perhaps less marked (Hohenburg, 1977). Except in Ireland the potato was not widely adopted in the eighteenth century, and its contribution to the West European diet only became significant after 1815; but by the mid-nineteenth century it was an important part of the diet of the poor in many parts of Western Europe; in Ireland it occupied some 30–40% of the arable acreage in the 1840s, in Norway 13% in the 1870s. However, in some places potatoes seem

Table 1.1. *Seed-yield[1] ratios in the regions of Europe, 1500–1820*

Period	Seed-yield ratio in each zone			
	I	II	III	IV
1500–49	7.4	6.7	4.0	3.9
1550–99	7.3	–	4.4	4.3
1600–49	6.7	–	4.5	4.0
1650–99	9.3	6.2	4.1	3.8
1700–49	–	6.3	4.1	3.5
1750–99	10.1	7.0	5.1	4.7
1800–20	11.1	6.2	5.4	–

Notes:
Zone I England, The Low Countries
Zone II France, Spain, Italy
Zone III Germany, Switzerland, Scandinavia
Zone IV Russia, Poland, Czechoslovakia, Hungary
[1] for wheat, barley, oats and rye
Source: Silcher van Bath (1977), p. 81.

to have been substituted for cereals in the diet whilst some of the crop went for distilling alcohol or as a cattle-feed (Drake, 1969; Bourke, 1967–68).

Perhaps more important was the upward trend in the yield of the major cereals; unfortunately reliable crop yields were not collected in many parts of Western Europe until the later nineteenth century, and before then one must rely upon contemporary estimates and informed deductions made by historians. The most comprehensive collection of data on European crop yields has been made by B.H. Slicher van Bath. His data are seed-yield ratios, that is the ratio between the amount sown and the amount harvested (Table 1.1). Yield per hectare of wheat are available for most West European states for the last hundred years (Fig. 1.5 and Table 1.2). A number of tentative conclusions can be drawn from these data. First, there are marked regional variations in average yields which have persisted for nearly five hundred years. The highest yields in 1500 were in England and the Low Countries; the adjacent parts of northern France and western Germany were probably also in this zone at that time. This inner zone has since extended to include Denmark. In 1850, 1909–13, 1948–52 and 1975–77 Denmark, Belgium, the Netherlands, Germany and the U.K. all had average yields markedly above those elsewhere in Europe; in these years, as in the period before 1820 (Table 1.1), average wheat yields in the north-west were two or three times those in eastern and southern Europe. Second, there was no major improvement in seed-yield ratios between 1500–49 and 1800–1830 in Eastern or Southern Europe: in England and the Low Countries the upturn seems to date from the second half of the seventeenth century, in Germany, Switzerland and Scan-

Table 1.2. *Wheat yields in Europe, 1850 to 1977–79 (100 kg/hectare)*

	c. 1850	1909–13	1934–35	1948–52	1977–79
Denmark	c.12	33.1	28.1	36.5	52.3
Belgium	10.5	25.3	27.7	32.2	48.2
Netherlands	10.5	23.5	30.9	36.5	59.0
Germany	9.9	24.2	20.0	26.2	45.6
United Kingdom	9.9	21.2	21.5	27.2	51.2
Austria	7.7	13.7	18.0	17.1	36.9
France	7.0	13.1	14.1	18.3	46.7
Italy	6.7	10.5	10.1	15.2	25.4
Norway	5.7	16.6	19.5	20.6	40.7
Romania	–	12.9	8.0	10.2	25.8
Hungary	–	13.2	11.3	13.8	38.6
Bulgaria	–	6.2	9.2	12.4	38.3
Spain	4.6	9.2	14.7	8.7	16.3
Greece	4.6	9.8	9.2	10.2	23.9
Russia	4.5	6.9	8.1	8.4	16.5

Source: J. Blum (1961), p. 303; League of Nations (1927), pp. 38–9; (1936), pp. 90–1; F.A.O. (1963), pp. 34–5; F.A.O. (1980), pp. 96–7.

dinavia from the second half of the eighteenth century. In most countries in Western Europe wheat yields in the late 1970s were at least five times what they were in the 1850s, and in most yields have at least doubled since the 1930s. What the trends were before the 1850s is difficult to establish. In England, which may be exceptional, estimates of the national wheat yield have been put between 1.0 and 1.4 metric tonnes in 1700, about 1.5 in 1800 and 1.9 metric tonnes by the 1850s (Craigie, 1883; Bennett, 1935). In France there was comparatively little increase in the eighteenth century (Morineau, 1968). What seems certain is that the rate of increase in yields after 1850 was more rapid than before and that the period of most rapid increase has been since the 1930s (Fig. 1.5).

The chronology of revolution

The overwhelming conclusion to be drawn from the limited statistics available is that output increases and productivity changes in the last thirty or forty years are more rapid than at any time in the past. Before 1850 it is difficult to make any confident estimates of growth, but some conclusions can be drawn. Until the 1850s increases in yield were slow and were obtained by the wider adoption of established techniques; the adoption of legumes was important, which had begun earliest in the Low Countries and then spread to England in the seventeenth century. Considerable proportions of the increase in output came from increases in the cultivated area and the adoption of new high yielding crops such as potatoes, maize and sugar-beet, whilst the extinction of the fallow increased the area that was sown. Until the 1850s the labour supply in agriculture increased everywhere in Western Europe, and farming became more labour-intensive. This period saw few innovations of labour-saving machinery, although output per head certainly rose.

The mid-nineteenth century was a turning point in England as the labour supply began to decline; it also saw the slow adoption of new inputs provided by industry, a major break with the past. The provision of factory-made implements accelerated from the 1820s, and machines overtly aimed at saving labour were widely diffused, most noticeably the reaper. Artificial fertilisers began to be used from the 1840s, and efficient underdrainage became more common. In the rest of Western Europe the decline of the labour force was generally after its beginnings in Britain, and the adoption of labour-saving machinery thus also generally later. The period between 1850 and the 1930s was characterised by slow gains in crop yields and labour productivity, a stagnant or slowly declining labour force, and few increases in the arable area except locally.

It is thus the period since the 1930s which has been truly revolutionary in West European agriculture. The arable area has not increased; the labour force has fallen dramatically; crop yields have risen remarkably, even in those countries of the north-west where yields were already high in the 1930s, due largely to the unprecedented rise in the consumption of artificial fertilisers, the adoption of new high-yielding cereal varieties, and the chemical control of pests, disease and weeds. Most dramatic have been the increases in labour productivity due to the fall in the labour force, and the use of tractors instead of horses and the use of a wide range of machines.

A picture of progressive increases in output and productivity since the late eighteenth century casts little light on the controversy as to when the agricultural revolution began. That modern increases have become ever more and more rapid is well illustrated by the estimates of the average wheat yield in

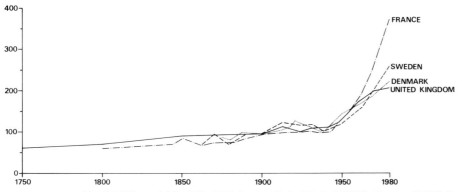

Fig. 1.5. Wheat yields, 1750–1980. Source: B.R. Mitchell (1975); Bennett (1935); Toutain (1961); F.A.O. (1963, 1980).

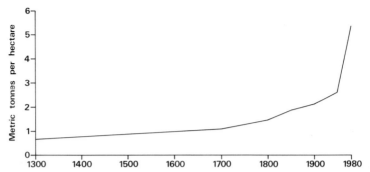

Fig. 1.6. Wheat yields in England, 1300–1980. Source: Titow (1972); Bennett (1935); Craigie (1883); Ministry of Agriculture (1968).

England (Fig. 1.6). No earlier period can parallel the rate of increase since the end of the Second World War. Between 1300 and 1700 average yields rose only by 50%; even if this increase were compressed within a century, it hardly suggests any radical change before the mid-seventeenth century. Thus it seems that European agricultural change was evolutionary rather than revolutionary until this century. It is the period since the 1930s that merits the title.

REFERENCES

Bairoch, P. (1965). Niveaux de dèveloppement économique de 1810 à 1910. *Annales: Economies Sociétés Civilisations*, 20, 1091–117

(1969). *International Historical Statistics: the working population and its structure.* New York, Gordon and Breach

(1973). Agriculture and the industrial revolution 1700–1914. In *The Fontana Economic History of Europe: the industrial revolution*, ed. C.M. Cipolla, pp. 452–506. London, Collins

Bennett, M.K. (1935). British wheat-yields for seven centuries. *Economic History*, 10, 22–6

Bloch, M. (1966). *French rural history: an essay on its basic characteristics.* London, Routledge and Kegan Paul

Blum, J. (1961). *Lord and peasant in Russia from the ninth to the nineteenth century.* New Haven, Princeton University Press

Bourke, P.M.A. (1967–68). The use of the potato in pre-famine Ireland. *Journal of the Statistical and Social Inquiry Society of Ireland*, 21, 72–97

Chambers, J.D. & Mingay, G.E. (1966). *The agricultural revolution 1750–1880.* London, Batsford

Chorley, G.P.H. (1981). The agricultural revolution in northern Europe, 1750–1880: nitrogen, legumes and crop productivity. *Economic History Review*, 34, 71–93

Clark, J.G.D. (1965). Radio carbon dating and the expansion of farming culture from the Near East over Europe. *Proceedings of the Prehistoric Society*, 31, 58–77

Collins, E.J. (1969). Labour supply and demand in European agriculture, 1800–1880. In *Agrarian change and economic development: the historical problems*, ed. E.L. Jones and S.J. Woolf, pp. 61–94. London, Methuen

Connell, K.H. (1962). The potato in Ireland. *Past and Present*, 23, 57–63

Craigie, P.G. (1883). Statistics of agricultural production. *Statistical Journal*, 46, 1–47

Deane, P. & Cole, W.A. (1962). *British economic growth 1688–1959: trends and structure*. Cambridge University Press

Dobb, M.H. (1963). *Studies in the development of capitalism*. 2nd edn, London, Routledge and Kegan Paul

Dovring, F. (1965a). The transformation of European agriculture. In *Cambridge Economic History of Europe*, vol. 6, *The industrial revolutions and after: incomes population and technical change*, part 2. ed. H.J. Habakkuk & M. Postan, pp. 603–72. Cambridge University Press

(1965b). *Land and labor in Europe in the twentieth century: a comparative survey of recent agrarian history*. 3rd edn, The Hague, Martinus Nijhoff

(1969). Eighteenth century changes in European agriculture: a comment. *Agricultural History*, 43, 181–6

Drake, M. (1969). *Population and society in Norway, 1735–1865*. Cambridge University Press

Duby, G. (1954). La révolution agricole médiévale. *Revue de Géographie du Lyon*, 29, 361–6

Duckham, A.N. (1959). The current agricultural revolution. *Geography*, 44, 71–8

Eddie, S.M. (1968). Agricultural production and output per worker in Hungary 1870–1913. *Journal of Economic History*, 28, 197–222

Ernle, Lord (1968). *English farming, past and present*. 6th edn, London, Cass

Faucher, D. (1956). La révolution agricole du XVIIIe–XIXe siècles. *Bulletin de la Société d'Histoire Moderne*, 20, 2–11

Food and Agriculture Organisation (1958). *Production Yearbook 1957*, 11, Rome, F.A.O.

(1963). *Production Yearbook 1962*, 16, Rome, F.A.O.

(1977). *The fourth world food survey*. Rome, F.A.O.

(1980). *Production Yearbook 1979*, 33, Rome, F.A.O.

Grigg, D.B. (1966). *The agricultural revolution in South Lincolnshire*. Cambridge University Press

(1974). Agricultural populations and economic development. *Tijdschrift voor Economische en Sociale Geografie*, 65, 414–20

(1980). *Population growth and agrarian change: an historical perspective*. Cambridge University Press

(1981). The historiography of hunger; changing views on the world food problem 1945–1980. *Transactions of the Institute of British Geographers*, 6, 279–92

(1982a). Counting the hungry: the world pattern of undernutrition. *Tijdschrift voor Economische en Sociale Geografie*, 73, 66–79

(1982b). *The dynamics of agricultural change: the European experience*. London, Hutchinson

Hammond, J.L. & Hammond, B. (1911). *The village labourer, 1760–1832: a study in the government of England before the Reform Bill*. London, Longmans

Hayami, Y. & Ruttan, V.W. (1971). *Agricultural development: an international perspective*. Baltimore, Johns Hopkins University Press
Hohenburg, P.M. (1977). Maize in French agriculture. *Journal of European Economic History*, 6, 63–101
Jensen, E. (1937). *Danish agriculture, its economic development*. Copenhagen
Jensen, N.F. (1978). Limits to growth in world food production. *Science*, 201, 317–20
Jones, E.L. (1967). Introduction. In *Agriculture and economic growth in England 1650–1815*. ed. E.L. Jones, pp. 1–48. London, Methuen
Jones, G.E. (1967). The adoption and diffusion of agricultural practices. *World Agricultural Economics and Rural Sociology Abstracts*, 9, 1–34
Kerridge, E. (1967). *The agricultural revolution*. London, Allen and Unwin
Ladurie, E. Le Roy (1975). De la crise ultime à la vraie croissance 1660–1789. In *Histoire de la France rurale*, vol. 2. ed. G. Duby & A. Wallon, pp. 393–441. Paris, Seuil
Langer, W.L. (1963). Europe's initial population explosion. *American Historical Review*, 69, 1–17
League of Nations (1927). *International Statistical Yearbook 1926*. Geneva, League of Nations
   (1936). *Statistical Yearbook 1935–36*. Geneva, League of Nations
Marx, K. (1977). *Capital: a critique of political economy*. vol. 1. London, Lawrence & Wishart, pp. 671–701
McKeown, T. (1976). *The modern rise of population*. London, Edward Arnold
Mingay, G.E. (1977). *The agricultural revolution: changes in agriculture, 1650–1880*. London, Black
Ministry of Agriculture, Fisheries and Food (1968). *A century of agricultural statistics. Great Britain 1866–1966*. London, H.M.S.O.
Mitchell, B.R. (1975). *European Historical Statistics 1750–1970*. London, Macmillan
Morineau, M. (1968). Y-a-t'il eu une révolution agricole en France au XVIIIe siècle? *Revue Historique*, 239, 299–326
Newell, W.H. (1973). The agricultural revolution in nineteenth century France. *Journal of Economic History*, 33, 697–731
Osvald, H. (1952). *Swedish agriculture*. Stockholm, Swedish Institute
Overton, M. (1979). Estimating crop yields from probate inventories: an example from East Anglia 1585–1735. *Journal of Economic History*, 39, 363–78
Ross, E.D. & Tontz, R.L. (1942). The term agricultural revolution as used by economic historians. *Agricultural History*, 22, 32–8
Saville, J. (1969). Primitive accumulation and early industrialization in Britain. In *The Socialist Register 1969*, ed. R. Miliband & J. Saville, pp. 247–71. London, Merlin Press
Slater, W. (1961). The revolution in agriculture. *Advancement of Science*, 18, 249–56
Slicher van Bath, B.H. (1960). The rise of intensive husbandry in the Low Countries. In *Britain and the Netherlands*, vol. 1. ed. J.S. Bromley & E.H. Kossman, pp. 130–52. London, Chatto and Windus
   (1977). Agriculture in the vital revolution. in *Cambridge Economic History of Europe*, vol. 5. *The economic organization of early modern Europe*, ed. E.E. Rich & C.H. Wilson, pp. 42–133. Cambridge University Press

Thomas, D.S. (1941). *Social and economic aspects of Swedish population movements, 1750–1933*. New York, Macmillan
Thompson, F.M.L. (1968). The second agricultural revolution 1815–1880. *Economic History Review*, 21, 62–77
Timmer, C.P. (1969). The turnip, the new husbandry and the English agricultural revolution. *Quarterly Journal of Economics*, 83, 375–95
Titow, Z. (1972). *Winchester yields; a study in medieval agricultural productivity*. Cambridge University Press
Toutain, J. (1961). *Le produit de l'agriculture française de 1700 à 1958: 1. Estimation du produit au XVIIIe siècle*. Paris, Institut de Science Economique appliquée
Turner, M.E. (1980). *English Parliamentary enclosure: its historical geography and economic history*. Folkestone, Dawson
Vandenbroeke, C. (1971). Cultivation and consumption of the potato in the 17th and 18th centuries. *Acta Historia Neerlandica*, 5, 15–39
Whetham, E. (1970). The mechanization of British farming 1910–1945. *Journal of Agricultural Economics*, 21, 317–31
White, L.T. (1962). *Medieval technology and social change*. Oxford, Clarendon Press

2 Land reform as a pre-condition for Green Revolution in Latin America

CLIFFORD T. SMITH

In most Latin American countries, land reform has been a burning issue for many years, flaring into activity from the 1950s to the early 1970s, but dying down in recent years except in Central America, and particularly in Nicaragua. The list of land reform legislation is formidable, beginning with the legislation of 1917 which followed the Mexican Revolution, and most recently expressed in the land reform of Nicaragua which followed the overthrow of Somoza in 1979.

Declining interest by governments, and in some instances, notably that of Chile since 1973, outright reversal of land reform, has been accompanied by a sense of disillusionment among reformists: disillusionment that legislation has not been put into effect; that relatively few peasants have benefited from land reform, even where it has been partially carried out; that many peasants, even among beneficiaries of reform, have been reluctant to abandon subsistence farming; that agricultural production, especially in the reform sector, has not responded to expectations; and that the rural sector has not been able to fulfil the prediction that increased and more equitable rural income would create demand for national industrial production.

The real impact of land reform

Yet the most significant results of the land reform movement seem to lie in other directions: a substantial increase in the intervention of the State in the agricultural sector; and a massive stimulus to the extension of capitalism in agriculture. State intervention is, of course, implicit in the whole process of land reform itself, but various mechanisms ensure continued State involvement. The first is the creation of new and self-perpetuating bureaucracies dedicated to agrarian reform and the administration of the 'reform sector'. The second mechanism lies in the acquisition by the State of land resources on a massive scale, or its power to do so under agrarian reform legislation. And the third mechanism operates by way of the retention of a continued interest in land that has been distributed to beneficiaries, enabling the State to control the beneficiaries' ability to sell, lease or mortgage their holdings and also enabling the State to control the beneficiaries' access to credit, and thus to influence, directly or indirectly, the use to which the land may be put.

The effectiveness of State intervention in the reformed sector varies substantially from one country to another, and may have various purposes other than the promotion of agricultural improvement and efficiency, but in relation to the introduction of Green Revolution technology, the State's involvement is a critical factor, affecting both the reformed and the non-reformed sector.

Except in Cuba, the other major result of land reform movements has been to facilitate the deeper penetration of capitalism into agriculture. It has done so, in part, by sweeping away 'pre-capitalistic' modes of production characterized by those labour-service and sharecropping tenancies on the large estates that were frequently the major targets of land reform legislation. Other processes are involved, affecting both the non-reformed and the reformed sectors, and they are no less significant and deserve more detailed discussion at a later point, but the major effect has been to provide a framework within which new agricultural technology has been greatly expanded, often for the greater benefit of foreign-controlled or domestic agribusiness rather than that of the Latin American peasant.

If it can be argued that the advancement of the role of the State and the advance of capitalistic agriculture are the two most significant consequences of the agrarian reform movement, it is evident that they are not unrelated. Without necessarily entering into the debate over the relative autonomy of the State, it is clear that where the State is effectively controlled by the national bourgeoisie, the two major implications of agrarian reform noted above tend to converge, though on many detailed issues they may be at odds.

Reformists may be disillusioned with the results of agrarian reform, but from this point of view agrarian reforms have succeeded, as De Janvry suggests, in confirming the dominance of capitalist enterprise in agriculture, which is unlikely, under present conditions, to be successfully challenged by radical forces. On this basis, he concludes, 'new land reforms are unlikely to occur in the near future in Latin America, even though land reform remains an active political issue' (De Janvry, 1981, p. 223). In so far as land reform has been a pre-condition for Green Revolution, it has been so mainly through the release of capitalist enterprise and the influence of the State rather than through the invigoration of peasant enterprise – the route by which optimistic reformists had hoped and expected that land reform would bring amelioration to the lot of the peasant.

The need for land reform

If it is true that Latin American land reform is to be regarded more or less as a completed episode, culminating in the period from the 1950s to the early 1970s, what are the specific characteristics of this phase of development? Why has land reform failed, even where it was partially carried out as a redistributive mechanism, to deliver those substantial benefits to peasant farmers which were expected from it?

There are two major strands in Latin American programmes of land reform which might be labelled as the radical and reformist traditions. Both stem from the polarization of land ownership into a structure of large estates on the one hand and small peasant farms on the other, frequently too small to support an adequate income for a peasant family, and differentiated according to various systems of tenancy or peasant ownership–the *latifundio-minifundio* complex. Among peasant farmers a broad distinction is to be made between those who have access to land by forms of tenancy on large holdings and those who own land in their own right, either as individual holdings or in communities (*comunidades*) which have a link, however tenuous it may be in many cases, with pre-Conquest structures. The pattern of landholding, involving the formation of the classical *hacienda*, the plantation and the erosion of indigenous community structures, is deeply rooted in the colonial history of Latin America, though many would now argue that the colonial period merely set the stage for a much more aggressive phase in the expansion of large landholdings in the nineteenth and early twentieth centuries (Grieshaber, 1979; Magnus Mörner, 1973).

The radical tradition

The radical tradition in Latin American reform movements has always focussed intellectually on the broader need to destroy the social and political dominance of a land-owning oligarchy, usually seen as the key to a total reconstruction of society and, of course, closely tied to Marxist doctrine and a wide spectrum of left-wing political parties. Equally radical, pressures for land reform have come from below, from peasant farmers reacting against oppression, injustice and dispossession. Characteristically, peasant pressures have been localized, inchoate, disorganized and repressed with brutality. But union organization has at times been able to orchestrate protest, if only for short periods, and without great success, as for example among the peasant leagues in Brazil in the early 1930s or the pressures exerted in the late 1950s by the Federación Campesina Venezolana, or successfully in the *valle* region and the *altiplano* of Bolivia in the early 1950s. The radical tradition has had its successes, most notably in Cuba and also, for example, in the formulation of land reform laws in Mexico in the late stages of the Mexican Revolution, though execution of land reform in Mexico had to await the reforming zeal of the Cárdenas regime of the early 1930s. In Bolivia in 1952, peasant pressure was instrumental, in conjunction with leadership of the Movimiento Nacional Revolucionario, for a land reform movement which has never been totally reversed. But other radical or radicalized land reform programmes have been short-lived: in Guatemala, briefly, under the Arbenz regime of 1952–4; in

Chile the progressive radicalization of land reform from 1969 to 1973 was abruptly halted and reversed under Pinochet's military regime.

The reformist tradition

The reformist tradition of land reform or agrarian reform is more complex, and certainly much more hesitant, reflecting interests very different from those of the radical spectrum. But it is the reformist tradition which dominated the wave of interest and activity in land reform and agrarian reform from the late fifties to the early seventies. Agrarian reform legislation poured from government printing offices: Venezuela, 1959; Panama, 1962; Colombia, 1961; Peru, 1962, 1964, 1969; Ecuador, 1964, 1972; Chile, 1962, 1967; Costa Rica, 1962; Dominican Republic, 1962 (Wilkie, 1974).

Rhetoric about agrarian reform in the late fifties and sixties became part of the stock-in-trade of populist politics at a time when most Latin American countries still had at least the formal apparatus of elected government and the rural vote was worth courting. In the immediate context of the Cuban Revolution and the spread of rural guerrilla movements in Latin America (in Venezuela, Colombia, Peru, and Bolivia, for example), the promise of agrarian reform offered the prospect of halting the recruitment of discontented peasants and a hope that land reform would create a basis for a property-owning democracy. Support for this aspect of land reform was forthcoming briefly during Kennedy's presidency in the USA and was enshrined in those often quoted clauses of the charter of the ill-fated Alliance for Progress, which promised

To encourage . . . programs of comprehensive agrarian reform leading to the effective transformation, where required, of unjust structures and systems of land tenure and use, with a view to replacing *latifundios* and dwarf holdings by an equitable system of land tenure, so that the land will become, for the man who works it, the basis of his economic stability, the foundation of his increasing welfare, and the guarantee of his freedom and dignity. (Para 6, Title 1, Charter Objectives for the Alliance for Progress, 1961)

Immediate circumstances led many parties, even of the moderate right, to embrace agrarian reform in their platform programmes, but there were structural factors pointing towards it at a more fundamental level. While on the surface there appeared to be a convergence of radical and liberal opinion as to the need for agrarian reform, in reality the two traditions of land reform led in entirely different directions. The radical view saw land reform as part of, or a step towards, social restructuring and the elimination of the agrarian base of oligarchy; where sincerely held, the reformist view was essentially economic as well as populist, aiming at the 'modernization' of agriculture – or, to use a different mode of thought, the deeper penetration of capitalistic relations of production into the rural sector.

An agrarian crisis

One essential feature of the agrarian crisis of the period was the failure of agricultural production to keep pace with population growth. In 1975, agricultural production per head was less than it had been in the period 1961–5 in no less than nine out of twenty Latin American countries: Chile, Colombia, Cuba, the Dominican Republic, Ecuador, El Salvador, Mexico, Peru and Uruguay. Even in the mid-sixties food production had failed to keep pace with population growth over the previous decade in Argentina, Colombia, Chile, Ecuador and Uruguay. Weak agricultural performance was most apparent in the production of foodstuffs for domestic consumption rather than in the export sector, leading to rising imports of foodstuffs even where there was clearly a potential capacity for internal production. Between 1967 and 1973 rising imports of foodstuffs as a percentage of total imports were characteristic of Argentina, Chile, Colombia, Mexico, Nicaragua, Panama and Peru (Blakemore & Smith, 1983, p. 11). Until the 1950s, the most technically advanced agricultural systems were essentially those devoted to the production of export crops, but the explosion of urban, and especially of metropolitan populations created new demands for foodstuffs and raw materials which internal production seemed incapable of satisfying because of structural bottlenecks in agrarian organization. Influential studies, particularly those undertaken in the early sixties by the Interamerican Committee for Agricultural Development, brought to light the dimensions of the *latifundio-minifundio* complex in the countries surveyed, stressed the social injustice and rural oppression charactereistic of many areas, and also pointed to the agricultural inefficiency associated with the polarization of landholding. The dichotomy between extensively worked *latifundios* controlling most of the land resources and the proliferation of *minifundios* too small to employ peasant families or to supply adequate incomes was seen to be prevalent. One corollary of such distorted distributions of landholding was the small share of land in the hands of medium-scale proprietors who might be seen as the initiators of rural improvement.

Some of the large estates, particularly those in the export sector, could be regarded as highly productive and efficient in terms of innovation, capital investment and yields, but the image which most frequently emerged was that of the backward *hacienda*, operated by sharecropping or by burdensome and oppressive labour-service tenancies and owned by absentee landlords for whom the prestige of landownership mattered more than the maximization of income (Pearse, 1966; Barraclough & Domike, 1966). Levels of investment on the *haciendas* were low, partly because of 'a high propensity towards consumption' by the landowners, partly because profits from rural estates were more profitably invested in the expanding urban sector – in urban real estate, construction, commerce, industry or overseas investments. Internal social and tenurial institutions within the *haciendas* inhibited change and innovation in a variety of ways. The indirect exploitation of estates through sharecropping tenancies was not, in general, conducive to technical innovations in agricultural techniques. On pastoral *haciendas* labour-service tenants were accustomed to pasture their own native stock together with those of the *hacienda* owner. The introduction of improved stock or the improvement of pastures by landowners was therefore prevented unless investment in fencing and disease control was also forthcoming. The internal social hierarchy of the *hacienda* was often complex and delicately balanced (Bourricaud, 1962) to the point at which landowners were reluctant to attempt innovations, such as mechanized arable farming, or the introduction of new crops, which might disturb internal social relationships and traditional customary practice.

On the other hand, peasant communities had been subjected not only to the erosion of their land-base by the expansion of *haciendas*, particularly in the late nineteenth and early twentieth centuries, but they also suffered fragmentation of holdings as a result of the expansion of population. The *minifundios* were more intensively cultivated than the *haciendas*, though at a low level of technology, but as peasant holdings diminished in size and therefore in their capacity to provide a surplus over and above subsistence needs, so peasant farmers became more reluctant to undertake the risks in producing for commerce and became more concerned to preserve their capacity to produce for subsistence, earning income by the sale of labour (increasingly in the urban sector).

Thus, neither the large estate nor the small farms would, or could, respond to pressures making for agricultural innovation. Both the large estate owner and the peasant small-holder responded, in distinctive ways, to more rapid growth in urban, industrial and commercial sectors of the economy – the former by transferring capital to non-agricultural investment, the latter by transferring labour.

This image of the characteristic features of prevailing agrarian structures was highly influential in strengthening the case for a moderate land reform as an essential step towards breaking down the structural obstacles to the raising of agricultural productivity, particularly in relation to the supply of domestic markets, but it is important to stress that it was, to some extent, a simplistic image. Detailed community studies of the mid-sixties and early seventies indicated wide variations in the degree to which communities had responded to external commercial pressures or to the growth of population. Under favourable circumstances of location with respect to markets, of resource availability or of dynamic local leadership, small peasant-holdings had sometimes evolved stable and highly productive methods of cultivation or stock-raising in response to market demand (Whyte & Alberti, 1976). In other areas the picture was one of apathy, increasing poverty or hostility. The so-called traditional *haciendas* were sometimes becoming much more responsive to the need for raising productivity by the investment of capital, technical innovation, the eviction of labour-service tenants or their reduction to the status of a wage-paid proletariat. But it was the generalized image which pointed directly to the redistribution of land as a means of removing major obstacles to the improvement of agricultural production as well as eliminating social injustice in the rural sector.

The economic case for reform

In the hands of populist politicians, the social aspects of land reform (to eliminate social injustice, anti-social or 'neo-feudal' tenures and to give the land to those who work it) took precedence over economic arguments, but there were powerful supporters of the economic case for land reform of a moderate kind (Dorner, 1972; Thiesenhusen, 1972; Barraclough, 1973). One basic group of arguments rested on the image of the sturdy yeoman farmer as self-improver and potential innovator (in addition to his assigned role as individualistic defender of liberal democracy). Given enough land, or released from the bondage of share-cropping or labour-service tenancies, the Latin American peasant would respond rapidly to market forces by raising agricultural production. The ICAD reports, and others, suggested that economies of scale in agriculture were not significant, and brought abundant evidence to support the view that the intensity of land-use varied inversely with the size of holding (though labour productivity tended to vary directly with size of holding). The observable contrast between intensively cultivated *minifundios* and extensively used lands of the *haciendas*, often co-existing side by side in the same environment, allowed a further conclusion to be drawn. Underemployed peasant families would enhance their income and find additional work if the agricultural potential of the *haciendas* were more fully realized. Redistribution of land would make possible a greater degree of equality in the marginal product of land and labour. It is also noteworthy that this optimistic view of peasant capacity for self-improvement also rested on changing images of peasant attitudes to 'modernization'. In one sense, G.M. Foster, in his work on peasant society in the image of the limited good (Foster, 1965), had put a respectable, intellectual gloss on the stereotypes commonly held by elite and urban sectors of the peasantry as inherently conservative, stubborn in the face of change, and bound by tradition and custom. But other social anthropologists were taking a very different and more sympathetic view of peasant attitudes towards change, ranging from the opportunism of Sol Tax's penny capitalists to the appraisal of peasant strategies towards risk avoidance and response to change within the context of a household strategy for which the use of land was only one of several parameters (Pearse, 1975).

A second major element in the economic case for land reform of existing landholding structures was more concerned with its potential effects on demand. A redistribution of income in favour of the *campesino* would increase overall levels of effective demand in the countryside for cheap manufactured goods of a type which could be produced by national industries: clothing, textiles, footwear, paraffin stoves, roofing materials and the like. Other corollaries of this argument follow, though rarely stressed in the literature: increased income in the hands of peasant farmers would be reflected in greater and more varied consumption of foodstuffs, and a shift from basic grains and potatoes towards meat, milk, fruit and vegetables, itself providing a stimulus to local agricultural specializations. Furthermore, redistribution away from absentee landlords should reduce the drain of rural incomes into the cities in so far as rural populations relied for their modest supplies on local towns and provincial capitals rather than the major regional centres. In the event, the results of land reform have only partially confirmed theoretical expectations in this direction. Imported transistor radios and bicycles have tended to follow increased income in the hands of reform beneficiaries; national industry may have benefited from increased demands for clothing etc., but often at the expense of traditional local artisan production; the tendency towards more varied diet is expressed in demand for manufactured, packaged foodstuffs as likely as not to be imported, and often less nutritious but more prestigious than traditional diet. Yet where affected by land reform, peasants have eaten better (sometimes at the expense of produce formerly routed to the urban sector, as in the early stages of land reform in Bolivia), and the emergence of new peasant towns for marketing rural produce in the *altiplano* of Bolivia expressed, in part, the replacement of provincial and regional capitals by more local centres as the source of supplies and the destination for rural produce (Preston, 1969; von Marschall, 1970).

Underlying both the populist appeal to peasant emancipation and acceptance of the economic possibilities of land reform, as they were perceived in the late fifties and sixties, were fundamental changes in the economic and social structure of many Latin American countries. The shift from export-oriented development towards import-substitution industrialization, combined with the urban expansion closely associated with it, gave new emphasis to that sector of the bourgeoisie whose interests were involved in industrial expansion, commerce, banking and urban construction, rather than with the export sector or *rentier* profits from the ownership of land. A reformed rural sector could provide raw materials, cheap food supplies for the urban population, and provide a market for industrial output. It was among these groups and among the expanding state bureaucracies that support was forthcoming for 'reformist' land reforms, producing an apparent, and politically convenient, convergence with more radical views of the need for land reform.

Towards socialism or capitalism?

The fundamental difference in aims is obvious – land reform as a step towards socialism, and land reform as a step towards the more complete penetration of capitalism into the rural sector, or towards the 'modernization' of the rural sector. Yet many different interpretations could be put on programmes for *'reforma agraria'*, the fashionable coin of political discourse. In its usual sense, *reforma agraria* implied both land reform – the expropriation of land and its redistribution for the benefit of small farmers – and also the improvement of physical and social infrastructure: roads, agricultural extension services, cheap rural credit, education and even the commercialization of agricultural production (Warriner, 1969). It was under this banner, broader and less precise than the simple concept of land reform, that the peasantry, landless labour, the urban-based trade unions and their intellectual spokesmen of the left could be united briefly with sectors of the urban-based middle classes and populist politicians. The essential ambiguity of the term *reforma agraria* permitted universal support at one level; at another level it allowed lukewarm governments to ignore the explosive issues involved in land reform and to divert their efforts towards agricultural colonization of public land, the provision of rural credit, creation of irrigation projects and other peripheral activities, labelled by Ernest Feder as 'false agrarian reforms' and 'counter-reform' (Feder, 1970).

Agrarian reformism, as adopted by Ecuador, Colombia, Venezuela, Peru in 1964, and Chile in 1967, had economic aims which pointed towards a 'modernizing' concept of change, far removed from radical land reform. The target of increasing production of foodstuffs and raw materials involved the facility (not always executed, by any means) to expropriate unused land reserves of private owners, or lands deemed to be inefficiently or 'anti-socially' worked. Producers deemed to be efficient were normally exempt from expropriation or could retain substantial parts of their former estates. 'Neo-feudal' or 'anti-social' tenures were to be abolished, to be replaced by wage-paid labour, cooperative structures or individually-held peasant farms. Compensation for expropriated estates were substantial, sometimes encouraging landowners to divest themselves of unprofitable parts of estates (as in Venezuela) and thus to realize assets for investment elsewhere. Consolidation of *minifundios* into viable peasant holdings was often envisaged in legislation, but peasant opposition invariably made such provisions inoperative from the beginning.

The effectiveness of land reform measures

It has repeatedly been demonstrated, indeed, that there is a very large gap between land reform legislation, however modest and tentative, and its execution, and it is a gap in which many apparently well-meaning attempts at reform have disappeared without trace. Legislation not backed by political will and continuous budgetary support has achieved little. In Ecuador the Institute of Agrarian Reform and Colonization (IERAC) founded in 1964, eliminated labour-service tenancies, achieved some redistribution of land in its first two years of operation, chiefly in the *sierra*, but effectively achieved little more until a revival of interest in agrarian reform after 1972 and then again, a subsequent decline of activity. By 1979 agrarian reform had affected less than 20% of the peasant population and less than 15% of the agricultural land. A substantial part, even of this, had formerly been public land leased to large landowners (Handelman, 1980). The vast majority of large landowners had succeeded in maintaining their position by 1979, particularly in the coastal region. In Mexico, land reform was envisaged as a major solution to the agrarian problem as early as 1917, but little was done until the radical regime of President Cárdenas in the 1930s, and for most of the period since then land reform has made little further progress, except for a brief flurry of activity in the early seventies. In Colombia, as early as 1936, a law allowed for expropriation of land, and especially idle land, in the public interest and with a view to increasing food production. It also offered some protection for tenants. Some squatters were evicted as a result, and some landowners sold off land to small- and medium-scale holders. But little fundamental change occurred. A new agrarian reform law of 1961 set up a National Institute of Agrarian Reform and Colonization, but land reform was virtually a dead letter from the start and effort was diverted towards colonization of public land and provision, for example, of supervised credit. By 1970 less than 1% of the agriculturally exploited area had been affected by land reform, and since 1970 agrarian reform has been virtually abandoned (Sanders, 1980).

The diversion of agrarian reform programmes towards the colonization of new land or to State-owned land is nowhere better illustrated than in Venezuela, where public land constituted 73% and privately owned land only 27% of land transferred to the National Agrarian Institute (IAN), and much of the private land had been acquired before 1965 (Cox, 1978). In principle, peasant farmers in need of land may petition for the expropriation of underused or idle land in large estates, but in practice very little land has been expropriated against the wishes of landowners, and compensation terms have been very generous. But colonization has, in fact, been responsible for the new settlement on a fairly large scale to the south of the Andes and on the margins of the Orinoco basin (Smith, 1974). Venezuelan experience, with abundant public land at the disposal of the State, demonstrates very clearly that under favourable conditions a large number of peasant farmers can be accommodated with land without impinging seriously on the status and wealth of large landowners or impeding the penetration of the agricultural sector by foreign-controlled agribusiness. In Ecuador IERAC concentrated much of its attention on colonization, and the regularization of spontaneously settled new land in the eastern region and in the coastal zone, as well as in the densely populated *sierra*. 1.2 million ha or 74% of the land adjudicated between 1964 and 1977 represented colonization rather than agrarian reform (Handelman, 1980). In the tentative first stage of Peruvian agrarian reform of 1963-9, the relatively advanced agriculture of the coast was virtually untouched, a few estates in the *sierra* were affected by reform, but ambitious colonization programmes were mounted in the sparsely settled eastern regions.

Much of Latin American land reform legislation, particularly that which issued forth in the early sixties, was either formulated in such a way as to protect the interests of landowners, especially the 'modernizing', capitalistic estates, or it was never implemented as a true land reform. Exemptions, long bureaucratic delays, low budgets and policy fluctuations as a result of changing political circumstances have delayed or inhibited significant progress in redistribution.

There are some exceptions, of which Cuba is the most obvious example, of a revolutionary land reform. In Mexico, by 1969, the reformed sector (the *ejidos*) accounted for 61% of the total cultivated areas of the country. The authoritarian military regime in Peru between 1968 and 1975 achieved substantial reform against the wishes of landowning groups, and by the end of the period had expropriated and adjudicated about a half of the agriculturally exploited land in the coastal region and the *sierra*. The old traditional *haciendas* have virtually disappeared from the *sierra*, and former sugar and cotton estates on the coast have been transformed into cooperatives. The Allende government in Chile pushed land reform against powerful opposition until its policies were overturned after the coup of 1973. The Bolivian land reform, following the 1952 revolution, and affecting chiefly the *altiplano* and the region around Cochabamba, has never been reversed. And in Nicaragua, a rapid land reform has been taking place since 1979, greatly helped by the expropriation of the vast Somoza estates.

Productivity of the reformed sector

Where land reform has taken place on a significant scale, the performance of the reformed sector has, in general, been disappointingly poor, and Latin American experience can offer few examples of land reform leading directly to substantial increase in agricultural production from the reformed sector itself. In Mexico expropriated land was allocated to *ejidos* by which beneficiaries (*ejidatarios*) effectively received the use of individual plots of land within a loose communal framework. A perennial problem in the Mexican agricultural sector ever since has been the relatively slow growth of agricultural production in the *ejido* sector. In the 1940s the situation almost reached crisis proportions (Whetten, 1969), yet it has been argued that although output in the private sector increased much more rapidly than in the *ejido* sector in the fifties, output measured against the value of *inputs* did increase more rapidly in the *ejido* sector than in the private sector (Mueller, 1970). Obviously, the verdict depends in part on the indices of change which are adopted. There has long been considerable concern about the failure of Mexico's land reform in terms of the production of basic food crops for domestic consumption, notably maize, a crop which is given an almost mystical symbolism above and beyond its immediate utility. The problem of the *ejido* sector in Mexican agriculture is still not totally solved by any means, and current concern with its problems has stimulated the SAM (*Sistema Alimentaria Mexicana*) programme for the provision of credit and extension services, though recent accounts suggest that it has been of greater benefit to the independent medium-scale producers than to the *ejidatarios*.

In Venezuela, the relatively low productivity of the reformed sector has, again, been the subject of much comment and criticism. Part of the problem in Venezuela has been that the reformed sector has concentrated its production on staple foods (maize, rice, beans, etc.) of relatively low value, in which *yields* are often *above* those of the private sector, but aggregate value of agricultural production is less (Smith, 1974). To some extent, as in Mexico, there is a reluctance by small farmers to abandon the production of subsistence crops. And the private sector has retained its grip, not only on the best agricultural land near urban markets, but also on the more profitable crops of high value such as sugar, coffee, fruits, vegetables, poultry and stock production. Nevertheless, the charge can still be made that the reformed sector has been slow to experiment in the production of new crops or new strains, and indeed, the share of the reformed sector in total crop production *declined* from 33% in 1967–8 to 20% in 1975 (Cox, 1978). In Bolivia, the major advances in agricultural production have taken place in the eastern regions basically unaffected by land reform. And although the output and variety of arable production on the reformed lands near Lake Titicaca and La Paz-Oruro has greatly increased, the potential for more intensive stock-rearing on the *altiplano* by irrigated production of fodder crops, improved breeds, etc. has not been tapped (Zuvekas, 1977). In Peru, the years following the land reform of 1969–75 have been marked by a substantial fall in agricultural output, which dropped by 12% from 1970 to 1980. Decline is the result of many factors, including three successive years of drought and economic crisis, but there have been depressingly few signs of resilience in the reformed sector as a whole.

Reasons for failure

Why has land reform failed, even where it has been partially carried out, to deliver the kinds of results that were expected from it? Perhaps it is too soon to ask the question, in the sense that much more time is needed for peasant initiatives to flourish? Yet the Mexican, Bolivian, and Venezuelan experience of reform all date back over twenty years or more. Do the reasons lie in the inadequacy either of legislation or of the mechanisms adopted to carry it out? How far have inadequate land reforms been devised as an inevitable result of inadequate or incomplete concepts of previously existing structures and processes? Is it necessary to take refuge in the idea that no land reform can be successful unless it is part of a total restructuring of society? Or can it be argued that the limited changes already accomplished are sufficient to permit a deeper penetration of capitalistic, 'modernized' agriculture in the changing circumstances of the eighties?

The deficiencies of land reform legislation and of the mechanisms to carry it out are legion. Much may reasonably be attributed to a deliberate intention to avoid the confrontation of powerful landowning interests, but even in 'well-intentioned' reforms there have been many basic problems. For example, one of the major problems arising even before agrarian reform legislation is put into effect has been the tendency for landowners either to disinvest by running down their installations, selling stock, or to break up estates into smaller, but nominal holdings, often distributed to members of the family network in order to evade the provisions of the anticipated law (e.g. in Chile in 1964–5, or in Peru from 1964 to 1970). The agricultural census of Peru in 1972 suggests a dramatic fall in stock population, especially on surviving large estates, which may be due to under-registration, but must also reflect to a large extent a real decline from which recovery has been relatively slow. Peruvian sugar estates suffered from the flight of experienced and skilled managerial and technical staff following the land reform of 1969, as did the Cuban reform of sugar estates from 1959.

In all but revolutionary reforms, the processes involved in expropriation, valuation, compensation and the allocation of land to beneficiaries have not only tended to be costly and long drawn out, but have also led to the bureaucratization of land reform organizations. Nowhere is this better illustrated than in Venezuela, where it has been estimated that over 50% of the budget for land reform went to administrative costs, and in the early seventies, at any rate, the funds budgeted for the acquisition of land from private owners was little more than the budget for travelling expenses of agrarian reform officials! In Peru, the diversion of agrarian and legal expertise into land reform appears to have resulted in a virtual breakdown in the provision of agricultural extension services (World Bank Report on Peru, 1980).

Other problems have resulted from misconceived images of the agrarian reality or a sheer lack of knowledge. The Peruvian reform of 1969, like many others, was predicated in part on the idea that expropriation of the large estates and the emancipation of tenant farmers and landless labour working on them would go far to satisfy rural unrest. Some limited measures were undertaken to reach *minifundios* by the creation of associations between former tenants on the estates (organized in cooperatives) and neighbouring communities (SAIS), but in the event they affected very few of the vast numbers of peasant farmers owning their own plots or organized in communities. Indeed, calculations suggested that land reform in the *sierra* could only make available enough land to satisfy 9% of qualified candidates (Smith, 1976). The execution of land reform was, not surprisingly, accompanied by unrest and rural rebellion (e.g. in Andahuaylas in 1973), particularly among those very large numbers of small-holders who had not in any way benefited, nor saw any prospect of benefiting, from land reform. In the highlands of Peru, in spite of the active pursuit of genuine land reform to 1975, there was never enough land to go round.

Other criticisms that have been widely voiced relate to the treatment and organization of the beneficiaries of land reform. Initial assumptions that agrarian reform involved the improvement of infrastructure, the provision of rural credit, agricultural extension services, etc. have rarely been fulfilled. In Venezuela, a complaint of the early 1970s was that beneficiaries received little or no help on land allocated to them. Land distributed was often of poor quality, partly because landowners had been able to divest themselves, with good compensation, of the poorer parts of their estates or because landowners were able legally to retain the best located and most productive land for themselves (e.g. in Mexico). Delays in the granting of title to beneficiaries of reform effectively precluded access to rural credit (e.g. in Bolivia and Ecuador), while restrictions on the disposition of lands acquired from land reform agencies have meant that peasant beneficiaries' access to rural credit has been confined to specific agencies controlled by government or the land reform agency itself, since collateral for commercial credit cannot easily be offered. (This has been a recurrent problem in Mexico and Venezuela.)

One of the consequences of the inadequacy of support systems for land reform beneficiaries and particularly for those in remote locations distant from urban markets, on poor land and perhaps with not enough of it, has been the tendency for peasants in the reformed sector to give high priority to the production of subsistence crops. The concentration of the Venezuelan reform sector on staple foodstuffs – maize, beans and rice – is indicative of their priorities. In some former *haciendas* of the Peruvian *sierra*, cooperatives created by the Institute of Agrarian Reform have virtually disintegrated as peasant farmers insist on individual cultivation of land for their own subsistence crops. In the Bajío of Mexico, a detailed comparison of innovation and diffusion of hybrid maize and sorghum demonstrated clearly that while *ejidatarios* adopted hybrid maize fairly readily, their rate of adoption of sorghum was slower and less complete than that of private medium-scale farmers. Again, the importance of preserving a subsistence base to land-use by farmers in the reformed sector appears to have been demonstrated (quite apart from their readiness to adopt new varieties of maize where the advantage was clear (Ellis, 1978).

Not least among the factors which have inhibited the success of the reformed sector are the constraints imposed by post-reform organization – or the lack of it. In Venezuela, one of the criticisms of reform in the sixties was the lack of support given to beneficiaries after land had been adjudicated (Smith, 1974); in Peru, the emphasis placed upon cooperative forms of post-reform organization has led to many problems. Lewis Taylor's work suggested that where *haciendas* were formerly worked by wage-paid labour and were relatively advanced agriculturally, cooperatives were more successful than on traditional *haciendas* in which former tenants and peasant neighbours have tended to take their own initiative in dividing land into plots at the expense of the cooperatives (Taylor, 1980). On technically advanced and unionized sugar estates in Peru the cooperative members have effectively become privileged groups working minimal hours themselves, but hiring cheap labour on a casual basis for much of their labour needs.

Agrarian reform in Latin America has not fulfilled the great expectations that were raised by it, not least in the economic sphere. It is true that the status of many former tenants has improved; many of the beneficiaries seem at least marginally to have reached higher levels of material welfare, though it is sometimes difficult to disentangle the effects of agrarian reform from effects due to other circumstances. In one sense, as it was suggested initially, agrarian reform has facilitated and encouraged the extension of capitalism into agriculture. To a substantial extent, it was, of course, designed to do so by those who saw agrarian reform as a means of 'modernizing' the rural sector. Within the reformed sector, labour-service tenancies and sharecropping have been eliminated. In some cases, the threat of agrarian reform was enough to persuade landowners to follow a general tendency towards the conversion of labour-service tenancies to wage-paid labour, more stable forms of tenancy, or even to the sale of parts of their estates to peasant farmers. In other cases, land was adjudicated individually to tenant farmers or organized as cooperatives. The loss of paternalistic relationships between landlord and peasants, and their replacement by a cash nexus or by the bureaucratic government of a cooperative has sometimes been regretted, but these trends are symptomatic of the removal of constraints upon more capitalistic relationships: from landlord and tenant towards employer and worker. Similarly, land reform or the threat of it has resulted in landowners either making some attempt to exploit idle land or disposing of it to land reform agencies or to small and medium farmers. Former landowners, left with the rump estates allowed to them by reform legislation (in Mexico and Chile, for example), have been thus encouraged to use the land remaining to them more intensively, with greater use of capital investment and hired labour.

Green Revolutions and State interventions

The major advances in agricultural development have taken place in the 'non-reformed' sector. In Mexico, river basin irrigation projects have made available new land for medium-scale and large-scale agricultural operations which have been capitalistically organized from their inception. It is in such areas, and among the medium-scale farmers left by land reform elsewhere, that agricultural innovation and much more capital-intensive farming has made the most substantial contribution to the expansion of agricultural output. In Bolivia, the eastern regions were untouched by the agrarian reform of the fifties, and capitalist farming associated with the production of sugar, rice and beef has expanded considerably in these areas in the last twenty years. Large stock-raising estates are being re-created on a large scale, often at the expense of small and medium farmers (Clarke, 1974). It is in such areas of post-reform development, especially perhaps in Mexico, that the Green Revolution, with its emphasis on high yields and intensive investment in inputs as well as improved or new crop strains, has been most widely adopted. Indeed, in Mexico at least, innovation and high technology in agriculture appears to be very closely linked either with the direct participation of international agribusiness, or with systems of contract farming associated with multinational companies (Burbach & Flynn, 1980).

Land reform obviously implies the intervention of the State in the rural sector, and in itself represents an extension of government responsibilities far greater than the generally accepted role of government to provide basic infrastructure, agricultural extension services, rural education and even cheap rural credit. But agrarian reform has often involved more far-reaching consequences through the continuing involvement of agrarian reform agencies. In general, the direction of State involvement has been, in principle, towards raising agricultural production, hastening the transition from subsistence to commercial production and above all, perhaps, facilitating or encouraging the transition towards capitalistic forms of production. In practice, the results of State involvement have sometimes been less than effective in bringing about the desired aims.

In the allocation of land, for example, the State usually retains the right of reversion of the land it allocates, and as in Mexico, restricts the right of beneficiaries to sell, mortgage or lease their lands. Adopted in the interest of protecting holdings from fragmentation or amalgamation into new large estates, such restrictions, where operative (and they have been commonly ignored at various phases in Mexico and Venezuela), tend to fossilize the units created by land reform, and more importantly, limit the access of land reform beneficiaries to commercial sources of credit since the land cannot be offered as collateral. Rural credit for the reform sector is therefore available only through State-controlled sources (often in insufficient quantities), but vastly extending the capacity of government to guide production along desired lines. Thus, in Ecuador:

The agrarian reform which has been carried out in the rice zone is seen as a significant move in the realization of development objectives on the part of the Ecuadorian state. In return for the distribution of land titles [to former rice-tenants] the state bureaucracy expected to increase their control over the marketed surplus of rice . . . By selective inputs of agricultural technology and the close management of rice cultivation it was also hoped to increase rice production dramatically. (Redclift, 1978, p. 162)

In Venezuela, however, the multiplicity of government agencies involved with reform beneficiaries and the bureaucratic delays involved have been a common cause of complaint and frustration (Eastwood, 1974).

In the Peruvian agrarian reform of 1969–75, more sweeping than most in its expropriation of the large estates, the emphasis given to the formation of cooperatives reflected the ideology of the Velasco regime, but one major underlying characteristic was the firm intention to exercise continued control by government over management and the allocation of resources in the new cooperatives. In many instances, particularly in the *sierra*, however, the cooperative structures have been disintegrating or, at least, falling far short of initial objectives. The attempt at State control has by no means been successful, and current reorientation of policy has been towards the stimulation of medium-scale farming on an individual rather than a cooperative basis.

Conclusion

In their broadest sense, programmes of agrarian reform represent an effort, in economic terms, to change rural structures in ways which will lead to increased agricultural production, yet it is also seen as a political necessity that low food prices should be maintained for the benefit of urban consumers. Rises in the prices of staple foodstuffs are generally greeted by riots and strikes, and opposition not only from the urban working class and the informal sector, but also from industrial and mining interests concerned to maintain low wages. In a sense, the question of food prices is symptomatic of a more general tendency to subordinate the agricultural sector to the overriding priorities given to industrialization. Yet controls over prices of staple foodstuffs do not often extend to luxury and highly processed foodstuffs oriented to middle-class markets. But it is precisely in this area of innovation that the agrarian reform sector is least well able to participate because of restrictions on credit availability and the investment required for new agricultural technologies. Current tendencies, such as the trend towards monetarist policies, and the participation of foreign capital in processing, packaging, marketing and production, favour the medium-scale farmer and the re-creation of large-scale units in a capitalistic rather than a traditional form. The beneficiaries of the agrarian reform sector are in danger of becoming marginalized, starved of credit, sometimes more concerned with subsistence than with production for the market, generally endowed with holdings too small to benefit from current advances in agricultural techniques, and often too remote from urban markets to specialize in highly intensive production.

REFERENCES

Barraclough, S. (1973). *Agrarian structure in Latin America.* Lexington Books, Lexington.

Barraclough, S. & Domike, A.L. (1966). Agrarian structure in seven Latin American Countries. *Land Economics*, 42 (4), 391–424

Blakemore, H. & Smith, C.T. (eds.) (1983). *Latin America: geographical perspectives.* Methuen, London

Bourricaud, F. (1962). *Changements à Puno: Étude de sociologie Andine.* Institut des Hautes Études de l'Amérique Latine, Paris

Burbach, R. & Flynn, P. (1980). *Agribusiness in the Americas.* Monthly Review Press, New York

Clarke, R.J. (1974). Landholding structures and land conflicts in Bolivia's lowland cattle regions. *Inter-American Economic Affairs*, 28, 15–38

Cox, P. (1978). *Venezuela's agrarian reform at mid-1977.* Research Paper No. 71, Land Tenure Center, University of Wisconsin

De Janvry, A. (1981). *The agrarian question and reformism in Latin America.* Johns Hopkins University Press, Baltimore

Dorner, P. (1972). *Land reform and economic development.* Penguin, London

Eastwood, D. (1974). Agrarian reform in Venezuela: principles and practice. In C.T. Smith (ed.), *Studies in Latin American agrarian reform*, Centre for Latin-American Studies, University of Liverpool, Monograph No. 5, 19–38

Ellis, P.R. (1978). The diffusion of recent agricultural innovations in the Bajío, Mexico. Unpublished Ph.D. thesis, University of Liverpool

Feder, E. (1970). Counterreform. In R. Stavenhagen (ed.), *Agrarian problems and peasant movements in Latin America*, Anchor Books, New York, 173–224

Foster, G.M. (1965). The peasant in the image of the limited good. *American Anthropologist*, 67 (2), 293–315

Grieshaber, E.P. (1979). Hacienda-Indian community relations and Indian acculturation. *Latin American Research Review*, 14, 107–128

Handelman, H. (1980). Ecuadorian agrarian reform: the politics of limited change. In. H. Handelman (ed.), *The politics of agrarian change in Asia and Latin America.* Indiana University Press, Bloomington, 63–81

Lehmann, D. (ed.) (1974). *Agrarian reform and agrarian reformism.* Faber & Faber, London

Lindqvist, S. (1979). *Land and power in South America.* Penguin, London

Marschall, K.B. von (1970). La formación de nuevos pueblos en Bolivia. *Estudios Andinos*, 1, 23–37

Mörner, M. (1973). The Spanish American hacienda: a survey of recent research and debate. *Hispanic American Historical Review*, 53, 184–215

Mueller, M.W. (1970). Changing patterns of agricultural output and productivity in the private and land reform sectors in Mexico, 1940–1960. *Economic Development & Cultural Change*, 18 (2), 253–78

Pearse, A. (1966). Agrarian change trends in Latin America. *Latin American Research Review*, 1 (3), 44–77

(1975). *The Latin American peasant*. Cass, London

Preston, D.A. (1969). The revolutionary landscape of highland Bolivia. *Geographical Journal*, 135 (1), 1–16

Redclift, M.R. (1978). *Agrarian reform and peasant organization on the Ecuadorian coast*. University of London, Institute of Latin-American Studies, Monograph No. 8, London

Sanders, T.G. (1980). Food policy decision-making in Colombia. In H. Handelman (ed.), *The politics of agrarian change in Asia and Latin America*, Indiana University Press, Bloomington, 82–102

Smith, C.T. (1974). Agrarian reform in Venezuela: recent changes and regional variations. In C.T. Smith (ed.), *Studies in Latin-American agrarian reform*, Centre for Latin-American Studies, University of Liverpool, Monograph No. 5, 39–60

(1976). Agrarian reform and regional development in Peru. In R.M. Miller, C.T. Smith & J.R. Fisher (eds.), *Social and economic change in modern Peru*, Centre for Latin-American Studies, University of Liverpool, Monograph No. 6, 87–119

Taylor, L. (1980). Main trends in agrarian capitalist development: Cajamarca, Peru, 1880–1976. Unpublished Ph.D. thesis, University of Liverpool

Thiesenhusen, W.C. (1972). A suggested policy for industrial reinvigoration in Latin America. *Journal of Latin-American Studies*, 4, 85–104

Warriner, D. (1969). *Land reform in principle and practice*. Clarendon Press, Oxford

Whetten, N.L. (1969). *Rural Mexico*. University of Chicago Press

Whyte, W.F. & Alberti, G. (1976). *Power, politics and progress*. Elsevier, New York

Wilkie, J.W. (1974). *Measuring land reform, supplement to the Statistical abstract of Latin America, 1974*. University of California: Los Angeles, Latin American Center

Zuvekas, C. (1977). *Technological change in Bolivian agriculture: a survey*. Working Document Series: Bolivia, No. 4, Rural Development Division, US Agency for International Development

3 Frogs and farmers: the Green Revolution in India, and its murky past

CHRISTOPHER J. BAKER

The Green Revolution seems to have suffered from one of those optical illusions bound up with the business of ageing. Things which seemed enormous when seen through the eyes of the child look much more modest when viewed again after a passage of years. Green Revolution watching has been around long enough to have developed a fair bit of middle-aged spread. The shining skyscraper seen in childhood now looks like a fairly ordinary apartment block.

In the early years of the Green Revolution, the major criticisms and the major sources of controversy revolved around the effects on distribution. Few doubted the potency of the new technology, but many believed that it would be solely or largely available to a richer minority of the rural population and that as such it would tend to accentuate class divisions in a society which was already badly divided. More recently this topic has been joined and perhaps overshadowed by two other critical commentaries. The first is the observation that the Green Revolution has really caught on in only a few regions and production regimes. In India it has succeeded with wheat, but results have been more equivocal in the case of rice. It has become established in the areas selected for the intensive programme (and of course these areas were selected on the grounds that they were likely to deliver success), but it has not developed a lot of momentum outside these areas (e.g. Dasgupta, 1977). The second is the contention that the Green Revolution never happened. According to this view, production trends in the Indian subcontinent as a whole show no marked shifts in the mid-sixties and thus the Green Revolution was really more ballyhoo than bread (e.g. Rudra, 1979).

But what happens to this unsteady scene if we take a pace backwards and view it from a little further off? What happens to these criticisms of the Green Revolution when we set them against a slightly longer-run view of India's agrarian development? In particular what should we make of the present fashion for statistical proofs that the Green Revolution has not happened since the graph of India's agricultural growth shows no dramatic shift in trend around the magic year of 1966–7?

The agrarian revolution in history

The historical perspective is very practised at making molehills out of mountains. Seen from a sufficient distance, almost any graph looks pretty smooth. The temptation to see Indian agriculture as something timeless and unchanging has always been very strong. For a long time it has been standard practice for historians to make scathing remarks about the common nineteenth-century view (usually attached to the nicely bipolar pair of Marx and Maine) that made a fundamental distinction between the rural and urban contributions to India's history. According to this 'hovercraft' view, the dynamic and changing forces of the state and the urban sector flew across the timeless seas of Indian rural society without making more than a few insignificant ripples, and without meeting any obstruction more imposing than an occasional cloud of spray. But critical comments on this classical view have not until very recently gone so far as to propose an entirely antithetical view – that the pattern of Indian history has emerged from the arcane forces of the deep. With many qualifications and appended details, the conventional view of India's rural history has remained 'nothing much new under the sun'.

Rural resurgence

The hovercraft theory was only a particularly structured version of the more general, and more generally accepted, notion that the message of modern history is that change comes from the town. With their very different final perspectives, Marx and Maine were both fascinated by the power of Europe's industrial revolution. It is hardly surprising that this general view gained a new lease of life in an era when attempts were being made to reproduce the effects of industrial revolution in non-western parts of the world. However, the more recent industrial difficulties of the advanced industrial countries, the knowledge gained from the failures of the instant industrialisation policies of the early development age, and the new concern for the supply of primary commodities, have forced economists and other apprentice magicians to take a more enlightened and optimistic view of agriculture. It is difficult not to believe that there is a connection between this shift of perspective, and the resurgence of interest in historical studies of agrarian change.

That is not to say that agrarian history was ever downgraded in its own right. But it has not always, as it has recently, ventured out of its own narrow pathways and become a truly imperial force. In the last decade, several studies of the long-term development of the western world have concentrated chiefly, if not exclusively, on the rural and agricultural roots of change. In these several works, the keys to explanation and analysis of course differ enormously – the relations between landlord and peasant, the demographic and productive implications of different kinship systems, the timing and location of breakthroughs in agricultural technology, the pattern of trade in rural produce – but the principal message is the same. The modern history of the western world, however much it may seem at first to be dominated by urban forces, cannot be understood apart from the intricacies of the rural part of the story.[1] And what is more, this rural part of the story is full of change and movement. Unlike the style of the courtly portrait painters of the age of Marx and Maine, the countryside is not just the 'background'.

This perspective has been applied to Asia some time ago. T.C.Smith's *Agrarian Origins of Modern Japan* (1959) is now over twenty years old. But South Asia would seem to be a more difficult terrain to invade. In his cross-country comparison of the agrarian transformations of the modern world, Barrington Moore (1967) ended up with only negative conclusions about India. In the end he used the sub-continent as the example of changelessness which served as a contrast for the dynamic histories of the other regions. Moreover, the end product of the agrarian history of India would seem itself to be sufficient proof of a lack of dynamism. Comparisons between statistics from the end of the colonial era and those available from the Moghul period have suggested (not without controversy) that the level of production remained unchanged across three centuries. The technologies employed in much of Indian agriculture do not *look* as if they have changed in aeons. The only serious attempt to analyse the statistics of agricultural production across the whole sub-continent in the first half of the twentieth century cannot produce much evidence of growth (Blyn, 1966). The basic premise of the Green Revolution programme was that the stagnation of Indian agriculture in the colonial period left behind a terrifying shortage of basic foods.

Change and torpor in the Indian countryside

In recent years there has been enough piecemeal study of India's agrarian history to make possible a view of the subcontinental pattern of change in the colonial period which is rather cannier than the blunt 'did it grow or decline' theme which preoccupied earlier writing. Of course it is not yet possible to reach anything like an assured and acceptable conclusion. The extremely bitty and biassed nature of the data on the one hand, and the extraordinary ideological importance attached to the basic conclusion ('Was colonialism a bad thing or a very, very bad thing? Answer to within not fewer than three decimal places and associated *t* statistic') make sure of that. But it is now possible to see some preliminary outline.

The major paradox of agricultural change in India's recent history would seem to be this. At the most general level, India's agricultural sector seems to have been torpid and unresponsive, as is evident in the long-term failure to produce enough food for everyone to eat. But at a more particular level, in specific areas and in specific periods, there have been many examples of rapid growth, technological change, and sensitive response to forces of the market. The argument for a general condition of torpidity (whether attributed to the climate, the capacity of the people, the social structure, or the state) is continually cut short by examples of specific dynamism.

A few of these examples must be mentioned. The Punjab's first Green Revolution took place in the second half of the nineteenth century. Farmers responded to the provision of water from the new canals by moving to the production of fine rice and sugar cane, and by adopting three sets of 'new varieties' of sugar cane within the space of a single generation. In the early years of the twentieth century, Gujarat agriculture grew rapidly, with sugar cane and cotton leading an expansion of acreage which in some districts like Surat amounted to a 50% increase over a decade. After the First World War, when most of the agriculture of eastern India seemed to be in a hopeless state, the farmers of the Presidency Division of Bengal put more land under the plough, planted more barley, gram and jute beside their usual crops of rice, and kept the growth of output comfortably ahead of the galloping pace of the population. In the Kongu area of Madras and in parts of Maharashtra, farmers transferred half of their cropped area from ordinary dry grains and sundry crops to cotton cultivation within the space of five to ten years around the same period.

All these examples involve cash crops which enjoyed a fair pull from urban or overseas sources of demand, but there were some similar spurts in areas dedicated to food crops. In the upland areas of the very far south of India, large but indeterminate tracts of forest and scrub were cleared and planted with rice and good dry grains between the 1810s and 1830s. The north Indian canal building of the pre-Mutiny period prompted a boom in rice and gram production in the west of U.P. and the Doab region in the 1840s. Wheat cultivation grew rapidly in the Narmada valley in western-central India in the 1870s and 1880s (Stone, 1979; Charlesworth, 1979; Islam, 1978; Baker, in press; Stokes, 1978).

This pattern of sporadic growth probably defies any general explanation. Certainly in different instances the 'trigger' for change seems to have come from different origins, and from both the demand and supply sides. The pattern of change, however, had some features in common. First, whatever single factor started off the spurt, other changes tended to accumulate. For instance a new provision of irrigation might prompt the adoption of new crops, new varieties of seed, different manurial practices, new marketing methods and different organisation of labour. Thus institutional and technical changes tended to be concentrated together in these short periods. Second, the periods of spurt or boom were generally short and were followed by lapse into stagnation or even a subsequent decline. The reasons why such growth never seemed to be sustained are certainly complex and different in individual cases, but there may be a general pattern. In his study of the Narmada valley wheat boom of the last years of the nineteenth century, Eric Stokes (1978) strongly denied the simple suggestion that the new opportunity for wheat cultivation and export was simply 'taken up' and finally exhausted by the logic of demographic growth and demand elasticities. Indeed after the end of the boom there was still plenty of room for expansion (still a low man-land ratio), and plenty of demand for wheat (subsequently supplied by the Punjab). The reasons, Stokes argued, lay in the development of agrarian society. Those local farmers and investors with a properly capitalist outlook stacked up their profits from the wheat and took it off to the town. Those who stayed and who bought up the land of those departing settled back to a life of rentier ease rather than a life of continued accumulation. Starved of truly active capital, farming in the Narmada valley shifted down to a lower level of intensity and the boom passed. It is possible that other booms have ended in a similar way with the usual range of rural predators – the rentier, the usurer, the carpet-bagger and the State – fastening on like leeches to any red-blooded example of growth.

Studies of one or two of these waves of growth and collapse suggest that the shape of local society may undergo several phases of change in the course of one such wave. In the early stages, when new opportunities are first becoming available, the scene is dominated by the small handful with the resources and entrepreneurship to grasp them. They have the necessary access to land, capital and markets, and they seem able to translate early profits into local monopoly. Theories of the dominating role of kulak-like rich peasants are born out of studies of such periods (Kumar, 1968; Washbrook, 1973). But later, opportunities diffuse, not by some automatic principle, but through the intervention of a small army of middlemen. The business of supplying capital, inputs and market access to a dynamic local economy becomes so attractive that many dive into this pool and farmers of all levels find they can get access to these services at competitive rates. Wealth spreads a bit. Monopoly is eased a bit. But as the boom passes, the middleman army moves away, and the incipient rentiers who remain begin to assert control not only over land but over all the links between the local and the outside economy so that they may take a rentier-like income from 'ownership' of these assets as well (Charlesworth, 1978).

Long swings?

But amid this confusing pattern of spurt and stagnation, is there any long-term trend, any 'long swing' analogous to the many different long-term trends which now compete with one another to explain the evolution of modern Europe? Overall trends in the political economy of the countryside are difficult to describe at the level of subcontinental generalisation because of the immense variety of local and regional detail. There have however been some spatial shifts which may soon be invested with the kind of explanatory importance recently attributed to shifts between east and west, north and south, in the history of Europe.

Until the Moghul period, the richest agricultural areas of India were the rice-growing regions, mostly positioned along the major river-systems, or the coastal plains of the peninsula. The lower Gangetic plain, and the coastal strips of Gujarat, Kerala and Tamil Nadu were the attractive areas, and the consequences still show up on the demographic map of India. Most of the remaining areas were more sparsely populated, more dangerous, less well provided with basic infrastructure, and less productive. Beginning in the Moghul times, and quickening in the colonial period, a new trend has emerged. The old rice-growing areas have often declined, or at least have been swamped by the accelerating pace of increase in their already substantial populations. The signs of decline appear both in these areas' productive capacity and in their social development. It is in these areas that it has been possible to find evidence of stagnant yields by comparing modern data with readings from Moghul records. One probable reason for such stagnation or decline lies in the exhaustion of the soil. The attempts to drive the land harder in order to feed more stomachs per acre have run through the stage of diminishing returns to the stage of actual degradation. More is taken out of the land than is put back. Other possible reasons are tied up with the accompanying pattern of social change. These areas have seen the development of something which might be called small-scale landlordism. Over the long term, population pressure has fragmented land holdings into a very small mean size. It has also made available a large and cheap labour force. The declining capacity of the land reduces the incentive for the land-owner to aim at increasing production through careful investment and careful husbandry (the effort would simply not be repaid), while the availability of cheap labour makes possible an easier alternative. The small plot owners thus work their land through various systems of tied labour and share-cropping – systems which are inefficient in terms of the gross production which results, but which are understandable in terms of the alternatives facing the individual petty landlord or rentier.

Over the same period of stagnation and decline in these old rice-growing regions, there has been a steady drift of population into the other tracts of the sub-continent. This has had two very different results in two rather different sorts of tract. On the one hand, arable agriculture has been extended into areas which until recently had been forest, marsh or semi-desert and which had supported perhaps only some shifting cultivation, gathering activities, seasonal fishing, or livestock husbandry. As agriculture extended in these tracts, it was always prone to the seasonal disasters of drought and flood. The combination of labour and simple technology could never deliver more than a small surplus, and any accumulation of such surpluses would regularly be wiped out by the inevitable bad year. State investment in such areas never looked like a sensible proposition in comparison to investment in other areas. These tracts thus begin and end as relatively poor. Much of the Deccan, and some insecure patches of the great riverine plains, fall into this category.

On the other hand, there were other areas where the increase in population and the accompanying advances in security and in infrastructure unlocked considerable opportunities for growth and prosperity. Many such tracts had been settled for some time, but were made considerably more attractive and productive by some combination of better security, better irrigation and better communications. The land was good, and nature moderately benign, and investment in rather more intensive cultivation often paid good returns. Also in these areas the pattern of agrarian society was shaped out of the defensive co-operative communities, or the society of individual homesteaders, which characterised the early stages of expansion in such difficult and often dangerous terrain. While the pioneer ethic may have faded pretty fast, the development of forms of rentierism and unfree labour ran far behind the pattern of the old rice-growing tracts (Stokes, 1978).[2]

These intermediate tracts were the scene of much of the agricultural growth in the colonial period. They had the space, the flexibility and the incentive to adopt the new paying crops like cotton, sugar and wheat. Owner-farmers were the rule rather than the exception, and they responded well to the stimuli of the market and were praised by the British ('sturdy' Jats, Patidars and Gounders) as fine examples of unfettered individualism. 'In this way', wrote Eric Stokes, 'over the course of the nineteenth century Lakshmi, the fickle goddess of fortune, betook herself with uneven tread westward from the lush verdure of Bengal until she has come to fix her temporary abode on the Punjab plain between Ludhiana and Lyallpur' (Stokes, 1978: p. 228). But this has not simply been a north Indian swing, though in other parts of the sub-continent it does not have quite the same geographic clarity. Around the peninsula, the shift has been from the riverine coastal tracts to their immediate hinterlands, and to occasional pockets of prosperity (Narmada, Kongunad) further into the interior.

The obscure history of agricultural technology

The growth in Indian agriculture in the colonial period, both in the sporadic spurts and in the long-term move towards the 'intermediate' tracts, was not simply a matter of extending the area. Commentators who think that 'technological change must involve something with several wheels and a noxious smell' are inclined to career past some of the less noisy and smelly changes which have taken place. But in its own fashion Indian agriculture was highly developed, and was still developing through the colonial period, despite all sorts of checks and hindrances. The agricultural consultants called in by the

British rulers in India – Dr Voelcker of the Royal Agricultural Society in the 1890s, the personnel of the Royal Commission on Indian Agriculture in the 1920s, and W. Burns who wrote a report on the technological possibilities of Indian agriculture in the 1940s – all reported their appreciation (and indeed surprise) at the complexity of technical change and adaptation in Indian agriculture. In particular they mentioned intricate crop rotations and fallowing systems designed to conserve and replenish the soil, elaborate methods of moving and distributing water, and knowledge of basic plant biology (Voelcker, 1894; Royal Commission, 1928; Burns, 1944). Periods of expansion in acreage tended also to be periods of technological change and diffusions. Since this kind of technical change is often easily ignored, I shall have to abandon the wider scope and concentrate on Madras in order to provide some illustration.

The adoption of transplantation in Indian rice cultivation has gone strangely unnoticed. In Madras in the later nineteenth century, it was reported that the practice was very rare. In the next thirty years or so there are stray mentions of moves to transplantation. By the 1930s, most contemporary writers appear to assume that the practice is the norm. Adoption of new seeds and practices for cash-crops were more often reported. New strains of cotton crop discovered in the 1910s, had taken over about half the acreage within fifteen years. Between the 1890s and the 1930s, there were three generations of new groundnut seeds, and two of new varieties of sugarcane, and all were adopted very rapidly. The adoption of new crops often led quickly to the adoption of new cultivation systems. As farmers in the Tamilnad interior took to more valuable crops they also moved towards more intensive cultivation practices, particularly repeated ploughings and more application of water using wells, tanks and various sorts of water-lift. These methods created a demand for more powerful draught animals, and led to the establishment of an ancillary cattle-breeding industry. When a few pumps appeared on the market as Second World War surplus, these farmers snapped up these new-fangled devices immediately and started bombarding the foreign-trade department for permission to import some more (Baker, in press).

Many of these advances, like transplantation and pumps, were of course no more than importations of known techniques and devices. But there was also a local research effort which had some important results. Agriculture departments appeared in most provinces of India in the 1880s and 1890s, and got involved in research work over the next two decades. The departments in the Punjab and Madras were particularly active (Hirashima, 1978). They spent a good deal of their severely limited resources trying to discover an implement which would revolutionise Indian agriculture, a strategy which reflected certain assumptions carried over from European experience (seed drills, etc.). The heavy ploughs which were an early favourite were later abandoned when it was realised that their major contribution was to increase the chances of soil erosion and to reduce the life-span of the bullocks required to drag them. In other respects, the departments and their research station were enormously hampered by the incomplete scientific understanding of tropical agriculture – particularly of soil and plant chemistry – and the often dangerous tendency to assume that the scientific lore from the temperate regions would apply (the heavy plough fixation was affected by such an assumption). In matters like plant breeding and improving cultivation practices they thus tended to proceed by the slow process of experiment and observation. The agricultural research journals of the first half of the century are full of reports on experiments in which the results are detailed but no analytical explanation is offered for them.

In such circumstances these departments had considerable success in breeding or acclimatising new crop strains, and passing them on to the farmers. Cash-crops like sugar, cotton, jute, tobacco and groundnut enjoyed the most attention, but there was also some success with foodgrains. It is not often credited that by independence quite a large part of India's rice acreage had already been transferred to new varieties of seed, and that these new seeds promised as large an incremental gain over the old types as that claimed for the new strains of the 1960s and seventies.

There were of course many reasons why these innovations did not have a larger impact on the general health of Indian agriculture, but one important set of reasons lay in the tentative and partial nature of the research and its application. By the 1930s, the officers of the research stations were puzzling over the reasons why so many of the new strains of crops which they had been growing for several decades had begun to show unmistakable signs of long-term fall-off in yields, even under research conditions. They had enough knowledge at least to guess at the reasons. New seeds delivered better yields but also took more out of the soil, and there had not yet been any attempt to counteract this effect. Next, increasing the number of farms irrigated under a riverine system often meant that an increasing proportion of farmers got their supply of water rather later than the optimum time; experiments showed that this could have a truly drastic effect on yield per acre, with the result that providing water to more farmers could mean a net decrease in overall output. Both of these informed guesses pointed to the dangerously partial nature of the research and development work in progress (Tamil Nadu Archives, 1947).

By the 1940s, those in the forefront of India's agricultural research had started to point out that it was all very well doing a lot of experiments using the oldest known research technique (hit or miss), but they could do with some more systematic thought and analysis. One of those who came to this conclusion was the Madras Director of Agriculture, Dr B. Viswanathan. When he was asked to submit his proposals to be included in the Government of India's first proper attempt at rural planning, he replied not with the usual shopping list for funds and personnel, but with a critical essay on the strategy of agricultural research and development. He noted that all the work on Indian research stations had produced an unprecedented amount of empirical data on tropical/sub-tropical agriculture, and that there had been a fair number of useful practical results. However, little had been done to advance a properly scientific understanding of tropical agriculture in general and the Indian variety in particular, and without such an advance progress was bound to be limited. The failure to build up a systematic body of knowledge about Indian agriculture, he noted, meant that after every pace which they lurched forwards, there appeared a little gremlin who forced them to take at least half a pace backwards:

We do not know the particular deficiencies of soils, the plant foods taken out by crops, plant foods supplied by manures and the response of crops in increased yield. We are not yet in a position to say with any degree of certainty, the amount of manure or fertiliser or water that can be applied to a given crop in a given locality. This is so because the studies on soils and manures in relation to crop growth have been of an isolated character and lack co-ordination necessary for attaining greater fertiliser and manure efficiency in terms of crop yields. (Tamil Nadu Archives, 1945a)

They could breed a super new seed, in other words, but they did not really know how it delivered the extra yield, and Viswanathan among others was beginning to suspect that at least one reason for the declining trend in foodgrain yields was buried among the attempts to make those same yields increase.

The Green Revolution and its past

What light can we reflect back from this ramble around India's recent agrarian history on to the evaluation of the last fifteen years of that history, the period of the Green Revolution? First, the peculiarly uneven impact of the new technology should be seen against a long historical pattern of strangely sporadic growth. In other words, the Green Revolution has not been a sudden break from stagnation into change, and the fact that the impact of change has been uneven fits in well with an established pattern. Over the long-term, Indian agriculture has not been the hopelessly inert toad that is often presumed. Rather it has been more like a collection of sleepy frogs, each of which makes an occasional, spirited hop between long bouts of torpor.

Second, the Green Revolution should not be considered something which was essentially generated outside India. Protagonists tend to see it as a supreme achievement of international co-operation and modern science, while critics see it as a nefarious plot by the trustees of late American millionaires. Of course, the important seeds did come from Mexico and the

Philippines, and the cash came from all over the place. But two other elements which were vital to such success as has been achieved were entirely indigenous – the demand for such technological advance (and hence the willingness to use it), and the organisational capacity to distribute the goods. On the first point, it is clear that by the mid-twentieth century there were farmers who were pressing anxiously against the frontiers of the available technology. Over the past half-century, they had eagerly adopted various types of new crops and seeds thrust on them by the market or the departments of agriculture, had harassed government for more help with irrigation, built wells whenever it was a technically and commercially sensible undertaking, and snapped up pumpsets as soon as they knew what they were.

The organisation of revolution

On the second point, the organisational capacity, two points need to be made. First, long before the magic year of 1966, India's agricultural development officers had plotted a course towards the Green Revolution. Seed technology had occupied India's experimental stations since the early years of the century. What those such as Madras' B. Viswanathan saw by the time of the Second World War was that agricultural change would require a much more rounded effort on the part of government, and that meant more knowledge and more administrative machinery. After its first development efforts in the crash wartime campaign Grow More Food, one Madras department concluded:

In economic affairs and planning partial views tend to be false views. Government will probably do more harm than good by its intervention unless it is provided with a complete (or nearly complete) and very carefully analysed statement of the facts. Such a statement cannot be obtained from administrative departments engaged in handling urgent matters of detail, nor from private students with limited resources. (Tamil Nadu Archives, 1945b)

Dr Viswanathan argued that the kinds of technological advance which were needed could only come from communal effort: 'The days of individualism are gone', he wrote, 'either the farmers should organise themselves or the State should organise them and teach them ways and means of obtaining a decent and secure living.' And he set out a menu of the research that would have to be done: breeding of crops that were more productive, more adaptable, and better able to withstand the climatic vagaries which were the norm for most of India; more small-scale irrigation, particularly from wells; more research on the use of water and manure to make optimum use of available resources; more research on pests and diseases (thitherto an almost untouched subject); and the establishment of a machinery through which the state could supply co-ordinated packages of improved inputs (seeds, fertiliser, pesticide), technical assistance with irrigation and cultivation practice, and supporting finance. Viswanathan also noted (in 1944) that it would take about twenty years for such a programme to bear fruit. It would take that long to acquire the knowledge to develop and multiply the seeds, and to construct the administrative machinery (Tamil Nadu Archives, 1947). Twenty years was in fact a rather optimistic guess.

Second, the administrative aspect of the Green Revolution has been truly revolutionary – but it was a revolution that took place about a quarter of a century earlier. The nub of the change was a decision to commit a sizeable chunk of the government's administrative resources to an attempt to quicken agricultural change. The colonial government had worked on the principle of holding the rural economy at arm's length, and at the end of 1942 the Viceroy was still arguing that any attempts to intervene in the business of foodgrain production and distribution were 'not likely to yield results comparable to the panic they would create'. Within two years of this statement, a major government commission had concluded that 'a policy of laissez-faire in the matter of food supply and distribution is impossible in the future'. The contrast between these two statements represented not only a change of attitude but an enormous shift of resources. Again the example comes from the province of Madras, but the same pressures were operating elsewhere in the subcontinent. In 1942–3, the Madras Government sank no capital at all in the grain trade; in 1946–7 it put up Rs 291.4 million. In 1942 food administration took up half the time of one official; in 1946 there were fifteen thousand foodgrain officers. In 1942 food administration cost government virtually nothing; in 1946–7 it swallowed a quarter of the provincial budget. In 1942, the idea of agrarian planning would have seemed moonshine, but by 1944–5 officials were wrestling with a ramshackle attempt at planning known as the Grow More Food campaign, and writing memos to one another about three-year plans, five-year plans, ten-year plans and even longer strategies. Viswanathan was busy telling Delhi that just for starters he would need a thousand more men for research and extension work in his agriculture department (Baker, 1981).

Of course the immediate reason for this sudden shift was the war, the consequences of Britain's recruitment of the Indian economy for the war effort, and the resulting disaster in Bengal. But the fact that the shifts turned out to be more permanent than the war or the empire indicates that there were longer-run reasons of more lasting weight. Naturally there have been steps backwards as well as steps forwards in the subsequent history of India's agricultural administration, and naturally the units of India's agricultural and food administration departments are riddled with the petty corruptions and enormous inefficiencies which swarm through any huge and sprawling bureaucracy. But the point is that some things work; seeds and fertilisers do get distributed, and crops do get purchased, and research does get done. In the wartime crisis large numbers of general administrators suddenly found themselves trying to tell experienced farmers what they ought to be doing, and to dictate to the traders who ran one of the biggest distribution networks in the world. The reaction of these officers, once they had been catapulted forward in the promotions that followed independence, was to create a more professional and more knowledgeable service. There were few existing models for the kind of extension work that was envisaged, and a lot had to be found out by simple trial and error. But in comparison to many other countries, it is the bureaucratic complexities behind the Green Revolution which are particularly impressive.

Old problems rather than new ones

The Green Revolution itself is not really an imported variety, but more like a cross between a foreign concoction and some hardy local plants. Thus it is hardly surprising that the little leaps forward of the sixties and seventies look suspiciously like the old frog-hops of Indian agricultural growth. If so, what else can we learn from this analogy? The first point is that much of the concern about increasing inequalities and technological indivisibilities may have been too hasty. Certainly it seems that in the early years of the new technology, the larger farmers were better able to take the new opportunities and the result was a measurable concentration of control over assets and income. However, as we have noted above, a similar kind of pattern has been evident during previous spurts of local agricultural growth. Rural society has always been quite remarkably plastic in this respect. Yet in these past examples, the initial direction of change towards greater inequality and stratification was not sustained. After a time, the new opportunities did tend to percolate through to a wider group, not through the action of some economist's law of gravity, but through the designs of agents and middlemen who could see the chance for a profit. It seems possible that a similar development has been taking place in the recent case. Subsequent reports have been more confused and equivocal about the question of advancing disparities, and the picture is no longer so clear. Besides, the main argument supporting the case for a definite structural bias in the new technology revolved around the alleged indivisibilities – the fact that it is difficult or uneconomic to make available the inputs in units appropriate to the small farmer. Yet this idea somehow fails to ring true in the Indian context, where the practice of miniaturisation and division is extremely well-developed. In effect the Green Revolution technology is probably only a little less divisible than a packet of cigarettes, and already there is a great deal of the 'one cigarette, one match' style of trading in Green Revolution inputs.

The real problem, past examples suggest, lies not in the lurch towards capitalist rationality and all its horrors (accumulate, accumulate), but in the subsequent drift into lazy rentierism (vegetate, vegetate). Previous spurts of local agricultural growth often lapsed back towards inertia within a couple of decades, well before the opportunities available in the market or the available technology had been exhausted. Many explanations are possible for this pattern, but one description might go like this. When new marketing or technological opportunities become available, a relatively small group of large or enterprising farmers are able to secure most of the benefits, partly through monopolising access to the new opportunities, partly through their ability to recruit their lesser neighbours as subordinate assistants, and partly through a readiness to reinvest, particularly in the acquisition of more land to exploit. At a later stage, however, agents and middlemen appear and make the new opportunities available to a wider group of farmers; they sell inputs, or mediate access to markets. Once they have these facilities, the smaller farmers may be able to compete successfully with their bigger neighbours simply because the former are prepared to discount the price of their own labour. As far as the big men are concerned, this fouls up the market and changes the balance of attractions between re-investment in expanding production and shift to a more rentier style. The big men may find it makes more sense to rent out their assets of land and liquid capital rather than put them to work directly, and anyway, a charpoy is more comfortable to drive than a plough. Once this trend begins, a phase of gradual degeneration sets in. The middlemen and rentiers take such a large skim from the surplus of production that the re-investible portion is steadily diminished and the impetus to grow gradually dwindles away.

An end or a beginning?

Finally in the long trends of India's agrarian history, the Green Revolution looks more like an end than a beginning. The successes have largely come in the 'intermediate' areas which have been generally in the ascendant over the past century. Indeed many of the most impressive sites of the Green Revolution appear to be places which saw rapid agricultural growth in the period from the 1880s to the 1920s and then marked time – Punjab and Doab, Godavari, Narmada, Gujarat. The problems of the dry lands and of the old rice lands remain. Some commentators have argued strongly that the relative lack of success in the rice tracts has a simple technological cause – the new wheat technology was better than the new rice technology – and the barrier will be breached once the labs get it right. But this may be a delusion.

Certainly there have been problems with rice strains and cultivation techniques, but it is doubtful if these are more than a contributing cause. The old rice tracts have not served as frontiers for a long time, and have passed up several opportunities to invest in growth. It will take more than some good chemistry and botany to shift them into a higher gear. And that in the end seems to be one of the most important messages of Ben Farmer's interrogative *Green Revolution?* (1977). As the book's conclusion suggests, the project's battery of different research techniques uncovered a whole array of small changes which had taken place over the past ten to fifteen years, but also an underlying constancy which overwhelmed any sense of a general pattern of change. While starting out by asking the conventional question about how new technologies have influenced the shape of rural society, the book's reflective conclusion ends up pointing out that the shape of society has controlled the development and adoption of technology, both at the national and local levels. The arrival of the new technology in the project's south Indian study area had not precipitated the violent changes which the catastrophists had predicted in the late sixties; but equally the adoption of the technology had hardly proceeded at a revolutionary rate. The project's south Indian study area was not inside the main rice-growing delta tracts, but nevertheless it was in one of the oldest-settled tracts of the region. If agrarian change and agricultural growth are to spread to these areas, then the time-hardened structure of local society will either have to be softened up or cracked open.

NOTES

1. Barrington Moore's *The Social Origins of Dictatorship and Democracy* is the best known, but was only a nose ahead of J. Kautsky's similar work. More recently the agrarian theme has played a large part in I. Wallerstein's *The Modern World System*, A. MacFarlane's *The Origins of English Individualism*, and E.L. Jones' *The European Miracle*. And then of course there are the ranks of the *Annalistes*.
2. See, for example, Eric Stokes' article on 'Dynamism and enervation in North Indian agriculture: the historical dimension', in *The Peasant and the Raj*, although his perspective is rather different. I have borrowed the idea of 'intermediate' areas from David Ludden, but he would be as surprised as any with what I am trying to do with it here.

REFERENCES

Baker, C.J. (1981). Colonial rule and the internal economy in twentieth-century Madras. *Modern Asian Studies*, 15, 575–602
 (in press). *The Tamilnad Countryside*. Oxford University Press
Blyn, G. (1966). *Agricultural Trends in India, 1891–1947: Output, Availability and Productivity*. University of Pennsylvania Press, Philadelphia
Burns, W. (1944). *Technological Possibilities of Agricultural Development in India*. Lahore
Charlesworth, N. (1978). Rich peasants and poor peasants in late nineteenth century Maharashtra. In C.J. Dewey & A.G. Hopkins (eds.), *The Imperial Impact*, Athlone, London, pp. 97–113
 (1979). Trends in the agricultural performance of an Indian province. In K.N. Chaudhuri & C.J. Dewey (eds.), *Economy and Society: Essays in Indian Economic and Social History*, Oxford University Press, Delhi, pp. 113–42

Dasgupta, Biplab (1977). *Agrarian Change and the New Technology in India*. UNRISD, Geneva

Farmer, B.H. (ed.) (1977). *Green Revolution? Technology and Change in New Rice-Growing Areas of Tamil Nadu and Sri Lanka*. Macmillan, London

Hirashama, Shigemochi (1978). *The Structure of Disparity in Developing Agriculture*. Tokyo

Islam. M.M. (1978). *Bengal Agriculture 1920–1946: A Quantitative Study*. Cambridge University Press

Kumar, Ravinder (1968). *Western India in the Nineteenth Century: A Study in the Social History of Maharashtra*. Routledge & Kegan Paul, London and Toronto

Moore, B. (1967). *The Social Origins of Dictatorship and Democracy*. Allen Lane, London

Royal Commission (1928). *Royal Commission on Agriculture in India: Abridged Report*. Government Central Press, Bombay

Rudra, Ashok (1979). Organisation of agriculture for rural development: the Indian case. In Dharam, Ghai, A.R. Khan, E. Lee & S. Radwan (eds.), *Agrarian Systems and Rural Development*. Macmillan, London for I.L.O., pp. 72–112

Smith, T.C. (1959). *The Agrarian Origins of Modern Japan*. Stanford University Press, Stanford, California

Stokes, E. (1978). *The Peasant and the Raj: Studies in Agrarian Society and Peasant Rebellion in Colonial India*. Cambridge University Press

Stone, I. (1979). Canal irrigation and agrarian change. In K.N. Chaudhuri & C.J. Dewey (eds.), *Economy and Society: Essays in Indian Economic and Social History*, Oxford University Press, Delhi, pp. 86–112

Tamil Nadu Archives (1945a). Board of Revenue proceeding 1030, dated 11 July 1945

(1945b). Board of Revenue note dated 3 January 1945 in Revenue Department file 238 dated 6 February 1945

(1947). Development Department file 910, dated 3 March 1947

Voelcker, J.A. (1894). *Report on the Improvement of Indian Agriculture*. Eyre & Spottiswoode, London

4 Agrarian change and the Merchant State in Tamil Nadu

BARBARA HARRISS

In this chapter I analyse agricultural mercantile policy in Tamil Nadu State in South India. I do not consider the originally intended effects of mercantile policy. Rather I consider the way in which policy has *actually* been implemented. As Schaffer (1981, p. 32) suggests, 'Public policy is, after all, what it does. The point is to explain what that is, and then see if that explanation can be an instrument for change and improvement.'

My approach has been to examine the way in which institutional decisions about the sphere of exchange alter the mobilisation, distribution and use of resources in Indian society. These resources I have disaggregated so far as possible into four types: commodities, physical infrastructure and technology, finance, and labour. I have examined each state intervention in isolation, and also in relation to others and to 'civil society' (Harriss, 1983). The concept of state which I have used is not, therefore, the all-encompassing Althusserian one, that where power exists there is the state, but a more limited one, consisting of the creators and executors of public policy: that part of the economy involved in the mobilisation and distribution of public resources.

Methodology

I have examined each implemented intervention by the State at the level of aggregation, spatial and administrative, at which the policies motivating it have been conceived. I have then examined each intervention as it exists in one, long-commercialised, dryland region, part of Coimbatore District in Tamil Nadu State. Some structural and behavioural aspects of the private mercantile system have been considered (Harriss, 1981a, 1981b). Finally, I have investigated the means whereby the private mercantile sector moulds and influences public policy at its formulation and in its implementation, and also the power of the mercantile section *vis-à-vis* other sectors of society (Harriss, 1981c).

The character of actually implemented interventions in agriculture and industry is not covered in a complete way. While I have considered the means whereby agricultural producers exert pressure on policy formation, the further pursuit of these subjects, necessary for a finished analysis of the political economy of the state, has yet to be carried out. I have also been unable to assess the importance of investment, the costs and returns to mercantile interventions relative to those in the economy as a whole. In these respects the research is partial, and this partiality can also be seen as inevitable given the type of resources which exist in the Indian countryside, and the nature of their control. It is hypothesised that their control operates through 'conglomerate property' relationships, which consist of linkages of ownership over many sectors of the economy, operating by the extraction of resources through different modes. If this is the case, then the rates of return to one sector, or even to trade in one commodity, cannot be dissociated from gross returns right across the portfolio of conglomerate property (Chattopadhyay, 1981).

Despite this incompleteness we shall characterise in this chapter the nature of *the Merchant State*, referring in particular to Tamil Nadu. There are two aspects of our characterisation of the State as mercantile. One aspect is the importance of the private mercantile sector in the resource base of the State, its role in the formulation of policy, and the extent to which state intervention operates in the interests of private merchants. The second aspect concerns the nature and role of state mercantile activities and state intervention in the mercantile sector.

Private merchants' capital

Let us enlarge first on the latter aspect: the degree of domination, if any, of merchants' capital over the rest of the economy, both agrarian and non-agrarian. Any such domination would be a relationship which is not adequately represented in existing statistics. At the outset we therefore encounter problems of measurement, and we have to proceed by simplifications and by proxies. Mishra (1981) has most thoroughly discussed these measurement problems, and the difficulty of assessing the role of merchants' capital by means of existing data sources.

As a simple indicator, the importance of mercantile activity can be gauged from its contribution to the income of each State. Fig. 4.1 shows that in the 1950s the mercantile sector was of greater relative importance in the economy of Madras (now Tamil Nadu) than in any other State of India except Maharashtra and West Bengal. This suggests the importance of the conurbations found in these three States: the economic contribution of the mercantile sector in states without such types of city is uniformly low. We can deduce that, as well as their other economic activities, these large cities are substantial concentrations of mercantile activity. As such they may exert a special type of influence over the rural areas surrounding them.

Fig. 4.2 gives more recent details of the relative importance of commerce in the income of Tamil Nadu State. If we compare the broad category of trade

Green Revolutions: an overview

in Fig. 4.2 with Fig. 4.1, we can see that over a long time period it has remained constant, both as a percentage of net domestic product and in real value. Agriculture's share has declined while that of registered manufacturing industry has increased. The largest rate of increase, especially interesting for our own study, has been in the share of net domestic product comprising public administration: the State itself.

We can also assess the importance of mercantile activity from its share of state employment (see Fig. 4.1). While 63.5% of the population in Tamil Nadu in 1960–1 produced 45.5% of the output in agriculture, 4.9% of the population produced 14.2% of the output in the broad category of trade. Average earnings per person in the wholesale trade, at Rs 16,200, were higher than those in any other State except for Maharashtra, while earnings in retail trade were low and suggest considerable polarisation within the mercantile sector. However, from these data it is extremely difficult to draw conclusions about the nature of rural-urban trade, rural-rural trade and trade in agricultural products (Mishra, 1981, ch. 9).

By the 1970s much of the Indian mercantile sector was trading in industrial and/or manufactured goods. Manufactured products in 1977 made up 50% of

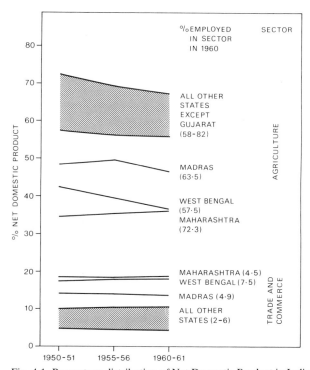

Fig. 4.1. Percentage distribution of Net Domestic Product in India, by States, 1950–51 to 1960–61. Numbers in brackets show, for 1960–61, the percentage of employment in each State contributed by agriculture and by trade and commerce, respectively. Data after Mishra (1981), citing NCAER (1965, pp. 145–8) and NCAER (1967, pp. 60–2).

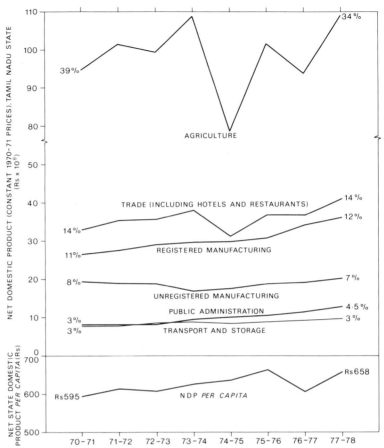

Fig. 4.2. Net Domestic Product for Tamil Nadu, by industry of origin, 1970–71 to 1977–78 at constant 1970–71 prices. Data after Govt. of Tamil Nadu (1978, pp. 56–68).

the total value of traded commodities in India as a whole, textiles alone constituted 11% while food articles comprised only 30% (Chandok, 1978). And Mishra (1981, ch. 9) shows that the wholesale and retail margins for the wide variety of industrial goods exceed those of least processed agricultural products. One feature of mercantile domination will be the terms on which agricultural and industrial products are exchanged in rural areas. Ulyanovsky and Pavlov (1973, p. 28) have ventured to assert:

In India . . . merchants' capital mediates not so much between different spheres of production as between owners of the surplus product received from those spheres of production. Merchants' capital does not invade the lower levels of the redistribution system but concentrates at its higher level.

Actually there are no statistics which can substantiate this statement over and above the type reported already here, and of such a position in the economy there are only faint circumstantial hints.

State mercantile activities

We can now introduce the nature and role of state interventions in the sphere of exchange. In India the state sector is assigned a decisive role in progressive and planned economic change, in the mobilisation and redistribution of social resources and in changing relations of production and exchange. All the while it is both state-owned means of production *and* the market itself which regulate the economy (Tyagunenko, 1973, pp. 106–24).

It is the policy of the present Government to enlarge the share of state trading in the economy (*Hindu* 7.3.80). We have already seen from Fig. 4.2 that in Tamil Nadu the share of state administration in state income is growing rapidly. Yet the share of state trading and commercial enterprises in the revenue of the State has actually declined from 9% in 1969–70 to 3% in 1978–9. These trends suggest that in the 1970s there occurred *both* an expansion in state activities in accordance with Central Government public policy *and* a crisis in the profitability of these activities. At the same time Central Government is increasing its budgetary control of States: in Tamil Nadu the share of Central Government in state revenue has increased from 25% in 1969–70 to 31–2% in 1978–80. The Central Government share derives from revenue which largely comes from taxes on traded goods, a further indication of the importance of the market, which now contributes about 60% of the revenue of the State. State planning in Tamil Nadu appears to be moving in the opposite direction to that suggested in Ulyanovsky and Pavlov (1973, p. 131): 'the goal of planning is to convert the public sector into the basis of reproduction' (of society).

The State as merchant

The earliest stated objectives of state intervention and planning as they evolved after Independence were to capture the commanding heights of the economy from which position its lower slopes and less commanding summits could be strategically regulated. The extent of public intervention in the private mercantile sector may be interpreted as one indication of the latter's commanding position in the economy, for there are on paper a great many such public interventions. In Tamil Nadu we have considered the regulation of agricultural markets, state trading in food and the public distribution system, state kind payment schemes, state trading in cash crops, co-operative marketing, state intervention in storage, the taxation of traded goods by the state and finally the state finance of private trade (Harriss, 1983). In other regions there may be even more. One important result of our research has been the varying strength and changing permutations and combinations of interventions over different regions (Harriss, 1980, 1981d). In this chapter we shall concentrate on general characteristics.

The ideology of State mercantile interventions

The entire panoply of state interventions in the sphere of exchange had original intentions stated as anti-mercantilist. State trading had the stated objective of crushing mercantile power and regulating and controlling international trade as well. Co-operative marketing was aimed to eradicate middlemen 'where they are exploitative', regulated marketing was aimed to codify transactional practice and to reduce mercantile power by rendering the agricultural trading sector more competitive. Storage and anti-hoarding laws had the purpose of reducing price fluctuations caused by mercantile speculation as did controls over future trading contracts. State storage schemes aimed to reduce the oligopolistic control by merchants of commodities over time. State finance on the face of it set severe constraints on lending to the mercantile sector. These interventions were not meant to benefit merchants.

Their intended beneficiaries were for the most part the undifferentiated sector of agricultural producers. Regulated marketing legislation, originally conceived as a means of improving the quantity and quality of crops exported to Britain, has more recently been justified (without much change in the content of the legislation) as a means of protecting 'small' farmers and raising the prices they receive for their produce. According to the legislation, farmers should participate in the management of these markets (Harriss, 1980, 1981e). State trading had as its objectives not only the raising of producer prices to 'support' levels but also the provision of production credit to producers with marketed surplus. State trading in cash-crops was originally intended to raise and stabilise producer prices. So was co-operative marketing, which had the additional advantages of being decentralised, participative, not inconsistent with free market operation yet able to administer non-market distribution if such a system of exchange was expanded. State warehousing at the outset had the unambiguous purpose of enabling farmers to have access to state credit on production of a warehouse receipt. State finance was intended to channel funds for production on concessional terms to the priority sector: agriculture.

To a lesser extent certain mercantile interventions were conceived as benefiting other sectors of society. The public distribution system, in addition to its regulating role, is the result of an attempt to channel cheap food to economically vulnerable people (mainly urban), and in the form of kind payments public distribution is now to benefit the rural landless. The coalescence of these interventions would represent an intention to set formidable constraints upon the freedom of activity of private merchants.

Growth of intervention

These interventions did not pose simultaneous threats to private merchants.

In Tamil Nadu regulated marketing legislation was enacted in 1933. Public procurement and the public distribution system came into being during, and have operated intermittently since the Second World War, although independent state trading corporations came much later: Food Corporation of India (F.C.I.) in 1965 and Tamil Nadu Civil Supplies Corporation (T.N.C.S.C.) in 1972. The marketing co-operatives were set up in the early 1950s. State storage schemes date from 1964, state curbs on the finance of trade date from the nationalisation of banks, and the introduction of the priority sector conditions on loans began after 1969. State trading in cotton started in 1972, though the Cotton Corporation of India (C.C.I.) did not expand operations in Tamil Nadu until 1976. Kind payment schemes to rural labour were initiated in 1978. *The mercantile sector has therefore had to adapt to a phased rather than combined assault on its freedoms*, which does not mean to imply that this phasing was in any way the product of deliberate planning.

Interventions have multiplied numerically. Each of them has also been marked by a peculiar form of expansion, not necessarily in sheer physical turnover (this is not a salient feature of most state interventions) but in terms of the range of functions assumed under each intervention. The number of agricultural commodities notified under regulated legislation has greatly expanded. The Food Corporation which started trading in wheat and rice has had added pulses, gram, coarse grains, oil and sugar, and fertiliser to its brief. T.N.C.S.C. has had incorporated grain, pulses, oil, salt, kerosene and cement. C.C.I., originally set up to canalise international cotton imports and exports, has had added a vast domestic cotton procurement network and cotton seed trading to its mandate and its directors want to expand ownership of storage, ginning and cotton seed processing facilities. Co-operative marketing institutions, besides being multi-produce in conception, have reassumed investments in storage infrastructure which they originally had shed, and have re-expanded into retail marketing from which they had formerly been split off and which is now duplicated institutionally. Actually public sector retailing is triplicated, for the T.N.C.S.C. has its own outlets. *This functional diversification and institutional fission is accompanied by regional diffusion. It is not necessarily or invariably accompanied by a physical expansion in total turnover.*

Tendencies in management and infrastructure

The evolution of the functions of institutions of state intervention is furthermore characterised by *tendencies in management towards standardisation, bureaucratisation and centralisation* in control of commodities and financial resources. The marketing co-operatives and regulated market committees which were the most autonomous forms of state intervention in exchange are now highly centralised in terms of the control of finance and in terms of decision making. They are no longer popular or participative institutions if, indeed, they ever were. Despite the contrast between such trends and rural development planning rhetoric, these may be the only means of ever regulating the private mercantile sector. In the case of state trading institutions, information, decisions, the location of management, and controls over finance are immensely more centralised than are the equivalent aspects of the private mercantile sector. Interventions in warehousing are centralised simply by dint of the large-scale storage technology used.

Yet another aspect of state mercantile expansion is the installation of physical infrastructure owned by these institutions and frequently financed using concessional international capital mediated by the Agro-Refinance Development Corporation: markets, warehouses and silos, and agro-processing machinery. The characteristics of such infrastructure are its relative 'modernity', its very large absolute size and scale and, often, its foreign origin. This equipment has high capital and fixed cost components. It is often locally *un*employment creating. Its break-even points are at the type of high rates of capacity utilisation at which remarkably few Indian factories normally run (Harriss, 1976, 1977, 1979; Harriss & Kelly, 1982). This has profound implications for the organisation of supplies in terms of quantity, quality and homogeneity, and further for the type and location of state control of commodities, finance, maintenance equipment and spare parts. Even further, such technologies require very stable policies relating to supplies. This means policies on prices, extent of procurement and its finance, all of which have been historically unstable. We shall see why later on. It is only in a few regions (such as Punjab and Haryana and at certain ports) where this technology may be viable and supplies guaranteed.

The expansion of this particular type of physical infrastructure and 'vertical integration' can be explained to some extent by the absence of co-ordination on the policy peripheries and the physical peripheries of each institution of intervention. Such problems occur whether the interface is with private trade, other state corporations or departments of state government. We hypothesise that the greater the number of other institutions with which the intervention grows to interact, the greater is the internal pressure for the diversification of its functions and for the expansion of its own physical infrastructure, in order to reduce its operational instability.

Diversification leads to state trading institutions holding a portfolio parodying that, perhaps, of conglomerate property in the private mercantile sector. The rationale behind such portfolios must be to reduce risk, to allow state trading institutions to cross-subsidise, and to allow the maximisation of gross returns across the range of commodities, policy on the trading of which may be unstable. The annual directors' reports of these corporations make this abundantly clear. But the multiplication of certain forms of technology under different institutional control, and the existence within the State of equipment with high depreciation costs and fixed costs result in its vulnerability to subsidisation if supplies are unstable. Actually, and in contrast to 'conglomerate property', they represent a force tending to reduce the profitability of State trading.

Employment by the State

State intervention in exchange has not taken employment in directions which reduce exploitation. We have noted two of its features already: *firstly the tendency to remove responsibility from participative and decentralised institutions to increasingly bureaucratised centres, and secondly the technology-induced creation of unemployment in co-operative marketing, storage and state trading.* State mercantile interventions furthermore combine high cost machinery with low labour productivity. Often this contradiction is only resolved by state subsidies. Yet employment in state trading institutions is expanding at a faster rate than the rate of expansion in turnover and, in cases where turnover is on a secular decline, it contracts more slowly than the rate of decline in commodities handled. Contraction, in such cases as the Civil Supplies Corporation, is at the expense of the lowest paid. The para-State generally provides secure employment at the highest levels and most geographically central parts of its institutions and deteriorates further down and further out. At the top, as with F.C.I. and C.C.I. for instance, the secure but complex administration may thwart the speedy decision making which these institutions were set up to accelerate.

By contrast the conditions of employment of casual and piece-rate labour give no indication whatsoever of progressive relations of labour within the spheres of statised exchange. F.C.I. pays its unskilled labour (which load, unload, hump and stock) at rates lower than those prevailing on the 'free market' for coolies, such that indigents from another district, brought 70 miles by a contractor, are the only people who can work at F.C.I.'s go down in and around Tirupur. The Cotton Corporation's ginning operations are no different from those of the private sector. They depend on a vast army of ununionised women to pluck impurities from *kapas*, paid minimum daily wages won by union activists in related industries, and mediated through an only slightly less exploited forewoman (Harriss, 1983, chs. 8–9).

The crisis of profitability

Hence in the state commercial sector *there is a crisis of profitability*. This is not to say that all are in deficit. Nor is it to say that all state trading ought necessarily to be profitable, though it is interesting and significant that the annual reports of all these institutions are dominated by obsessions with profits. Regulated markets are a profitable intervention, since fees in excess of local costs are fairly easy to collect even when there is massive evasion and when the intervention amounts to *nothing* more than fee collection. State storage is profitable, since capacity utilisation commonly exceeds 100%, though no farmers use these stores where space can be cleverly double-booked and double-charged to serve the uncertain needs of state corporations and large agri-business companies. The nationalised banks also make profits, of course, despite problematical lending to the priority sectors.

By contrast both the produce marketing co-operatives and the F.C.I. are chronically in deficit, kept in operation by subsidies from Central Government in both cases, offset to varying extents by more profitable fertiliser trading, and by small components which do operate profitably. The T.N.C.S.C. and the C.C.I. have fluctuating profitability, now declining into loss as their activities are circumscribed by the outcomes of implemented policies in other sectors to which their activities are subordinated, and as their role as buffer stock-holders is enhanced.

This crisis of profitability is not a characteristic unique to the state mercantile sector. It is part of a general decline in profitability in the public sector in India (Reserve Bank of India, 1980a; Krishnaswamy, 1980). It occurs despite concessional finance, and despite concessional exemptions from a number of fees and taxes.

To some extent factors 'internal' to each intervention, though remarkably similar throughout this whole sector, explain its low profitability, and even its failure to compete (with all its advantages and concessions) with and therefore to regulate the private mercantile sector. We are thinking here of factors such as the structure of employment, the centralisation of management, and the costs of technology controlled by these institutions. But this is by no means all. Relevant to our explanation of the character of the State-as-merchant is the effect of the interrelationships between all these institutions.

Relationships between institutions of intervention

Relationships between state interventions are characterised by lack of co-ordination. Insofar as the state trading institutions (F.C.I.; T.N.C.S.C.; C.C.I.) by-pass the regulated markets (which they all do in practice), they stunt the resource base of the latter, and perpetuate the rural decentralisation of trade which has for many years actually been illegal under the Agricultural Produce (Markets) Act (Harriss, 1981e). In turn F.C.I. derives its ability to qualify for massive subsidy from its diffuse institutional dependence, and its vulnerability to changes in policy in sectors over which it has no control. The same is true, though the subsidy is absolutely and relatively less, for Tamil Nadu Civil Supplies Corporation. Its working capital is not allocated by an institution over which it has much influence, and its profitability is qualified by political directives which do not take cognisance of economic viability (for instance the expansion of Fair Price Shops as employment schemes for village youth) and the incurring of expenditures which are frankly outside its brief. The C.C.I. is not linked with, rather it is dependent upon, policies of several Government Ministries (Finance, Industries, Commerce, Foreign Affairs) not all of which are co-ordinated and all of which are lobbied by Mercantile associations promoting anti-State-mercantilist stances. Co-operative produce marketing is affected by other interventions affecting supplies (levies, movement restrictions, state procurement) and prices. *This lack of co-ordination explains the unstable and* ad hoc *nature of mercantile policy and interventions.*

From these cases we can see that it is not only a question of lack of co-ordination, *it is also that certain interventions are subordinated to certain others*. Regulated market legislation is ignored by some institutions to the extent that it adds to the costs of their operation. Information provided by fees registers and transaction slips may, however, be used by those same institutions, to monitor levies, storage laws, sales taxes, and excise. And of course market regulation does not affect producer prices (in either direction) as much as can the implementation of support and/or procurement prices by state trading institutions. Food trading corporations depend most crucially on financial institutions. Banks have quite frequently exacerbated uncertainty regarding the quantity and exact timing of funds for state trading. The Reserve Bank of India's credit policies are extremely flexible, and the evidence we have garnered suggests that the Finance Ministry does not always act in a way that is supportive of state trading. Even so state foodgrains trading credit takes priority over state cotton trading credit. Thus to this extent the C.C.I. depends on the activities of F.C.I. All the trading corporations depend on decisions made by Government Ministers for their physical targets and locational directives which condition the size of operation. The C.C.I., which feeds a major industry rather than final consumers, is decisively dominated by a state industrial corporation (the National Textiles Corporation) which decrees the quantity and quality of its supplies and which can, by delaying payment to the C.C.I., determine the power of the latter's market interventions (Harriss, 1983, ch. 9).

The produce marketing co-operatives make losses and are subsidised. *Insofar* as these losses result from the circumscriptions of other interventions to which the activities of the co-operatives are subordinated, and *insofar* as these losses are exacerbated by small scale operations, the dependence of these institutions upon financial subsidies from State Governments and the National Co-operative Development Corporation is perpetuated. The warehouse corporations depend for their own profits in part on the subsidies given to the State Trading Corporations which patronise these large stores. The diffuse nature of these dependencies qualifies unprofitable interventions for their subsidies (Harriss, 1983, chs. 10 and 12). Lest it be forgotten, we will repeat that the emphasis on profitability is the institutions' own, not ours.

Finally, it is to improve state institutions' profitability that international finance has come to invest in the instruments of state intervention. The physical infrastructure of market places is justified in terms of the scope it offers for small traders to 'serve' small farmers (F.A.O., 1979; F.A.O./D.S.E., 1980). Finance from the I.D.A. and F.A.O. as well as bilateral aid from countries such as Britain and West Germany mediated by the Agro-Refinance Development Corporation has supported the installation of market place infrastructure and of large-size and large-scale technology for storage and processing that may require permanent subsidy from the national fisc in order to permit operation at low capacity. But the *proposals* for this technology suggest considerable profitability at market prices while the operational assumptions embodied in such proposals may be grotesquely unrealistic.

Conclusions

Let us now compare the history of these interventions with their objectives. *The landless, originally stated to be beneficiaries of public distribution and kind payment schemes, do not benefit very much*. In our study region the public distribution system, even in two taluks where it has been very considerably extended at the behest of the Chief Minister, is overwhelmingly confined to urban areas. The kind payment schemes provide patchy opportunities for earning food, negligible additions to demand for labour if taken on the aggregate, with no effect on wages and prices. Substituting, in the main, existing obligations to maintain roads, they are timed to coincide with, rather than to complement, peak demands for agricultural labour. The urban 'vulnerable' may be benefited by the public distribution system (Harriss, 1983, ch. 8).

We do not know the extent to which all the interventions in cotton actually result in a lower price for the finished textiles since there is no relationship between raw materials price movements and those for the finished products. Imports policy both for artificial fibres and for extra long-staple cotton may reduce the prices of the finest cloth for the social elites, and not all of this cloth is re-exported as was originally intended.

However, most of the interventions in exchange were originally justified in terms of their impact on an undifferentiated 'agricultural community'. While co-operative marketing has been a successful and significant channel for fertiliser, it has failed conspicuously in its objective to link farm production credit with marketing. So, similarly, has F.C.I. failed. Co-operatives have also failed to be a source of credit to farmers on receipts of stored produce. In the same way the Central and State Warehousing Corporations have failed. In fact, despite their occasional (profitable) successes, *co-operative produce marketing societies are on the whole massively avoided by producers* (Harriss, 1983: ch. 10).

State Trading Corporations do not benefit farmers when they operate according to a perverse logic of procuring in times of scarcity (with an element of coercion in the 'support' price), and opening ration shops and inaugurating food for work programmes in times of relative abundance (Harriss, 1981e). Their operations are also characterised by spatial patchiness. Above all, none of these interventions has caused any reversal in the tendency towards an increasingly imperfect market for commodities, as shown by our analysis of the behaviour of co-efficients of variation of wholesale prices of sixteen agricultural commodities in Tamil Nadu over the last twenty years (Harriss, 1981b). Indeed, it is possible that the interventions have exacerbated these tendencies. This is a comment not only on state trading but also on market regulation.

It is possible that the quality of intervention is affected by its quantity – by the size of operations of each institution. The quantities of grain traded and distributed by the State in our particular study region (which is a deficit district for foodgrains) are so negligible as to be unable to affect producer prices. In the South, unlike North India, procurement prices are, except in a few localities, not support prices being at all times below the level of the private market, sometimes up to 40% below (as in 1974). The same observation about the lack of effect on prices of low volumes traded is even true for cotton, and lags in finance and in decisions based on price information mean that the effect of the market procurement of C.C.I. is not consistent. C.C.I. has not in the past been conspicuously successful in scaling sufficient of the commanding heights of the cotton trade to ensure the National Textiles Corporation its ordered supplies. The co-operatives have totally failed to market produce as ('unexploitive') commission agents for producers.

So, with isolated exceptions, the expansion of state intervention is not benefiting its intended beneficiaries. This is not a criticism. Our purpose is rather to reveal the nature of state intervention. In fact the State would be acting as an unusual sort of merchant if it did benefit a sector other than itself. The State is, however, acting as an unusual sort of merchant in other respects. We have seen that the apparatus of the State generally is growing just as the contribution of State commerce to the net domestic product of the State has dropped by 60% in real terms during the 1970s.

The State expands into the sphere of exchange and experiences failure or increasing crisis of profitability. Yet it expands further. We must conclude from this the existence of interests inside the State which benefit from this expansion and this failure.

The merchant as State

In the state of Tamil Nadu the mercantile sector shows a far higher degree of inequality than does the agricultural production sector. We outlined above the sheer size of the mercantile sector, but to analyse its structure requires additional information on the pattern of control of resources. Despite differences between individual commodities (exemplified by primary data from a region in Coimbatore District), and despite the exemption from all official statistics of the petty trade which actually deepens this inequality in control over turnover of commodities, *there is an underlying structure of polarisation* (Harriss, 1981b). This polarisation is evident whether we use data on physical turnover, on the value of turnover or on the value of assets in mercantile firms. Oligopsonistic and oligopolistic trade co-exists with petty or subsistence trade. Furthermore it is likely that the latter depends on the former, kept small because of the terms and conditions on which petty trade is financed. While the crucial determinants of competitive trading, namely entry barriers, may be low for subsistence trade they may be very significant for oligopoly trade.

Polarisation in the mercantile sector

In the case-study region there are strong links between merchants' capital and usurers' ('finance') capital, especially among the bigger mercantile enterprises. These links imply inequality in the control over traders' money for production loans, but this is hard to demonstrate quantitatively because not all merchants would discuss their moneylending. Even in large firms, however, the coalescence of mercantile and finance capital is less than perfect: there is some delinking of commodity trade and finance within the bigger business units as family managerial combines split. While one branch of a family at the top part of the structure of control may deal only in commodities, another branch may manage a finance corporation lending to industry and trade as well as to agriculture and being repaid in cash, a reflection of the relatively profound monetisation and commercialisation of the local economy.

Our data shows that the production credit emanating from merchants exceeds that from co-operative and nationalised banks (Harriss, 1983: ch. 12). Big merchants in certain commodities are actually net bankers, receiving deposits from farmers, on which depositors get interest at rates equal to or higher than those obtainable in 'proper' scheduled and nationalised commercial banks.

We also have evidence of another type of *coalescence*, that *between command over commodities and mercantile control of land*. In the study area agricultural land was owned by 80% of a random sample of agricultural wholesale merchants in cotton, paddy rice, coarse grains, groundnuts and tobacco. Although the Gini co-efficients summarising concentration of land ownership among merchants registered lower values than those for concentration over commodities, they were higher than those for land-holding as a whole in the local region. The average farm size for merchants was three times that for the region. We have yet to combine the three sources of income and wealth: land, trade and moneylending in a single index of the concentration of property. Nor have we yet considered other sorts of coalescence of control and ownership, in industries and in other property. In our region, it would be nothing short of astonishing, however, if such inclusions *reduced* the value of the gini co-efficients.

Our data also allows the inference that *mercantile control of industrial goods is even more polarised than that of agricultural commodities*. We have no information about the degree to which polarisation is changing, whether there is differentiation in the sphere of exchange as in production. But there is certainly growth: the average mercantile firm grew by 75% in real terms between 1970 and 1978. As well as being economically polarised, trade is striking in its geographical concentration. Although the omission of sales taxes on a number of rural and agricultural commodities together with widespread rural evasion by traders of those commodities which are taxed overemphasises the true spatial distribution of mercantile activity, nevertheless 60% of the revenue from sales taxes comes from the city and region of Madras alone.

The behaviour of agricultural markets

Over the years between 1958 and 1978 (the latest for which we could get statistical material) the wholesale markets for agricultural produce have been characterised by irregular price rises and irregular though cyclical fluctuations around rising trends. The co-efficients of variation of wholesale prices for 16 commodities mostly show rising trends or increases in variability, even in commodities such as foodgrains, commerce in which has been most controlled by the State. *There is a general tendency towards deterioration in the competitive integration of wholesale prices over space and through time* (Harriss, 1981b).

Despite the greater apparent polarisation of control over commerce in industrial commodities than in agricultural commodities, and mindful of the unavailability of statistical material covering the last three crucial years, *we have no evidence of a long-term trend against agricultural products in the crude barter terms of trade*. What we have observed, however, is *massive regional variations in the increase in value of agricultural production*, which would inform debate on the income terms of trade. The range of value of total agricultural production per hectare of districts representative of differing ecological conditions has widened by a factor of three over the last twenty years. That of rainfed agriculture (Tirunelveli District) has increased least and is most variable and unstable. Those of the deltaic rice bowl (Thanjavur), and an intermediate district where rice production is fed by tanks and wells (North Arcot) have increased far less than has the value per hectare of Coimbatore District: very dry but with a long-commercialised agriculture based on well irrigation, and supplying local industry.

It is significant that it is in those crops whose wholesale prices have risen most greatly (and which most exceed the index of price rises in manufactured goods), and it is in those regions where the value of production per cultivated hectare has risen most rapidly and is highest in absolute terms, that farmers' agitations have arisen and been concentrated. We shall refer back to this phenomenon later.

Dependence of the State upon merchants

This, then, is what we know of the character of the mercantile sector and of its relation to agriculture. We are in a better position to attempt to characterise the relationship between private (agricultural) merchants and the State.

The first aspect of this relationship is the paramount *importance of traded goods in the resource base of the State*. The rate of growth of government is the fastest of any sector in Tamil Nadu. The rate of decline of state commerce in the net domestic product of Tamil Nadu is also fastest of any sector. Accompanying these tendencies is an increase in the allocation to the state fisc of revenue from the Central Government. This revenue is mostly derived from internal and external excise duties. But the main generator of revenue for the state government comes from sales taxes which it administers. The change from multi-point towards single-point taxation is being accompanied by an increase in its rate and an increase in the intermediate goods taxed. The conclusion to be drawn from this is not that trade is a weak point at which taxation can be applied. The level of evasion, which we have suggested is likely, puts paid to that idea at the outset. Rather, in the absence of large financial surpluses from public enterprises, and in the absence of feasibly taxable resources from the agricultural sector, the *State is dependent on a large and growing private mercantile sector*, to provide it with 50% of its revenue. Moreover, the private mercantile sector is large (absolutely and in comparison with all other states except for West Bengal and Maharashtra – see data in Mishra, 1981), and it is growing.

Role of merchants in state policy

The second aspect of the relationship between merchant and government is more problematical because we have not considered other sectors of Tamil

Nadu's economy in such detail. This aspect is the role of the mercantile sector in the interactive process of formation and implementation of state policy. We have had to confine our studies to mercantile policy, and some aspects of policy towards the finance of exchange.

Although big merchants with varying degrees of willingness and subject to varying coercion are involved in the finance of all political parties including the Communist Party of India, merchants for the most part strive to preserve a calculated political neutrality. In turn the mercantile policies of all political parties except the C.P.I. (Marxist) have been shown to be very confused at the local level, and generally ignored in party manifestos. Moreover cabinet and administrative responsibility for the mercantile sector is highly diffuse. *The nature of decision making at the party political level and within the administration and executive does not lead to coherent policies or coherent decision making with respect to the mercantile sector*, not even with respect to the individual commodity subsectors within it. But the evident lack of mercantile involvement in party political activity ought not to be interpreted as apathy or political weakness on the part of agricultural merchants. The process through which their power is exercised is simply not through political parties.

I have elsewhere presented evidence (Harriss, 1981c) to suggest *the importance of mercantile associations in the formation of mercantile policy*. Mercantile associations (of which there are eleven operating in our study region, covering five commodities) are set up for purposes other than this. Their closest direct connection with party politics is the extent to which merchants' associations have been a response to the demands of unionised labour organised by political parties. They have also been set up in response to a need for the auto-regulation of trade as the process of commercialisation results in commodity specialisation, regional diffusion and in the expansion of long-distance commodity flows. But even if they were set up for these other purposes, they are activated and perpetuated by the need to counter threats embodied in public policy which, as we saw at the beginning, has evolved a side regulatory potential. The means of defence and of retaliation is the lobby, and merchants are organised so as to lobby any level of the political and the executive system.

To generalise about the agricultural mercantile sector's role in policy making would be wrong, for there are significant differences within the sector itself in the degree to which industrial capital is involved in the transformation of the commodity. It would seem that where industrial capital is relatively small (in the cases of rice, groundnuts and tobacco in our study region) merchants lobby in order to preserve their independence. They lobby sporadically, when under threat. Their impact is greatest not at the point of policy formulation but on the discretionary decision-making powers at lower levels of the executive in the course of implementation.

Where industrial capital is relatively strong (as in the case of cotton) merchants lobby almost continually, which may be a sign of the threat to their independence. However, they will align themselves with lobbies representing apparently competing interests (cotton producers, spinning and weaving industries) in a fluid and unstable manner depending on specific circumstances. Examination of the interaction of these various lobbies suggests considerable concessions by the State to mercantile interests rather than to industrial ones. In other words, even in the case of cotton the mercantile sector seems far from being a passive wing of industrial capital. This sort of mercantile lobby operates not merely at the level of discretionary executive power but at the level of policy formulation and decision making.

Lobbies therefore operate simultaneously on policy formulation and policy implementation, so that *the appearance of a regulatory policy may conceal the reality of an outcome with an emasculated effect or an opposite effect*. It is the character of these outcomes and the social processes giving rise to them which reveals the true nature of the State. Let us turn now to this difficult subject.

Indirect involvement in party politics

It is not through party politics that merchants exercise power over the enactment of public policy. Only 37% of my sample of 150 agricultural merchants acknowledge party affiliation, the number of active participants is much smaller, and support is spread evenly between all parties. Rather than acknowledging affiliation to political parties, merchants owned to have held office in local participative institutions such as the co-operatives. Some structural conditions therefore exist for the subordination of municipal or co-operative interests to private mercantile ones. A president of such an institution is hardly likely to allow measures which threaten his very livelihood.

Merchants are also active in social institutions (Lions, Rotary Societies, etc.). Here particularistic acts of prestige-enhancing, redistributive charity are of small importance beside the forging of social ties with middle levels of the local bureaucracy. That the Collector steers clear of such involvement also is of small importance, besides demonstrating in a negative way the potentially compromising nature of such societies for the administrative cadre. Merchants are also active in the trusteeship of local temples. What is important here is not only their real piety but also the degree to which they exercise control over land (often urban) and property owned by the temple.

Collaboration in state interventions

Rather than through direct political action, merchants operate indirectly, firstly through lobbying (see above) and secondly through *collaborating in measures designed to curb their power, and thereby actually increasing that power.*

If we consider the implementation of market regulation in Tamil Nadu as a whole, although it was dryland cash crops that were first to be notified, and though the first regulated market was a dryland one, it is now the dry regions of the state (in particular Salem, but also Ramnad, Trichy, Tirunelveli) where regulation is most defectively implemented in terms of original objectives, and merchants most antagonistic. This failure of regulation stems from the power of merchants, rather than from the limited importance of dryland produce. Before the political Emergency, merchants on the local Regulated Market Committee in our study area were able to block and quash some 150 cases against traders registered by the market committee's secretary, who was not a trader and who was finally dismissed (Harriss, 1981e).

During the Emergency (when some interventions – sales taxes, for instance – functioned much more efficiently than before or after) traders were bold enough to try to get scrupulous officials transferred from their markets. The cotton lobby succeeded in persuading the Director of Agriculture to stop the enforcement of the part of the Agricultural Produce (Markets) Act which stipulates that all transactions should be supervised within the regulated market yard, an order which had apparently come from Delhi. It is alleged that merchants have blocked the investment of the chronic surpluses made from fees by regulated markets, in such commodities as land on which expanded regulated markets and 'farmers' stores can be built. This is done through the courts and through delays and discrepancies in valuation by revenue authorities. A local court has also seriously delayed the case by organised farmers to evict cotton commission agents from their shops inside the regulated market. The action of police in outlawing an organised protest march by farmers against these commission agents at one day's notice and by brutal suppression of farmers' demonstrations on other occasions (personally witnessed) is also not against mercantile interests. Sharad Joshi (the farmers' leader) has also alleged (1981) that merchants have been able to persuade the police to repress a campaign for higher *bidi* tobacco prices. It is almost impossible, however, to find any direct evidence of the mechanism of collusion between merchants and the police.

Market regulation is not necessarily a full-time intervention. In the major market of our study area, Tirupur, open auctions are only held on two days of the week. Even then commission agents charge for giving information on prices to farmers. Then, as on other days, merchants can flout the law by not paying on the spot for commodities purchased but by paying without interest within 21 days, a period which allows considerable speculative activity with this finance. The degree to which the law can be enforced is compromised by the fact that the staff of regulated markets may be kin of merchants. The staff is also numerically inadequate to administer the law in a minimum way and extract fees on village transactions. In villages the behaviour of the merchant is unregulable unless by other interventions his transactions can be tracked.

Control of the food trade

The power of merchants in the implementation of state trading in food, especially rice, lies in the two factors. Firstly, the largest wholesale traders almost invariably control processing plant as well. *The layer of industrial capital involved in the transformation of paddy to rice is thin. It is a subsector or extension of merchants' capital.* In such combined firms we hypothesise that most profit is profit on alienation deriving from buying cheap and selling dear rather than profit related to surplus value extracted through processing.

Secondly, the corporations, as we have seen, own storage and processing technologies of large size, with high capital and fixed cost components and with problems of supply and maintenance. They also operate under unstable policies with regard to supplies and price margins. Expansion in ownership of such technology is lumpy, rather than incremental. Shifting the ownership of such technology to the co-operative sector so that it can be enlisted as and when policies demand it has resulted in the necessity for large subsidies to the co-operatives. *Therefore the para-statal trading corporations have come to depend on the very private mercantile sector that state trading officially seeks to challenge and to eliminate.*

The technologies of storage and processing in private ownership are smaller in size (though the simple expedient of multiplying the number of hullers can solve capacity constraints if or when they arise). They have lower starting financial and fixed cost components than do Modern Rice Mills for a given capacity. Their break-even points are far lower. They can operate to high quality specification if the raw material is of high quality. (This is something which international 'experts' dispute.) They also happen to create between seven and twelve times more employment than does a Modern Rice Mill for a given throughput (Harriss, 1976, 1977, 1979). Since they are in private ownership they are expendable as and when policies affecting the supply of paddy through state trading institutions change. The fixed costs of the corporations are thereby reduced. *It is in the interests of the directors of state trading to use private processing agents*, in order to justify their position on grounds of cost effectiveness.

Merchants as agents of the State

The interests of private merchants in being agents of state trading institutions are not straightforward. On the one hand their collective purely mercantile interests are threatened, for movement restrictions cut off their supplies. They are forced, coerced, into being passive agents for state trading institutions. They have no alternative. Yet to be agents of the State is not necessarily against their individual interests. *If* the state trading corporation ensures them high and even rates of capacity utilisation (and this is indeed the case with the relation between F.C.I. and its hulling agents in our study area), then this arrangement may be to the merchant's advantage. The extent to which this happens depends on his portfolio of other investments. Certainly his profit on alienation from buying and selling is abolished, but he still has surplus value extracted through the mill. Even if the fixed fees paid by the state corporation do not vary in the fashion of free market prices, and therefore lower his rate of exploitation, the merchant is compensated in other ways. High capacity enlarges his absolute profits and costs are reduced because the State, not the merchant, bears the costs of raw material. Despite the fact that the bank guarantees, necessary to render the merchant eligible to be an agent of the State, require the depositing of a certain quantum of money, this arrangement enables money to be released from the paddy-rice trade to another part of the merchants' multiple enterprise, a part less constrained by the State. When policies change and 'free' trade is again liberalised, the merchant can return to commodity processing and speculation. These arguments assume no criminal activity on the part of the merchant.

To be an agent of the State is very much to a merchant-processor's advantage should he be interested in illegal profits. For a start, since movement restrictions and the imposition of procurement at prices *lower* than those of the market almost always lead to a deterioration in the spatial integration of markets, exacerbated further at times of changes (or anticipated changes) in policy, merchants may reap excess profits from evasion of the restrictions. The type of evasion that is possible by a hulling agent concerns the few percentage points of outturn of rice from paddy between the specifications of the state trading corporation and the maximum that his machines can achieve. In turn this will depend on the quality of the raw material. This physical difference may be removed and the rice traded privately. Then both merchants who are agents of the State and those who are not may smuggle. The directors of state corporations naturally expect their subordinates to be vigilant on this issue but the large costs of litigation and the long delays involved in prosecutions prevent them from pursuing punishment for all but gross offenders. We saw that the cases registered by the Civil Supplies Corporation involve large tonnages (989 in one district in 1980) and very large sums of money (Rs 5.8 million). In a negative way, since these cases are the tip of an iceberg, these are illustrative of the advantages of state trading to a merchant prepared to flout the law.

Control of the cotton trade

The Cotton Corporation has enlisted merchants directly. They are part of the corporation's salaried labour-force, used to train 'technically qualified personnel' in the arts and sciences of buying and selling, and used to supervise the processing at ginning factories. They also mediate linguistically. The C.C.I. is supposed to purchase from farmers. When this was implemented strictly, in 1980 in our study area, purchases dropped to 8% of those over the equivalent period during the preceding year. The C.C.I. buyers use the reason of poor implementation of market regulation in order to purchase from traders. The lags in information and in finance inside the C.C.I. allow unrecruited merchants to mediate financially for the purchases made by C.C.I.'s own merchants. Because the entry of C.C.I. onto a local market is a public event and because the C.C.I. buys in bulk, private merchants can speculate in a way which may lead to the C.C.I.'s purchase operation's having the reverse effect on prices from that intended. It would seem that in South India, procurement prices are not so high as to invariably act as price supports. The influence of merchants' capital is centripetal, leading to a spatial concentration in Tirupur where few *bona fide* farmers market their produce. Because Tirupur is a cotton marketing centre of cardinal importance in South India, the C.C.I. locates its activities there. Yet this is not in the interests of farmers. It is actually in the interests of merchants. In fairness to C.C.I., it is beginning to purchase in regulated subyards at periodic markets, directly from farmers. But the quantities involved are very small as yet.

The layer of industrial capital comprising the textiles industry above the C.C.I. is thick, and fractions of this may collaborate with mercantile interests to mutual advantage. The C.C.I. hires in ginning factories, and the arguments we have used with respect to paddy and rice merchants appointed as agents of the State apply also to *kapas* and lint merchants who own ginning factories. Furthermore, although it is illegal, the C.C.I. cannot prevent ginning factory owners from trading on private account unless they can guarantee to supply the factory at maximum capacity. Again it is private merchants who can offer such bulk supplies.

The C.C.I. is, as we saw, dominated by a state industrial corporation, the National Textiles Corporation. It can also be manipulated and exploited by private industry. The rate at which private spinning mills and/or the N.T.C. repay the C.C.I. for lint constrains C.C.I.'s purchase operations. Private spinning mills may slow their repayments and use this money to finance other parts of their industry. The purchases and stocks of C.C.I. are publicly known. Hence private spinning mills can manipulate their own stock levels so that C.C.I. bears the costs of maintaining short-term buffers. Since even the Committee on Public Undertakings (1975) doubted the capacity of the Indian

State to acquire the functions of private trade, the influence of private merchants' capital, working inside the organisation, is pervasive.

Control of co-operatives and storage

With respect to produce marketing co-operatives, we know one case where the co-operative has successfully established a monopoly in a free market in a new commercialised product: maize. Co-operative cotton ginning is also successful in Tinupur though a negligible proportion of the total produce passing through the town enters either the co-operative or the regulated market yard on regulated market days. For the most part the managers of co-operative marketing societies are themselves private merchants. *They have not eradicated the middleman.* He is at the heart of the co-operative.

In states such as Karnataka and Andhra Pradesh, warehousing corporation space has been taken over by traders as well as big business and by parastatal corporations (Harriss, 1981d). In Tamil Nadu there is no mercantile takeover of public sector space. Merchants do not use these facilities but neither do the farmers for whom they were intended.

The manipulation of interventions

Merchants manipulate a number of interventions simultaneously. At the grass roots level, merchants encounter vigilance over the level of their stocks (storage and hoarding laws), prices (regulated markets, sales tax and civil supplies, public distribution), and the direction of their commodity flows (movement restrictions, sales taxes and civil supplies). In our study area, and in commodities affected by combinations of interventions, there are very *strong forces favouring the perpetuation of a system of mis-implemented interventions.* At one and the same time local low-level officers in the administration benefit from bribes, unsolicited gifts and from creaming off parts of the 'legitimate' on-the-spot fines exacted from miscreants by the State. Merchants benefit from these badly implemented interventions for the high and illegal profits which stem from their evasion.

State finance of merchants

In the area of finance, the State sets very severe limitations on the finance of private trade, though the finance of state trading is, of course, a major banking activity. However, subject to restrictions which vary over time, the wholesale trade and storage by private merchants can be financed. It can even be financed by Co-operative Banks (Reserve Bank of India, 1980b). The scrutiny and vigilance over banks that is supposed to be provided by the R.B.I. is totally incommensurate with the magnitude of the task. It is difficult to argue that mercantile enterprise is not financed considerably by nationalised banks.

Again, in their reluctance to lend the quantities planned by parastatal corporations and at the right point in time, these banks betray a position favourable to private trade. Their support of regulated marketing, the granting of permission by the R.B.I. for the installation of urban and semi-rural bank branches in regulated markets dominantly visited by merchants, cannot be interpreted as an anti-mercantile stance. Nor can be their active financial guaranteeing of agro-processing firms on contract to state trading institutions (Harriss, 1983: ch. 14).

Lastly the State finances the private merchant through other elements in the merchant's portfolio which qualify for loans on concessional terms. Agro-processing facilities are small-scale industries and are in the priority sector. Agricultural production is squarely in the priority sector, in which the diligent branch bank manager strains to approach the fulfilment of targeted investments. Merchants are landowners and control small-scale industries. Loans to these are fungible. They release the merchant's private funds for other enterprise.

Success in the curbing of mercantile activity

We have been able to find comparatively little evidence for the *operation of effective interventions of the State successfully against the interests of merchants. Where this exists it is of a particular form, consisting not of the curbing and constraining of mercantile activity by competition but by oppression and compulsion; and this mainly to weaker isolated individuals.* For example, the interventions meant to protect a labour-intensive, rurally located, oil-pressing technology operated by very small merchants guarantees them exemption from sales tax, yet it allows a competitive advantage only if the quantities of raw material (groundnut pod) purchased by them are restricted to supply for a week's operation. These tiny firms cannot speculate on the market, over a period longer than a week and with supplies greater than that for a week. Under these conditions it is not possible for them to accumulate the resources to render them eligible for the State's concessional matching loans for the upgrading of the technology (Harriss & Kelly, 1982).

Our case study of oppression and of the extortion of a not inconsiderable amount of cash out of a private groundnut-expeller factory owner by the upper levels of the Civil Supplies Corporation against the advice of the lower levels of the Corporation, reveals how an inevitable need for vigilance becomes a recipe for real oppression when combined with low quality and defective supplies of raw material and packing equipment (Harriss, 1983: ch. 8).

But these are hardly evidence to support a conclusion that the relation between merchant and State is ambivalent. They are isolated examples. And while in theory the role of merchants' capital in its pure form is ambivalent, *in practice and in its concrete and impure form, private merchants' capital dominates state merchants' capital especially in a rural area such as that of our case study.*

Conclusion

Merchants profoundly infiltrate all interventions which have the purpose of curbing their activity. Merchants occupy the commanding heights in the sphere of exchange, not the State. The weakness of state intervention in some areas, its strength in others, is an expression of the degree to which it serves mercantile interests in the form in which it is implemented.

This is not a criticism but a characterisation. There is no conspiracy at work but there are tendencies within this economy. Not all events taken in isolation, not all runs of events, support this interpretation, but taken as a whole the dynamics of the sphere of exchange do not seem to be satisfactorily explained in other terms.

Alternatives

There is no indication of ways in which, under the present form of the State, alternative types of intervention, or alternative degrees of intervention, would have effects materially different from those we have described. This has profound implications for the implementation of the stated objectives of current and future Government plans (Govt. of India, 1981a; 1981b: pp. 79–84, pp. 111–14). In our study area, it is under a dynastic succession of five-year plans, of projects and programmes, of commissions and corporations, that the mercantile sector has evolved, and taken its present form and role. The present form of both the mercantile sector and implemented interventions are the product of the historical interactions of both.

It is contended with evidence that private merchants dominate the entire sphere of exchange. We have yet to explore systematically the relationships between this and the sphere of production in agriculture and industry to see the extent to which the mercantile sector dominates the entire economy. It is at this level that we may find major contradictions. For while it ought to be clear that I do not espouse theories of urban bias propagated by Sharad Joshi and Narayanasamy Naidu (see Shakia & Sonalkar, 1981) and earlier articulated to the academic community by Lipton (1977), there is no doubt that the relations between the merchant sector and the rest of the economy will vary according to dominant forms of relations of production in agriculture, the location and type of capital in industry and relations of industrial production. For *in its concrete, impure form merchants' capital and the portfolios gener-*

ated by it are not independent of the mode of production but bound up in it, very probably determinants of it, and determined by it in a dialectical relationship.

If society and State are not transformed and socialised in a socialist revolutionary manner, and there is at present absolutely no indications of authority for such changes, then we must look at the sectors of productive capital for challenges to mercantile power. Any such investigation far exceeds the boundaries of my present research project, but for some semblance of completeness let us consider the following.

There is a continuing debate about whether the Indian State functions autonomously, or whether it is subjugated to the interests of capitalism, either 'monopoly' and 'retrogressive', or 'state' and considered by most as 'progressive' (see Arora, 1981, for a statement of the first position, and Clarkson, 1979, for a review of the latter). Important unpublished work by Sharma (1981) has, however, shown that the distributive shares (the relationship between profit and wages) in organised, large-scale Indian manufacturing industry derive from mercantilism rather than from the appropriation of the surplus value of productive industry. Research on small-scale industry by Streefkerk (1978, 1981) reveals the kindred phenomenon of 'commercialism'. It is at least possible that it is mercantile capital which dominates Indian industry; and this domination is the more likely the thinner the layer of industrial capital in an agrarian economy. In Tamil Nadu this layer is thin (Kurien & James, 1979). Where agricultural production contributes more than any other sector to the state product, and engages most people, then we must look to productive agricultural capital to crack the economic domination of the merchants.

Agrarian unrest

This of course is precisely what the farmers' agitations in South India are really about, and prices are the weapons of war. In Tamil Nadu as elsewhere the movement has a large mass base despite the fact that it is led by capitalist farmers. The continual protests in favour of raising product prices have the purpose of raising rates of return to production, which, if conceded, would *change investment patterns within the economy*. They are a very decisive threat to the top end of the polarised mercantile sector for two reasons. Firstly in the south, procurement prices for grain have contained an element of coercion since the open market rarely drops below their level. Even the market support operations of the C.C.I. have not invariably been at or above the level of the market by virtue of the effects of information lags and centralised decision making within that institution. To raise producer prices would be impossible without a major expansion in state intervention. Our description of the manner in which merchants penetrate such institutions or are incorporated by them suggests that effective expansion is highly unlikely.

Secondly, the agitation is strongest over commodities where wholesale price rises have most exceeded those of manufactured goods and in regions where the values per hectare of agricultural produce are greatest and have risen fastest. However, these price rises have been marked by great fluctuations over space and through time. The farmers' agitations can be interpreted as a demand to have their cake and eat it; a cry for stability of (high) returns to production as a basis on which to consolidate capitalist agriculture. The stabilisation of prices by whatever means and the upward destabilisation of farm incomes would also be a decisive threat to mercantile power.

This movement is unequivocally backed by all opposition parties. Such behaviour is opportunist, a characteristic political style 'traceable to the freedom struggle and consisting of ready support to any interest once it is organised' (Mehta, 1980).

Progressive or retrogressive?

The movement is found controversial by academic commentators and analysts. On the one hand since higher prices will cover the higher costs of production of small farmers (an argument which accepts that small farmers are 'inefficient', *pace* Lipton, 1977) and since under monopsonistic pricing the average commodity prices for all farmers are below the true costs of production, the mass movement is progressive (Bokare, 1981; Shankar, 1981).

On the other hand, higher produce prices will raise the retail prices of wage goods and hit poor consumers whether urban or rural. They will add inflationary forces to the general price level (Patel, 1980). They will benefit those who already exert massive control over the highly differentiated agricultural sector (Paranjape, 1981). As such the movement is retrogressive.

Policy prescriptions of these protagonists coalesce around some degree of positive discrimination towards small farmers and the landless (often by fiscally redistributivist reforms), negative penalisations on the control of property and assets by the rural and urban elites (often also implemented by taxation), and measures in the sphere of exchange such as increased state trading and the state provision of physical infrastructure (Shankar, 1981; see also Govt. of India, 1981b: p. 79). We have commented at some length on the latter two measures and this is not the moment to dwell on the history of the first two.

Very few of these commentators analyse the implications of the existence of private trade on these policies. Shakia and Sonalkar (1981) are exceptions. They write (referring to the benefits of higher prices to small farmers and to the landless): 'Sharad Joshi abstracts from the reality of the agricultural product market in which sale and purchase of cash crops is everywhere mediated by contractors, traders of co-operative institutions dominated by big farmers.' The same is true of the ideology of Narayanasamy Naidu, the farmers' leader in Tamil Nadu. Both reveal ambiguous views about the nature and role of state action in the sphere of exchange.

The State is criticised and protested to, yet it is expected ultimately to solve on behalf of farmers their problems of exchange. This can be interpreted on the one hand as an abrogation of responsibility on the part of farmers. On the other hand it can be recognised as a sign of the weakness even of capitalist agriculture in the face of market forces in these commercialised parts of rural India. Historically the solution of problems of exchange in the interests of producers is something which the State has not been able to do with conspicuous success. Indeed its manipulation by private mercantile interests has allowed the perpetuation and in some cases the worsening of relations of exchange which are problematical for producers. Thus this set of demands by farmers does not just raise difficulties connected with the social distribution of potential beneficiaries. It challenges the independence of the State and the ability of the State to act.

The response by the Central Government (Govt. of India, 1981a) contains the same abstraction from the reality of oligopolistic markets and linkages between money and commodity markets as does Joshi's ideological justifications for raised producer prices. An expansion in state trading is avoided. Producer prices are to be raised and stabilised by squeezing the margins of the private mercantile sector. Margins are to be squeezed and stabilised by an increase in state-financed physical infrastructure in storage, transport, processing and in communications technology. Farmers themselves are then to use this infrastructure to organise their own marketing by (state-organised) marketing co-operatives, and by regulated markets (managed by a majority of farmers).

Mercantile manipulation of agrarian unrest

From the vantage point of Tamil Nadu, there is yet no evidence that such interventions will not be manipulated by the evolving mercantile sector, as in the past. Besides, very little attention has been paid to the provision of production credit and credit on stored produce, areas of linkage between commodities and money which still define mercantile power.

But the farmers' movement has, in this respect, two crucial and revealing internal debilities, drags on the process of any agrarian bourgeois revolution. Firstly there is a contradiction inside the farmers' movement over credit. The strategy of non-repayment of state credit for production in order to draw attention to problems of the rates of return in agriculture enables large farmers to lend money to the smaller farmers comprising the mass base of the movement. The default of individuals within a co-operative renders the entire branch co-operative ineligible for credit, hence small farmers, who may or may not have repaid co-operative loans, will borrow from larger farmers who have resources from nationalised banks and who may also be traders. The delinking of production credit from commodity trade is a crucial area of progressive marketing reform. The State is asked to solve this problem as with many others. The State cannot expand its agricultural credit provision unless farmers repay loans. Farmers refuse to repay loans as a strategy of protest. Secondly, the movement is infiltrated by merchants. The merchants who are members of the Agriculturalists Association in my study area in Tamil Nadu are larger than average merchants and larger than average merchant-farmers.

Farmers wish to evict a group of local commission agents in the study area. These commission agents act as bankers. To evict them would lead to a cessation of their money-lending activities. Until the State intervenes to replace this substantial and wide-ranging network of production credit, the commission agents cannot be threatened. The State cannot intervene.

It is for such reasons that agricultural capital cannot as yet crush merchants' capital in its concrete manifestation. Neither can the State. It is in this sense that we can characterise Tamil Nadu as a Merchant State.

ACKNOWLEDGEMENTS

This chapter attempts to thank B.H. Farmer for the qualities which, to me, characterise his academic life and work. Among these are research which is interdisciplinary in scope and undogmatic in argument, thorough work which is empirical, oriented towards policy issues, stamped with a sense of region, and finally work written not just with style but from an experience equivalent to his oft-quoted 'feet muddy from the paddy fields'. In my case, only this last is a certainty. This essay springs from the dirt and chaff, the incense and the diesel fumes of many market places, and from evidence sifted from the dust of mouldering, mice-eaten Government files. It represents a practice of fieldwork learned almost completely through his good auspices. I am grateful also to John Cameron, Bernard Schaffer and the editors for helpful responses to the draft.

REFERENCES

Arora, D. (1981). Big business, influence generation and decision-making in India. *Economic and Political Weekly*, 16 (9), Feb. 28, pp. M2–M14
Bokare, M.G. (1981). Prices of farm products. *Mainstream*, 19 (29), 22–4
Chandok, H.L. (1978). *Wholesale Price Statistics, India, 1947 to 1978*, vol. 1. Economic and Social Research Foundation, New Delhi
Chattopadhyay, B. (1981). An approach to the research design for the study of market circuits in eastern India. CRESSIDA, Calcutta (mimeo)

Clarkson, S. (1979). *The Soviet Theory of Development*. Macmillan, London
Committee on Public Undertakings (1975). *Cotton Corporation of India, Ministry of Commerce*. Lok Sabha, Delhi
F.A.O. (1979). *Rural Markets: A Critical Link for Small Farmer Development*. F.A.O., Bangkok
F.A.O./D.S.E. (1980). Rural market development programme in Asia: general review of progress. Bangkok (mimeo)
Govt. of India (1981a). *Major Recommendations of the Group on Perishable Agricultural Commodities*. Krishi Bhavan, New Delhi
  (1981b). *Sixth Five-Year Plan 1980–85*. Planning Commission, New Delhi
Govt. of Tamil Nadu (1978). *Statistical Handbook of Tamil Nadu 1978*. Dept. of Statistics, Madras
Harriss, B. (1976). Rice processing technology: the case for modernisation in South Asia. *Tropical Science*, 18, 161–86
  (1977). Paddy milling – problems in technology and the choice of policy. In B.H. Farmer (ed.), *Green Revolution?* Macmillan, London, pp. 276–300
  (1979). *Paddy and Rice Marketing in Northern Tamil Nadu*. M.I.D.S./Sangam Publishers, Madras
  (1980). Regulated foodgrains markets: a critique. *Social Scientist*, 88, 22–31
  (1981a). The distribution of mercantile economic power in Tamil Nadu. *CRESSIDA Transactions*, 1 (1), Calcutta
  (1981b). The behaviour of farm prices in Tamil Nadu. *Madras Institute of Development Studies, Working Paper* No. 22, Madras
  (1981c). Agricultural mercantile politics and policy: a case study of Tamil Nadu. *Economic and Political Weekly*, 16, 10–12, 441–58
  (1981d). Coarse grains, coarse interventions. *Food Systems and Society Working Paper*, United Nations Research Institute for Social Development, U.N.R.I.S.D., Geneva
  (1981e). Inaction, interaction and action: regulated agricultural markets in Tamil Nadu. *Social Scientist*, 9 (100), 96–137
  (1983). *State and Market (State Intervention in Agricultural Exchange in a Dry Region of Tamil Nadu, South India)*. Concept, New Delhi
Harriss, B. & Kelly, C. (1982). Food processing policy for rice and oil technology in South Asia. *Institute of Development Studies Bulletin*, 13, 3, 32–44
Joshi, S. (1981). Countdown to an agitation. *Business Standard*, 7 May, Calcutta
Krishnaswamy, K.S. (1980). What ails the public sector? *Reserve Bank of India Bulletin*, 34 (12), 969–79
Kurien, C.T. & James, J. (1979). *Economic Change in Tamil Nadu, 1960–1970*. Allied, New Delhi
Lipton, M. (1977). *Why Poor People Stay Poor*. Temple Smith, London
Mehta, B. (1980). Politics and economics of farm agitations. *Mainstream*, 19 (14), 6–8, 41
Mishra, S. (1981). Patterns of long-run agrarian change in Bombay and Punjab. Ph.D. dissertation, Cambridge University
N.C.A.E.R. (1965). *Distribution of National Income by States*. Delhi
  (1967). *Estimates of State Income*. Delhi

Paranjape, H.K. (1981). Prices of agricultural products. *Mainstream*, 19 (23), 19–25
Patel, I.G. (1980). Policy framework for Indian agriculture. *Reserve Bank of India Bulletin*, 34 (12), and *Mainstream*, 19 (17), 15–23
Reserve Bank of India (1980a). Finances of Government companies 1977–78. *Reserve Bank of India Bulletin*, 34 (11), 871–7
  (1980b). Report on trends and progress of banking in India, 1980. *Reserve Bank of India Bulletin, Supplement*, June
Schaffer, B.B. (1981). To recapture public policy for politics. Institute of Development Studies, University of Sussex (mimeo)
Shakia, M. & Sonalkar, V. (1981). Farmers' agitations and the Left. *Mainstream*, 19 (26), 11–13, 27
Shankar, K. (1981). Question of agricultural prices. *Mainstream*, 19 (29)
Sharma, S.C. (1981). Distributional shares: received theories and empirical evidence. A case study of the Indian manufacturing industry with particular reference to the jute industry. Ph.D. dissertation, School of Social Sciences, Jawaharhal University, New Delhi
Streefkerk, H. (1978). *Sluip-en Omwegen, eenleine Indiase Stad, Ondernemers en Arbeiders in Zuid Gujarats Sinds 1900*. Amsterdam
  (1981). Too little to live on, too much to die on: employment in small-scale industries in rural South Gujarat. *Economic and Political Weekly*, 17, 659–68, 721–8, 769–80
Tyagunenko, V.L. (ed.) (1973). *The Industrialisation of Developing Countries*. Progress, Moscow
Ulyanovsky, R. & Pavlov, V. (1973). *Asian Dilemma*. Progress, Moscow

PART II
Agrarian change at village level

5 Agrarian policy and agrarian change in tribal India

STUART CORBRIDGE

There has not been a Green Revolution to speak of in tribal India – certainly not in tribal Bihar. It is of course true that a number of individuals in Bihar's tribal belt have introduced improved varieties of seeds and have begun to apply chemical fertilisers to their crops, but this has not been a general trend (Table 5.1). It should be emphasised that this has little to do with any cultural backwardness or with any lack of an entrepreneurial spirit amongst the tribals of the Jharkhand.[1] It simply reflects the constraints imposed by the region's geology. The absence of suitable groundwater supplies means that tubewell irrigation – so much the precondition for the Green Revolution in the rest of India – is impracticable over much of the region.

Yet this failure to undergo a Green Revolution has not been without certain ironic consequences. For whilst it is now well established, not least by Benny Farmer (1977) and his co-workers, that the Green Revolution has succeeded more in differentiating the peasantry than in raising the living standards of the rural poor, it is true also that these and other findings are beginning to encourage the Indian Government towards a reappraisal of its agrarian policies. No longer can it be taken for granted that agricultural development can be secured by pumping a range of agricultural inputs and techniques into essentially undifferentiated rural 'communities' or 'peasantries'. The literature on the Green Revolution has finally scotched the belief that such communities exist – at least in caste India. Unfortunately no such lesson has been learnt by the planners responsible for India's tribal areas. The absence of a quickly polarising Green Revolution has merely confirmed these planners in their belief that in tribal India one can still legislate for, and develop, culturally and economically intact and undifferentiated rural communities.

This chapter challenges that belief. Without getting too embroiled in the wider relationships between tribal policy and tribal politics it is written in the conviction that a tension exists between a series of repatterned, but structurally unchanging tribal policies, and a seies of economic, demographic and political developments which have transformed the tribal economy of the Jharkhand. The former are all predicated on an assumption of communal integrity which the latter have effectively rendered obsolete. Moreover this notion of tension, I would argue, helps to explain why many tribals are now

Table 5.1. *Bihar: percentage of net sown area under high yielding varieties, 1976–77*

Area	% Net sown area under HYVs
Bihar state	25.83
Jharkhand region	5.84
Hazaribagh	5.99
Dhanbad	5.92
Ranchi	7.0
Palamau	4.46
Singhbhum	4.16

Source: Bihar Statistical Handbook, 1978, Tables 3.1 and 3.6 (1979).

turning their back on a Government which supposedly protects them and discriminates in their favour. It helps us to understand why many tribals are instead demanding radical agrarian policies and some degree of political autonomy.[2]

Of course a full examination of this tension, and of its importance for an understanding of the emergence of such political action in the Jharkhand, is beyond the scope of one short chapter. At the very least such an examination would demand an interrogation of planning documents for signs of continuity and change, and an investigation of the transformation of the tribal economy of the Jharkhand – recording its recent industrialisation, its changing demographic structure and its restructured relationships with the local forestry economy.

But if such issues cannot be at the centre of this discussion they remain important contextually. I will thus want to make reference to such themes in the course of an analysis of three necessarily more limited objectives. These objectives are all situated firmly within an agrarian context and are as follows. The first objective is to briefly review the main contours, assumptions and debates of tribal policy generally. The aim here is to set the scene for the more specific discussions which follow, and to show that even within its own restrictive terms tribal policy has been a failure. The second objective is to explore the tensions which exist in the Jharkhand between tribal agrarian policies and the changing agrarian structure of the region. The third objective is to continue this theme by looking at how these same contradictions manifest themselves at village level. This section comments too on the possible implications of tribal agrarian policies remaining unresponsive to changed local circumstances.

Isolation or assimilation? The tribal policy debate

It is impossible to understand the direction of tribal policy in India today without first setting it in the context of a debate that raged most intensely in the 1940s, between the so-called isolationists and the so-called assimilationists. For it is the vocabulary of that debate which structures the vocabulary of policy now, and which, in the process, sets limits to current initiatives.

This is true in two ways. On the one hand, adherence to the terms of this debate indicates that both pre- and post-Independence governments are in agreement, perhaps unwitting agreement, in one crucial respect. Both believe that tribal policy can and should take the form of government's legislating for, and protecting, identifiable and basically homogeneous tribal communities. I shall want to comment on this shared assumption later on. On the other hand, and more immediately, the vocabulary of isolationism/ assimilationism means that the ultimate justification of post-Independence policies has always been an antithetical one. The final argument in favour of these policies is that they are not tardy, and that they are not isolationist. Rather they seek to protect the tribals only in the short term. The longer-term aim is to uplift the tribals by means of positive discrimination.

But is this true? I want to begin this section by briefly reviewing the isolationist and assimilationist positions, and by asking whether it is the case that current tribal policies do discriminate significantly in favour of tribals. In other words I want to begin by tackling tribal policy on its own limited ground, looking at its own claims and boasts.

Isolationism

Let us start with the isolationist position. An attack on this has become almost a tradition in a tribal studies literature dominated by the perspective of assimilation (e.g. Das, 1967; Sharma, 1977; Ghurye, 1980). Perhaps as a result even the better placed of these attacks tend to forget to what extent the term isolationism itself is the product of specific historical circumstances. In fact its origins are very much as a term of abuse coined by nationalist politicians in the 1930s and 1940s to denounce a British tribal policy which they believed to be just one further weapon in the divide-and-rule arsenal. This is important. Because the term was coined in the heat of a political struggle, it had more than a significant air of caricature about it. In fairness therefore, it should be recognised that not all British politicians, planners and anthropologists deserved to be tarred with the same brush.[3]

Nevertheless the clear thrust of British tribal policy did leave itself open to a charge of being isolationist. Above all the government of tribal areas remained resolutely of an executive type, even after the Montagu–Chelmsford Reforms of 1919 had introduced a limited measure of self-government into the rest of India. At that time the tribal areas were designated either as Excluded or Partially-Excluded Areas and ultimate responsibility for them rested with the Governor-General or the Governor – always a colonialist. Tribal administration and the budgeting for tribal areas thus remained a Reserved Subject. Power was not transferred to the newly formed Provincial Legislatures. (In practice this meant that in the Partially Excluded Areas like the Jharkhand the Governor retained the right to modify or withhold, in the scheduled areas, any laws passed by his Provincial Legislature.)

Moreover, the explanation offered for this executive rule by the British – that the tribals needed personalised and simple administration to protect them from exploitative non-tribal outsiders – did not fully stand up to nationalist interrogation.

Firstly, it was apparent that such 'simplified rule' helped to camouflage the Raj's lack of expenditure on the tribal areas. No serious effort was being made by the British to 'develop' the tribals. As K.K. Srivastava put it recently, 'Prior to Independence the policy of isolation and drift left the tribals to themselves and almost no efforts were made to develop their lot' (1981, p. 146). As a result, the nationalists concluded, not entirely without reason, that executive rule was merely a front for mummifying tribal culture and for isolating the tribals from the Indian National Congress and mainstream Hinduism.[4]

Secondly, the nationalists saw through, and rightly rejected as offensive, the implication of the Montagu–Chelmsford Reforms and of the later Simon Commission proposals that only the British could be expected to rule tribal areas in a simplified, personalised and paternalistic fashion. And there can be no doubt that the British did make such an assumption. Colonel Wedgwood, speaking in the House of Commons in 1935, perhaps put it as bluntly as anyone when he urged:

The only chance for these people is to protect them from a civilisation which will destroy them, and for that purpose, I believe, direct British control is the best . . . Unless you have our experience of the last 50 or even 150 years in dealing with this problem it is impossible to say that any other race on earth can look after them as well as we can. (Govt. of UK, 1935, 299, col. 1549)

Thus it is not without good reason that British tribal policy is enshrined in today's literature as isolationist and berated as such. Moreover when stretched to its extremes a caricature of isolationism does provide a neat counterfoil against which to base the claims of an alternative philosophy, assimilationism, which we can now consider.

Assimilationism

The lodestar of assimilationism in India is the belief that the structures and the machinery of exclusion can be turned to assimilationist ends by providing them with a developmental impulse. In other words the aim must be to use the paraphernalia of scheduling for a measure of protection in the short run (and in this way the Scheduled Areas and the Scheduled Communities have replaced the Excluded Areas and the Backward Tribes of colonial days). During this time the areas and communities would be uplifted by means of positively discriminating financial and legislative policies, so that in the medium and long term scheduling and protection would no longer be necessary. At this point the tribal communities will have been 'assimilated' – which broadly means that they will have the same opportunities and values as everyone else.

Once again it is a term which goes back at least as far as the 1940s, when it was consciously used in contradistinction to British aims and policies. It did not receive any concrete endorsement, however, until the Constitution was drawn up between 1947 and 1950. It was only then that Sardar Patel declared that the Constitution should be formulated so as to, '. . . endeavour to bring the tribal people up to the level of Mr Jaipal Singh[5] and not keep them as tribes – so that, ten years hence, the word "tribes" may be removed altogether when they would have come up to our level' (Govt. of India, 1947: p. 467). What this meant, in practical terms, was that post-Independence Indian governments committed themselves to a whole series of measures designed to protect, uplift, and generally to discriminate in favour of the scheduled communities – including the scheduled tribes. Probably the most important such commitments were these:

Article 46 of the Constitution, which promises that the state shall promote with special care the educational and economic interests of the weaker sections of the people and, in particular, of the Scheduled Castes and the Scheduled Tribes, and shall protect them from social injustice and all forms of exploitation.

Article 164, which declares that in the States of Bihar, Orissa and Madhya Pradesh there shall be a Minister in charge of tribal welfare.

Article 244, which empowers the President to declare any area where there is a substantial population of tribal people as a Scheduled Area under the Fifth Schedule or, in Assam, as a Tribal Area under the Sixth Schedule. Under the Fifth Schedule the executive power of a State extends to the Scheduled Area subject to the Governor's authority to modify State and Central laws and to make regulations for the maintenance of peace and good government.

Article 275, which makes provision for the payment, from the Consolidated Fund of India, of grants-in-aid of the revenues of a State for the purpose of promoting the welfare of its Scheduled Tribes or for raising the level of administration of the State's Scheduled Areas.

Article 330, which sponsors the reservation of seats in the Lok Sabha for the Scheduled Castes and the Scheduled Tribes, except those Scheduled Tribes in the tribal areas of Assam or those in the [ex] Autonomous Districts of Assam.

Article 335, which promises that the applications of members of the Scheduled Castes and the Scheduled Tribes for certain public service posts will be given priority – subject to their appointment being consistent with the maintenance of an efficient administration.

Article 338, which allows the President to appoint a Special Officer (Commissioner) for the Scheduled Castes and Scheduled Tribes. This officer is to investigate all matters relating to the Constitutional safeguards for the Scheduled Castes and Scheduled Tribes and he is to report his findings, via the President, to each House of Parliament.

Article 342, which amounts to a mechanism for scheduling tribes by public notification. Such notification must be by the President, following consultations with the Governor of the concerned State.

(All are Directive Principles of State Policy)

Taken together this is an impressive string of commitments indeed. It provides for positive legal employment and financial discrimination. Moreover it charts out very clearly the Government's conception both of the tribal problem and of the time-scale necessary to solve it. Tribal policy amounts to the protection and uplift of identifiable (scheduled) communities, and this assimilationist goal was expected to be fulfilled within ten years. (Articles 275, 330, and 335 were to run only between 1950 and 1960, in line with Sardar Patel's belief that by then the word 'tribes' would be meaningless.)

Paper commitments are not always easy to translate into tangible action, however, and the simple fact remains that these same commitments have had to be re-validated three times since 1950 – in 1960, 1970 and 1980. This raises the question of whether the tribal policies of post-Independence governments, based on positive discrimination, have failed even within their own terms – discounting for the moment whether these terms are the right ones. I want to argue now that, sadly, this is the case.

Why positive discrimination has failed

Briefly, successive governments' policies have failed for two reasons. Firstly, because the Constitutional provisions which were enacted were shot through with legal loopholes, the exploitation of which the Government has since encouraged. Secondly, because fiscally the Government has not been prepared to adopt either a meaningfully progressive taxation system, or to distribute those revenues which it does collect significantly in favour of the Scheduled Communities.

In a little more detail, my major criticism of the Constitutional positive discrimination clauses is that they were still-born. In the first place the relevant articles are only Directive Principles of State Policy. They are not Fundamental Rights of the Constitution and as such they are non-justiciable. Indeed rather the reverse is true. There have been a number of cases where Government promises to reserve seats or jobs for the Scheduled Communities have been taken to the Supreme Court on the strong legal grounds that these promises contradict certain Fundamental Rights of the Constitution. Specifically they clash with Articles 15 and 16 which prohibit discrimination on the grounds of religion, race, caste, sex or place of birth, and guarantee equality of opportunity in the realm of public employment.

Secondly, even supposing that the Government is willing to sort out these clashes with Amendment Acts in favour of the Directive Principles (Prasad, 1980), there remains a get-out clause for employers worried by positive discrimination demands – namely that the appointment of all employees must be consistent with the maintenance of an efficient administration. It is this clause which has really emasculated positive discrimination. Thus it has been used by – amongst others – the Ministry of Finance on behalf of the State Bank of India in 1973, when its response to a request from the Commissioner for the Scheduled Castes and Scheduled Tribes to discriminate positively for these communities read as follows:

The Bank stated that it is not in a position to adopt the recommendation in view of the fact that having regard to the need to preserve certain minimum standards of efficiency and in view of the fact that the clerks in the State Bank of India are considered for promotion as officers at early stages in their career, the waiving of the minimum qualifying standard in the written test will not be in the interests of the institution. (Govt. of India, 1973, p. 1)

And the bank is not the only or the worst culprit. Although few statistics are available, those that I have seen make it clear that this same loophole is exploited by a number of public corporations, making positive discrimination a farce. At present the Scheduled Communities are being helped to acquire jobs almost exclusively as Class III workers and as sweepers – jobs they would probably get anyway.[6]

So much for the constitutional side of positive discrimination. What about the financial side of things? This is much less of a clear-cut issue, mainly because it is impossible to accurately quantify the financial resources that flow between the Government and tribal men and women. The reason for this problem is that the financial statistics break down only by area, and not by ethnic community, and one of the arguments of this chapter is that tribal areas and tribal communities are no longer one and the same thing. However, it can be stated with confidence that the Government's fiscal activities, generally, are weak, and that in respect of the Special Tribal Spending budget the Government's performance has by no means been as rosy as most authorities claim.

This is not to say that the efforts of post-Independence governments have not eclipsed the efforts of the Raj – clearly they have. But, as the Government and its supporters never tire of telling us, this is not saying much. Nor is it to say that a chart of Special Tribal Spending would not reveal increased expenditure from Plan period to Plan period – clearly it would. Indeed it is almost

Table 5.2. *Special plan provision for the Scheduled Tribes – 1*

Scheme	First Plan		Second Plan		Third Plan		1966/69	
	Total spent (Rs Crore)	Per capita spent (Rs)	Total spent (Rs Crore)	Per capita spent (Rs)	Total spent (Rs Crore)	Per capita spent (Rs)	Total spent (Rs Crore)	Per capita spent (Rs)
Education	5.1	0.48	7.84	0.78	13.51	0.98	9.32	NA
Economic uplift	4.6	0.41	20.00	1.78	30.71	1.82	24.07	NA
Health, housing, Communications	10.1	0.90	15.08	1.34	6.31	0.78	1.93	NA
Total	19.8	1.79	42.92	3.90	50.53	3.58	35.32	NA

Source: Sinha (1981), p. 72, Table 6.3.

another tradition of tribal studies to begin a paper discussing tribal Plan outlays with a chart like Table 5.2, taken from Sinha (1981).

What I would say is that such Special Tribal Spending remains small in comparison to General Account Spending (which probably discriminates against tribal areas), and that in real terms, and as a percentage of total Plan outlays, the commitment of governments has withered over the years (Table 5.3).

To sum up: there is some evidence to suggest that in intention at least post-Independence Indian governments have dropped isolationist tribal policies in favour of a more assimilationist approach, and that they have far exceeded the British in their attempts to give the tribals a fair crack of the financial whip. Ultimately, though, these assimilationist, 'positively discriminating' policies have not succeeded, even in their own terms. The gap between the living standards of people in the tribal areas and those in the non-tribal areas has hardly narrowed since 1947.

Continuity in policy

It is important, however, that a critique of current tribal policies should not stop at this point. Just as worrying as a policy's failure to live up to its own terms of reference, is the possibility that its terms of reference may be seriously flawed. It is this possibility that I wish to explore for the rest of this chapter. I want to argue that the isolationist/assimilationist dichotomy, though it helps us to detect certain contrasts in British and Indian tribal policies, serves equally to occlude an important continuity in policy.

At times this continuity is clearly visible. It is evident, for example, in the

Table 5.3. *Special Plan provision for the Scheduled Tribes – 2*

	1st Plan 1951/56	2nd Plan 1956/61	3rd Plan 1961/66	1966/69	4th Plan 1969/74
Special Scheduled Tribes spending (constant prices, Crores)	19.40	37.32	32.18	17.20	32.92
Special STs spending as a percentage of total Plan outlays	1.0	0.92	0.59	0.49	0.45

Computed from: Govt. of India (1977); Selbourne (1977), Table 2; Draft Fourth Five-Year Plan 1969–74 (1969).

prolongation of forms of executive rule in tribal areas, and in the fact that the tribals are still assumed to reside in Scheduled Areas. It is evident too in the continued notification of tribal communities – though the designation 'backward' has now given way to the less offensive 'Scheduled'.

Most of the time, however, the continuity is implicit. It resides in a shared, if perhaps unspoken, conception of what exactly the 'tribal problem' is, and of how it is to be solved and by whom. Put most bluntly it consists in a shared belief that there exist clearly identifiable tribal communities in clearly identifiable geographical areas. These communities are held to be culturally distinct, economically and socially undifferentiated and only loosely integrated into wider structures of market exchange and politics. They are, however, open to abuse from non-tribal outsiders. As such they require, as communities, official outside help of one sort or another – either to preserve their cultural integrity (as the British argued) or to uplift them into the general mass (as it is argued today).

Of course it is unlikely that any one authority (academic or official) would phrase it in precisely these terms. It is true also that these parameters allow for a good deal of policy change – of the sort we have seen. But it surely is a common belief of this sort which underwrites the strong element of continuity in tribal policy, and which finds expression in policy statements such as these, from 1935 and 1978 respectively.

The members of these tribes are such as to endear themselves to Members of the Committee. They are of attractive disposition, free and friendly. Some Honourable Members who have had the opportunity perhaps of meeting them in a shooting expedition in Central India know that they would do their best to provide any Honourable Member with game, either large or small, and that by their general sportsmanship and attractive character they would endear themselves to any Honourable Member who had the privilege of having contact with them. (Govt. of UK, 1935, 301, vol. 1393)

A tribesman likes to enjoy the sunlit day, the starlit sky by night, forested land with its wild profusion of tinted flowers, murmuring brooks, the enchanting streams and green hills. We feel that planners have to be in tune with tribal lore and sentiments, hopes and aspirations, and their idiom, in order to prepare a practical plan for their development. (Govt. of India, 1978a)

Revealing comments indeed – but ones which serve only to prompt, and not to hold back, the question that must follow: does it make sense to conceive of tribal life, and thus of the tribal problem and its solution, in these terms today? I shall suggest that it does not. But this time I want to argue my case at another scale – at the level of tribal agrarian policy in Bihar. Specifically I want to look firstly, if schematically, at the transformation that has occurred in tribal Bihar over the past eighty years or so, and at the tension that must exist when this changing reality is set against a rather more constant agrarian policy. And, secondly, I shall attempt to indicate something of the gap that now exists between policy and reality at the village level.

The Jharkhand: agrarian policies and agrarian realities

It is a matter of some debate as to whether the villages of tribal Bihar even one hundred years ago approximated the stereotype of closed, backward and essentially unstratified communities. There can be little room for such debate today however. The Jharkhand has been transformed (Fig. 5.1).

Of course this transformation has been uneven, both in time and in space and in its less immediate effects. But a transformation there has been and its broadest contours cannot be submerged by even the more foreshortened accounts. At the very least the following changes would emerge:

(i) Since 1921 the Jharkhand has been an area migrated to rather than migrated from and this net immigration has been expanding steadily since the heyday of emigration to the Assam tea plantations. The effect of this reversal is clear enough: population densities in the Jharkhand have risen from 208 persons per square mile in 1911 to 526 persons per square mile in 1978. As a result the percentage of tribals in the Jharkhand is now less than 50% in each of the region's districts, Ranchi excepted.

(ii) Secondly, although such population densities might seem low by West Bengal or Kerala standards, they are still indicative of strained man/land relationships in the Jharkhand. Mainly for geological reasons the region is far from the most fertile, and only 7% of the net sown area is currently irrigated. As a result subsistence landholding sizes have always been larger in this region than in most parts of India. When land was freely available for reclamation this was not much of a constraint. Today, however, land that has not already been colonised is a rarity.

(iii) This man/land pressure has been further heightened by the reservation of the forests in the Jharkhand, which has been going on since the 1880s. Land and forests previously freely available for employment, production, grazing and reclamation purposes are now subject to strict controls. Today they are run in the 'national interest' – not in the interest of the 'Lords of the Forest' whose dependence on the forests is the natural complement of a less than full agricultural

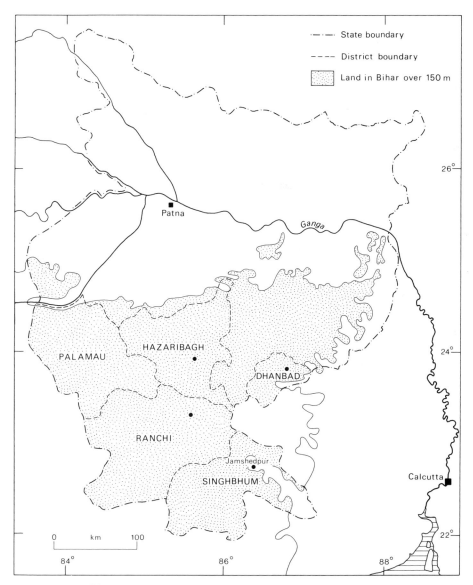

Fig. 5.1. Bihar State, showing the five districts of the Jharkhand.

calendar. As the Government itself admits, 'What were once rights, and later privileges, are now concessions.'

(iv) Further land has been lost to industry, which has boomed in the Jharkhand since 1900. Besides the older industries of coal and mica mining, there is now an iron and steel industry (at Jamshedpur and Bokaro), an iron ore mining industry at Singhbhum District, an enormous heavy engineering complex near Ranchi and numerous small businesses. All of these have demanded land from the Jharkhand, the so-called resource triangle of India. Equally they have brought new jobs and opportunities to the region and freed some Jharkhandis from a tenuous dependence on agriculture.

(v) Finally there is evidence of widespread agricultural commercialisation and change. Local cereals and pulses, for example, take up less land than they once did. Rice and more straightforwardly commercial crops have begun to push them aside. Similarly there would appear to be more markets now, meeting more often, and cash is the normal medium of transactions.

Taken together these changes amount to a transformation (Table 5.4). No longer is it the case that the terms tribal and Jharkhandi are synonymous. No longer can one ignore the pressure for land in the region. No longer can one assume that the tribal people of the area are divorced from industrialisation and from the sway of commercialisation. And no longer can one assume – and the Government bases its tribal policy on the assumption – that tribal society is undifferentiated.

Yet despite these changes, and despite the invalidity of its key assumptions, tribal policy still exhibits a stronger sense of continuity than of change. Agrarian policies in tribal India are a case in point. Such policies still hold tight to the assumption that, 'The tribal economy is generally undifferentiated and that each individual possesses a variety of skills necessary to eke out a living in those regions' (Govt. of India, 1978b, p. 77), and to the rather vaguer belief that, 'The simple tribal communities are not used to complex and formal systems: they need a much more sympathetic and humane approach' (p. 25). As such it is not surprising that their aim is to ' . . . uplift tribal communities which show little division of labour and a poor understanding of markets', and that 'more funds are essential for the task'.[7]

As will be shown below, such continuity in the most basic policy assumptions can only generate tensions, locally, when it cuts against the grain of changed material circumstances. But before we move on, it is important to document the practical effects of such assumptions as they have manifested themselves in the agrarian policies of tribal Bihar specifically. This requires that some attention is paid to the twin prongs of current agrarian policy in the Jharkhand. One of these prongs is concerned with protection and preservation and it takes its lead from a tenancy act introduced by the British as far back as 1908. The other consists of a more recent series of initiatives designed to develop the communities protected by the tenancy legislation. We can look at them in turn.

Table 5.4. *The agrarian transformation of the Jharkhand*

	Population density per square mile	Net sown area as % of total area	% of net sown area given over to millets and pulses	% of forests reserved or protected
1911/12	208	40.3	26.0	72.1
1975/76	526	60.1	15.4	99.9

Sources: *Agricultural Statistics of Bihar and Orissa, 1911/12*, Table A; *Census of India 1911*, vol. 5 *Bihar and Orissa*, Part III; *Report on the Agricultural Census of Bihar*, 1970/71 (1974).

Protective legislation

The protective impulse is by far the longer standing of the two, and still the stronger. Today it is codified in the form of the Bihar Scheduled Areas Act of 1969, but really this Act is only an amended version of the Chota Nagpur Tenancy Act of 1908. And that Act, in its turn, was very much the culmination of a series of tenancy acts passed by the British in the nineteenth century, all of which were drafted in response to revolt or the threat of revolt. In 1908 it happened to be the millenarian Birsa Rebellion of 1900 that the Government was responding to, but the precise character and demands of any particular rebellion seemed to be lost on the Raj. The administrator responded in the usual fashion. Believing that the cause of the revolt had its roots in the alienation of tribal lands to rapacious non-tribals, and not in any tribal/Government clash, the Raj acted to tighten up the regulations governing the transfer of tribal lands in Chota Nagpur (the Jharkhand).[8] In 1908 it tightened up quite considerably.

Simplifying somewhat what it did was this. The Act starts with an omnibus restriction on transfer by tribal raiyats to non-tribal raiyats of their rights in land, except in ways specifically permitted. In effect this meant that transfer by sale, gift or by other contract or agreement was forbidden except for certain industrial or religious purposes and only then with the consent of the Deputy Commissioner of the District. These restrictions still continue although the 1969 Act does allow the mortgaging of land for a five-year period. Similarly usufructuary mortgages are now allowed for up to seven years, with the provision for an extension to fifteen years if the mortgagee is a registered co-operative society (Bandyopadhyay, 1979).

Thus set out, and passed, the Act has been a force to reckon with. It would be churlish to deny this. Most observers believe that the Act has gone some way to serving its basic purpose of protecting and preserving those tribal landrights which still remained in 1908. In all likelihood the alienation of tribal land has slowed down since that date, and this finds some reflection in the low sales prices that are recorded when transfers do legally take place. By common consent, too, the Act (or the 1969 Act anyway) has few unforeseen loopholes, and it amounts to the most comprehensive restriction of transferral rights in India outside of the North-Eastern States.

That said, however, the Act is only as good as the assumptions on which it is built. The most important of these assumptions is undoubtedly the presupposition that what has to be guarded against is the transfer of land from tribals to non-tribals. The Act has less to say about the problem of land alienation between tribals – presumably because the notion of unwelcomed intra-tribal alienation of land is anathema to a conception of an undifferentiated tribal society. As a result transfers between tribal raiyats need only the permission of the Deputy Commissioner, so long as the transfer is between raiyats resident within the jurisdiction of the same police station. Moreover no limit is set on the land area that can be transferred in this way, and to obtain the permission the tribal need only show 'reasonable or sufficient purpose'. (In practice this is a formality.) One last point, which is a corollary to the above, is that the Acts were drawn up on the assumption that nearly all, if not all, tribals were occupancy tenants. Very few, if any, were assumed to be under-tenants, and thus under-tenancy is not ameliorated by the Acts.

The Acts, then, have built in limitations. They certainly protected landed tribals against the alienation of their land to non-tribals, and this was presumably a reasonable goal in 1908. What they do not do is to offer tenurial protection to the non-tribal residents of the Jharkhand, or to the growing body of under-tenants. More importantly the Acts, especially the 1969 Act, refuse to face squarely the possibility that transfers of land between tribals ought to be strictly regulated.

Development initiatives

Nevertheless the Tenancy Act is no longer the sole representative of agrarian policy in the Jharkhand. Since Independence it has had to coexist, not always happily, with a series of developmental initiatives. These initiatives reflect the Indian Governments' belief that the tribal communities are at present closed and undifferentiated, and in need of protection, but that such protection must only be a springboard for development. Accordingly those same 'tribal communities' whose landowners find themselves protected by a Tenancy Act, find themselves in line too for Government credit and for Government subsidies. Much like any other Indian 'community' the villagers of the Jharkhand are serviced by the community development apparatus (by an equivalent of a Block Development Officer, by village-level workers and so on), and can ask for Government funds to help them sink wells or tanks, to improve their land, to purchase bullocks and so forth. Similarly there is in the Jharkhand the full range of extension services: the co-operatives, the seed multiplication farms, the demonstration farms are all present. Indeed there is perhaps more than the normal range since there are also the special multi-purpose LAMPS, which are specific to the Integrated Tribal Development Projects.[9]

Once again there is much here to be applauded. But once again, too, the worth of such 'developmentalism' cannot transcend the assumptions on which it rests. The Government is assuming, as governments have always assumed, that money and skills can be pumped into a tribal community without the benefits being creamed off by an elite. To the extent that this assumption is unfounded, such policies can only go the way of the community development projects generally.

Is such an assumption unfounded, then? Is tribal policy now at odds with a new tribal reality, and if so what are the implications for the tribals and for the Government? Certainly we have grounds for believing that a tension does exist, and our study of agrarian policies and realities at the regional level has helped to suggest what forms these conflicts might take. But to answer such questions in any more detail, we really must move down the scale-ladder one step further: to the village.

Sarbai: agrarian policies and agrarian realities

The village where this fieldwork was carried out can be called Sarbai and it is located in the Khunti subdivision of Ranchi District. It is just within walking distance of the Jamshedpur/Ranchi road, but it is not within the hinterland of either of these cities, or of any other large town. It would therefore be difficult to ascribe its character to any proximity to the urban fringe. The main field research was carried out between February and May 1980, in the slack season, with the help of a local tribal research assistant.

As will become clear the chief characteristics of the village are strikingly similar to those which might have been 'predicted' by our earlier historical overview. The village is a mixed ethnic community; intra-tribal differences are apparent and resented; some seasonal migration to industrial areas is common; and a good deal of contact with the market is the norm. Only the fact that the main landowner in the village is a Rajput seems palpably exceptional.

The village was not deliberately chosen to be 'typical'. A host of more pragmatic considerations dictated its choice. Nevertheless the fact that it is not untypical must have a bearing on the relevance of the results of the fieldwork – the main thrust of which was to uncover the distribution of operational land-holdings in a 'tribal village' and to examine the local effects of actual or feted Government policies. The results can most easily be conveyed in a summary form and they are as follows.

Population and land tenure

(i) Firstly, regarding the community: the village has a population of 372 people or 71 households. This comprises the following groups: Rajputs, Yadavs, Mundas, Oraons, Ghasis, Turis, Dhahris and Bhoktas. Although numerically it is a 'tribal village' – in so far as Mundas and Oraons predominate – Sarbai is far from being the home of tribals exclusively (Table 5.5).

(ii) Secondly, regarding land, there is a considerable difference between land owned and land operated in Sarbai. Just how great this difference is, it is not easy to assess, but it is enough to suggest that the tenancy legislation governing the area is not watertight. The direction of this difference is easier to specify. It is such as to increase the inequality in land-holdings operated relative to land-holdings owned, which is perhaps the reverse of the usual situation in India. This reflects the stickiness of the land market of course. Land transfers have not been stopped, but they have been driven underground. It reflects, too, the limitations of even well-designed tenancy legislation in changed circumstances. These limitations are well brought out by Asit Bandyopadhyay an ex-Land Reforms Commissioner of Bihar, writing in his personal capacity in an unpublished paper. He says, 'the protective wall built up by legislation for land held by tribal communities is too weak to hold against the onrush of economic pressures constantly seeking to batter it down' (1979, p. 32). More succinctly still, he concludes that ' . . . legislative measures, however well conceived and skilfully framed, but devised in abstraction from the socio-economic milieu in which they are meant to be implemented, cannot be very effective' (p. 33). Sadly, recent developments in Sarbai can only confirm that conclusion. As inequalities of wealth in the village have widened under the impact of commercialisation, industrialisation, and intensified man/land pressure, so land in the village has increasingly become a commodity to be bought or sold, legally or illegally. Indeed all of the now landless tribal families in the village claimed to have been land-owners until quite recently (between five and fifteen years ago). All claimed to have 'lost' their land because of indebtedness and other reasons, the land being transferred (legally as far as I could ascertain) to other tribal families in the village.

Distribution of land-holdings

(iii) Thirdly, this sale and purchase of land has ensured that the distribution of operational land-holdings in Sarbai is highly skewed. Four households control 19% of the land, a further 19 households control a further 40% of the land, and 39 households control the remaining 41% of the land. Nine households are landless. More importantly the restricted opportunities to gain employment and income from forestry activities or from local industries, means that a household's relationship to land is now the major determinant of its income and wealth. In this respect Sarbai is not unlike a number of 'non-tribal' villages which have been the subject of close study in India.[10]

(Just how closely a household's access to land determined its level of income I cannot say because the calculation of precise annual household incomes is

Table 5.5. *Sarbai village: ethnic and caste composition*

Ethnic/caste group	Households	Population
Rajputs	3	20
Yadavs	5	22
Scheduled Tribes:		
Mundas	34	178
Oraons	19	98
Scheduled Castes:		
Ghasis	3	12
Dhahris	3	17
Turis	2	16
Bhoktas	2	9
Total	71	372

Source: author's field surveys.

Table 5.6. *Sarbai village: operational land-holdings by caste/ethnic group of households*

Caste/ethnic group of household	Land-holding (hectares)					
	Landless	0.1–2	2–6	6–10	10–15	15+
Rajputs	–	–	–	1	1	1
Yadavs	–	–	4	1	–	–
Mundas	1	2	16	10	3	2
Oraons	3	3	9	3	–	1
Scheduled Castes	5	2	3			
Total	9	7	32	15	4	4

Source: author's field surveys.

beyond the scope of four months' fieldwork. Simple observation and questioning, however, revealed that the distribution of operational land-holdings does underwrite a visibly skewed distribution of incomes in Sarbai. Those without land all recognised this fact. For them, making ends meet meant either working for their more prosperous co-villagers, or periodically migrating to the Calcutta brickfields and the mines of Dhanbad.)

(iv) Fourthly, this unequal distribution of land does not correspond to any neat ethnic division within the village. The four largest landholdings are operated by a Rajput family, by two Munda families and by one Oraon family. Of the landless households five are Scheduled Caste families (though there are only ten Scheduled Caste families in the village); the other four are Scheduled Tribes families (three Oraon families and one Munda family) (Table 5.6).

It is thus not the case that all tribals stand in a similar relationship to the land. Some tribals control more land than they legally own. Some tribals are effectively tenants of land that is legally theirs but which, de facto, is in the hands of other families, both non-tribal and tribal. And some tribals are simply labourers on the farms of others. Finally, because there is still a tendency to hire such agricultural wage-labour on a kinship/ethnic basis, it is more likely that tribal wage-labourers will be exploited by other tribals than by non-tribals. (Wages are pitifully low no matter what the kinship connection, and neither kinship nor ethnic affiliation could suppress resentment of this fact.)

(v) Finally, the distribution of land-holdings 'owned' in practice, cannot be explained in terms of demographic cycles at the household level (Table 5.7). This is important. It means that the level of inequality in Sarbai cannot be explained away along the lines of the Chayanov model. The ownership of land is not at present primarily dependent on the size of households as Chayanov suggests it should be, though this is a secondary factor. For this reason current inequalities are unlikely to be transitional or cyclical, as the Chayanov model further predicts.

Taken together these five sets of observations must call into question the very foundations of Government tribal policy, and especially its agrarian dimensions. They reveal that it makes little sense to talk of protecting distinct 'tribal' villages, or to talk of injecting funds and skills into entire Tribal Project Areas in the belief that the benefits will be roughly equally shared out amongst unstratified tribal communities. Indeed if our analysis is correct, action in support of such policies is more likely to exacerbate, than to ameliorate, the current 'tribal problem'. This is the paradox of tribal policy as it is now formulated. Precisely because the tribal communities are so fractured, and not just along ethnic lines, action in favour of the tribal community generally often amounts to action in support of an emergent tribal elite only.

This is certainly what happens in Sarbai. By definition it is the land-owning tribals only who are protected by the Bihar Scheduled Areas Act, and in practice only the non-marginal tribal cultivators at that. Similarly it is the wealthier tribal families who are taking advantage of Government schemes and advice, as Table 5.8 shows. It is they who have made use of Government loans and of Government scholarships, and it is they who have been encouraged to visit Government demonstration farms and seed multiplication units. Finally it is members of this elite, too, who are beginning to introduce some new seeds and new agricultural techniques into the village. If ever there is to be a Green Revolution amongst the tribals of the Jharkhand, it will clearly be pioneered by these richer tribal cultivators.

Conclusion

It is to be hoped that a full-blown Green Revolution will not be needed to alert the Government to the changes that are transforming the nature of the

Table 5.7. *Sarbai village: household size in relation to operational holding*

Household size	Land-holding (hectares)					
	Landless	0.1–2	2–6	6–10	10–15	15+
1–2	1	1	3	–	–	–
3–4	3	3	8	4	2	–
5–6	2	2	13	5	2	2
7–8	2	1	5	3	–	1
8+	1	–	3	3	–	1
Total	9	7	32	15	4	4

Source: author's field surveys.

Table 5.8. *Sarbai village: impact of Government schemes on the Scheduled Tribal population*

Government	Tribal household's operational land-holding (hectares)					
	Landless (4)	0.1–2 (5)	2–6 (25)	6–10 (13)	10–15 (3)	15+ (3)
Government loans	–	–	3	–	1	2
Government scholarships	–	–	–	–	1	2
Know the name of Local Extension Officer	1	2	12	8	3	3
Know of Government demonstration farms	–	–	6	5	2	3
Introduced improved seeds	–	–	2	1	2	2

Source: author's field surveys.

'tribal problem' in India. But one cannot be confident on this score. After all, not even the many demands for political independence for the tribal regions have provoked the Government into reviewing anything other than the organisational effectiveness of its tribal policies. And although such reviews have their place (they have led recently, for example, to the setting up of the Chota Nagpur Autonomous Development Authority), they do not bring into question the deeper assumptions on which tribal policies are built. These deeper assumptions remain disturbingly the same, being locked within the isolationist/assimilationist dichotomy. Tribal policies are thus still predicated on the colonial belief that governments can and should act in favour of culturally distinct and internally undifferentiated tribal societies.

It is this shared underlying assumption which this chapter challenges. It contends that tribal policy in India today is flawed in two major respects. Firstly, it fails to live up to even its own terms of reference – its commitment to discriminate positively on behalf of the Scheduled Tribes. Secondly, more importantly, it fails because it refuses to recognise that these terms of reference are no longer appropriate. Until tribal policy does recognise this fact, until it does face up to a changing 'tribal problem', it can only sponsor developments in tribal society which are entirely at odds with its stated aims. This is the central, if unwitting, paradox of tribal policy today.

ACKNOWLEDGEMENTS

I would like to thank Asit Bandyopadhyay, Benny Farmer, Anil Gupta, Steve Jones, Nirmal Sengupta and Dennis Tete for their help at various stages of the research project upon which this paper is based: of course, none are responsible for my conclusions. However, my main thanks are due to the people of the village I call 'Sarbai'.

NOTES

1. In this chapter the terms, 'the Jharkhand', 'Chota Nagpur' and 'the tribal belt of Bihar' are used interchangeably, although only Chota Nagpur corresponds to a clear administrative unit. I prefer to use the term Jharkhand (meaning land of the forests) wherever possible because it is popular locally and because it is the rallying point for much of the region's politics. Various political parties in the area are demanding a new State – the Jharkhand State.
2. The Jharkhand Mukti Morcha Party especially, and its MP, Sibu Soren, ally regionalist political sentiments with a radical agrarian programme. It is interesting that this 'tribal' party is challenging the political hegemony of the tribal elite identified in this chapter.
3. As a crude generalisation one could perhaps say that the further the British administrator was from the tribal village the more he deserved the isolationist label. Certainly the perception of the tribal problem in the District was very different from that in Delhi or in the India Office.
4. Even the British authority Grigson noted that the Indian National Congress, at their 1936 Faizpur meeting, saw exclusion as ' . . . yet another attempt to divide the people of India into different groups, with unjustifiable and discriminatory treatment, and to obstruct the growth of uniform democratic institutions in the country' (Grigson, 1946, p. 83).
5. Jaipal Singh was the Oxford-educated tribal who led the Jharkhand Party to its first Parliamentary successes.
6. What evidence there is comes in the various Reports of the Committee on the

Welfare of the Scheduled Castes and the Scheduled Tribes. The 5th and 9th of these Reports cover, respectively, the Sini Railway Workshops (Bihar) and Air India. They reveal that at Sini no tribals got Class I or Class II jobs; along with 18 Harijans and 341 others, 25 tribals gained Class III jobs. At Air India no tribals were interviewed for/appointed to the 41 Class I posts. Similarly the two tribals who applied with 783 others took none of the 135 Class II posts. But at Class III level 69 tribals out of 193 were successful. The tribals were 'successful' as sweepers too: they took all seven 'posts'. See CWSCST 9th Report (1970) and CWSCST 5th Railways Report (1977).

7. Interview, December 1979, New Delhi, with a senior official of the Ministry of Home Affairs.
8. An alternative explanation of the late-nineteenth-century rebellion in the Jharkhand would focus on precisely this tribal/Government clash. Indeed the timing of the revolts seems to bear this out: the revolts followed rent enhancements in the wake of revenue hikes, and/or the withdrawal of forestry rights. (This is not to dispute, of course, that land alienation was a serious problem in the Jharkhand; it was.)
9. The LAMPS are tribally-oriented credit-cum-marketing agencies. They were set up to service the Integrated Tribal Development Projects of the Fifth Five Year Plan Period.
10. I have quickly compared the extent of inequality in Sarbai with two village studies that I am familiar with. It is clearly not as unequal as Thaiyur village in Tamil Nadu, studied by Djurfeldt and Lindberg (1975), but the degree of inequality in Thaiyur does seem exceptional. It is not, however, so very different from Randam village (again in Tamil Nadu) studied by John Harriss (1979).

REFERENCES

Bandyopadhyay, A. (1979). The status of landholders in tribal Bihar. Typescript

Das, N. (1967). The safeguards for tribes – past and present. *Adibasi*, 8 (2), 55–61

Djurfeldt, G. & Lindberg, S. (1975). *Behind Poverty: The Social Formation in a Tamil Village*. Scandinavian Institute of Asian Studies Monograph Series, 22, Lund

Farmer, B.H. (ed.) (1977). *Green Revolution? – Technology and Change in Rice Growing Areas of Tamil Nadu and Sri Lanka*. Macmillan, London

Ghurye, G.S. (1980). *The Scheduled Tribes of India*. Transaction Books, New Brunswick

Govt. of Bihar (1974). *Report on the Agricultural Census, 1970/71*, S.R. Adige (ed.)
  (1979). *Bihar Statistical Handbook, 1978*

Govt. of India (1947). *Debates of the Constituent Assembly of India, Vol. III*
  (1960–73). *Committee on the Welfare of the Scheduled Castes and Scheduled Tribes – 5th, 9th, 18th Reports*
  (1977). *Twenty-First Annual Report of the Commissioner for Scheduled Castes and Scheduled Tribes*
  (1978a). *Interim Report of the Study Team on Social Services in Tribal Areas During the Medium Term Plan, 1978–1983*. Ministry of Home Affairs

(1978b). *Report of the Working Group on Tribal Development During the Medium Term Plan, 1978–1983*. Ministry of Home Affairs

Govt. of United Kingdom (1935). *Parliamentary Debates – Official Reports, Fifth Series, Vols. 299–301*

Grigson, W.V. (1946). The Aboriginal in future India. *Man in India*, 26 (2), 81–95

Harriss, J. (1979). *Capitalism and Peasant Farming: A Study of Agricultural Change and Agrarian Structure in Northern Tamil Nadu*.Monographs in Development Studies 3, School of Development Studies, University of East Anglia

Prasad, A. (1980). *Social Engineering and Constitutional Protection of Weaker Sections in India*. Allied, New Delhi

Selbourne, D. (1977). *An Eye to India*. Penguin, Harmondsworth

Sharma, B.D. (1977). Administration for tribal development. *Indian Journal of Public Administration*, 23, 515–39

Sinha, S.P. (1981). Tribal development administration. In L.P. Vidyarthi (ed.), *Tribal Development and Its Administration*. Concept, New Delhi, pp. 65–82

Srivastava, K.K. (1981). Planning for tribal development. In L.P. Vidyarti (ed.), *Tribal Development and Its Administration*. Concept, New Delhi, pp. 143–60

Vidyarthi, L.P. (ed.) (1981). *Tribal Development and Its Administration*. Concept, New Delhi

6 Migration and agrarian change in Garhwal District, Uttar Pradesh

WILLIAM WHITTAKER

Labour migration has been viewed as an instrument of economic development, transferring labour from a subsistence agricultural sector of low productivity to a capitalist, industrial sector where high productivity, efficiency and profitability are believed to prevail (Lewis, 1954). The key feature of this process is a permanent transfer of labour, labour which is surplus to production requirements in the agricultural sector and which thereby reduces the agricultural sector's total consumption requirement. The resulting surplus of agricultural production over domestic subsistence requirements is believed to provide a source of capital for financing economic improvements in the agricultural sector, for the manufacture of industrial sector products, and for increasing the effective demand for them (Mellor, 1969). In the Himalaya, however, migration and agrarian change have taken on a different guise. The majority of moves undertaken by hill labour are circular in nature, not extending beyond the duration of an individual's working life, and they are a response to declining per capita production levels in the agricultural sector. The purpose of migration is therefore to provide cash support through remittances and pensions earned outside the hill area, for a resident population which operates an agricultural system that is unable to meet its subsistence requirements and which possesses a weak facility for structural transformation. My purpose in this chapter is to examine the structural characteristics of sedentary hill agriculture, and to review the historical development of migration from Garhwal District, Uttar Pradesh (Fig. 6.1). It will mainly be concerned with district-level developments which have led to the emergence of a remittance economy supported by subsistence agriculture.

Garhwal District

Garhwal District, one of seven hill districts in Uttar Pradesh, India's most populous state, lies between the High Himalaya on India's northern frontier and the *Terai*, formerly a belt of steamy, malarial jungle bordering the Gangetic plain to the south.[1] The altitude varies from 500 m to 3500 m, and with the exception of a narrow strip 5–8 km wide along the southern edge called the Bhabar there is very little naturally flat ground (Fig. 6.2). The western boundary is formed by the Alaknanda river which, below its confluence with the Bhagirathi river at Deoprayag, becomes the Ganga. The whole district, comprising numerous steep-sided valleys with narrow, often stony, floors, is drained by tributaries of this system. Altitudinal variation results in a variety of climatic zones, from sub-tropical in the lowest parts of the lowest valleys to warm temperate near the crests of the higher hills. The rainfall is monsoonal in character and averages 1450 mm per annum, but there is high annual variability, 955–2300 mm, as well as marked seasonality.[2] Over 75% of annual precipitation occurs between mid-June and mid-September, the *kharif* growing season.

The total population in the 1971 census was 553 028 persons, comprising 261 054 males and 291 974 females. When adjusted for a suspected 5% undercount of females at the state level in the 1971 census (Visaria, 1971), the sex ratio is 1177 females per 1000 males. When compared with the state figure of 879 females/1000 males this hints at substantial emigration of males. Provisional totals from the 1981 census reveal that between 1971 and 1981 the population increased 12.9% to 624 259 persons. Rural population growth was much lower than the state average, 7.9% c.f. 19.7%, whilst the urban growth rate was higher, 86.8% c.f. 61.2%. Nevertheless 93.7% still lived in rural areas. Important urban centres are Pauri, district headquarters (population

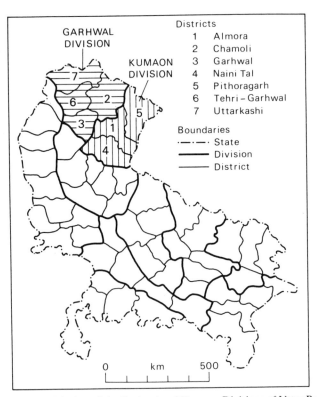

Fig. 6.1. Districts of the Garhwal and Kumaon Divisions of Uttar Pradesh.

Agrarian change at village level 111

13 600 in 1981), Srinagar, market staging post and university town on the Alaknanda (9200 population), Lansdowne, regimental centre of the Garhwal Rifles (8100 excluding military establishment), and Kotdwara, principal market, industrial centre and only railhead in the district (19 400) (Fig. 6.3).

Occupationally, 81% of the workforce were engaged in agriculture, 97% as owner-cultivators. The percentage employed in agriculture has declined from 89.6% in 1951 to 80.9% of the workforce in 1971, with increases in service sector employment accounting for most of this change (Table 6.1). The district is poorly endowed with commercially exploitable mineral resources and possess a weak industrial establishment employing only 1.2% of the workforce. Industry is predominantly small-scale and is restricted to Kotdwara and environs. Communications are poor and frequently disrupted

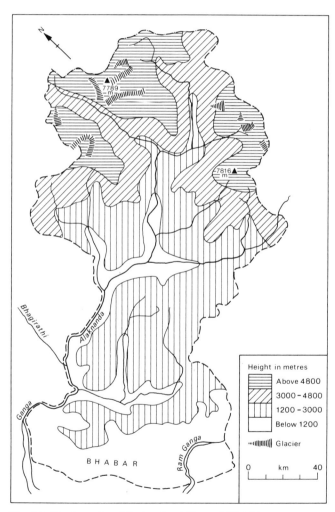

Fig. 6.2. Physiography of Garhwal and Chamoli Districts.

Table 6.1. *Distribution of working population of Garhwal by occupation 1951–1971*

Occupation type	Per cent of total population		
	1951	1961	1971
Agriculture & related activities	89.6	86.3	80.9
Mining		3.2	0.02
Household industry		1.9	0.8
Manufacturing	3.0	0.8	0.6
Construction		0.9	0.6
Trading	1.3	0.8	1.6
Transport	0.3	0.7	0.7
Services	5.7	5.2	14.6

Source: Census of India.

during the monsoon by landslides. The length of surfaced roads in 1971 was 4.4 km/100 km^2, which is low when compared with the State figure of 42.0 km/100 km^2, although some increase has occurred since 1971.

Within the old boundaries of Garhwal are several centres of pilgrimage for devotees of the Hindu and Sikh faiths. Today an estimated 100 000–300 000 pilgrims each year make their way up the Alaknanda valley from Hardwar, where the Ganga issues forth from the Himalaya, to the places of purification: Gangotri (source of the Ganga), Yamunotri (source of the Yamuna), Badrinath and Kedarnath for Hindus, and Hemkund for Sikhs. The pilgrimage season lasts from April to September.

Because of the comparatively small area under cultivation, estimated at 24.5% of the total area in 1979 (State Bank of India, 1980), the overall population density figure of 102 persons/km^2 (Census of India, 1971) conceals the fact that in Garhwal, as in other Himalayan districts, there is considerable population pressure on land. Population density in the U.P. hill districts was 522 persons/km^2 net sown area in 1971, a level as high as in the most fertile regions of South Asia (Shah, 1981, p. 440). But whereas on alluvial soils 2–3 crops per year can be grown with high yields, in the hill areas, because soil fertility is easily and rapidly exhausted, only three crops are grown per unit of arable land every two years. In the light of low agricultural productivity, population pressure and weak economic diversification, it is perhaps hardly surprising to learn that many Himalayan regions from Kathmandu to Kashmir should be deficit grain producers and dependent on migration as a means of securing employment and cash to meet domestic consumption requirements (Cool, 1967; P. Caplan, 1972; MacFarlane, 1976; Parry, 1979; G.B. Pant University, 1976; State Bank of India, 1980). Before examining the historical antecedents of the current situation, the characteristics of hill agriculture will be considered. This will be followed by a brief theoretical appreciation of structural, ecological and economic constraints to agricultural development and, in the context of population growth, the pressure towards migration.

Ecology of hill agriculture

The basis of life in Garhwal is an elaborately organised agriculture, characterised by high labour intensity and low productivity. Sustained cultivation on the steep slopes encountered is only possible by means of terracing, often covering entire hillsides with steps 1.5–2.5 metres high and 3.5–6.5 metres wide (Spate, 1954, p. 402). In some places as many as 500 of these terraces can be counted on continuous flights, and in some villages there are more than 6000 pocket handkerchief-sized fields (Pant, 1935). The cumulative labour input involved in their construction, by cut and fill behind a retaining wall, is enormous, and to allow soil development it is spread discontinuously over 4–5 years. Thereafter, assiduous maintenance is necessary in a region where even properly built roads are often swept away by landslips: usually 25–40% of the cultivation terraces give way during each rains (Spate, 1954, p. 403). The average size of fields for the Ramganga catchment area in the mid-1970s was estimated at 0.024 ha (Ghildyal, 1981, p. 131).

Irrigation is obviously desirable in a region experiencing such marked seasonality and annual variability of rainfall, but the possibilities are limited. Of the net cultivated area, only 7.8% is irrigated (State Bank of India, 1980). Of this 57% is located between Dogadda and Kotdwara. Over the remainder of the district irrigation is distributed in a piecemeal fashion. The method usually adopted is the construction of small channels (*guls*) contoured round hillsides from small headworks upstream. Only the smaller streams can be tapped; the larger ones are too turbulent and too variable to be easily harnessed. The majority of cultivation is rain-fed and therefore subject to the vicissitudes of the climate.

Upland soils are for the most part shallow and skeletal with low water-retention capacity (Ghildyal, 1981). Soil fertility can only be maintained by constant manuring and the use of crop rotations which allow resting periods. Only irrigated land permits continuous cropping. The crop rotation most commonly used on rain-fed terraced land has changed little since first described by Traill (1828, p. 26). It includes in the *kharif* season dry rice, *mandua* (*Eleusine coracana*) and *jhangora* (*Oplismenus frumentaceus*), two hardy millets, and either wheat or barley in the *rabi* (Table 6.2).

Village lands are divided into two *sars* with one remaining fallow each *rabi* season. This possesses the advantage of allowing livestock to graze on stubble without damaging crops growing in the other *sar*. Pulses are often intercropped with cereals, whilst vegetables and spices are cultivated in garden

Table 6.2. *Standard two-year crop rotation on rainfed upland terraces*

Year	Crop season	Crop grown on each category of land	
		Sar I	Sar II
1	*Kharif* (May–Oct)	Rice	*Mandua/jhangora*
	Rabi (Nov–Apr)	Wheat/barley	Fallow
2	*Kharif*	*Mandua/jhangora*	Rice
	Rabi	Fallow	Wheat/barley[a]
3	*Kharif*	Rice	*Mandua/jhangora*[b]

[a] Barley grown on inferior quality land.
[b] *Jhangora* grown on inferior quality land.

plots around the homestead. Approximate yields are shown in Table 6.3.

If soil productivity is to be sustained in the absence of synthetic fertilisers, then there must be a net transfer of fertility from commercially-held pastures or, more often, from the forest to arable land (Blaikie et al., 1980, p. 16). This is usually in the form of fodder given to stall-fed animals and later applied as manure to the fields. If this does not occur in sufficient quantity, soil nutrient levels will not be maintained at the level necessary to prevent a decline in fertility. Livestock are therefore important for their provision of manure (all animals), draught labour (cattle) and dairy produce (buffaloes and cows). Milk production per lactating animal is only 3 litres per day approximately. Buffaloes are considered too large and unwieldy for plough labour and are therefore kept only for milk and manure.

Farm implements are simple: metal-tipped wooden ploughshares, hoes, and scythes for cutting fodder and crops. Judging from various descriptions over time, farming technology has not undergone any radical structural transformation since the beginning of the nineteenth century (Traill, 1828; Atkinson, 1886, pp. 262–4; Pauw, 1896, pp. 11–24; Walton, 1910, pp. 30–7).

In this farming system the absolute amount of land that is needed to support long-term cultivation and the maintenance of yields depends, therefore, on the productive capacity of the forest. If the system were closed then an optimum balance between human and livestock populations, arable land, and forest resources would at least be hypothetically feasible.

Soil and nutrient losses

On a healthy vegetated slope a dynamic balance exists between the rate of erosion and soil formation. Removal of natural vegetation cover, even with substitution by cultivated crops, results in soil erosion, i.e. removal at a faster rate than formation. Thus, cultivation in the hills is obtained at the expense of environmental stability. First, removing forests and other natural vegetation from the hillsides increases the water yield. In other words, precipi-

Table 6.3. *Approximate yields of principal crops*

Crop	Yield (kg/ha) 1896	Yield (kg/ha) 1979	% of 1979 gross cropped area
Rice	1120	1133	17.6
Wheat	898	538	25.4
Barley	N.A.	362	5.7
Mandua	1120	924	24.6
Jhangora	1100	924	13.7

Sources: Pauw, 1896; Dept. Agriculture, U.P., 1980.
N.A. – not available.

tation is in excess of the absorptive and retentive capacity of the soil. Erosion is intensified because water flow through the system becomes less regulated and more unmanageable. Run-off therefore increases and with it soil removal. Tempany and Grist (1958, p. 58) calculated that if heavy rains double the water flow, the scouring capacity of surface water is increased four times, its carrying capacity thirty-two times and the size of particle that can be transported sixty-four times. Even where water management systems are practised, such as *gul* irrigation, floods caused by excessive rainfall may enter the canal and in places spill over from it causing serious gully erosion on the land below (Tautscher, 1974, p. 8).

Second, removal of large volumes of timber without the replenishment of minerals that is normally accomplished through the decay of wood and litter leads to the impoverishment of ecosystems, particularly in montane forests where the pool of nutrients is already limited (Odum, 1971, p. 100). Land under sustained crop cultivation, even with fallow periods, requires a faster rate of nutrient recyclement than land under natural vegetation. For cultivated land, however, the efficiency of nutrient recyclement is much lower than under natural conditions because nutrients are lost through the removal of crops for consumption and because the production of animal manure requires the expenditure of energy. Furthermore, removal of forest resources for fuel, house construction and farm implement manufacture contributes to the net loss of energy and nutrients from the ecosystem. Forest fertility, therefore, is diverted to arable land to maintain soil fertility, and then is transferred to the village to satisfy human needs. This transfer impairs the forest's regenerative capacity. Secondary successions of vegetation will consequently be poorer in nutrients, and as further net losses are incurred to ensure stable crop yields, the store of nutrients will decline. Destruction of biological recycling mechanisms will inevitably result in the impoverishment of the ecosystem, and, in the context of population growth and the increased energy demands that result, hill agriculture will enter a downward ecological spiral.

Alternative options

To increase total agricultural production, the growing population has a number of options. Extension of the cultivated area, by exposing more of the total area, will result in increased erosion and water flow irregularities. Aggregate yields of the farming system may in fact decline, reducing the average product of labour. In any event, increasing the net sown area and attempting to maintain soil fertility will reduce the marginal productivity of labour because of the time required in the construction and maintenance of terraced fields, increased time expended in fodder collection and manure distribution, and the probability that more marginal land is being brought into cultivation. An expanding population completely dependent on agriculture as a means of livelihood will therefore find it increasingly difficult to meet consumption requirements merely by extending the area under cultivation.

Fragmented family holdings, a product of the nature of the terrain, the historical development of village agriculture and the land inheritance system (partible inheritance), preclude the introduction of labour-saving technology. The smallness of fields and their difficult access, invariably by footpath across or skirting other villagers' fields, discourages the mechanisation of those farm operations that other more suitable environments permit, for example, field preparation, crop cutting and transport of crop inputs to the field and produce from it. The fact that economies of scale cannot be enjoyed in the transportation of a surplus, should one exist and be for sale, to a distant market, obviously reduces the actual and potential profitability of hill agriculture. Thus, capital substituton for labour is hardly applicable in this farming system.

Under the current crop rotation system, intensifying agricultural production by increasing the frequency of cropping will result in declining yields. *Mandua*, a hardy, coarse millet of comparatively high calorific value and favoured by the hillman because it is slow to digest, is ideally suited to climatic conditions in the hills (Census of India, 1961, p. 14). From Table 6.3 it can be seen that yields are high by comparison with other cereals. It is, however, an extractive crop, leaving the soil with insufficient moisture to support any *rabi* crop (Shah, 1981, p. 438). The standard crop rotation illustrated in Table 6.2 is believed to optimise soil fertility in the long run yet maximise aggregate yields obtained per unit area. As yet no substitute rotation has been demonstrated to yield a comparable subsistence output for a similar capital investment.

As noted earlier, over most of Garhwal the possibilities for intensifying production through irrigation are limited by high variability in water supply and because of the difficulty in harnessing water resources. The adoption of Green Revolution type packages of higher yielding varieties of seeds and their complementary fertilisers and pesticides is thus restricted by water availability (Shah, 1981, p. 438).

The future

In view of the limited adaptability of the farming system, and despite the deleterious consequences, it seems likely that extension of the cultivated area will be the first method adopted to increase production. In the long term this will undoubtedly lead to ecological degradation and declining yields but this will affect the whole community rather than a specific individual. If production fails to meet consumption requirements, collective organisation and action against environmental deterioration may collapse in the face of a mad scramble for land. Steep slopes may be brought into cultivation even though the cultivator may know that he may thereby threaten the future interests of the community. The individual will take action as soon as he needs to avoid the possibility that someone else may do so first. Competition for limited resources is of the essence but, as Reiger notes: 'there is one common characteristic: individual and collective rationality are at variance' (Reiger, 1981, p. 373).

As population increases, then, more land may be cultivated but the average product will become insufficient to provide a minimum standard of subsistence. Because the agricultural system possesses a weak facility for upward transformation and for increasing productivity per capita, population in excess of the number that can be supported by agriculture will have to turn to non-agricultural wage employment, either locally or elsewhere. This does not mean, however, that the presence of migration implies zero marginal productivity of labour (Lewis, 1954). Removal of part of the labour force may compel the residual agricultural labour force to work harder, longer or more efficiently, or may require them to draft in additional labour such as children to replace labour lost through changes in employment, and to ensure the maintenance of levels of output (Lipton, 1964). The availability of wage employment and the opportunities this creates for saving may enable a larger population than can be supported directly by the land to remain in the village, providing that deficits can be made up by migrants' remittances and locally earned cash. With further population growth, agricultural extension may proceed further, calling for higher inputs of labour but lowering still further per caput production levels and increasing domestic dependence on non-agricultural and external earnings.

It is likely that the availability of local off-farm employment will be limited. This will be the product of two principal factors: first, the inability of the agricultural economy to finance economic development, and second, the geographic and structural features of the hill economy which contrive to place it at an economic disadvantage in relation to other regions in the national system. The typical characteristics of hill farming, i.e. labour intensiveness, low productivity, and an ecological straitjacket, limit the possibilities for the production of a surplus. Furthermore, geographical factors such as large distance from markets and poor communications and transport facilities, and the low value per unit weight of the main subsistence products available (e.g. grain), make commercial farming either unprofitable or uncompetitive. Indigenously financed economic development is therefore limited whilst inter-regional disparities and disadvantages inhibit externally-initiated economic development (Myrdal, 1957). Thus, apart from population control, migration out of the area may offer the only rational, immediately available course of action to a population that has outstripped the absorptive capacity of the local system and is unable to redress this imbalance through structural transformation of the economy. It remains to be seen how far the experience of Garhwal supports this conclusion.

Labour migration from Garhwal District

From patchy, ill-authenticated data, often based on qualitative assessments by officials, the following historical outline has been constructed. My purpose is to review the development of migration in Garhwal against the background of population growth and economic change, so as to test the validity of the general conclusions outlined above concerning the functional role of migration.

Early history

Two major ancestral stocks are generally believed to have contributed to the present *pahari* (Hindi generic term, 'of the hills') population. One, usually assumed to have been indigenous, appears as the *Doms*, or Scheduled Castes (Berreman, 1974, p. 14); the other, the *Biths*, is believed to be an admixture of *Khasas* of Central Asian origin, and degraded Brahmin and Rajput immigrants from the plains (Hitchcock, 1978, p. 112). These *Biths* comprise the present day Brahmin and Rajput caste groups, which are numerically dominant over the socially inferior and economically subservient Scheduled Castes (21% of the total population in 1971).

In the fourteenth and fifteenth centuries Garhwal was transformed from a loose federation of fifty-two petty principalities, from which the title 'Garhwal' meaning 'land of the forts' (Hindi) appears to have been derived, into a kingdom approximating to the current areal extent of Garhwal Division (see Fig. 6.1). In Kumaon there was a similar process of state formation. Over two centuries of internecine warfare followed, before both states were overrun by the newly consolidated and expansionist Gurkha kingdom of Nepal: Kumaon in 1790, Garhwal after a struggle in 1803.

Little is known of economic conditions prior to the Gurkha invasion. Ferishta, the Moghul court historian, wrote in a confused and, one suspects, exaggerated fashion of the Raja of Garhwal's impressive hoard of gold and his army of 80 000 men (Walton, 1910, p. 116). However, no concerted effort was made to subjugate the hill kingdoms, which remained economically as well as politically isolated from the plains. Among the fiscal arrangements of the native Rajas, there were sixty-eight taxes to which the landholder was liable. Although all were not vigorously levied, the effect, nevertheless, was to leave the agriculturalist with little beyond the means of subsistence. This revenue appears to have been used primarily for the maintenance of court and army (Pauw, 1896, p. 58).

Perhaps it was the stiff resistance put up by the Garhwalis that fashioned subsequent relations between victor and vanquished. Whatever the cause, the Gurkhas

> regarded the devastated condition of Garhwal and the barbarity of much of the population more as justifications for plunder than as incentives to constructive administration. The land revenues were grossly over-assessed, and the occupation troops left to squeeze from their assigned estates rents which bore no relation to their yield. Arrears increased and there was armed resistance followed by brutal retaliation, depopulation and an increase in the trafficking of human slaves used as a supplementary currency. (Pemble, 1971, p. 19)

Anxious to stem the rising tide of rural depopulation and the abandonment of the more accessible, and often most fertile land, the Gurkha overlords promulgated laws designed to tie male labour more firmly to the village (Atkinson, 1886). An estimated 20–40% of the total population of Garhwal, which numbered 132 774 persons in a census of 1811, is believed to have been sold into slavery during this period (Fraser, 1820, p. 379; Regmi, 1971, p. 120).

Population and environment in the nineteenth century

Compelled to action by encroachments on their territory around Gorakhpur, the East India Company expelled the Gurkhas from Garhwal and Kumaon in 1815. The removal of war and misery as Malthusian checks to population growth, and the replacement of a harsh oppressive rule with a benevolent and despotic administration (Atkinson, 1886), provided the stability and long-term security necessary for agricultural restoration and development. The attitude of the British was essentially laissez-faire. No special measures were adopted to improve the backward tracts within the region, but proprietary rights were bestowed on those bringing land under the plough (Atkinson, 1886, p. 243). Whether or not the practice of polygyny originated during this period is unknown but the gazetteer Atkinson interpreted this feature of nineteenth-century social life in Garhwal as a response to 'the great difficulty in cultivating the large amount of waste land available' (Atkinson, 1886,

p. 255). Certainly in the first twenty to thirty years of British rule the land waxed fat. There was a modest export of foodstufff, including 'grain of all kinds' (Traill, 1828, p. 226), which were traded down the Alaknanda valley during the dry season which followed the *kharif* harvest (Girdlestone, 1867, p. 61). Exceptional crop yields were noted but this was because many fields had benefited from fallow periods of several years' duration after abandonment. However, Bishop Heber was alarmed at the rate of deforestation, which he attributed to population increase and wasteful travellers' practices. On his tour of the region in 1824 he forecast that 'unless some precautions are taken, the inhabited part of Kemaoon [then Garhwal and Kumaon divisions] will soon be wretchedly bare of wood and the country, already too arid, will not only lose its beauty but its small space of fertility' (Laird, 1971).

Then as now, agriculture was dependent on the vagaries of the climate. Periodic crop failure resulting from uneven distribution of rainfall within the growing season was an unavoidable feature of the agricultural economy. British Garhwal (Garhwal and the Chamoli districts) could be divided into two complementary climatic zones: the north of the district in the shadow of the glacier-garlanded peaks of the High Himalaya, in which the *kharif* (monsoon) harvest was liable to suffer from excessive rainfall, and the south where it was drought-prone. For as long as the district remained self-sufficient, a poor harvest in one part was usually compensated for by a good harvest in the other. Consequently, public famine relief measures were felt by the administration to be unnecessary until *c*. 1880 when the domestic population was too large to be accommodated by this indigenous redistributive mechanism alone. The import of foodstuffs was not easy. The malarial jungles of the *Terai* formed an almost impenetrable barrier between the plains and hills, and during the monsoon tracks through this area became impassable mires. The nearest railway line was at Saharanpur, a distance of 100 miles from Srinagar.

Demographic data for the nineteenth century is quite inaccurate prior to 1872, land-use statistics prior to 1896 hopelessly so. During the period 1872–1981, population growth in 'British Garhwal' (i.e., since 1961, Garhwal and Chamoli Districts combined) was unchecked but generally increasing in rate (Table 6.4).[3] In the early nineteenth century agricultural extension appears to have kept pace with population growth, but this process came to an end about 1880. The crossover of sex ratios suggests, though hardly proves, increasing numerical significance of male migration over the whole period (Fig. 6.4). State Famine Relief was instituted when crops failed in 1890 and 1892, and in 1896 the Settlement Officer Pauw wrote

> Garhwal as a whole does not produce sufficient to feed its inhabitants as the small exports to Tibet are far more than balanced by enormous imports from the plains. It is hardly possible that with its increasing population, Garhwal will ever again be able to pay its land revenue out of the produce of its fields. (Pauw, 1896, p. 1)

Table 6.4. *Population growth in Garhwal and Chamoli Districts ('British Garhwal' pre-1961), 1872–1981*

Year	Population Total	Males	Females	% Total population change per decade
1872	310 258	155 750	154 538	–
1881	345 629	170 755	174 874	+ 11.4
1891	407 818	200 319	207 499	+ 17.9
1901	429 900	211 588	218 312	+ 5.4
1911	479 641	235 554	244 067	+ 11.5
1921	485 186	232 863	252 323	+ 1.1
1931	533 885	257 987	275 898	+ 10.0
1941	602 115	289 956	312 159	+ 12.8
1951	639 625	301 298	338 327	+ 6.2
1961	735 464	342 984	392 480	+ 14.9
1971	845 599	403 016	442 583	+ 14.9
1981	988 546	N.A.	N.A.	+ 16.9

Source: Census of India.

Crop cutting experiments from 1897 to 1912 revealed that yields were no different from those obtained in the plains (Nelson, 1916, p. 31). The damage wrought by excessive rains was felt to be minimal (Atkinson, 1886, p. 257). A comparison of accounts on farming techniques indicates that technology at the end of the century was virtually the same as the beginning (Atkinson, 1886; Traill, 1828). It was noted, however, that crop yields depended almost entirely on the amount of manure put into the ground (Pauw, 1896, p. 24). From this we might infer that population growth, in the context of an unchanged farming technology, had pushed the cultivated area to its critical limit by the end of the century. Yields could still be maintained by manure applications and soil erosion was held to be at an acceptable level.

Non-agricultural employment

At the end of the nineteenth century some improvements occurred in internal communications. The extension of a Northern Railway branch line to Kotdwara in 1897 ensured passage through the treacherous *Terai* and facilitated the bulk imports of grain now needed in many parts of the district. Kotdwara, enjoying the comparative advantage a rail link offered in addition to its location at the interface between plain and hills, developed as a break of bulk, distribution and market centre. Elsewhere, trading was monopolised by immigrants from the plains, but on the whole the economy remained weakly diversified. Cultivation and trading of tea in Central Asia at one time gave great hopes of proving remunerative (Atkinson, 1886, p. 258). However, this was curtailed by the imposition of prohibitive duties on all articles imported from India by Russia. In addition, planters complained that the reduction in duty on Chinese teas affected them injuriously, and consequently the tea industry never progressed beyond infancy.

The railway spawned some small-scale industrial activity in Kotdwara and the annual influx of pilgrims, estimated at 30 000–50 000 (Raper, 1810, p. 540; Traill, 1828, p. 166), generated demand for restaurants, tea shops, porters, etc. Those villages situated near the Alaknanda benefited from this through the sale of some grain, dairy products and labour. But much of the profit from the pilgrim trade flowed back down to the plains, to be invested in more lucrative areas. Locally, then, 'there was little to attract the mass of people from their hereditary pursuits beyond the demand for unskilled labour on the public works and coolies' (Atkinson, 1886, p. 251), activities which Biths generally found degrading.

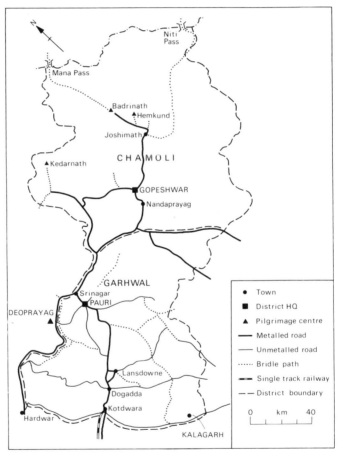

Fig. 6.3. Urban centres and the transportation network in Garhwal and Chamoli Districts.

Labour migration

Against this background of an insufficiently productive agricultural base and a poorly developed non-agricultural economy, both seemingly unable to absorb increases in population, migration can be viewed. There had always been some mobility of labour but it was not until the latter half of the nineteenth century that commentators became aware of its increasing quantitative and economic significance. Pauw lists three main sources of employment outside traditional agriculture: seasonal labour in the forests of the southern part of the district, temporary labour in the hill stations, and the army (Pauw, 1896). Forest labour, undertaken during the slack *rabi* (winter) growing season when forest roads were negotiable, entailed cutting timber and bamboo and offered daily wages of 4 annas (¼ rupee) in 1879. Of the amount paid to labourers in that year, it was estimated that Rs 50 000 (200 000 man-days) was to Garhwalis, the largest portion of the earnings accruing to inhabitants of the villages bordering the forested tracts.

The second type saw Garhwalis serving as menials to the vast army of memsahibs, who, accompanied by their offspring, sought refuge from the blistering heat of the pre-monsoon summer months of the plains in the cool

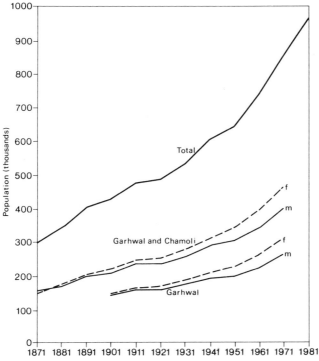

Fig. 6.4. Population growth in British Garhwal (1871–1961) and in Garhwal and Chamoli Districts (1961–1981).

hill stations of Mussoorie and Naini Tal. It is quite probable that many originally seasonal workers were taken on as full-time employees and thenceforth accompanied their new employers back to the plains. This offers a plausible explanation for the fact that even today Garhwalis are unflatteringly regarded as good servant stock, a characteristic most better educated Garhwalis view with embarrassed disdain. Certainly Garhwalis were widely distributed over northern India by 1900 and awareness of the less acceptable aspects of migration, such as separation of families, had become an established feature of folklore: 'even at Delhi one remembers or thinks of his home' (Upreti, 1894, p. 115). Initially, therefore, the seasonal nature of much of the migration observed suggests that if migration was necessary as a means of supplementing income derived from the fields, targets could be met by recourse to temporary moves of a few months' duration.

Service in the armed forces, particularly the army, is a feature common to most Central Himalayan societies (L. Caplan, 1970; P. Caplan, 1972; MacFarlane, 1976; Parry, 1979). Since at least the seventeenth century, soldiery was an important economic activity in Garhwal. After serving in successive Rajas' armies, Garhwalis were either conscripted into, or operated as mercenaries in the Gurkha army. In 1814, during the first year of the Anglo-Nepalese war, General Ochterlony of the British army is known to have recommended the recruitment of Garhwalis and Kumaonis (Bolt, 1967, p. 59). Subsequently many joined the ranks of the 3rd Gurkhas. It was not until 1887 that a native regiment was raised at Lansdowne which afterwards became the Royal Garhwal Rifles. Growth of the regiment was at first steady: two battalions served in World War I and by the end of World War II there were six. Thereafter growth was spectacular: by 1977 there were fifteen battalions, drawing all 'other ranks' from Garhwal Division. There are now at least as many again serving in other corps of the Indian army, as well as a similar number in the police and other para-military forces. It has been calculated that one in six of all eligible males were enlisted into the armed forces during World War II, Garhwal District returning the best recruiting figures in the province (Mason, 1974, p. 411; *Victory Record*, 1945, p. 2).

The attraction of the army lies not only in the economic benefits that it confers on the soldier, for example assured reasonable pay, clothing and board, a pension and/or gratuity on leaving the service, but also it offers an avenue of upward social, as well as economic, mobility for even the barely literate (Parry, 1979, p. 42). Nowadays, it also offers a vehicle for the acquisition by some of practical skills of use on discharge from the service, for example driving. The concept of *izzat* (Hindi, honour) and attendant social prestige, encapsulated in the martial ethic associated with the dominant Rajput caste group, should not be underestimated. Brahmins also joined up, but at the end of the nineteenth century the armed forces were all but closed to hill Doms (Evatt, 1927, p. 34).

Table 6.5. *Population growth in Garhwal District, 1901–1981**

Year	Population Total	Males	Females	% Total population change per decade
1901	283 760	139 657	144 103	–
1911	316 938	155 650	161 288	+ 11.7
1921	320 602	153 872	166 730	+ 1.2
1931	352 782	170 473	182 309	+ 10.0
1941	397 867	191 598	206 269	+ 12.8
1951	422 653	197 784	224 869	+ 6.2
1961	482 327	222 892	259 435	+ 14.1
1971	553 028	261 054	291 974[a]	+ 14.6
1981	624 259	N.A.	N.A.	+ 12.9

*Territory as existing at 1981 Census.
[a]Enumerated total.
Source: Census of India.

Population and environment in the twentieth century

In Garhwal District during this century, population growth has been unmatched by a commensurate increase in either the area under cultivation or the volume of agricultural production. Between 1901 and 1981 the total population rose from 283 760 persons to 624 259 persons, an increase of 119% (Table 6.5). The two periods of comparatively low intercensal growth, 1911–21 and 1941–51, were due to the influenza epidemic which raged across Northern India in 1918–19 and the prolonged absence of males serving in the armed forces during World War II. The cultivated area, however, increased by only 51% from 88 222 ha in 1896 to 133 500 ha in 1980, the cropping intensity from 140% of the net cultivated area to 154% and the irrigated area from 3.2% of the cultivated area to 7.8%. Fertiliser application was only 1.10 kg/ha, a figure too low to have any significant effect on the principal crops which, with the exception of rice, have probably declined in yield per hectare (see Table 6.3). Because there has been little or no capital substitution for labour, production levels per caput have also fallen. The density of livestock has, however, increased, from 342 animals/km^2 in 1896 to 474 animals/km^2 in 1980. These figures tend to confirm the hypothesis advanced earlier, that extension of the cultivated area is the principal means by which agricultural production can be raised, and that in order to maintain yields more animal manure is required per unit area of land. In turn, greater demands are placed on forest resources by the larger human and animal population.

Statistics on forested areas do not bear this out. In 1916 less than 60% of the total area of the district was recorded as being under forest of one kind or another (Nelson, 1916, p. 7). By 1927 this proportion had risen to 65.7% (Ibbotson, 1933, p. 4), and by 1971 'forest' was 68.9% of the total area (Dept.

Agriculture, 1971). These figures tell us nothing of the quality of forest resources and merely purport to indicate the area classed as forest. As such, they must be regarded with suspicion. It is quite likely that some of the increase in the cultivated area has been obtained at the expense of the forested area rather than cultivable wasteland, a category of land used for land revenue assessment which in other parts of India has been found in a number of cases to be uncultivable (Farmer, 1974, p. 29). There is also the probability that some *de jure* forest land is *de facto* cultivated land, the result of illegal and unrecorded encroachments. But even if we accept the statistics as correct, in the knowledge that forests in the hills are still the primary energy source, there can be no denying that because of increases in dependent human and animal populations as well as in the cultivated area, forests are subject to much heavier demands for fuel fodder than in 1896. An average decadal rate of population increase of at least 10% is twice that of the rate of natural forest growth and is bound to have diminished the size of the forests and depleted their reproductive capacity (Mauch, 1976, p. 2). Moddie (1981, p. 347) believes that in the Garhwal and Kumaon Divisions as much as 80 000 ha of Civil Forest lands are now virtually treeless.

Local population pressure is not the only cause of deforestation. The forests of the Himalaya also serve as a source of timber and wood products for the population of the plains. With the gradual opening up of the hill areas in this century, for strategic as well as economic purposes, the forests have become more accessible, and by extension, more exploitable. Certainly, during the 1939–45 period prodigious amounts of timber were extracted for railway sleepers (*Victory Record*, 1947, p. 26). Today the rate of extraction is believed by outside observers to be excessive (Eckholm, 1975, p. 765), but to regard the hill populations as being impassive to these developments would be erroneous. The *Chipko Andolan* ('Hug a tree campaign'), the result of spontaneous action by hill women aimed at preserving dwindling forest resources from continued commercial exploitation, originated in Chamoli District, has gained a substantial following, and demonstrates a growing local awareness of the dangers of deforestation. It is believed that chir pine (*Pinus roxburghii*), a major source of raw materials for the paper and resin industries, is extending aggressively over all types of broad-leaved species (Bandyopadhyay & Shiva, 1979, p. 1733). As pine forests do not possess abundant forest floor vegetation and because their leaves are not suitable as fodder, the availability of fodder for the increased numbers of livestock is being reduced even further, thereby posing an additional threat to the maintenance of the agricultural system.

Migration at the present day

During recent years emigration has certainly increased. Because only data on

Table 6.6. *The population of Garhwal District classified according to place of birth and place of registration in 1971*

	Per cent of total Garhwal population, by place of enumeration			
	Rural areas		Urban areas	
Place of birth	Male	Female	Male	Female
Place of enumeration	36.5	23.7	1.2	1.0
Elsewhere in the district	4.7	24.6	0.2	0.1
Other districts in U.P.	2.5	2.0	0.9	0.8
Other states in India	0.3	0.1	0.3	0.3
Other countries	0.6	0.1	0.05	0.05
Total	44.6	50.5	2.65	2.25

Source: Census of India.

in-migration is collected at the district level in census enumerations, a derived measure of the extent of out-migration is desirable. The sex ratio is believed to furnish this on the grounds that immigration is small and not sex specific (Table 6.6). Moreover sex specific fertility rates and mortality rates conform to the state level pattern, and there are no regionally exclusive cultural practices which might account for the excess of females over male, e.g. male infanticide or senilicide.

The sex ratio approach to migration estimation is best applied to rural areas only because urban growth is due to natural increase of urban populations and in-migration of persons born outside the district. Nevertheless it only offers an indication of the type of migration which separates families, e.g. a male member working outside the district and the rest of the family remaining in the village. Family migration, because it involves roughly equal numbers of each sex, leaves the total sex ratio unaffected. Similarly, outward and return migration in intercensal periods is lost. If we assume that without migration a sex ratio similar to that recorded at the state level would be obtained, then by adjusting the 1971 population figures for suspected undercount, and by subtracting the actual male population from the expected figure, we can obtain an approximate figure of the volume of accumulated migration of males. By this method, and for the rural population only, we find that in 1971 there were at least 40 000 male migrants outside the district or 31% of the working age group, i.e. those aged 20–59 years. If we acknowledge that not all migration is undertaken by males, then the true extent of out-migration will be higher. Over time, the sex ratio of Garhwal has continued to widen and followed a trend opposite to those of the state and national level figures (Mitra, 1979). Migration, though, has only been incre-

Table 6.7. *Sex ratios (females per 1000 males) for All-India (1921–71), Uttar Pradesh (1881–71), and Garhwal and Chamoli Districts (1872–1971)*

Year	Sex ratio – females per 1000 males		
	All-India†	Uttar Pradesh	Garhwal & Chamoli
1872			992
1881		925	976
1891		930	1036
1901		937	1032
1911		915	1036
1921	955	909	1083
1931	950	904	1069
1941	945	907	1076
1951	946	910	1123
1961	941	909	1144
1971	930	879	1168*

*Adjusted for suspected undercount of females
†Territory as existing at 1971 Census.
Source: Census of India.

mental, i.e. it has skimmed off a part of the natural increase of the population (Table 6.7 and Fig. 6.5).

Still using sex ratios as an indicator of accumulated migration rather than rates of migration (Wasow, 1981, p. 436), and employing multiple regression analysis, we find that 65% of the explained variance of intra-district variations between the fourteen Development Blocks in the district can be attributed to two variables: the extent of local non-agricultural employment (negatively correlated with the sex ratio) and the female participation rate (positively correlated with the sex ratio). The first suggests that potential migrants will remain in their home Block if there is wage employment available. As noted earlier, the decline in agriculture's share of the workforce has been caused by a rise in service sector employment. Nevertheless, the district population is still primarily dependent on agriculture even though 69.5% of cultivating households own less than 1 ha of land (Census of India, 1971), and only 1.3% of the agricultural workforce were classified as agricultural labourers.

The second feature, a result of migration, is that as male emigration increases, the percentage of the total female population in employment increases. This suggests that zero marginal productivity of labour does not exist prior to migration and that removal of labour through migration will affect agricultural production. From a consumption viewpoint migration may be necessary, but in labour-for-production terms it may be that it can only take place without disrupting the volume of production if compensatory

Agrarian change at village level

measures are undertaken, i.e. drafting in more labour to replace that lost through migration.

Survey of six villages

Despite this, the region is still believed to be a deficit economy producing only 40% of its grain requirements (State Bank of India, 1980, p. 6). Remittance receipts are high, with money-order receipts alone standing at Rs 125 per caput in 1979. Money-orders, however, only represent a fraction of total remittance receipts. A study of the remittance patterns of six villages in the district by the author in 1980 revealed that money-orders accounted for half the total remittance receipts by value. It is likely, therefore, that domestic income derived from migrants' remittances is higher than that obtained locally. The per caput income for the district exclusive of remittances was Rs 155 in 1976–77 (State Bank of India, 1980, p. 2). Over time, what has emerged is a dual economy, or as Parry has described for a similar situation in Kangra, 'a remittance economy backed up by subsistence agriculture' (Parry, 1979, p. 45).

This economic shift has been accompanied by changes in the type and nature of migration from that described by Pauw in 1896. Nowadays, seasonal or short duration moves appear to be unable to generate sufficient income to meet consumption deficits. Most moves are semi-permanent, i.e. for working life, and specific places and occupations dominate the pattern. For the same group of six villages, from which 50% of the total male population had migrated, 24.6% of these were serving in either the armed forces or the police, and 43.9% were clerical workers in various organisations, mostly public sector. Only 2.1% were professionals, e.g. accountants,

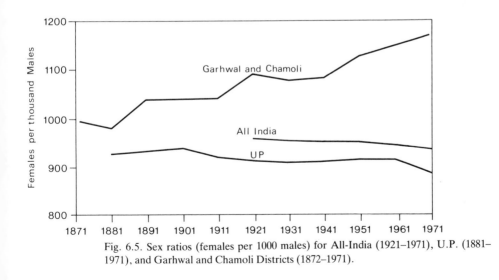

Fig. 6.5. Sex ratios (females per 1000 males) for All-India (1921–1971), U.P. (1881–1971), and Garhwal and Chamoli Districts (1872–1971).

teachers, etc., 0.7% were engaged in agricultural activities, and 3.8% were unemployed at the time of survey. The remainder tended to gravitate towards catering and related service activities, some as private servants, a relic of previous occupational patterns. Only 1.6% were self-employed, and only one person migrated seasonally to the hill station of Mussoorie to work as a bearer during the high season.

By place of work, 42.7% of all migrants worked in Delhi, 20.2% in Field and Camp Post Office areas (military installations of unknown location), and a further 20.7% in cities and towns in U.P. Migration within the district was minimal at 2.0% of the total. Migrants were concentrated in the northern, Hindi-speaking part of the country, and with the exception of armed forces personnel the majority had moved to urban areas and were drawn from the educated part of the village community. Higher castes showed a higher propensity to migrate than Scheduled Castes.

Contact between migrant and village

Concentration of migrants in certain cities, most notably Delhi, and in particular occupations, most notably public sector clerical work, is both the cause and consequence of special features of the migrant system whose purpose is to increase the new migrants' chances of securing worthwhile, long-term employment and to prevent the disintegration of the village structure. Whereas twenty years ago employment was relatively easy to obtain in urban areas, now new migrants generally undergo initial periods of unemployment and/or fairly brief spells in the informal sector, where entry is easier but remuneration and security of tenure are lower (Todaro, 1969, p. 139). Informal sector employment often takes the form of a menial job in a roadside canteen or restaurant adjacent to, and serving, government offices. Relatives and friends already working in these government establishments are able to place migrants initially, and then effect introductions to recruiting officers, in the hope that the migrant 'in transit' will eventually be able to secure a more permanent and more promising position.

Security of tenure is what most migrants aspire to, and it is one of the chief attractions of public sector employment. This is understandable when one considers that the migrant has a long-term commitment to providing for the rest of his family who, more often than not, are unable to gain subsistence from family lands in the village. Reasonable rates of pay once confirmed in one's post, pension rights, subsidised housing and access to low-interest credit are all significant too. Pensions provide security for old age when, on retirement, the loss of service privileges such as cheap housing and the prohibitively high costs of urban living force the majority back to the village, where even the smallest holdings offer a degree of security and where the cost of living is lower.

The success of the dual economy, that is, the village family system supported by the urban migrant system, depends on sustained contact between migrant and village. Organisations run by members of a village or a group of contiguous villages fulfil this requirement. These associations ostensibly exist primarily for the provision of low-interest credit to their memberes but their importance runs much deeper than this. The loans that can be drawn are comparatively small, Rs 500 to Rs 1000, but along with other similar associations of Garhwalis in specific offices and departments, and in addition to service benefits, these have effectively eliminated subservience to the rural moneylender whose standard interest charge is 25% of the amount borrowed. To avoid tax liability, these societies are unregistered and therefore have no recourse to courts of law in cases of repayment default. As such, they depend on the mutual trust of their members and provide a focus for migrants' attentions, a sense of attachment to the village community and a channel for communication with it. They should therefore be seen as extensions of village society.

Conclusion

It has been noted that the principal indigenous responses to declining per capita production in agriculture have been male labour migration out of the area and extension of the cultivated area. Increased dependence on cash derived from labour migration has resulted in the replacement of seasonal and temporary migration by moves of a semi-permanent nature, and the emergence of a relatively efficient migrant system to support local subsistence agriculture. The low investment potential of hill agriculture has been recognised in a study undertaken in Almora District which revealed that capital investment in agriculture tended to be in land and livestock, elements perpetuating the current system, rather than farming technology which would represent a conscious attempt to alter it (Tewari, 1970). Land capability studies, however, suggest that the balance between forest and arable land has been irrevocably disturbed, with a much higher percentage of the total area actually under cultivation than that which can support sustained cultivation (Ghildyal, 1981, p. 130).

The future of the Garhwal economy would therefore appear to rest on the continued availability of wage employment outside the district and/or an increase in local non-agricultural employment within it to absorb population increases, and the success of exogenously initiated attempts to modify the agrarian system by raising land and labour productivity. Few would deny that permanent urban employment in India is becoming increasingly harder to acquire. Similarly, the potential for expansion of the armed forces is limited. Therefore, male labour migration out of the district in the future may not be an adequate response to the problem of gaining subsistence from insufficiently productive resources employing inflexible exploitative techniques.

The expansion of state apparatus occurred ostensibly to promote and manage economic growth, but it was not accompanied by any fundamental reorganisation of the economy, nor by the removal of the twin elements of underdevelopment in agriculture, labour intensiveness and low productivity of land and labour. As a result, so-called economic development in Garhwal has been fiction rather than a fact. Without a marketable agricultural surplus, indiscriminate extension and improvements of the communications network will indirectly encourage further migration, the export of valuable forest resources, and a growing dependence on, and subservience to, the wider economic system. It has been noted in Nepal that

> The provision of metalled roads . . . which seems to be a prerequisite for breaking out of low and stagnant levels of production, cannot in these circumstances have a significant effect in promoting economic development given the lack of *sufficiently radical* improvements in basic productive capacity. (Blaikie et al., 1980, p. 8)

In Garhwal labour migration, migrant organisation and remittance flows may be seen as conservative responses to the stagnation of domestic agriculture, and as attempts to prevent the total collapse of the agricultural system. An ineffective economic diversification in the hills and the poor prospects for any immediate change imply a greater reliance on migration in the future. But, as employment opportunities in other parts of India worsen, the efficiency of the current migration/remittance system may be reduced, and as an increasing population exerts heavier pressure on limited resources locally, future movement out of Garhwal is likely to involve increasingly the very impoverished, and increasingly whole families as well as individuals. Meanwhile domestic agriculture, as predicted by Heber, will continue to 'lose its small space of fertility'.

NOTES

1. '*Terai*' is the name given to the flat belt of country bordering the southern edge of the Himalaya from the Ganges gorge at Hardwar, U.P., to the northeast corner of Bihar State. Under natural conditions (still to be seen at Corbett National Park, Garhwal District) the *Terai* was tiger-infested jungle, but much has now been cleared and settled (see Farmer, 1974).
2. Based on data from Pauri for the period 1901–51.
3. There have been a number of boundary changes during the period covered which makes clarification of the term 'Garhwal' necessary. Prior to, and during, the Gurkha occupation (1803–15), Garhwal included present day Chamoli, Garhwal, Tehri Garhwal and Uttarkashi districts (see Fig. 6.1). Following the dissolution of the Gurkha empire in 1815, Garhwal was divided into British Garhwal (Garhwal and Chamoli districts in Fig. 6.1) and Tehri Garhwal (Tehri Garhwal and Uttar-

kashi districts in Fig. 6.1), the latter tract being granted to the deposed Raja of Garhwal in an act of clemency by the British. Administratively, the entire hill region of U.P., excluding the princely state of Tehri Garhwal, was treated as one Division, Kumaun until 1825 when it was divided into two Divisions, Garhwal (British Garhwal) and Kumaon (Kumaon Division in Fig. 6.1). From 1825 to 1961 British Garhwal remained virtually unchanged in area although on Independence in 1947 the prefix 'British' was dropped. In 1961 Garhwal was divided into Garhwal and Chamoli Districts. Wherever possible, an attempt has been made in the text to clarify the area referred to.

REFERENCES

Atkinson, E.T. (1886). *The Himalayan districts of the North-Western Provinces of India*, vol. 3. Allahabad, N.W.P. & Oudh Press
Bandyopadhyay, J. & Shiva, S. (1979). Agricultural economy of Kumaon hills. *Economic & Political Weekly*, 14 (41), 1733–6
Berreman, G.D. (1972). *Hindus of the Himalayas: Ethnography and change*. Berkeley, University of California Press
Blaikie, P., Cameron, J. & Seddon, J. (1980). *Nepal in crisis: growth and stagnation at the periphery*. Oxford, Clarendon Press
Bolt, D. (1967). *Gurkhas*. London, Weidenfeld
Caplan, L. (1970). *Land and social change in East Nepal*. Berkeley, University of California Press
Caplan, P. (1972). *Priests and cobblers: a study of social change in a Hindu village in Western Nepal*. London, Intertext
Census of India (1961). *Village Thapli – U.P. (District Garhwal)*. Village Survey Monograph Series, Allahabad
Cool, J.C. (1967). The Far Western Hills: some longer term considerations. Report to His Majesty's Government, Kathmandu (mimeo)
Eckholm, E.P. (1975). The deterioration of mountain environments: ecological stress in the highlands of Asia, Latin America and Africa takes a mounting social toll. *Science*, 189, 764–9
Evatt, J. (1927). *Handbook for the Indian army – Garhwalis*. Calcutta, Government of India
Farmer, B.H. (1974). *Agricultural colonization in India since Independence*. London, Oxford University Press
Fraser, J.B. (1820). *Journal of a tour through part of the snowy range of the Himalaya mountains and to the source of the Jumna and Ganges*. London, Rodwell & Martin
G.B. Pant University of Agriculture and Technology (1976). *Rural area development: research, planning and action in the Naurar watershed in Bhikiasen block of Almora district, U.P. Pantnagar (Naini Tal)*. G.B. Pant University
Ghildyal, B.P. (1981). Soils of the Garhwal and Kumaun Himalaya. In J.S. Lall (ed.), *The Himalaya: aspects of change*, pp. 128–37. Delhi, Oxford University Press
Girdlestone, C.E.R. (1867). *Report on past famines in the N.W. Provinces*. Allahabad, Govt. Press

Hitchcock, J.T. (1978). An additional perspective on the Nepalese caste system. In J.F. Fisher (ed.), *Himalayan anthropology: the Indo-Tibetan interface*, pp. 111–20, The Hague, Mouton

Ibbotson, J. (1933). *Report of the Eleventh Settlement of Garhwal District (1926–1930)*. Allahabad, Govt. Press

Laird, M.A. (1971). *Bishop Heber in Northern India: selections from Heber's journal*. Cambridge University Press

Lewis, W.A. (1954). Economic development with unlimited supplies of labour. *Manchester School*, May

Lipton, M. (1964). Population, land and diminishing returns to agricultural labour. *Bulletin of the Oxford University Institute of Economics & Statistics*, vol. 26

MacFarlane, A.D.J. (1976). *Population and resources: a study of the Gurungs of Nepal*. Cambridge University Press

Mason, P. (1974). *A matter of honour: an account of the Indian Army, its officers and men*. London, Jonathan Cape

Mauch, S.P. (1976). The long term perspective of the region's forest resources – and the associated availability of firewood, cattle fodder and construction material for the local population. Integrated Hill Development Project, East Nepal. Zurich (mimeo)

Mitra, A. (1979). *Implications of declining sex ratio in India's population*. New Delhi, I.C.S.S.R.

Moddie, A.D. (1981). Himalayan environment. In J.S. Lall (ed.), *The Himalaya: aspects of change*, pp. 341–50. Delhi, Oxford University Press

Myrdal, G. (1957). *Economic theory and under-developed regions*. London, Duckworth

Nelson, J. (1916). *Notes from the Forest Settlement Report of the Garhwal district*. Lucknow, Govt. of India

Odum, E.P. (1971). *Ecology*. London, Holt, Rinehart & Winston

Pant, S.D. (1935). *The social economy of the Himalayans*. London, George Allen & Unwin

Parry, J.P. (1979). *Caste and kinship in Kangra*. London, Routledge & Kegan Paul

Pauw, E.K. (1896). *Report of the Tenth Settlement of Garhwal District*. Allahabad, Govt. Press

Pemble, J. (1971). *The invasion of Nepal: John Company at war*. Oxford, Clarendon Press

Raper, F.V. (1810). Narrative of a survey for the purpose of discovering the sources of the Ganges. *Asiatic Researches*, 11, 446–563

Regmi, M.C. (1971). *A study in Nepali economic history 1768–1846*. New Delhi, Manjusri

Reiger, H.C. (1981). Man versus mountain: the destruction of the Himalayan ecosystem. In J.S. Lall (ed.), *The Himalaya: aspects of change*, pp. 351–76. New Delhi, Oxford University Press

Shah, S.L. (1981). The dynamics of a changing agriculture in a micro-watershed in the Kumaun hills of Uttar Pradesh. In J.S. Lall (ed.), *The Himalaya: aspects of change*, pp. 434–46. New Delhi, Oxford University Press

Spate, O.H.K. (1954). *India, a general and regional geography*. London, Methuen

State Bank of India (1980). *Credit plans for Garhwal District (1980–1982)*. New Delhi, State Bank of India
Tautscher, D. (1974). *Torrent and erosion control. Report to the Government of Nepal*. Rome, F.A.O.
Tempany, H. & Grist, D.H. (1958). *Introduction to tropical agriculture*. London, Longmans
Tewari, S.C. (1970). Capital investment in agriculture in hilly terrain of U.P. *Agricultural Situation India*, 24 (1), 981–3. New Delhi
Todaro, M.P. (1969). A model of labour migration and urban development in less developed countries. *American Economic Review*, 59 (1), 138–48
Traill, G.W. (1828). A statistical sketch of Kamaon. *Asiatic Researches*, 16, 137–234
Upreti, P.G.D. (1894). *Proverbs and folklore of Kumaun and Garhwal*. Lodiana, Lodiana Mission Press
Victory Record of the War Effort of Garhwal District 1939–45 (1947). Lucknow, Nami Press
Visaria, P.M. (1971). Provisional population totals of the 1971 Census: some questions and research issues. *Economic and Political Weekly*, 6 (29), 1459–64
Walton, H.W. (1910). *British Garhwal: A gazetteer, comprising Vol. XXXVI of the District Gazetteer of the United Provinces of Agra and Oudh*. Allahabad, Govt. Press
Wasow, B. (1981). The working age sex ratio and job search migration in Kenya. *Journal of Developing Areas*, 15, 435–41

7 Agricultural development in Tamil Nadu: two decades of land use change at village level

ROBERT W. BRADNOCK

Earlier views of the stagnation and changelessness of Indian agriculture have more recently given way to the widespread acceptance of extensive changes occurring within many aspects of agricultural activity and of rural life in general. As Kurien (1981) has argued, 'Over the past quarter of a century the rural areas of Tamil Nadu have experienced a new dynamism unknown in the days of the past – substantial increase in output, major changes in production techniques and in organisational patterns.' Despite the unquestioned fact that agricultural output has risen since Independence, and that Tamil Nadu remains one of India's most developed States, there is still controversy surrounding many of the fundamental characteristics of agricultural change in the State.

In part such controversy reflects continuing problems with the accuracy and comparability of the data, in part the contrasting backgrounds and interests of those engaged in research. Studies have ranged from State-level analyses of economic development to anthropological studies of villages (Kurien, 1981; Beteille, 1965). Some have focussed on thematic questions in specific regions of the State (Farmer, 1978), while yet others have examined such diverse questions as irrigation systems in Tamil Nadu (Adiceam, 1966), or the progress and implementation of land reform (Badrinath, 1970; Sonachalam, 1969). All such studies have either an explicit or implicit relevance to questions of agricultural change. In view of the diversity of the subject and the inadequacies of the data it is unsurprising that there is frequently little agreement as to precisely what changes are taking place. In the absence of such agreement it is even less surprising that, as Chambers and Harriss (1977) argued, there should be no accepted theoretical framework in which to place studies of agricultural change, nor universal agreement on the interpretation of the processes of change at work in the State.

The role of village studies

Despite these problems the growing body of research on agriculture in Tamil Nadu has shed light on a number of important variables and aspects of change. One component of such research which has a long Indian tradition is that of empirical research based on the study of individual villages. Indeed the flow of village studies in India, well established by the beginning of this century (Slater, 1918), has continued unabated to the present day (Das Gupta, 1977; Chambers & Harriss, 1977; Fujiwara, 1980). Some such studies have been masterpieces of detailed presentation and analysis, Chambard's (1980) Atlas of Piparsod being an outstanding recent example. Yet as Das Gupta pointed out, such village studies also pose many problems, and it might well be judged that the marginal returns to further village studies would be very slight. That such a judgement is premature is illustrated by the insights gained into questions surrounding the Green Revolution by Farmer et al. (1977), which successfully blended village-level research with regional level analysis.

One reason why village-level studies still have a role to play in the analysis of agricultural change in Tamil Nadu is the enormous problem posed by making sense out of what data exists at higher levels of aggregation. Successive censuses, National Sample Surveys and unofficial research reports present almost as many difficulties in their use as they provide answers to the questions they set themselves. But there are also positive reasons for continuing research at the village level. The complex factors which ultimately determine whether or not change occurs are finally and crucially operating through the medium of the farmer and the village. The extent to which individual farmers are more than passive instruments of wider forces over which they exercise no control is also the extent to which an understanding of their patterns of operation and their response to the opportunities for change is important to wider analyses of change.

This chapter attempts to answer only a limited range of questions in the context of one village in Tamil Nadu. It is concerned with the fundamental question of the dynamics of land use change since Independence, and more particularly in the twenty years after 1957, when the land settlement was finalised in eastern Ramanathapuram District following the abolition of the *zamindari* estates.[1] In studying land use and cropping patterns an attempt is made to look beyond the descriptive mapping which has characterised so much early geographical work of this kind in India, to an analysis of the processes by which land-use patterns emerge, and the ways in which they reflect the forces for change in the village environment.

Despite its limitations, land use is a particularly important and sensitive indicator of changing agricultural practice. Within the constraints imposed by environmental conditions, the choice of which crops will be grown is a decision which has to be taken at least once a year. What might be termed therefore the 'nominal opportunity' for change is present regularly and with some frequency. Almost certainly a change in cropping patterns reflects a number of other changes both in the relation of the farmer to his land (cultivation techniques, labour use and technical inputs) and in his relation to the outside world (markets and prices, government incentives, transport and the communication of information). At the same time, changed cropping patterns have to be related back to their relation with the physical environment if they are to be successfully sustained. Thus both directly and indirectly the extent to which land use has changed and the manner of that change are significant pointers to the functioning of the village agricultural system and the forces stimulating and inhibiting change.

Pooranur village

The choice of one village for study rules out any possibility either of 'representativeness' or of statistical randomness, but it does not preclude a degree of rationality in the selection. The choice of Pooranur in eastern Ramanathapuram District reflects two main concerns. On the one hand it lies in one of India's 'backward regions'. Such areas, identified officially at the beginning of the 1970s, are characterised by the apparent slowness of agricultural progress. Generally located in dry regions with limited or non-existent irrigation, they tend also to be remote from the infrastructure through which change is mediated. Corresponding in large measure to the extensive tracts of 'backward' land there are also great areas which have been left largely untouched by research work. As Harriss (1977a) pointed out, despite the large number of village studies in India they tended to be highly concentrated. The irrigated wheat lands of the north-west and the rice-growing deltas of the south-east have been seen as laboratories in which the experiments of agricultural change can be tested in preparation for the transfer of successful models across the country. The inadequacy of the assumptions on which such a concentration of research efforts was based is now widely recognised, but despite the development of the work of ICRISAT in Hyderabad and of a number of independent studies, there remain large gaps to fill.

Pooranur lies astride the Madurai–Ramanathapuram railway line some 16 km west of Ramnad town. Now connected by frequent bus service both to Ramnad and to Madurai, it is none the less relatively remote from South India's major transport network and urban system.

Climatic constraints dominate traditional agricultural activity. Throughout India water is by far the most important variable for agriculture, and Pooranur is no exception. Fig. 7.1 shows that its rainfall is highly concentrated in October, November and December, nearly half of the mean annual total of 700 mm falling in October and November alone. This precarious water supply is only marginally augmented by outside sources. Located at the eastern tail of the Vaigai River, it only occasionally receives supplementary water through the Vaigai system. Furthermore, despite the permeability of the surface rocks the underlying aquifer is universally saline throughout the village. These factors, coupled with the flat nature of the terrain, have combined to make eastern Ramanathapuram what Spate and Learmonth called

Agrarian change at village level

'tank country par excellence'. The largest of the tanks, including that of Pooranur, are linked to the Vaigai distributary canals, but despite post-Independence works on the Vaigai little water reaches the eastern end of the system.

Pooranur itself lies on one of the larger tanks in Paramagudi Taluk, stretching 2 km north-south (Fig. 7.2). To the west, though still in the village, is a smaller channel-fed tank and there are three small rain-fed tanks on the village lands. Pooranur tank is the heart of the village. Along its bank are spread out the various hamlets and settlements which make up the main part

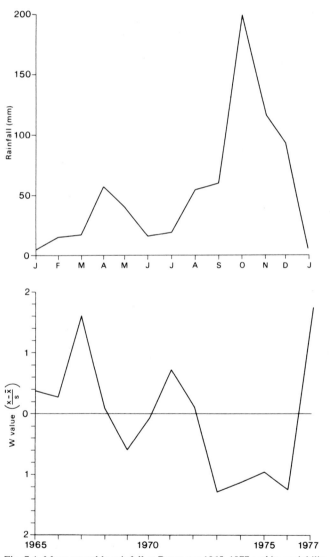

Fig. 7.1. Mean monthly rainfall at Pooranur 1965–1977 and its variability.

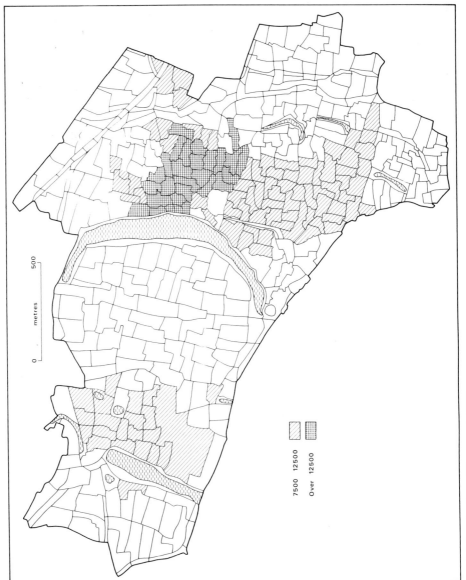

Fig. 7.2. Land values at Pooranur in 1977.

of the village: a mixed caste hamlet in the north, a Harijan colony and a Muslim hamlet a few hundred metres apart in the centre, and a small cluster of houses occupied by land-owning Pillais in the south.

Categories of land

Apart from the tanks and the hamlets there is little superficially to differentiate the landscape. While thin sandy alluvium dominates a little further to the east, Pooranur's soils are the friable granular earths 'free of stones with a small residue of granite and quartzite, known locally as *Pottal*' (Ramnad District Manual, 1910). Set in the almost totally flat Ramnad Plain, there is in the words of the Ramnad District Manual 'nothing in the way of scenery that one would ever care to see again'. Despite the apparent uniformity of landscape and soils the villagers' perception of the land quality is very different.

There are three major categories of land, with revenue assessments varying from Rs 0.81 per acre to Rs 6.75 per acre. The differences in value are related more to accessibility to water than to differences of soil quality, however, as is shown by Fig. 7.2. This shows land values above the mean, values being in terms of the sale value per acre. It is clear that all of the land of above average value is in the areas irrigated by the two channel-fed tanks.

The first category of land, *nanjai*, comprises the irrigated land of the major tanks, an area of just over 266 hectares. *Punjai*, or dry land, is out of reach of any source of irrigation water. Covering 495 hectares, it is the most extensive category but also the most risky to farm. The third category, *manavari punjai*, is intermediate between the irrigated and the dry land, being that area immediately above the tank which is often flooded for a brief period when the tank is absolutely full. It covers 146 hectares of land, which is sown with crops as the tank waters recede. Its fine clayey soils are relatively moisture retentive, making an additional and important contrast with the dry or *punjai* land.

Many other characteristics of the village may be thought *a priori* to have significance for agricultural change: the caste and social structure, patterns of land ownership and tenancy, access to Government development agencies and credit, accessibility to markets – all these and others are essential components of the agricultural system. We shall examine their significance in brief when analysing the patterns of land use change themselves.

Agrarian change, 1957–1977

Cropping patterns[2]

Table 7.1 shows that in 1957 paddy was by far the most extensive crop, dominating all three categories of land. The figures are slightly misleading,

Table 7.1. *Land use in Pooranur, 1957–1977*

| Crop | Proportion of each land category under each crop |||||||||
| | *Nanjai* land ||| *Manavari* land ||| *Punjai* land |||
	1957	1967	1977	1957	1967	1977	1957	1967	1977
Paddy	220 (86%)	209 (80%)	204 (79%)	64 (87%)	37 (55%)	36 (31%)	248 (57%)	201 (44%)	126 (29%)
Ragi	21 (8%)	25 (10%)	24 (9%)	3 (4%)	–	–	43 (10%)	42 (9%)	29 (7%)
Chillies	12 (5%)	23 (9%)	27 (11%)	–	–	–	5 (1%)	3 (1%)	9 (2%)
Cumbu				3 (4%)	24 (35%)	42 (37%)	4 (1%)	135 (29%)	167 (39%)
Gingelly				1 (1%)	6 (8%)	37 (32%)	–	–	86 (20%)
Vali				3 (4%)	–	–	84 (19%)	25 (6%)	4 (1%)
Varagu							32 (7%)	7 (1%)	3 (1%)
Cultivated area (ha)	255	260	258	74	69	116*	437	459	430

*The tank was deepened in 1967 and an increased area of *manavari* became available.
Source: *Adangal* records.

concealing as they do the fact that there was a wide variety of minor crops grown within the village. Some of these are listed, but in 1957 there were over fifteen other crops excluding vegetables. Furthermore, paddy cropping was far from uniform, with a number of different local and improved varieties being grown on different types of land.

Despite the overwhelming importance of paddy, there were clear contrasts between the different categories of land which are illustrated in Fig. 7.3. While over 85% of the *nanjai* and *manavari punjai* land was under paddy, only 57% of the *punjai* (dry) land had paddy cultivation. Nearly 20% of the dry land was under *vali*, a small millet with low yields but good drought resistant qualities, and other small millets such as *varagu* were also of some significance.

As can be seen from Table 7.1 the twenty years after 1957 witnessed some important changes in the overall land-use patterns. In contrast both to State-level changes in cropping patterns during the period (Kurien, 1981) and to

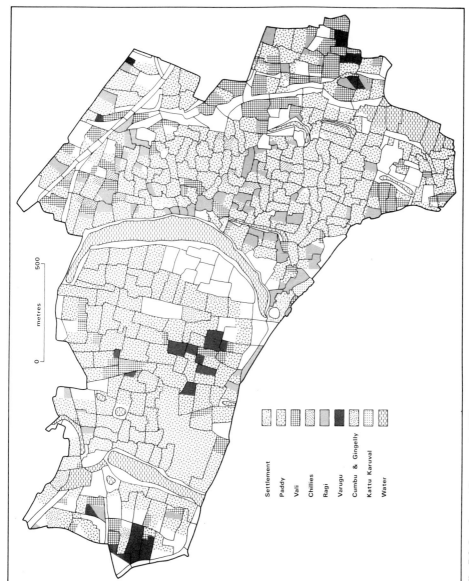

Fig. 7.3. Land use at Pooranur in 1957.

villages in other parts of Tamil Nadu (Harriss, 1977b) the total area under paddy decreased significantly on all categories of land. The most marked change occurred on the *manavari* land, where in 1977 less than one third was under paddy. There was also a major decline in the cultivation of paddy on the dry land, where already by 1967 the area under paddy had decreased by nearly 50 hectares and that under *vali* by nearly 60 hectares. On both the *manavari* and the *punjai* land their place was taken almost entirely by *cumbu* and *gingelly* (pearl millet and sesamum), sown either separately or intercropped. On the *nanjai* land the chief change was in the expansion of the area under chillies, which increased from 12 to 27 hectares, over 11% of the *nanjai* land. The distribution of these changes in land use is illustrated in Fig. 7.4.

Green Revolution technology

The gross changes in cropping pattern illustrated in Table 7.1 and Figs. 7.3 and 7.4 do not reveal the full scale of change which has occurred in Pooranur's agriculture. Alongside the innovation of different cropping systems have to be set new cultivation practices and new varieties of seed which have also contributed to changing the nature and output of the agricultural system in the village.

Most of these changes have affected paddy cultivation, and most have been confined almost exclusively to the *nanjai*, irrigated land. They can be summarised under four heads: double cropping, seed innovation, transplanting, and the use of chemical fertilisers. Mechanisation is still restricted to the use of half a dozen diesel pumpsets to extract the last pools of water from the bed of the tank, and many of the other agricultural operations continue to be performed in an entirely traditional way.

Of the four innovations, double cropping has made the least significant inroads. In 1977–78 less than 5% of the wet land was double cropped, a reflection of the scarcity of water. Seed innovation has been far more significant. Innovation in Pooranur, as elsewhere in Tamil Nadu (Farmer, 1977), long pre-dates the introduction of the high-yielding varieties. However, by 1977–78 two HYVs had been introduced on a significant scale, IR20 and Kannaigi, the latter as recently as 1976. Both were being grown as main season crops, sown in October, with growing periods of 130 days and 110 days respectively. Their distribution within the village was confined entirely to the *nanjai* land, and detailed analysis shows that they were restricted to those areas closest to the main distribution networks of the largest tanks. In all some 20% of the wet land was under HYVs in 1977–78.

It is pertinent at this stage to outline some of the factors which were inhibiting more widespread adoption of HYVs, although for a remote and backward district the adoption rate may cause little surprise. As with double cropping, the crucial factor differentiating land under HYVs from those under

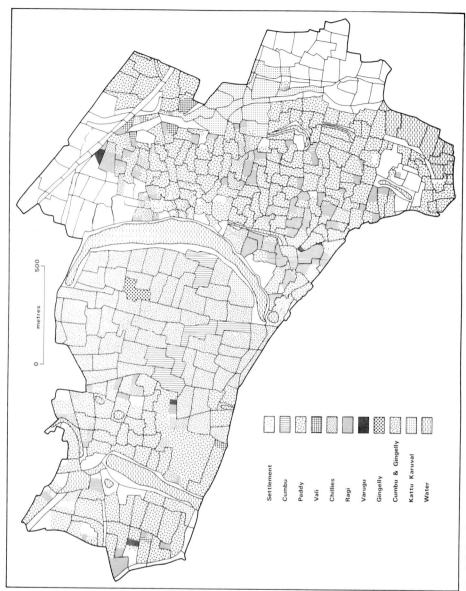

Fig. 7.4. Land use at Pooranur in 1977.

traditional varieties stands out as the duration and reliability of water supply. The cultivation of HYVs involved costs approximately twice as great as those for local varieties (Rs 1250 per hectare). Although yields were potentially very much larger, both of the HYVs available in the village were relatively water intensive. The fastest growing local variety available, *Pungar*, matured in 90 days when sown broadcast. Even when the tank was full, water could only be guaranteed for three months, and then to only a part of the *nanjai* land. Thus HYVs which could take as long as four months to mature stretched water resources to the limit. Even on some of the wet lands the risks of water failure could be seen to outweigh the possibilities of higher yields.

The same constraints can be seen to have influenced the extent of transplanting and the use of chemical fertiliser. Both were totally absent in 1957, but both were common by 1977–78. It is widely recognised that transplanting both paddy and ragi can increase yields significantly, but its use in Pooranur was restricted to the HYVs. Even Kannaigi was commonly sown broadcast, the common reason given being that transplanting delayed maturation by up to fourteen days, thereby again extending the period of risk of water scarcity.

Chemical fertilisers were first used in Pooranur in the late 1960s, though farmyard manure had been used on the *nanjai* land for many years. Despite the fact that the potential benefits of chemical fertilisers are now known throughout the village, use is entirely restricted to the irrigated land, and cost was frequently cited as a reason for using well below the recommended doses. The only exception was in chilli cultivation, where all farmers reported meticulous application of the recommended level of 2 bags of nitrate and 2 bags of urea per acre, thus highlighting the new importance of chilli cultivation suggested by its increased area.

From this brief outline it can be seen that despite superficial appearances to the contrary there have been major changes in the cropping patterns and some other aspects of agricultural operations in Pooranur. These changes have been directly reflected in improved output for some crops, but they also suggest a changed pattern of production with respect to the balance between subsistence agriculture and commercialised production. Improvement in yields were most marked in those areas sown with HYV paddy. However, even the farmers getting the highest return counted themselves fortunate to obtain yields of 2500 kg/ha which by standards elsewhere in the State was only mediocre. Harriss (1977b), for example, found yields of over 3340 kg/ha for *samba*-season HYVs in Randam, North Arcot District. None the less, HYVs in Pooranur were achieving more than double the yield of traditional varieties, and thus even though they were sown on only 20% of the *nanjai* land they were making an important contribution to increased production of paddy.

This increase undoubtedly compensated for the transfer of other land to crops produced directly for sale to the market. Of these, chillies were almost exclusively a *nanjai* land crop while cumbu and gingelly were *manavari* and *punjai* crops. In all cases the transfer out of paddy represents the perception of new economic opportunity outside the village, for all three crops are produced very largely for sale. Traditionally chillies were grown on a very small scale to meet village demand, though they were also valued as a crop to rotate with paddy as they were held to improve soil texture and to help to replace nitrogen (though they are not a leguminous plant). During the period after 1957 urban demand for chillies grew dramatically, with a corresponding increase in price. Thus despite intensive cultivation and higher input costs than for HYVs, returns were still attractive. Yields of between 1000 and 1300 kg were common in 1977–78, and although the price varied widely (between Rs 40 and Rs 100 per 10 kg), returns were sufficiently attractive to tempt some farmers to experiment on *punjai* land, in most cases with lamentable results.

The introduction of cumbu and gingelly has also augmented the cash flow into the village, for while some of the cumbu is retained for use within Pooranur all the gingelly is sold on the local market for oil pressing. Both crops are relatively drought resistant and quick growing, and it is significant that gingelly should have replaced paddy on the *manavari* land, where it can benefit from the moisture retentive soils as the tank waters recede.

Population change

The scale and importance of changes both in land use and key aspects of agricultural technology have been clearly demonstrated. However, such changes have not taken place in isolation, but have been paralleled by and inter-related with changes throughout Pooranur's economic, demographic and social system. So how are those changes which have characterised agriculture specifically to be interpreted, and how are they inter-linked with other aspects of village life?

The changes in land use which have taken place can be summarised as representing increasing intensity and increasing commercial involvement. In this Pooranur would seem to have followed a path common to many of Tamil Nadu's villages. In some respects there are also similarities in demographic and social change. As Fig. 7.5 shows, Pooranur's population grew dramatically between 1951 and 1971 after fifty years of stability. Population growth has been accompanied by an increasingly balanced sex ratio, which has steadily reduced from a maximum of 1445:1000 (female:male) to 1156:1000. In a region of seasonal and sometimes permanent male outmigration, this changing balance suggests that despite population growth there are greater opportunities for male employment in Pooranur at the end of the 1970s than for many years. As there is virtually no off-farm employment, that labour must be predominantly engaged in agriculture and related activities.

Size of holdings

The growth in population is reflected in the growing sub-division of Pooranur's land. Such sub-division is far from uncommon, but how has it affected both equality of ownership and productivity? To what extent have the landless been brought into the cultivating class? In 1957 when the land settlement was completed following the abolition of the *zamindari* estate there were 457 *pattadars*, or persons holding *patta*, the written document settling title to land. By 1978 the number of *pattadars* had more than doubled to 936. In 1957 the average size of holding was under 2 hectares, but one family alone owned over 200 hectares. With the increased number of *pattadars* the average size of holding has fallen to under 1 hectare, and the implementation of land ceilings legislation has reduced the area owned by the largest families. Even so in 1977 the largest ten landholders owned 25% of the land. Table 7.2 shows the distribution of ownership for both *nanjai* and *punjai* land in Pooranur in 1977. The respective Gini coefficients are 38.3 and 38.2, which according to Agrawal & Bansil (1969) is considerably lower than for South India as a whole (G = 47.6), suggesting a more equitable distribution of land.

A considerable body of literature suggests that the technological changes associated with the Green Revolution are strongly affected by the distribution of land holdings, with the larger land owners being in a position to command the necessary resources to benefit from and stimulate agricultural change (Byres, 1972; Kurien, 1981). In Pooranur no such relationship appears to hold. Chilli cultivation may serve as one example.

In 1977–78 *pattadars* (nearly 11% of the total) were growing chillies. Their mean holding size was 1.88 ha, nearly double the average size of holding for

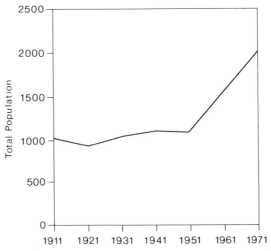

Fig. 7.5. Population change at Pooranur, 1911–1971.

Table 7.2. *Land ownership and size of holding in Pooranur, 1977*

Size category (ha)	Nanjai land						Punjai manavari land					
	Area			Pattadars			Area			Pattadars		
	Ha	%	Cu.%	No.	%	Cu.%	Ha	%	Cu.%	No.	%	Cu.%
0–0.25	29.08	10.7		174	39.4		19.90	3.1		116	18.3	
0.26–0.5	39.47	14.6	25.3	107	24.2	63.6	54.82	8.5	11.6	147	23.2	41.5
0.6–1.0	72.23	26.7	52.0	105	23.8	87.4	130.40	20.2	31.8	180	28.4	69.9
1.1–2.0	39.36	14.5	66.5	28	6.3	93.7	160.05	24.8	56.6	117	18.4	88.3
2.1–3.0	39.29	14.5	81.0	17	3.8	97.5	105.39	16.4	73.0	44	6.7	95.0
3.1–5.0	28.96	10.7	91.7	8	1.8	99.3	70.48	10.9	83.9	18	2.8	97.8
5.1+	22.49	8.3	100	3	0.7	100	103.28	16.0	100	12	1.9	100
	270.88			442			644.32			634		

Mean holding size: *Nanjai* 0.61 ha
Punjai 1.02 ha

Gini coefficient *Nanjai* 38.3
($G = ½ X_i - Y_i$) *Punjai* 47.6

Source: *Adangal* and *Chitta* records.[2]

the village, but this figure was distorted by the inclusion of the two largest farmers. 20% of those growing chillies owned less than one quarter of a hectare, even though as has been shown above the costs of chilli cultivation are higher than for any other crop. There was little evidence that this was the result of being forced to turn to cash cropping as a measure of distress, but rather that it reflected the high market prices obtainable for chillies. It suggests that in Pooranur neither the knowledge of a profitable crop nor the financial ability to take advantage of it were restricted to the largest landowners. It is particularly noteworthy that 16 of the 98 Harijan landowners were growing chillies in 1977, a slightly higher percentage than that of any other group.

More telling evidence that innovation is related not so much to ownership classes as to ecological constraints is provided by a comparison of Fig. 7.2 with Fig. 7.6. The latter shows the distribution of land owned by *pattadars* with more than two hectares. It can be seen that this land is scattered through all the major categories of land, and if anything is under-represented in those areas of the *nanjai* and *manavari* land where innovations have been most pronounced.

Conclusion

In the period between 1957 and 1977 significant changes in Pooranur's agriculture took place. The changes must be seen in the context of one of Tamil Nadu's semi-arid backward districts. It is an area in which direct Government intervention through Community Development Schemes, credit and marketing arrangements has been minimal.

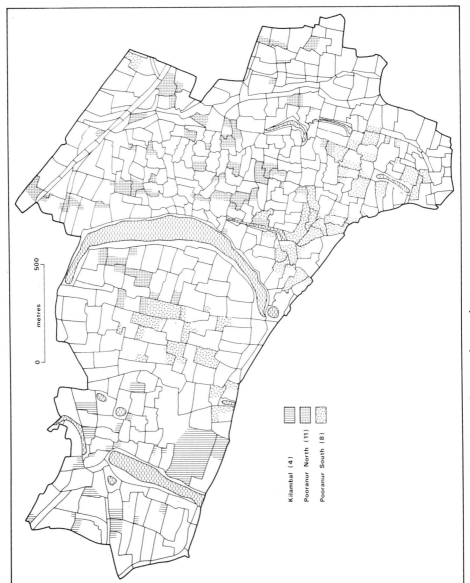

Fig. 7.6. Land holdings of *pattadars* owning more than two hectares.

Two factors have undoubtedly played an important role in stimulating agricultural change within the village. On the one hand there have been very significant external developments which have brought Pooranur into contact with the urban market of South India. While in terms of Tamil Nadu eastern Ramnad is remote, compared with many other parts of India it enjoys greatly improved urban accessibility. This has not only greatly increased the frequency of individual contact with towns but has facilitated the movement of goods and allowed high urban prices to act as a real incentive for change. But there has also been the influence of a few 'progressive' farmers, who have consistently taken note of developments and been willing to innovate, giving others in Pooranur an opportunity to judge from experience.

That experience has reinforced the influence of water as the most crucial constraint on all agricultural activity. When the guaranteed water supply is restricted to a tank of uncertain reliability land that can be regarded as potentially suitable for intensive and progressive agriculture is very limited. In adapting to new economic opportunities in agriculture the farmers in Pooranur have shown a strong sense of the importance of environmental constraints.

ACKNOWLEDGEMENTS

Fieldwork for this paper was made possible by the support of the School of Oriental and African Studies, University of London, and of the Central Research Fund, University of London. Their help is gratefully acknowledged. 'Pooranur' is a pseudonym, but the village and the farmers are real enough. Without the very real co-operation and help that I was given in 'Pooranur' this research would not have been possible.

NOTES

1. A *zamindar* is a landlord, or an intermediary between the farmer and the Government. The *zamindari* estates were estates owned by landlords, often absentee.
2. Data for the study of land use change were obtained from successive copies of the village *Adangal* and *Chitta*, the accounts and ownership records. Data on land values were collected by the village *karnam* as part of a survey in 1976–77 on the basis of recent land sales. The village *Adangal* is often an extremely unreliable source of information, despite its apparently universal coverage in South India. However, for Pooranur a detailed field survey in 1977–78 showed a remarkably high degree of accuracy in the register, and as the same *karnam* had kept the records since the permanent settlement it was assumed that the earlier records were also reliable.

REFERENCES

Adiceam, E. (1966). *La géographie de l'irrigation dans le Tamilnad.* Ecole française d'Extrême-Orient, Paris

Agrawal, G.D. & Bansil, C. (1969). *Economic Problems of Indian Agriculture.* Vikas, Delhi

Badrinath, C. (1970). Tamil Nadu Land Registration Acts, 1969. Madras (mimeo)

Beteille, A. (1965). *Caste, Class and Power.* University of California Press, Berkeley

Byres, T.J. (1972). The dialectic of India's Green Revolution. *South Asian Review,* 5, 99–116

Chambard, J.-L. (1980). *Atlas d'un village indien: Piparsod, Madhya Pradesh.* Paris

Chambers, R. & Harriss, J. (1977). Comparing twelve South Indian villages: in search of practical theory. In B.H. Farmer (ed.), *Green Revolution?* Macmillan, London, pp. 301–22

Das Gupta, B. (1977). *Village Society and Labour Use.* Oxford University Press, Delhi

Farmer, B.H. (ed.) (1977). *Green Revolution? Technology and Change in Rice-Growing Areas of Tamil Nadu and Sri Lanka.* Macmillan, London

Fujiwara, K. (1980). *Geographical Field Research in South India.* Research and Sources Unit for Regional Geography, University of Hiroshima

Govt. of Madras (1910). *Ramnad District Manual.* Madras

Harriss, J. (1977a). Bias in perception of agrarian change in India. In B.H.Farmer (ed.), *Green Revolution?* Macmillan, London, pp. 30–6

(1977b). The limitations of HYV technology in North Arcot District: the view from the village. In B.H. Farmer (ed.), *Green Revolution?* Macmillan, London, pp. 124–42

Kurien, C.T. (1981). *Dynamics of Rural Transformation. A Study of Tamil Nadu 1950–1975.* Orient Longman, Madras

Slater, G. (ed.) (1918). *Some South Indian Villages.* University of Madras Economic Studies vol. 1, Oxford University Press, London

Sonachalam, K.S. (1969). *Land Reform in Tamil Nadu.* Oxford University Press, Madras

8 Energy flows and agrarian change in Karnataka: the Green Revolution at micro-scale

TIM P. BAYLISS-SMITH

Reviewing his project on agrarian change in rice-growing areas undergoing the earlier stages of a Green Revolution, B.H. Farmer concluded:

Macro-scale planning of agricultural development spreads far too coarse a net over the landscape, given the great variations between areas and, within areas, between villages . . . Those who only contemplate villages from capital cities or from their desks might reflect that conclusions on inter-village variation . . . could only be made by prolonged work in the villages and paddy fields of Tamil Nadu and Sri Lanka. (Farmer, 1977b, p. 205)

This chapter, unlike most of the work that Benny Farmer has inspired, does not result from the author's own 'prolonged work in the villages and paddy fields', but it does draw upon other people's data from detailed field studies that are entirely within the Farmer tradition. My objective is to explore a methodology for the comparative analysis of agricultural systems. This methodology was developed by agriculturalists and social scientists in response to the 'energy crisis', following the oil shortages and oil price fluctuations of the 1970s which were seen as threatening the whole basis of modern technology, including that of the Green Revolution (e.g. Makhijani & Poole, 1975; Leach, 1976; Pimentel & Pimentel, 1979; Pimentel, 1980; Bayliss-Smith, 1982a).

To discover the degree of dependence of an agricultural system upon new technology an analysis is required of energy flows within the system. Given the variability in peasant farming practice that Farmer refers to above, data on energy flows become meaningless unless they refer to a particular farming environment. We are therefore drawn towards the micro-scale of enquiry, towards particular villages, and within these villages to consider particular households. Such data are available for the Mandya district of Karnataka State, India, an area which was studied by the economic anthropologist T. Scarlett Epstein in 1954–56 and again in 1970, and which was subsequently studied by members of a Ford Foundation project based at Bangalore University (Epstein, 1962, 1973; Rebello et al., 1976).

In drawing upon these data from Mandya I do not intend to make general statements about energy use and agrarian welfare in South India before and after the Green Revolution. One case study, however carefully selected, cannot reveal more than a small corner of the general picture. In any case, without personal fieldwork, without that 'thoughtful period spent in the area concerned, living with the land and with the society that uses it' (Farmer, 1980), one is in no position to place the micro-scale study into its macro-scale context. Instead, my objective is to examine whether or not measures of energy flow and the efficiency of energy use are an appropriate way of describing agricultural systems and the welfare of persons operating within them, in a situation where enormous social and technological changes of Green Revolutionary character are known to be taking place.

Mandya district in 1955

The village of Wangala (a pseudonym) in Mandya district was one of two studied by Epstein, and in 1955 it was representative of those villages in the southern Deccan plateau which had benefitted from irrigation works begun in the colonial period. In this region only the south-west monsoon provides an adequate and reliable rainfall for paddy rice, so that in the absence of irrigation rice cultivation would be restricted to valley bottoms flooded by the monsoon rains between July and October. In the southern part of Karnataka (then Mysore) State irrigation works were started early this century: Wangala along with 1600 other villages received water from canals that were completed in the 1930s, and immediately farmers were presented with new opportunities to grow irrigated crops, particularly rice and sugar cane. Elsewhere in South India local tanks remained the most important source of irrigation water until the 1950s, when the introduction of electric pump sets enabled the area of 'wet land' once again to be extended (Harriss, 1977b).

Wangala village

The village studied by Scarlett Epstein is on the undulating plateau country known as the Maidan. It is an area of ancient crystalline rocks which are deeply weathered and form gentle relief. The soils are mainly red loams and clays, thin on the ridges but deep in the valleys as a result of slope wash under the intense rainfall characteristic of the monsoon.

The population of 958 persons in Wangala controlled a total land area of 670 ha (Fig. 8.1). Before the 1930s only 12% of the arable land was irrigated, and that unreliably from a local tank liable to run dry, but in the 1940s the land-use pattern was transformed. The village was linked by canal to the Krishnaraja Reservoir, and the roads leading to local market towns were also improved. The result was an agricultural revolution as profound if not more so than the more recent Green Revolution. It involved the transition from a pre-industrial agrarian society dependent on dry-land crops grown for subsistence, to a society where farmers have become increasingly innovative in technology and capitalist in mode of production, with wet-land crops (sugar cane and rice) as their main source of livelihood. By 1955 55% of the 377 ha of arable land was irrigated, with the former staple, *ragi* (finger millet), restricted to the dry lands remote from water supplies. There were also 219 ha of waste land, mostly hill tops and ridges with soils too eroded to support agriculture, but used by the villagers as rough grazing.

Social structure

Despite these changes in agriculture, the social organisation of Wangala remained highly traditional. Indeed, the caste structure of the village was a factor which greatly facilitated the development of market production. Two-thirds of the population of Wangala belonged to the Peasant caste, owning almost nine-tenths of the land. The rich farmers who emerged in Wangala during the 1940s were Peasant men who had enterprise, enough land, and a little working capital, and who in 1939 suddenly discovered an opportunity to make large profits out of the new cash crops, sugar cane and rice. To be able to exploit these crops the farmer needed to have irrigated land, cheap labour, access to bullock power, and in the case of cane an investment in fertiliser.

The means to benefit from irrigation were therefore not open to all members of the community. In particular, households with insufficient irrigated land or with no land at all had little option but to work for the larger farmers, many of whom were able to reinvest their profits by buying more land from poorer people who had fallen into debt. As the rich got richer many of the poor became poorer, especially the members of low castes or 'outcastes' like the Untouchables who had never had much land in the first place. The pro-

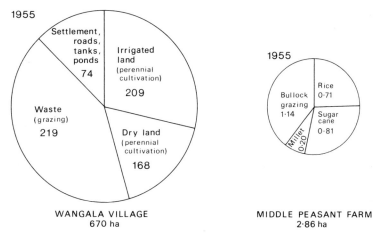

Fig. 8.1. Land use in Wangala, Mandya district, 1955. Data source: Epstein (1973, p. 55).

cess of differentiation was made worse by steady population growth and the small number of alternative jobs available in the vicinity.

B.H. Farmer (1981, p. 207) has suggested for the Green Revolution as a whole that 'while technology as such is scale neutral . . . the social system, including the skewness of the distribution of land holdings, generally creates a bias in favour of larger, wealthier and more influential farmers'. In Wangala, the increased provision of irrigation, markets and population growth combined to exacerbate existing divisions in society long before the Green Revolution itself. A small number of rich farmers and a large pool of under-employed casual labourers were created, the one group too powerful to be controlled by government legislation, and the second too numerous, too dependent, or too indebted to be able to improve its position except through emigration.

The new agriculture in Wangala was certainly more labour intensive, but the numbers seeking work were growing more quickly than the jobs – and of course the total land area available to the village did not increase at all. Epstein (1962) estimated that in 1955 at least 30% of the population could have been completely unemployed without total agricultural production being reduced in any way. Instead, no one was unemployed but the majority were under-employed, and many (especially the one-third belonging to Servant castes or Untouchables) were poor to the extent of being malnourished.

A middle Peasant's farm in 1955

As a case study of energy flow, we consider the agricultural economy not of the successful agrarian capitalists, nor of the landless labourers, but instead of the middle group of small Peasant caste farmers, who in 1955 constituted the majority of households. Scarlett Epstein collected detailed records of land holdings, income and expenditure from several households, and these data for a representative middle farmer and his household are shown in Fig. 8.2, expressed in terms of the major energy flows.

Within the farming system human labour constitutes 38% of the total energy input. This total excludes solar energy and animal traction as inputs, and also off-farm energy costs such as transport and food processing (Bayliss-Smith, 1982b). Human effort is supplemented by bullock power, used especially for ploughing, carting and threshing. The bullocks are given some fodder, mostly non-edible items from the farm such as rice hay, millet hay or cane leaves, and they also graze on harvested fields and on the village waste. In addition, a pair of she-buffaloes are kept by the household for their milk, but they receive no fodder and survive entirely by their own grazing efforts, tended by women or children. The farm animals do not therefore compete significantly with the human population for inputs, and they are managed at only a small energy cost in the form of human labour. As well as traction and milk the animals also supply manure for the wet land, but not in a quantity sufficient for more than one good paddy crop per year. By modern standards the yields of rice and finger millet are low.

The major energy subsidy is fertiliser, but at this time it was used almost entirely for growing sugar cane. Fertiliser was available on credit from the local sugar factory for farmers who contracted to sell a given acreage of cane at a given price. Few of the middle farmers could afford to buy fertiliser out of their savings. Unlike the subsistence crops sugar cane yielded well, but on the other hand the crop was also highly labour intensive, requiring 61% of the total human work on the farm and accounting for most of the hired labour.

Gross Energy Productivity

A useful index of the performance of farming systems is the Gross Energy Productivity statistic (GEP). This is defined as the total output of edible

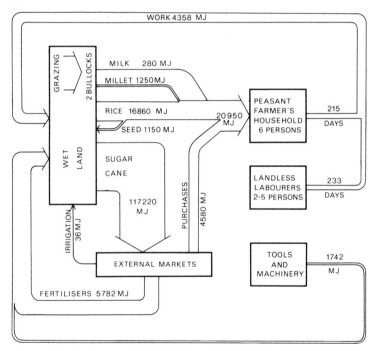

Fig. 8.2. Major energy flows on a middle Peasant farm of 2.86 hectares, 1955. Data sources: fertiliser is calculated by converting Epstein's (1973, p. 97) monetary inputs into quantities using data from Abraham (1965), assuming that N and P are used on a 50:50 basis, and the estimated total of 246 kg is converted into its energy equivalent using UK energy costs (Leach, 1976, p. 71); irrigation energy costs are based on per hectare costs of Punjab canal irrigation (Singh & Miglani, 1976); tools and machinery input is taken from Leach's (1976, p. 122) estimate of 225 kg × 90 MJ/kg, 20 year life, per hectare; all yields are from Epstein (1973, pp. 102 and 107).

energy per annum divided by the total agrarian population involved in its production, and it can be conveniently expressed in megajoules (MJ) of energy per person per day (Bayliss-Smith, 1982a, 1982b). The agrarian population in this case consists of the six persons who belong to the middle Peasant household plus a proportion of the population of casual labourers, of whom an estimated 2.5 persons would be supported by a farm of this size.[1] The data on energy flows in Fig. 8.2 show that these 8.5 persons produced almost 137 000 MJ in food, which averages 44.1 MJ per person per day. This level of GEP represents over four times more food energy than would be needed for actual dietary purposes, if we assume an average daily food intake of 9.57 MJ (2285 kcal) per person for Karnataka State (Kalirajan, 1976).

Surplus Energy Income: farmer's household

Unfortunately a large proportion of this GEP is production for exchange in the form of sugar cane, a product which is sold at prices which the farmers can do little to control. Obviously the actual incomes of the agrarian population will reflect the exchange value of production as well as its de facto energy value. In addition we must consider the distribution of income between farmers and labourers, rather than average welfare levels. The measure of *Surplus Energy Income* (SEI) reveals more effectively than GEP the actual – rather than potential – living standard of the agrarian population. SEI is defined as that proportion of net income which remains when all the requirements for subsistence food have been met. It is expressed not in monetary terms but in terms of the energy value of this 'surplus' income, using local food prices and needs. It can be expressed, like GEP, in MJ per person per day (Bayliss-Smith, 1982a, 1982b).

Epstein's household surveys provide us with the data for calculating how much of the food and income gained by farmers constitutes a real surplus. In 1955 the average middle Peasant farmer aimed to be almost self-sufficient in rice and millet, but he had to supplement these staples with some purchases, particularly vegetables, spices, oil, butter, and occasionally meat. The farmer's net income after all outlays in agriculture have been accounted for (e.g. wages, fertiliser, bullock hire, land tax), and after he has bought his household's food supply, amounts to Rs 1080. This 'surplus' income represents a food energy equivalent of 18 868 MJ for the entire household, or in other words 8.6 MJ per person per day of Surplus Energy Income.[2]

Surplus Energy Income: labourer's household

If we consider the other side of the coin, however, it becomes clear that this living standard is only made possible through the exploitation of the labour of the poor, most of whom are Untouchables with tiny landholdings or no land at all. In Wangala in 1955 each Untouchable caste household owned on average 0.62 ha, only 0.24 ha of which was irrigated (Epstein, 1973, pp. 56–7). Even assuming average yields this land would only supply 39% of the subsistence needs of a family of six. To purchase the remainder of its food at the Peasant caste standard would cost Rs 123 per person.[3] Epstein's surveys show that the total cash income of Untouchable households came mostly from wages, and amounted to only Rs 207 per person. Thus the surplus per capita income is Rs 84, equivalent to a Surplus Energy Income of 4.0 MJ, less than half that of the Peasant farmer.

In reality the Untouchable household would have eaten cheaper food (millet instead of rice, no meat), and they probably ate less anyway. Moreover many farmers provided their workers with a midday meal as well as wages, thus reducing the burden on the Untouchable household's food budget. Nevertheless, the gap between the farmer's SEI of 8.6 and his labourer's of 4.0 is a stark reminder of the inequalities which already existed in 1955 in Mandya district, inequalities which had been exacerbated by far-reaching agrarian changes occurring a whole generation before the onset of the Green Revolution itself.

Energy flows in rice cultivation

By 1955 aspects of Wangala agriculture were already modernised, but the production of paddy rice remained entirely traditional. Paddy was grown at this time as a half-year crop, with the land left fallow during the dry season. Bullocks were used for ploughing, and farmyard manure was the principal means of replacing lost nutrients to the soil. Little or no fertiliser was used, and the crop was almost entirely grown for subsistence. Improved varieties of rice had not yet arrived, but the Mysore State Agricultural Department had been advocating for some years superior Japanese methods of cultivation. These involved seed selection, better care of seedling nurseries, and a different technique of transplanting, but in Wangala only the richest farmers had experimented with these methods. Most farmers preferred a less intensive use of their labour and other inputs, reserving their capital investment for the more profitable crop, sugar cane (Table 8.1).

The result of this pre-industrial technology was a rather low yield but the minimum of risk and uncertainty. Inputs and outputs per cultivated hectare under wet-land rice are summarised in Table 8.1. Labour, seeds and tools are the major energy inputs, with irrigation a minor item because of the inexpensive canal network. The overall Energy Ratio suggests that 5.5 units of energy are being gained for every unit expended in cultivation. The ratio of food gained per unit of labour is 12.0, which is typical of subsistence crops grown under a pre-industrial technology (Leach, 1976).

Table 8.1. *Annual inputs and outputs for wet rice, Peasant farms in Wangala, Mandya district, 1955*

Item	Quantity per hectare	MJ/ha	Source
Inputs			
Labour	309 days	1978	Epstein, 1973, p. 100
Seed	88 kg	1329	Rutger & Grant, 1980
Irrigation	8.86 Hph	24	Singh & Miglani, 1976
Tools	225 kg, 20 year life	1013	Leach, 1976, p. 122
TOTAL		4344	
Output			
Paddy	2,348 kg		Epstein, 1973, p. 102
Rice	33% threshing and milling loss	23 752	Harriss, 1977a
Energy Ratio	$\frac{23\,752}{4344} =$	5.5	

Mandya district in 1975

The Green Revolution in Wangala

The new rice varieties developed by IRRI first became available to farmers in South India in 1966. Some of the early varieties were not altogether satisfactory, but by the mid-1970s a wide range of good high-yielding varieties (HYVs) were being grown. It was noticeable, however, that the spread of HYVs was less successful in the hill areas, where irrigation depends ultimately on local rainfall, than in the flood plains where too much water is often as great a hazard as too little. In South India HYVs were found to do extremely well in the sunny dry season, but only a few farmers could afford the technology to cultivate at this season, and in many places water is simply not available. During the cloudier monsoon period the yields of HYVs are less impressive, and since the product obtained is less palatable and fetches a lower price, market-oriented farmers often decided to continue with the traditional varieties (Farmer, 1977).

In Mandya district irrigation water from the canals is never available in the dry season, so that in 1970 most farmers were still restricted to cropping in the monsoon season only. Small farmers in particular were confronted with other problems: Scarlett Epstein found in Wangala that

> All farmers in the village now know that the improved varieties of seed can increase yields of paddy per acre, but they also know that more inputs are required to ensure increased productivity per unit of land. Farmers with less than 2 wet acres [0.8 ha] often cannot raise the necessary working capital to provide the additional inputs, and therefore are virtually forced to continue their customary paddy cultivation. (Epstein, 1973, p. 101)

Agrarian change at village level

Our case study, the middle Peasant farmer with 1.5 hectares in 1955, is well above this threshold size, and as such it is not typical.

Between 1955 and 1970 the land-use pattern at Wangala altered significantly (Fig. 8.3). A further extension of the canal network took place, enabling some dry land to be irrigated and some waste land to be cultivated for the first time. Part of the village tank was drained and brought into cultivation. Altogether the area of wet land increased by 60% in these fifteen years, but this compares with a 67% growth in population (Epstein, 1973, p. 57).

A large proportion of the new wet land was acquired by Wangala Peasants, including the 34 ha of government waste (half of which according to the law should have been reserved for persons belonging to scheduled castes and scheduled tribes). Peasant landholdings increased by 37% per household, Untouchable landholdings by only 11%, leading in 1970 to the following disparities:

	Peasant	Untouchable
Population as % of total	68%	13%
Landholdings as % of total	92%	5%
Average farm	1.30 ha	0.44 ha
Average wet land	1.05 ha	0.24 ha

The 1960s had thus been a period of opportunities but also severe inflationary pressures. Epstein (1973, p. 171) comments that 'Peasant middle farmers managed to hold their own . . . as long as they had at least three wet acres [1.2 ha] to grow most of their own food as well as some cash crops.' Only the more prosperous Peasant farmers actually improved their position substantially.

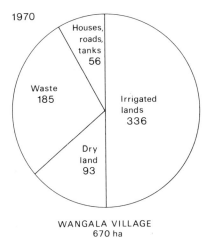

Fig. 8.3. Land use in Wangala, Mandya district, 1970. Data source: Epstein (1973, p. 55).

A middle Peasant farm in 1975

If we assume that, unlike many of his caste, the middle Peasant farmer of 1955 was not able to expand his holding, and if we assume also no change in household size or cropping pattern, then we can define a 1975 middle Peasant holding the same size as that of 1955 (Fig. 8.3). This farm would be larger than the average Wangala holding, but on the other hand the concept of an average farm is increasingly meaningless in this region of growing disparities. The purpose of this case study is to show how energy use has changed amongst the more prosperous farmers, those involved in the adoption of Green Revolution technology. We can assess the impact of the new technology on this farm by considering how the various agricultural inputs and outputs have changed. Data are available for 1975–76 from a project in Mandya district financed by the Ford Foundation and carried out by the Department of Agricultural Economics at the University of Bangalore. The project collected detailed records from 37 farmers, mostly intermediate in their scale of enterprise (Rebello et al., 1976).

The 1975 data are broadly comparable to Epstein's 1955 surveys, and they reveal quite substantial changes (Fig. 8.4). In 1955 the typical middle Peasant farm in Wangala had been a dual economy, with modernised sugar cane production but traditional rice subsistence. Twenty years later the modern technology prevailed throughout the irrigated parts of the farm. Overall yields had increased as a result of the adoption of HYVs and a greater investment in inputs. Both HYV rice and sugar cane were now cash crops, and most of the farmer's food supply was purchased rather than home produced.

On the other hand mechanisation was still limited. Bullocks continued to play their traditional role of providing mechanical energy at small human energy cost. During the 1960s, however, there were some changes in irrigation technology. The existing irrigation from tanks or canals was still cheap and reliable except in extreme drought years (e.g. 1966), but it only provided water for half the year or less, and so prevented the full potential of HYVs from being realised. Throughout South India there was an investment by innovative farmers in electric pump sets to extract ground water (Harriss, 1977b; Mencher, 1978). Up until 1970 the economics of pump set irrigation in Mandya was distinctly marginal, but the available machinery improved in the 1970s, increasing greatly the incentives. To make the middle Peasant farm of 1975 fully typical of the region, we assume that its irrigation is carried out by means of this new technology, enabling 30% of the paddy land to be double-cropped (Gurumurthy, 1976; Chinappa, 1977, p. 113).

Data on the 1975 farming system are shown in Fig. 8.4. It is clear that the Green Revolution has raised yields considerably in the wet land: sugar cane (already intensive in 1955) by 41%, and paddy by 159% per crop. Inputs have also risen, however: the wet-land crops are more labour intensive, with total work increasing by 27%, and much more capital intensive, with a 3.6 times greater energy subsidy from fossil fuel sources. Human work is now only 16% of the total energy input, compared to 38% in 1955.

The cash income of the farmer has risen substantially during the twenty years, but most of the apparent rise is accounted for by inflation. Rural prices in Karnataka State rose by 365% between 1955 and 1976, so that in real terms our farmer's net income only increased by about 22%. Not enough information is available to allow us to calculate the Surplus Energy Income, but it seems reasonable to estimate a comparable modest increase.

A significant change is that in 1975 the farmer and his family do less agricultural work than formerly, preferring to employ instead a larger number of casual labourers. In 1955 65% of the farm work in Wangala was done by members of the farm households. Twenty years later only 15% of work on farms in Mandya district was done by household labour, even though the total input had risen from 418 days per irrigated hectare to 534 days.

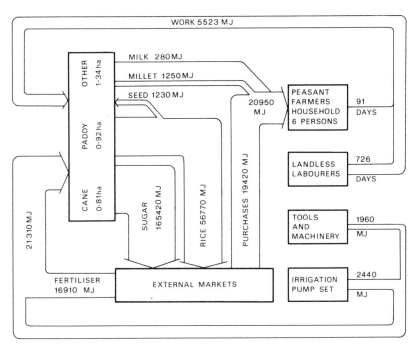

Fig. 8.4. Major energy flows on a 2.86 hectare farm in Mandya district in 1975. Data sources: wet-land work inputs, fertiliser and yields are calculated from data in Rebello *et al.* (1976), using conversion factors in Leach (1976); irrigation assumes electric pump-set technology, and is converted to energy terms using 415 Hph/ha for sugar cane and 227 Hph/ha for paddy (Singh *et al.*, 1976), to which is added 471 MJ/ha-yr capital depreciation cost (Leach, 1976, p. 124); pesticide assumes 7.28 kg/ha for paddy (Singh *et al.*, 1976) converted to energy cost at rate 311 MJ/kg (Pimentel & Pimentel, 1979, p. 146); the double-cropped area of 30% is the mean for Tamil Nadu in 1973–74 for farms of this size (Chinappa, 1977); dry-land inputs and outputs are unchanged since 1955, as are tools and machinery inputs/ha.

Increasingly, the more prosperous farmers are seeing their land as a business rather than a way of life, and they prefer to keep their wives at home and send their sons away for education rather than employ them at home (Epstein, 1973).

The declining work contribution from household labour and the larger number of underemployed casual labourers who are being supported imply that the Gross Energy Productivity of this system has probably declined. Unfortunately there are not enough reliable data to enable us to test this proposition with a GEP statistic comparable to that for 1955, and the same is true of Surplus Energy Income. Epstein (1973) found that between 1955 and 1970 the Untouchables, who are not even the poorest caste in Wangala, saw their real incomes decline by about one-third, which suggests a comparable decline in their SEI, but again the situation in Mandya district in the mid-1970s is not recorded.

In North Arcot, however, where conditions are broadly similar, the social impact of the Green Revolution upon the less fortunate has been summarised as follows:

In North Arcot . . . the very small cultivators and the agricultural labourers are trapped. If a new technology or mounting population pressure displaces them they have no chance of becoming small cultivators elsewhere . . . The prospect for many of the landless scarcely bears contemplation. Extruded from the bottom of the pile, forced in desperation to leave their villages, they will swell the numbers of urban migrants and of rural transients whose lot will be more terrible for being so often unseen and so easy to avoid seeing. (Chambers & Farmer, 1977, p. 417)

To prevent this process from continuing, a reduced rate of population growth is one measure which seems unavoidable, but without improvements in welfare it will be difficult if not impossible to achieve. But improved welfare cannot come about simply through relief measures such as rice handouts to the urban unemployed, and many would argue that radical political and social changes represent the only long-term answer. One thing is certain: in Mandya district, Karnataka State, the Green Revolution has not been revolutionary enough.

Energy and the Green Revolution

If we isolate the wet land under rice from the remainder of the 1975 Wangala system, then we can estimate the energy inputs and outputs per hectare for this particular crop (Table 8.2). These data indicate the magnitude of the revolution in technology which has occurred. Inputs per crop have almost tripled, while yields have risen about one and a half times. If we assume that 30% of the 1975 rice fields are double-cropped, then the difference is magnified still further. Fossil-fuel derived inputs (fertiliser, pesticide, irrigation, tools), which were negligible twenty years before, now contribute three-

Table 8.2. *Inputs and outputs for wet rice, farms in Mandya district, 1975, per crop and per annum*

Item	Quantity per hectare	MJ/ha
Inputs per crop		
Labour	317 days	2029
Seed	88 kg	1329
Irrigation	226.6 Hph	1259
Tools	225 kg, 20 year life	1013
Fertiliser	136 kg N, 48 kg P_2O_5, 50 kg K_2O	4964
Pesticide	7.3 kg dust	2271
TOTAL		12 865
Output per crop		
Paddy	6,080 kg	
Rice	33% threshing and milling loss	61 511
Annual input (30% double-cropped)		16 725
Annual output (30% double-cropped)		79 964
Energy Ratio =		4.8

Sources: seed, tools and threshing/milling loss – see Table 8.1; labour, irrigation, fertiliser, pesticide and yield – see Fig. 8.4.

quarters of the total energy input, indicating the thorough transition of this system from almost pre-industrial to almost full-industrial status (pre-industrial systems are defined as those with less than 10% of their inputs from fossil fuel sources, and full-industrial ones with over 95% – Leach, 1976).

Twenty-two rice-growing systems

A review of the literature reveals twenty other case studies where the energy flow in rice-producing systems has been quantified, to which we can add Wangala before and after the Green Revolution (Table 8.3). In technology these examples range from pre-industrial to full-industrial, and they include simple shifting cultivation systems (Sarawak, Tanzania), double-cropping systems of wet rice and beans (pre-Communist China), semi-industrial systems of perennial cultivation where animal traction is supplemented by machinery and fertiliser (Philippines, Japan, Hong Kong), and full-industrial systems which are highly intensive in all inputs apart from labour (Surinam, USA). Taken as a whole, the sample enables us to put the Mandya data into a wider context in which we can see alternative technological options.

If we consider first food yields in relation to labour inputs (Fig. 8.5), then we can perceive three different ways in which, historically, wet rice systems have changed. These options are represented by arrows in Fig. 8.5:

(i) The *Green Revolution* path has generally led to a large jump in yields, with 1500–

Table 8.3. *Pre-industrial, semi-industrial and full-industrial systems of rice cultivation: inputs and outputs per hectare-year*[zc]

Location	Technology (no. crops)[za]	Fossil fuel input	Labour per crop (days)	Labour as % total input	Total input[zb] (GJ)	Total output[zb] (GJ)
Pre-industrial						
a. Dayak, Sarawak (1951)	Forest fallow (0.1)	2%	208	44%	0.30	2.4
b. Dayak, Sarawak (1951)	Swamp fallow (0.2)	2%	271	51%	0.63	5.7
c. Kilombero, Tanzania (1967)	Grass fallow (0.15)	2%	170	39%	0.42	3.8
d. Kilombero, Tanzania (1967)	Grass fallow (0.55)	3%	144	35%	1.44	9.9
e. Iban, Sarawak (1951)	Forest fallow (0.1)	3%	148	36%	0.27	3.1
f. Luts'un, Yunnan (1938)	Irrigated rice and beans (2.0)	3%	882	70%	8.04	166.9
g. Yits'un, Yunnan (1938)	"	2%	1,293	78%	10.66	163.3
h. Yuts'un, Yunnan (1938)	"	4%	426	53%	5.12	149.3
Semi-industrial						
i. Mandya, Karnataka (1955)	Irrigated (1.0)	23%	309	46%	3.33	23.8
j. Mandya, Karnataka (1975)	Irrigated (1.3)	74%	317	16%	16.73	80.0
k. Philippines (1972)	Dry season, irrigated (1.0)	86%	102	5.3%	12.37	39.9
l. Philippines (1972)	Wet season, rainfed (1.0)	89%	102	4.1%	16.01	51.6
m. Japan (1963)	Rainfed (1.0)	90%	216	5.2%	30.04	73.7
n. Hong Kong (1971)	Irrigated rice and vegetables (1.0)	83%	566	12%	31.27	64.8
o. Philippines (1965)	Rainfed (1.0)	93%	72	13%	3.61	25.0
p. Philippines (1979)	Rainfed (1.0)	33%	92	16%	5.48	52.9
q. Philippines (1979)	Rainfed (1.0)	80%	84	11%	6.90	52.9
r. Philippines (1979)	Rainfed (1.0)	86%	68	7%	8.72	52.9

Table 8.3 (*cont.*)

Location	Technology (no. crops)[za]	Fossil fuel input	Labour per crop (days)	Labour as % total input	Total input[zb] (GJ)	Total output[zb] (GJ)
Full-industrial						
s. Surinam (1972)	Irrigated (1.0)	95%	12.6	0.2%	45.9	53.7
t. USA (1974)	"	95%	3.8	0.02%	70.2	88.2
u. Sacramento, Calif. (1977)	"	95%	3.0	0.04%	45.9	80.5
v. Grand Prairie, Ark. (1977)	"	95%	3.7	0.04%	52.5	58.6
w. Southwest Louisiana (1977)	"	95%	3.1	0.04%	48.0	50.8
x. Mississippi Delta (1977)	"	95%	3.9	0.05%	53.8	55.4
y. Texas Gulf Coast (1977)	"	95%	3.1	0.04%	55.1	64.7

Notes and sources:
a. Leach (1976, p. 119). Crop frequency retained as once in ten years (Geddes, 1954, p. 66), with added inputs of 108 kg seeds per crop and hand tools 69 MJ per crop (Pimentel & Pimentel, 1979, p. 75).
b. Leach (1976, p. 119). Crop frequency altered to once in five years (Geddes, 1954, p. 64), with seed and tool additions as in (a).
c. Leach (1976, p. 119), with seed and tools additions as in (a). See also Ruthenberg (1971, p. 39) for same data.
d. Ruthenberg (1971, p. 39), with seed and tools additions as in (a).
e. Pimentel & Pimentel (1979, p. 75), assuming cultivation once in ten years (Leach, 1976, p. 119), and with labour input recalculated at 0.8 MJ = 1 hour.
f. Fei & Chang (1949, p. 33), using rice yield of 60 piculs/acre (p. 71) and assuming 1 picul = 110.231 lb (p. 29). Seeds input for rice assumed as 88 kg (Pimentel & Pimentel, 1979, p. 76), and for beans 3 litres/kung or 76 kg/ha (Fei & Chang, 1949, p. 151), assuming 1 kung = 230 m^2 (p. 29). Beans yield used is median value of 2.3 piculs/kung (p. 70) at 11 MJ/kg. Hand tools and ploughs (25 kg × 10 MJ, 10 year life) as in Leach (1976, p. 119). Labour input is 20.3 labour units/kung where 1 unit = 8 hours (Fei & Chang, 1949, p. 33).
g. Fei & Chang (1949, p. 151), using paddy yield of 15 piculs/kung and conversion of paddy to rice of 30 piculs = 440 lb (p. 158). Seed and tools inputs and beans yield as in (f). Labour input is 29.73 labour units per kung of high-grade wheatfield (p. 159).
h. Fei & Chang (1949, pp. 208, 218), using paddy yield of 16 piculs/mow where 1 mow = 666 m^2 and where 1 kg paddy = 0.52 kg rice. Seed and tools inputs and beans yields as in (f). Labour input is 28.4 labour units/mow (p. 214).
i and j. Tables 8.1 and 8.2.
k and l. Rutger & Grant (1980), with labour inputs converted at 0.8 MJ = 1 hour.

2000 kg/ha of rice being increased to 3–5000 kg/ha. At the same time work inputs have been maintained, or have increased where labour is abundant (as in Mandya), to levels in the range 300–600 days per hectare, but elsewhere (e.g. Philippines) post-Green Revolution labour inputs have fallen to around 100 days/ha. This latter tendency would clearly be retrograde if it were to happen in areas suffering from rural underemployment.

(ii) The *agricultural involution* path shows that the Green Revolution is not the only way of raising yields and of increasing employment. Wet rice has the unique capacity of permitting more and more intensification in the face of population growth, the process described as 'involution' by Geertz (1963) in his classic study of agricultural change in Java. A similar process of extreme intensification occurred in pre-Communist China, as documented for Yunnan Province by Fei and Chang (1949). Here rice was double-cropped with broad beans in small fields that were intensively cultivated, irrigated and organically manured. These farms generated food yields (63–67% in the form of rice) that are among the highest ever recorded apart from under experimental conditions. In rice equivalent the level of output is two to three times the yield of Green Revolution peasant farms, and six to ten times the yield gained by means of shifting cultivation (Pearse, 1980, p. 109; Clark & Haswell, 1970, p. 43). Equally impressive is the labour requirement, which in the extreme case of Yits'un reaches almost 1300 days per hectare, in circumstances where 'the population pressure is merciless' (Fei & Chang, 1949, p. 159). There are aspects – but only aspects – of this form of agriculture which would be worth considering for areas like South India, where at present the innovative farmers are more drawn towards the western model of change than to any more labour-intensive alternative (Freedman, 1980).

Notes to Table 8.3 (*cont.*)

m. Pimentel & Pimentel (1979, p. 78), with labour input recalculated at 0.8 MJ = 1 hour.
n. Leach (1976, p. 124), excluding inputs of animal traction, domestic electricity, agricultural research and administration, and off-farm transport. A seeds input of 1551 MJ/ha is added, and the gross yield is revised, using the data in Newcombe (1975). Rice (at 3 t/ha) is about 31% of the total yield.
o. Leach (1976, p. 122), excluding animal traction input, adding seed input of 108 kg/ha (Pimentel & Pimentel, 1979, p. 76), and converting Leach's net yield to a gross figure by adding the same quantity.
p, q, r. Kuether & Duff (1981), with the direct energy input of animal traction excluded from the energy input of the 'traditional' system, i.e. from (p).
s. Leach (1976, p. 122) adding seed input at 157 kg/ha (Pimentel & Pimentel, 1979, p. 77) with energy content doubled to account for seed dressings, and the seed input added to the yield.
t. Leach (1976, p. 123), modified as in (s).
u, v, w, x, y. Rutger & Grant (1980), with labour inputs converted at 0.8 MJ = 1 hour.
za. Figures in brackets indicate the proportion of each hectare cropped per year over the long term.
zb. Inputs and outputs are calculated per hectare over the long term. To convert data to inputs and outputs per crop, divide by cropping factor (see note 3).
zc. Rice yields and, unless otherwise indicated, rice seed inputs are converted throughout at the rate 1 kg = 15.1 MJ.

(iii) The *industrialisation* path is illustrated in Figure 8.5 by Surinam and the USA, and represents a second alternative to Green Revolution farming practices. Yields are equally high (3–5000 kg/ha), but the substitution of labour by a fossil-fuel based technology has proceeded unchecked, so that by Third World standards labour inputs are quite astonishingly small: 13 days/ha in Surinam, and 3–5 days/ha in the USA. In the foreseeable future it is hard to envisage circumstances in South Asia where this low level of rural employment will be appropriate.

Conclusion

Rural unemployment is one reason for viewing with disquiet the prospect of a more complete industrialisation of rice cultivation. Another reason is the potential instability of the technology concerned, and in particular its large and inevitable energy subsidy, which derives at present predominantly from fossil fuel sources (Fig. 8.6). When food energy output from rice-growing systems is compared with the total energy input (both averaged out over the long

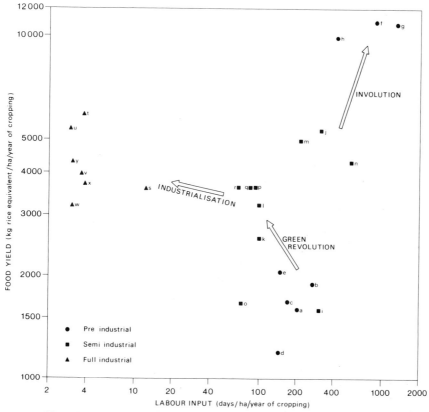

Fig. 8.5. Yield in relation to labour input: comparison of 22 rice-growing systems (for data sources see Table 8.3).

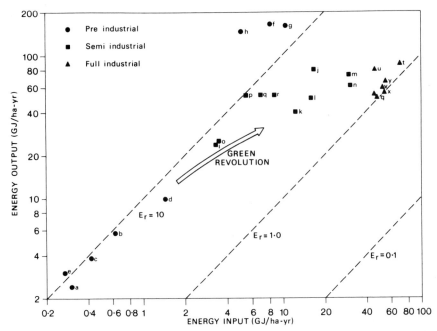

Fig. 8.6. Energy inputs and outputs for 22 rice-growing systems (for data sources see Table 8.3).

term), then it is clear that overall energy use is becoming less and less efficient. The pre-industrial systems have Energy Ratios of around 10, but with the Green Revolution this level is more than halved, and in full-industrial systems the ratio is close to one. As much energy is being expended in these systems as is being obtained from them in the form of food.

It is sometimes argued that the industrialisation of agriculture is necessary both to improve the welfare of the agrarian population and to improve yields. Our case study from Mandya, and much other work in South Asia, demonstrates very clearly that technological change alone is quite unable to reverse the existing social tendencies towards polarisation of rich and poor – indeed, it accelerates these tendencies. Nor are high yields uniquely associated with the application of Green Revolution technology. The analysis of energy costs and energy returns shows that a truly appropriate technology for the poorest regions of the tropical world has yet to be revealed.

NOTES

1. Epstein's (1973) data show that in 1955 a casual labourer's household lived off an annual cash income of Rs 148 per person (p. 163). The middle Peasant farmer's expenditure on casual labour can be calculated as amounting to Rs 368 (p. 97), which represents an outlay sufficient to wholly support 2.5 persons from the labouring class.

2. To calculate SEI we assume that the Wangala diet provided on average 9.57 MJ per person per day (Kalirajan, 1976). We also assume that a typical middle Peasant household in Wangala consumed in the year Rs 710 worth of purchased food (Epstein, 1973, p. 157), Rs 436 in subsistence rice (representing the market value of the 990 kg consumed), and Rs 55 of subsistence *ragi* (the market value of the 230 kg consumed) (Epstein, 1973, pp. 146 and 156). Rs 1201 worth of food is therefore being consumed by six persons each year, which represents Rs 200 per person, supplying 3493 MJ (i.e. 9.57 × 365) in total. The average cost of the diet is therefore 17.47 MJ per rupee, which when multiplied by the 'surplus' cash income gives the Surplus Energy Income.
3. Calculated as follows: total household income is Rs 1242 (Epstein, 1973, p. 163). Subsistence food supply is 5700 MJ from rice (0.24 ha yielding 23 752 MJ/ha, see Table 8.1), and 2390 MJ from *ragi* (0.38 ha yielding 559 kg/ha, with 12% waste and food value of 12.8 MJ/kg). The household's food deficit needing to be purchased is thus 12 860 MJ, costing Rs 736 at 17.47 MJ per rupee (see note 2).

REFERENCES

Abraham, T.P. (1965). Optimum fertiliser dressings and the economics of manuring. *Indian Journal of Agricultural Economics*, 20 (2), 1–20

Bayliss-Smith, T.P. (1982a). Energy use, food production and welfare: perspectives on the efficiency of agricultural systems. In G.A.Harrison (ed.), *Energy and Effort*. Taylor & Francis, Basingstoke

(1982b). *The Ecology of Agricultural Systems*. Cambridge University Press

Chambers, R. & Farmer, B.H. (1977). Perceptions, technology and the future. In B.H. Farmer (ed.), *Green Revolution?* Macmillan, London, pp. 413–22

Chinappa, B.N. (1977). Adoption of the new technology in North Arcot. In B.H. Farmer (ed.), *Green Revolution?* Macmillan, London, pp. 92–123

Clark, C. & Haswell, M. (1970). *The Economics of Subsistence Agriculture*, 4th edn. Macmillan, London

Epstein, T.S. (1962). *Economic Development and Social Change in South India*. Manchester University Press

(1973). *South India: Yesterday, Today and Tomorrow*. Macmillan, London

Farmer, B.H. (1977a). *Green Revolution? Technology and Change in Rice-Growing Areas of Tamil Nadu and Sri Lanka*. Macmillan, London

(1977b). Geography and agrarian research: experience from Tamil Nadu and Sri Lanka. In Indian Geographical Society, *The Golden Jubilee Volume 1976*. Indian Geographical Society, Madras, pp. 198–206

(1980). Some thoughts on the place of fieldwork in agrarian studies. *Sri Lanka Journal of Agrarian Studies*, 1, 1–11

(1981). The 'Green Revolution' in South Asia. *Geography* 66, 202–7

Fei, H.-T. & Chang, C.-I. (1949). *Earthbound China: A Study of Rural Economy in Yunnan*. Routledge & Kegan Paul, London

Freedman, S.M. (1980). Modifications of traditional rice production practices in the developing world: an energy efficiency analysis. *Agro-Ecosystems*, 6, 129–46

Geddes, W.R. (1954). *The Land Dayaks of Sarawak*. Colonial Research Studies No. 14, HMSO, London
Geertz, C. (1963). *Agricultural Involution: The Process of Ecological Change in Indonesia*. University of California Press, Berkeley
Gurumurthy, K.G. (1976). *Kallapura: A South Indian Village*. Research Publications No. 24, Karnatak University, Dharwar
Harriss, B. (1977a). Paddy and rice statistics in Sri Lanka. In B.H. Farmer (ed.), *Green Revolution?* Macmillan, London, pp. 20–9
(1977b). Rural electrification and the diffusion of electric water-lifting technology in North Arcot district, India. In B.H. Farmer (ed.), *Green Revolution?* Macmillan, London, pp. 182–203
Kalirajan, K. (1976). Calorie intakes of food: comparisons across states and classes. *Indian Journal of Agricultural Economics*, 30 (1), 53–63
Kuether, D.O. & Duff, J.B. (1981). Energy requirements for alternative rice production systems in the tropics. *IRRI Research Paper Series* No. 59, IRRI, Manila
Leach, G. (1976). *Energy and Food Production*. IPC Press, Guildford
Makhijani, A. & Poole, A. (1975). *Energy and Agriculture in the Third World*. Ballinger, Cambridge, Mass.
Mencher, J.P. (1978). *Agriculture and Social Structure in Tamil Nadu: Past Origins, Present Transformations, and Future Prospects*. Carolina Academic Press, Durham, NC
Newcombe, K. (1975). Energy use in the Hong Kong food system. *Agro-Ecosystems*, 2, 253–76
Pearse, A. (1980). *Seeds of Plenty, Seeds of Want. Social and Economic Implications of the Green Revolution*. Clarendon Press, Oxford
Pimentel, D. (ed.) (1980). *Handbook of Energy Utilization in Agriculture*. CRC Press, Boca Raton, Florida
Pimentel, D. & Pimentel, M. (1979). *Food, Energy and Society*. Arnold, London
Rebello, N.S.P., Chandrashekar, G.S., Shankamurthy, H.G. & Hiremath, K.C. (1976). Impact of the increase of prices in Mandya district of Karnataka. *Indian Journal of Agricultural Economics*, 31(3), 71–81
Rutger, J.N. & Grant, W.R. (1980). Energy use in rice production. In D. Pimentel (ed.), *Handbook of Energy Utilization in Agriculture*. CRC Press, Boca Raton, Florida, pp. 93–8
Ruthenberg, H. (1971). *Farming Systems in the Tropics*. Clarendon Press, Oxford
Singh, A.J. & Miglani, S.S. (1976). An economic analysis of energy requirements in Punjab agriculture. *Indian Journal of Agricultural Economics*, 31 (3), 165–73
Singh, R.I., Singh, G.N., Singh, R.K. & Prasad, V. (1976). Impact of input prices on productivity in agriculture: a case study. *Indian Journal of Agricultural Economics*, 31 (3), 100–5

9 Income and wealth disparities in a land settlement of the Sri Lanka Dry Zone

VIDYAMALI SAMARASINGHE and
S.W.R. DE A. SAMARASINGHE

The physical environment of the Dry Zone of Sri Lanka, with its fluctuations and variability of the rainfall regime, high potential evapotranspiration, relatively low water-holding capacity of the soil, and rapid release of soil moisture at low tensions, have imposed prohibitive limitations on the availability of water to crops (Farmer, 1956; Rasiah, 1980). Hence the provision of irrigated water becomes an essential prerequisite in the establishment of a viable agrarian economy within the area.

When the British took over the island in the nineteenth century the Dry Zone, which was the seat of the ancient kings (fifth century B.C. to thirteenth century A.D.), had long since been abandoned, and the region was jungle clad, rife with malaria, and scantily populated, and the man-made reservoirs which were built to provide water for paddy cultivation were damaged (see Farmer, 1957, pp. 8–18).

A typical settlement of the Dry Zone in this period was described in these terms: 'Here the air is heavy and unwholesome, vegetation is rank, malaria broods over the waters as they escape from the broken tanks . . . ' (Tennent, 1860, p. 611). Yet today this region is recognized as most attractive to internal migrants (ESCAP, 1976, p. 56), a transformation which testifies to the success of half a century of measures for regional development. The eradication of malaria in the 1940s contributed in no small measure to this success, but colonization schemes have been the major tool for state intervention.

Origins of Dry Zone colonization

The neglect of the Dry Zone continued until the 1920s, when the government in principle took over the responsibility for the provision of irrigation facilities for agriculture and land settlement. This process known as 'colonization' was defined as the settlement of peasants outside their native villages in small family-size farms, surveyed, mapped and blocked out for the purpose by the government (Govt. of Ceylon, 1929, 1958). The objectives of colonization were to increase the production of paddy, to ease the population congestion of the Wet Zone of Sri Lanka, and to preserve the peasantry by providing them with family-size farms (see Samaraweera, 1973, pp. 446–60). The policy framework for the establishment and the subsequent development of the Dry Zone colonization schemes was laid with the *Report of the Land Commission* of 1929, and its legislative foundations by the *Land Development Ordinance* of 1935. The policies thus laid down have been followed since with only minor modifications.

In a country where rice is the staple diet the importance of colonization schemes which became the major rice-producing units cannot be underestimated. Indeed most of the districts that came under the impact of Dry Zone colonization had become rice surplus regions as early as the 1950s (Farmer, 1952, p. 559). However, the preservation of the peasantry was valued not only for their capacity as producers of food, but also as a social group, and as a body of equal land holders (Govt. of Ceylon, 1957). Hence, in the words of Sir Hugh Clifford one-time Governor of the country, the newly settled peasantry in the Dry Zone should become 'a prosperous, self-supporting, and self-respecting multitude of peasant proprietors' (Clifford, 1927). Indeed, the emergence of an economically viable peasant community from among all the original settlers of a colonization scheme, who were believed to have started off more or less on an equal footing, seems to have been an important expectation of the policy makers. However, several studies have documented the existence of sharp income disparities within such communities in the Dry Zone today (Amerasinghe, 1974; AERU, 1969; Jogaratnam, 1971). The present study seeks to investigate the underlying reasons as to why such disparities in income and wealth have occurred, and identifies some of the key elements that should be included in models that can be developed for similar studies in the future.

Income disparity in the Dry Zone

It appears that off-farm incomes among the farmers of the colonization schemes do not constitute a major cause of income disparity because a very high proportion of the income of colonists is derived from agricultural production, chiefly paddy (Amerasinghe, 1974). Indeed, one study has suggested that since off-farm incomes are more important amongst lower income groups, their effect is if anything to reduce inequality (AERU, 1969). Farm incomes in turn are dependent on the productivity of land and farm size. There is a considerable amount of evidence to show that the availability of water is a crucial factor that determines the productivity of land in the Dry Zone, at least in relation to paddy cultivation (Farmer, 1957; Schikele, 1970; Jogaratnam, 1974). Paddy lands with an adequate supply of water show higher cropping intensity and better yields (ARTI, 1975a). However, yields are not a function of water availability alone but of better cultural practices as well (AERU, 1969).

Given all other factors, total farm income will be determined by farm size. In this respect, as one would expect, higher incomes accrue to households cultivating larger farms. It has also been found that high yielding varieties (HYVs) of paddy associated with the Green Revolution have benefitted the bigger farming units (Amerasinghe, 1974). Thus farm size becomes a critical factor determining income distribution. A concerted effort has been made by the Sri Lankan government in its land policy under colonization schemes to prevent variations in farm size becoming a source of inequality. From the very outset, the units of paddy land and highland allocated to new settlers within a given colonization scheme were equal in size. Initially, holdings with 2.0 ha of irrigated paddy land and 1.2 ha of highland were allocated in the older colonization schemes (Govt. of Ceylon, 1948). Later the size of allotments given to the colonist in new colonization schemes was first reduced to 1.2 ha of paddy land and 0.8 ha of highland, and subsequenbtly in 1964 to 0.8 ha of paddy land and 0.4 ha of highland (Govt. of Ceylon, 1966). Nevertheless two basic principles have remained inviolate throughout. One was that in any given colonization scheme every allottee was given an equal amount of land; and the other was that the land thus allotted could not be sold, mortgaged or alienated in any form without permission from the government, and sub-division of allotments for inheritance was restricted (Schikele, 1970).[1] Apart from the obvious social justice of this arrangement, it was also believed that this would help establish a farming community with a reasonably equitable distribution of income and wealth.

Three factors have been responsible for negating the original objective of the government to minimize farm-size variation. The first and foremost is the formal and informal sub-division of land among one's own children. The second is the encroachment of crownland by some allottees. The third is the acquisition of additional land, sometimes permanently through lawful purchase, but more frequently through 'temporary acquisition', i.e. informal and illegal mortgage, lease, or *Ande*, which is a system of share cropping.

It is generally recognized in the literature that all three factors mentioned above play a role in causing differences in farm size. However, it appears that the treatment of this issue in existing studies is inadequate in two respects, both of which relate mainly to the methodology adopted. The first is that most studies have considered a sample of all households of farming units now existing in a given colonization scheme. Such a method involves not only original colonists and their descendants but also the *purana* (precolonization) population, encroachers (mostly squatters on government reserves), and others who operate farms in the colony (ARTI, 1975b; Wanigaratne, 1979). The inclusion of these categories, whose circumstances may be significantly different to those of the colonists, makes it much more difficult to ascertain the true nature of income and wealth disparities among the latter. Secondly, many available studies acknowledge that the information that they have obtained on land encroachment, sub-division and especially temporary acquisition may not be all that reliable (Jogaratnam, 1971; ARTI, 1975b).

This is not surprising since colonists would naturally be reluctant to supply accurate information on activities which are considered illegal. In the present study an attempt has been made to design a methodology to minimize this problem.

Area of investigation and methodology

The present study is based on BOP 317, which is a small colony under a major colonization scheme known as the 'Parakrama Samudra' Scheme which was started in 1935, in the district of Polonnaruwa (Fig. 9.1).[2] BOP 317 covers a sizeable portion of the area known as Thalpotha and henceforth the present study will be referred to by that name. Colonists were settled in Thalpotha in the fourth quarter of 1951, during the third and final stage of the Parakrama Samudra Colonization Scheme. The terrain in BOP 317 is slightly undulating, a feature common to the district of Polonnaruwa, much of which consists of gently undulating lowland varying for the most part between 15–150 m above mean sea level.

Basic data on Thalpotha are provided in Table 9.1. Originally 254 colonist households were established in the village. At the end of 1981 there were 670 households with a total population of 5100. Thalpotha like a number of other colony villages met the basic criteria required for the present study. It was a sufficiently old colony which has at present a mixture of first- and second-

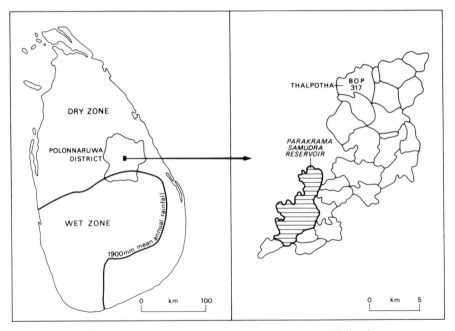

Fig. 9.1. Sri Lanka Dry Zone, showing the location of Thalpotha.

Table 9.1. *Thalpotha: basic data*

1. Number of households (farms) established in 1951	254
2. Number of households as at end of 1981	670
3. Population as at end of 1981	5100
4. Original allotment of paddy lands	514 ha
5. Encroached paddy land legalized in 1964	40 ha
6. Encroached paddy land not legalized	51 ha
7. Original allotment of highland	308 ha
8. Encroached highland not legalized	47 ha
Sample	
9. Number of original (1951) households in sample	30
10. Number of original households in sample which were found to be sub-divided	11
11. Total number of households in sample	43
12. Total number of households interviewed	41
13. Total population in interviewed sample	266
14. Owned paddy land (1951 allocation) in interviewed sample*	62 ha
15. Encroached paddy land in interviewed sample	7 ha

Notes: *Includes 6.4 ha purchased by three households from landowners who were resident in Thalpotha prior to colonization.
Current data refer to the situation as it existed during the period of the authors' field survey.
Source: Rows 1–8 from the Grama Sevaka, Thalpotha and the Kachcheri, Polonnaruwa. Rows 9–15 from the authors' survey.

generation farmers and a few from the third generation as well. The factor which prompted the choice of Thalpotha specifically was the opportunity of obtaining some reliable data about the issues that were of interest to the study. This was achieved by the employment of a graduate research assistant who had intimate knowledge of Thalpotha to gather the information. In the light of past experiences concerning similar studies where unreliable information reduced the usefulness of the study it was felt justified in considering this factor to be of overwhelming importance.

Several techniques were employed to gather information. A structured questionnaire was administered to gather the basic data. In addition unstructured interviews were held both with the respondents as well as third parties who often helped to fill some of the gaps. This was particularly important with respect to information on land acquisition. Furthermore, where necessary, the authors visited the paddy fields or land allotment concerned to verify the reliability of the data.

For the purpose of the study a random sample of thirty households from among the original household list of 254 was selected. This covered 12% of the list. Fourteen (47%) of the sample households were found to be undivided, i.e. with their paddy land not fragmented or divided either formally or informally, and they had the original settlers still remaining as their heads. Another five (16%) were also undivided but the heads of those households came from the second generation. Of the remaining eleven (37%), nine were divided into two households each, and two were divided into three each. The total of the divided households was twenty-four. Hence the total number of households to be surveyed consisted of forty-three households. The field study enabled the authors to obtain information from forty-one (95.3%) of the sample households, which included all the undivided households plus at least one each from all the divided households.

The relatively small size of the sample had the merit of enabling the authors to probe the respondents in detail, which probably helped to improve the quality of the data. On the other hand it reduced the scope for generalization. Both these considerations must be taken into account when the results of the survey are studied.

The field data was gathered over a period of six months, November 1981 to April 1982. This period included field testing of the questionnaire through a pilot survey. The information concerning income, production and other current activity spans the agricultural year 1981–82, covering *Yala* 1981 and *Maha* 1981–82.[3]

Income of Thalpotha households

The annual (1981–82) average net household income in the sample was found to be Rs 23 929. However, the income distribution was highly skewed (Fig. 9.2), with the top one-sixth of the households receiving one-third of the total income and the top two-fifths earning nearly two-thirds. The Gini Coefficient was estimated to be 0.27.[4] It is equally important to stress the absolute differences in income levels, especially those between the richest and poorest. The mean annual net household income of the top three households was Rs 65 892 (Rs 7907 per capita) and the average of the top seven was Rs 46 625 (Rs 6158 per capita). In contrast the mean annual net household income of the bottom three was only Rs 5760 (Rs 1737 per capita) and that of the bottom seven Rs 8665 (Rs 1957 per capita).

The undivided households generally enjoyed higher incomes than the divided ones (Table 9.2). Indeed fourteen (66%) of the divided households received annual net incomes of less than Rs 20 000, whereas only two (10%) of the undivided were in that category.[5] The remainder enjoyed a higher income.

The sample households derived 84.6% of the total income from paddy, and 3.9% from other crops[6] and animal husbandry, and 11.5 per cent from off-farm activity. Thus the impact of non-paddy agricultural production on income distribution was minimal. In point of fact it was found that any addition to incomes derived from such activity made almost no difference to the position of the Lorenz Curve.

Agrarian change at village level   179

Off-farm incomes

The position was slightly different with respect to off-farm incomes. The Lorenz Curve (Fig. 9.2) shows somewhat greater equity in the total income distribution, than when paddy income alone is taken into account. This difference is due to the impact of off-farm incomes. Data in Table 9.3 reveal the reason for this. In all groups except one, more than 50% of the households reported off-farm incomes. Such incomes were particularly important for the Rs 15–20 000 annual income bracket. In more general terms, the three lowest groups earned 17.6% of their incomes from off-farm sources whereas the

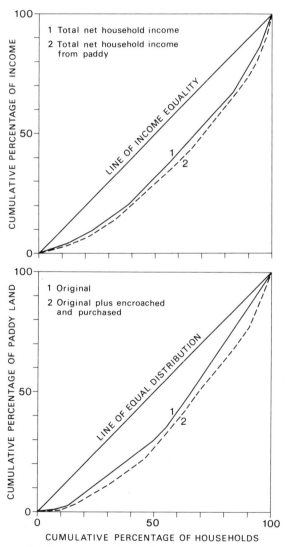

Fig. 9.2. Lorenz curves showing income distribution and paddy land distribution among Thalpotha households.

Table 9.2. *Distribution of income among a sample of 41 households in Thalpotha, 1981–82*

Annual net household income (Rs)	Number of households					Total income		
	Undivided	Divided	Total	%	Cumulative %	Rs ('000)	%	Cumulative %
Less than 10 000	–	5	5	12.1	12.1	37.0	3.7	3.7
10 000–14 999	–	4	4	9.8	21.9	50.1	5.1	8.8
15 000–19 999	2	5	7	17.1	39.0	120.3	12.3	21.2
20 000–24 999	3	4	7	17.1	56.1	157.0	16.0	37.1
25 000–29 999	8	3	11	26.8	82.9	290.3	29.6	66.7
30 000 and above	6	1	7	17.1	100.0	326.4	33.3	100.0
Total	19	22	41	100.0		981.1	100.0	

Source: authors' surveys.

Table 9.3. *Off-farm incomes of 41 Thalpotha households, 1981–82*

Annual net household income (Rs)	Total households	Off-farm income receiving households		Off-farm income	
		Number	Percentage	Total Rs	As a percentage of total net household income
Less than 10 000	5	3	60	4834	13.1
10 000–14 999	4	2	50	3240	6.5
15 000–19 999	7	4	57	28 374	23.6
20 000–24 999	7	1	14	810	0.5
25 000–29 999	11	6	55	39 332	13.5
30 000 and above	7	6	86	36 654	11.2

Source: authors' surveys.

corresponding figure for the three higher groups was only 9.9%. The greater dependence of the latter is only to be expected. Six of the nineteen households in this group received government food and kerosene stamps, which entitle the recipients to obtain these things free of charge. This item is included in the off-farm income estimates. Two households had people in regular government jobs, and several of the other households had members employed as casual labourers. In general it appears that those who had less land to cultivate relied more on off-farm activity to supplement their income, and this to a certain extent mitigated the overall income disparities. In contrast, off-farm incomes of the higher income groups were derived largely from the provision of services such as tractor and vehicle hire, rice milling and money lending – a feature which we will comment upon later.

Paddy incomes

In principle inequity in paddy incomes is caused by variations in cropping intensity, costs, yields and farm size. Typically in the Dry Zone cropping intensity is lower in *Yala* because of water shortages. However, this was not so in Thalpotha during the period 1981–82. The water supply of the Parakrama Samudra, the major irrigation scheme to which Thalpotha belongs, has been augmented from recent times by the Mahaweli River Diversion Project. As a result, in *Yala* the sample households cultivated all but 4.2 ha (6.1%) of the total of their paddy land, and in *Maha* almost the entire extent under paddy was cultivated.

It appears that the cost of production of paddy per hectare did not vary significantly among the sample households. In *Maha* the average cash cost of production per hectare was Rs 4970, with a standard deviation of Rs 1353, and a coefficient of variation of 0.272. The simple correlation coefficient between gross and net values of paddy was 0.97. Indeed, it may be surmised that the main reason for the stability of the cost of production per hectare is the adoption of new HYVs of paddy and similar input packages by all the cultivators in the sample. For example, the average expenditure on fertilizer per hectare was Rs 808 in *Yala* and Rs 1028 in *Maha* and the corresponding coefficients of variations were 0.31 and 0.30. It should be noted that the quantum of family labour available – which reduces cash cost of production – bears a positive relationship to farm size. Although in general the availability of family labour was less among those households in the sub-divided group because they tended to have fewer members of working age, even so their requirements of labour were also less because of the smaller farm size. This phenomenon may also have contributed towards the maintenance of a certain degree of stability in terms of cash cost of production per acre over the sample households.

Yields and soil variations

The coefficients of variation of 0.234 and 0.216 (Table 9.4) in the yield per hectare for *Yala* and *Maha* respectively indicate a certain measure of variability in land productivity. Such variations are usually attributed even in micro studies of small geographical regions, to differences in cultural practices. The evidence in relation to Thalpotha suggests that the physical environment exerted a decisive influence on yield. In this respect two factors must be considered. One is the texture of the soils, which were classified into three groups. They are, first, 'Sandy Clay Loam', which is considered to be best suited for paddy because of its relatively high clay content which ensures a high water and nutrient retention capacity. The second, which is the 'Sandy Loam', has a lower clay content and is considered to be moderately good for

Table 9.4. *Paddy yields and farm size, Thalpotha, 1981–82*

	Season	
	Yala	*Maha*
Average per hectare (kg)	3446	4007
Simple correlation coefficient between gross output and yield per hectare	0.39	0.26
Standard deviation of yield per hectare	806.0	866.1
Coefficient of variation of yield per hectare	0.234	0.216
Average cultivated farm size (hectares)	1.69	1.79
Simple correlation coefficient between cultivated farm size and gross yield	0.92	0.94
Standard deviation of cultivated farm size	0.89	1.09
Coefficient of variation of cultivated farm size	0.526	0.573

Source: authors' surveys.

paddy, and the third, which is the 'Loamy Sand' with very little clay content, is considered to be least suitable for paddy.

Another physical factor to be considered is the location of the paddy field. The fields located at the upper end of the sloping tracts close to the head of the field canal receive water first before those located at the lower end of the slope.[7] Although dependent to some extent on the water retention capacity of the soil in the fields, those at the upper end generally 'lose' some of their water through seepage to those located at the lower end. Thus by and large paddy fields with sandy clay loam soils located at the bottom end of the slope will have the best supply of water. Moreover, if the fields at the upper end of the slope have soils with poor nutrient retention capacity, then they stand to lose soil nutrients added by fertilizer, due to leaching. Based on these considerations the paddy plots of each of the cultivators in the sample were classified into three categories: 'good', 'fair' and 'poor'. The rule followed was to classify plots with sandy clay loam soil and located at the lower end of the slope as 'good' and those with loamy sand soil and located at the upper end as 'poor'. The remainder were classified as 'fair'.[8]

Table 9.5 shows the average yields with respect to each category. The results are in accord with expectations.[9] The relatively low average yield in the 'poor' category is particularly striking. Moreover, it is also interesting to note that yields are subject to greater variations in the 'fair' and 'poor' categories compared to the 'good'. This may be due to the fact that there is less uniformity in cultural practices among those who cultivate the lands in

Table 9.5. *Paddy yields, quality of land and expenditure on fertilizer, Thalpotha, 1981–82*

Type of land/ season	No. of plots	Yield			Per hectare expenditure on fertilizer		
		Average per hectare (kg)	Standard deviation	Coefficient of variation	Average expenditure (Rs)	Standard deviation	Coefficient of variation
Good							
Yala	8	3847	559.5	0.145	818	191.9	0.235
Maha	8	4378	451.6	0.103	1043	224.2	0.215
Fair							
Yala	24	3621	808.1	0.223	788	166.7	0.212
Maha	24	3965	1204.6	0.304	1006	336.1	0.334
Poor							
Yala	9	2609	485.2	0.185	850	468.9	0.552
Maha	9	3193	482.1	0.151	1003	478.3	0.478

the 'fair' and 'poor' categories. For instance, some farmers may attempt to offset the physical disadvantages by applying larger amounts of fertilizer. In this respect, the data in Table 9.5 are suggestive. Although there was no significant difference in the per hectare average expenditure on fertilizer among the three categories, it was seen that there was a higher degree of variation among the farmers of the 'poor' category. Indeed based on the above analysis it may be surmised that differences in yield arising from differences in the physical qualities of paddy land is a fixed long term factor which may give rise not only to disparities in current incomes but also to disparities in the accumulation of wealth, a question which will be considered later.

Size of land holdings

Tables 9.4 and 9.6 in conjunction with Fig. 9.2 indicate that the major factor which influenced income distribution in Thalpotha was the size of the paddy farm. As explained earlier, all original settlers of the region were legally entitled to two hectares of paddy land each. This implies an absolutely equal distribution.[10] The Lorenz Curve in Fig. 9.3 shows the actual distribution of paddy land. In principle, the inequity depicted in it could arise due to two factors. One is unequal sub-division in inheritance. The other, is the acquisition of land, permanent or temporary, through encroachment, purchase, mortgage, lease or *Ande*.

The major cause of unequal distribution was sub-division, both formal and informal and not necessarily involving any payment of 'rent'. Consequently, the bottom four households (10%) held only 1.8% of the entire area of paddy land allotted to the original settlers in the sample. The bottom half of the households could account for only a little less than one-third of the original paddy land. The sub-division of paddy land was partly dependent on the

Table 9.6. *Ownership of paddy land in relation to income, 41 households at Thalpotha, 1981–82*

Annual net household income (Rs)	Size of paddy land (hectares)			
	Less than 1.0	1.01–2.00	2.01–3.00	3.01 and above
Less than 10 000	4	1	–	–
10 000–14 999	2	2	–	–
15 000–19 999	1	7	–	–
20 000–24 999	–	5	2	–
25 000–29 999	–	5	7	–
30 000 and above	–	–	5	2

Source: authors' surveys.

demographic profile of the family and partly on the incidence of out-migration of sons.

Pressures for sub-division

In principle, the sub-division of colony land is legally controlled. The minimum unit of legally-allowed sub-division of irrigated paddy land which originally was 1.0 ha under colonization schemes was reduced to 0.6 ha in 1981. However, it seems that farmers resort to informal sub-division within colonies which, sometimes, results in paddy holdings as small as 0.2 ha.

As far as Thalpotha was concerned, the convention among the original households has been to divide the land among the male children of the family. In the sample taken for the present study, of eleven original households which have divided only two had given any land to the daughters. One household was in a situation where the family had no sons to inherit the land and 1.0 ha was given to a married daughter. In the second case, two married daughters had been given just 0.2 ha each.

Table 9.7 shows that there was no significant difference in the average number of male children in the two groups of households, i.e. households which have already divided the land at least partly, and those which remained undivided. The crucial determining factor appears to be the age structure of the sons. The average age of sons in the undivided group was about ten years less than of the divided group. Furthermore, it is also seen that with respect to the sons who have not migrated out, those in the undivided group were considerably younger than those in the divided group. Related to this is the question of marriage. In the case of the divided category of households, the land has been sub-divided among twenty-one married sons (and three married daughters). The remaining three sons in that category were still living in Thalpotha and were unmarried. They belonged to one family. How-

Table 9.7. *Demographic characteristics of the sample of 30 original Thalpotha households, 1981–82*

	Undivided	Divided
No. of original households	19	11
Sons		
Number	52	29
Average per household	2.74	2.64
Average age	31.3	41.3
Out-migrated	16	5
Resident in Thalpotha	36	24
Married	14	21
Unmarried*	17	3
Average age	26.4	41.1
Number above 30 years of age	12	21
Number below 30 years of age	24	3
Daughters		
Number	50	11
Average per household	2.63	0.91
Unmarried	17	3
Married	33	8
Resident in Thalpotha	3	1
Resident outside Thalpotha	30	7

Note: *Only those who were above 18 years of age at the end of 1981.
Source: authors' surveys.

ever, although the marriage of sons living in Thalpotha and dependent on farming usually leads to the sub-division of the original allotment, it is not always so. In twelve of the undivided households married sons were living in with their spouses. The explanation, it appears, is that five of the twelve married sons happened to be the only sons residing in Thalpotha and in five more these were the only sons who were married and they remained with the original household. In the two remaining households, there were two married sons each. In one, the marriage of the second sons had taken place comparatively recently in 1980 and had produced just one child, while in the other the second son had no children, both situations which would have reduced the pressure to sub-divide.

It is probable that out-migration of sons also reduced the pressure to sub-divide. About 30% of the sons in the undivided households had left Thalpotha to obtain employment elsewhere and all but one of them were reported to be married. It is possible that if they had remained in the colony after marriage, there would have been several married sons for each household which would have increased the pressure to sub-divide. Indeed demographic pressure on the land may have pushed out some of the sons from Thalpotha. In fact several of those who have migrated out have done so in order to obtain land from other colonization schemes. However, that does not explain conclusively the higher out-migration rate among the undivided group, because such households had 0.85 ha of paddy land per son if all sons remained in Thalpotha compared to 0.89 ha per son for the divided group.

The figures in Table 9.7 appear to suggest that the position of daughters in the demographic profile of the family had some influence on land sub-division. What is striking is the fact that, on average, there were almost three times as many daughters in the undivided group as in the divided. Moreover, there was an average of about one unmarried daughter in each of the undivided households. This could mean that a relatively high incidence of daughters in the family could exert some pressure to postpone sub-division. In principle, this could happen if the brothers postpone their marriage until the sisters are given in marriage. But, if this is true the average of sons in the two groups should not differ significantly. Another possibility is that the undivided households might have been under pressure to postpone sub-division to help accumulation in order to provide dowries for the daughters. Given all other factors an undivided household will have more of relatively cheap family labour. Furthermore, such undivided land could be considered as a kind of reserve asset that could be used to attract prospective suitors. Due to the same set of reasons the pressure on the sons to out-migrate could be greater.

Encroachment

Encroached paddy land constituted 6.9 ha (10.0%) of the total paddy land cultivated in *Maha*. Fig. 9.2 shows that encroachment together with purchased land aggravated the inequity of holdings. The Gini Coefficient rises from 0.25 for the original holdings to 0.29 when encroachments (but not purchases) are included.

Land encroachment by the original settlers to augment their paddy holdings usually consisted of either encroaching on state-owned 'reservations' set aside for canal bunds and to meet what were officially described as 'future government requirements' or encroaching on odd pieces of land such as rock outcrops left out in the original allocation because they were believed to be unsuitable for paddy. Typically, the colonists encroached upon such pieces of land that lay adjacent to their holdings. Since all paddy plots were not so located, encroachment depended partly on chance. However, it is also seen that more systematic factors did influence encroachment. In our sample of thirty original households twenty had got paddy allotments which gave scope for encroachment into adjacent land and the other ten had not. Five of those which belonged to the first category had failed to encroach whereas two of those who belonged to the second had encroached on land which was physically separate from their original allotments. Indeed these two held two of the largest encroached paddy tracts in our sample. The factors which influenced such systematic encroachment or its absence also contributed towards other forms of acquisition.

Land purchases

In the typical colony the scope for purchase of paddy land is highly restricted. Thalpotha is no exception. When available, such land belongs either to the pre-colony residents of the area or to colonists who have no heirs to whom the land could be transferred. All the purchased land in the sample used for this study belonged to the first category. Land was purchased from an area outside the BOP unit but which was located immediately adjacent to it.

Purchased land accounted for 6.4 ha (11.4%) of the total land cultivated in *Maha* and these belonged to just three households. Indeed land purchases made only a minor difference to the overall distribution of paddy land. The Gini Coefficient increased from 0.29 to 0.31 when the purchases were added to the sum of original land holdings and encroachments.

Temporary acquisitions

Land cultivated in the sample through temporary acquisition accounted for 4.7 ha (6.8%) of the total paddy land cultivated in *Maha*. This made only a little difference to the overall distribution of paddy land. Indeed the Gini Coefficient declined from 0.31 to 0.30 when such land was added to the sum of original, encroached and purchased land. From the point of view of the present study, it is more relevant to consider such temporary acquisitions in the past in their totality. It is the incidence of such acquisitions over the years that is conceptually relevant to the question of accumulation and the creation of disparities in incomes and wealth in the long run.

Concentration of acquired land

What is striking in land acquisition, be it permanent or temporary, is the high concentration of such land among a relatively small number of households. In encroachments nine out of the original thirty households had 0.5 ha or more of encroached land and accounted for 5.7 ha (82%) of the total of 6.9 ha. Indeed, three households held as much as 3.2 ha (47%) of the total. Land purchases were even more concentrated with just three households accounting for the total. One among them owned 3.8 ha (60.3%) of the total. A similar pattern could also be discerned in relation to temporary acquisition on a continuous basis for a period of five years or more. Among them, five had begun the practice before 1960 and one other in 1977. It is also interesting to note that all but one such household belonged to the undivided category.

Whatever the mode, land acquisition requires capital. Purchases are the most expensive, and encroachment and *Ande* the least. Once acquired all require working capital. In addition, purchases require an initial capital sum. Encroachments require some capital to develop the land. Mortgages and leases also require capital advances.[11] It follows that those households who got the physically better-endowed land which have consistently higher yields were in a position to accumulate wealth. Indeed such households would have stood a better chance of acquiring additional land. Also, those who succeeded in developing their original allotments before others would certainly have been at an advantage partly because it would have helped the process of accumulation and partly because households would normally have acquired additional land only after developing their own allotments. Table 9.8 produces some evidence to support the above hypotheses. Firstly, it is seen that three out of the eight paddy allotments in the 'good' category belonged to this group and that only one (10%) in the group had an allotment which got classified as 'poor'.

Secondly, it is also evident that a higher proportion of the households in category 1 had better highland allotments which had some degree of irrigation water supply.[12] These, reportedly, were an important source of income, mainly from short-term crops. In contrast the bulk of households in category 2 had highland allotments which had practically no irrigation water.

Thirdly, 80% of the households in category 1 reported cultivating their respective allotments in full by 1960. The percentage was a little lower for category 2 for the same period.

Fourthly, the reported relative availability of capital among the original households when they arrive in Thalpotha was also a relevant consideration.[13] Those who had some capital to spare had been more successful at land acquisition partly because such capital could have been directly invested in acquiring extra land and partly because it would have helped speed up the development of the original allocation. Furthermore, Thalpotha was badly affected by the drought of 1956 and the floods of 1957 which affected many parts of the Dry Zone. Those households which had some capital to spare would have been better able to survive these natural hazards. Indeed, there are indications that the incidence of temporary acquisitions increased in the late 1950s. For example, out of the nineteen households which reported ever having made a temporary acquisition, five did so for the first time between 1957 and 1960.

Acquisition of capital goods

Finally, it is useful to note that there were two four-wheel tractors, six hand tractors, one motor car, one power generator and two bullock carts owned by certain households in the sample. All but the six hand tractors earned a cash

Table 9.8. *Capital availability and land acquisition among 30 original colonist households*

Category		Number	Capital at beginning*			Year of full cultivation of original paddy allotment			Quality of paddy land			Availability of irrigation water for highland	
			1	2	3	1960 or before	After 1960	Not known	Good	Fair	Poor	Available	Not available
1	No.	10	6	2	2	8	1	1	3	6	1	6	4
	%		60	20	20	80	10	10	30	60	10	60	40
2	No.	20	2	6	12	12	6	2	5	10	5	6	14
	%		10	30	60	60	30	10	25	50	25	30	70

Notes: Category 1: Original households with the sum of encroached and purchased paddy land of 0.5 hectares or more or temporary acquisition of paddy land on a continuous basis exceeding five years or more.
    Category 2: All original households not included in Category 1.
*1. Capital available
  2. Some capital available
  3. Capital not available
Source: authors' surveys.

income for their respective owners. Except for the two bullock carts (which are mostly owned by the poorer sections of the community in Sri Lanka) and one hand tractor, the rest were owned by households receiving an annual income of Rs 25 000 or more. Moreover, there was a heavy concentration of these assets among a few households. The top income-earning household which also owned the largest area in paddy holdings (6.0 ha) owned one four-wheel tractor, one hand tractor and the power generator. The second highest income-earning household which also owned the second largest area of paddy holdings (4.7 ha) also owned the other four-wheel tractor, one hand tractor and the motor car which was hired out. All but the rice mill in the sample were post-1970 acquisitions and were preceded by land accumulation. This suggests that the surplus generated from agriculture formed the basis of non-agricultural wealth.[14]

Summary and conclusions

The survey data demonstrate the existence today of significant disparities in income and wealth among colonist households who were settled in a colonization scheme thirty years ago. The disparities could be attributed mainly to differences in income from paddy production, which in turn stem largely from differences in the size of holdings. Two characteristics have determined the size of paddy holdings of a given household today. One has been the degree of sub-division of the original allotment, and the other has been the ability to acquire additional land. Very significant differences have emerged among the colonist households with respect to the factors which influence these two phenomena.

The sub-division of land in any given household was determined mainly by the 'age of the family' and the number of sons per family. Among the first generation of colonists those families which had relatively older children resorted to sub-division earlier. The implication is that initial differences in household demography have created a 'demographic cycle' in the temporal pattern of land sub-division. This in turn has influenced income and wealth distribution in the colony. Related to this was the number of sons in the family. Those families which had more sons, and whose sons did not or could not out-migrate, had to sub-divide more.

The ability to acquire additional land has been determined partly by the availability of capital to the individual colonist households in the early period of settlement. In this connection, the assumption frequently made that all colonists started on an 'equal footing' is evidently incorrect. Those who had some capital when they arrived in the colony were at an obvious advantage. Also, those who were fortunate enough to get relatively better-quality land were at a still greater advantage in terms of accumulating capital. Such a process of accumulation, once begun, has had the tendency to perpetuate and widen disparities. Thus a small minority among the colonist households have succeeded in strengthening their capital base and income-earning capacity, both by acquiring an above average amount of agricultural land as well as other income-earning assets.

ACKNOWLEDGEMENTS

We owe a special debt to Mr H.W. Thilakaratne whose untiring efforts in helping to gather the field data made the study possible. We also thank Messrs A.R. Dissanayake and R.S. Wijesekera for doing the soil analysis and the University of Peradeniya for giving us a research grant (RG/82/AT/15) to finance this project.

NOTES

1. Until 1981 the minimum unit of sub-division was 1.0 ha for paddy and 0.4 ha for highland, but since then they have been reduced to 0.6 ha and 0.2 ha respectively. Since 1982 allottees have been permitted to mortgage the land to official lending institutions.
2. BOP refers to the 'Blocking-Out-Plan' undertaken at the planning stage of the colony. The BOPs under major colonization schemes are identified by numbers, and each of the BOPs shows the use to be made of all land in the colony including channels, roads, paddy and highland allotments, reservations for the purpose of conservation and for temples and other public buildings (see Farmer, 1957, p. 170).
3. *Yala* is the minor cultivation season (April–September) and coincides with the

South-West Monsoons and *Maha* is the major cultivation season which coincides with the North-East Monsoon (October–March). Hereafter unless otherwise specified *Yala* refers to *Yala* 1981, and *Maha* to *Maha* 1981–82. Incomes in Sri Lanka rupees can be converted into US dollars using the May 1982 exchange rate of 1 dollar = Rs 20.50.

4. This is lower than the Gini Coefficient of 0.35 for income distribution by spending units in the entire country in 1973, and 0.37 for income receivers in the rural sector in the same year (*Survey of Sri Lanka's Consumer Finances*, 1973, Central Bank of Ceylon, 1974, Colombo, p. 68).
5. It may be suggested that the undivided households on average were bigger than divided households, which correspondingly reduced the per caput incomes. This was not the case. The nineteen undivided households had a total population of 135 with a per caput income of Rs 4089 whereas the divided households had a population of 131 with a per caput income of Rs 3276. The Spearman's Rank Correlation between total net household income and per caput income generated a 'z' value of 4.84 which was significant at the 0.2% level. This suggested a close correspondence between the two variables.
6. Incomes from highland permanent tree crops only are included in this estimate. Incomes from short-term crops have not been included because of the unreliability of the data. There is evidence to suggest that there was significant variability in incomes from short-term highland cultivation, a factor which will be considered later.
7. Note that this is not the same as being located at the head, middle or bottom of the main canal, which can also influence the availability of water when it is in short supply.
8. Dry Zone soils are generally poor in the content of organic matter. Therefore nutrient retention capacity depends largely on the clay content. In addition, the degree of clay content also determines the water retention capacity (pers. comm., Dr S. Somasiri, Land Use Division, Government Department of Agriculture, Peradeniya). The farmers were asked to describe the supply of water (good, fair, poor) and the quality of the soil which in their terminology was either 'sandy' soil or 'good' soil. Their classification tallied closely with that arrived at by the authors by way of a laboratory soil analysis and field observations of the physical location of the fields *vis-à-vis* the upper end of the slope or the lower end of the slope.
9. The Variance Ratio Test was applied to the results in Table 9.5. The results of the test indicated that the differences between the standard deviations of the *Maha* yields of the 'Good–Fair' and 'Fair–Poor' categories were significant at the 5% level. The differences between the standard deviations of fertilizer use in *Yala* by the 'Good–Poor' and 'Fair–Poor' categories and in *Maha* by 'Good–Poor'categories were also significant at the same level.
10. In practice two of the thirty original households in the sample got only 1.9 ha each because 0.1 ha in each of the two allotments were not suitable for paddy, but this source of disparity is negligible.
11. In the early days of the colony there were instances where undeveloped land was given out on *Ande*, but even in such cases capital would have been required to

develop the land. Note that mortgages were taken by giving an interest-free loan which had to be returned in order to repossess the land.
12. The highland allotments located below the irrigation canals had a relatively better supply of water mainly due to seepage. The other highland allotments had to depend on rain. The first category were generally well developed whereas the latter were not. This difference is evident even to the casual visitor to Thalpotha.
13. There were numerous methodological problems in assessing this. A precise quantitative assessment was not possible. The technique we adopted was to question the respondents about the nature and extent of property (land and dwellings) they owned in their place of origin (1951), and also their original occupation. On the basis of information thus obtained the groups were classified using a rule of thumb. Those who were in receipt of a regular wage or owned 0.4 ha of paddy or 0.6 ha or more of highland were classified in the 'capital available' group. Those who did not own land and who were not in receipt of a regular wage were classified in the 'capital not available' group. The rest who owned lands in extents less than the minimum specified for the first group were classified in the 'some capital available' group. It should be noted that most who owned such property liquidated them before coming to Thalpotha. A minority either rented them or permitted a relative to use them.
14. Even the rice mill had been financed with capital accumulation from cultivation. The owner in question reported taking on *Ande* 1.2 ha of paddy in *Maha* 1959 and leasing in 2.0 ha in *Maha* 1960 to earn a surplus to purchase the rice mill.

REFERENCES

AERU (1969). *Summary Report of the Socio-Economic Survey of 9 Colonization Schemes in Ceylon, 1967–68, Part I – Highlights of Findings: Comparative Analysis*. Agricultural Economics Research Unit, Peradeniya
Amerasinghe, N. (1974). Impact of High Yielding Varieties of rice in a settlement scheme. *Tropical Agriculturalist*, 130 (2), 63–86
ARTI (1975a). *The Agrarian Situation Relating to Paddy Cultivation in Five Selected Districts of Sri Lanka*. Research Study Series No. 11, Agricultural Research and Training Institute, Colombo
   (1975b). *The Agrarian Situation Relating to Paddy Cultivation in Five Selected Districts of Sri Lanka, Part 3 – Polonnaruwa District*. Research Study Series No. 8, Agricultural Research and Training Institute, Colombo
Clifford, H. (1927). Some reflections on the Ceylon land question. *Tropical Agriculturalist*, 67, 283–307
ESCAP (1976). *Population Monograph No. 4*. Bangkok
Farmer, B.H. (1952). Colonization in the Dry Zone of Ceylon. *Journal of the Royal Society of Arts*, vol. C, no. 4876, 547–64
   (1956). Rainfall and water supply in the Dry Zone of Ceylon. In C.A. Fisher & R.W. Steel (eds.), *Geographical Essays of the British Tropical Lands*. London, Philip
   (1957). *Pioneer Peasant Colonization in Ceylon*, London, Oxford University Press

Govt. of Ceylon (1929). *Report of the Land Commission*. Ceylon Sessional Paper XVIII
    (1948, 1966). *Administrative Report of the Land Commissioner*. Colombo
    (1957). *Interim Report of the Land Commission*. Ceylon Sessional Paper XV
    (1958). *Report of the Land Commission*. Ceylon Sessional Paper X
Jogaratnam, T. (1971). *Report of the Re-survey of the Elahera Colonization Scheme in Ceylon*. Peradeniya
    (1974). Irrigation farming in the Dry Zone of Sri Lanka. Agricultural Economics Research Unit (mimeo)
Rasiah, V. (1980). Water management for rice cultivation in the Dry Zone of Sri Lanka. Paper presented at the Rice Symposium, Colombo, Sri Lanka (mimeo)
Samaraweera, V. (1973). Land policy and peasant colonization 1914–1918. In K.M. de Silva (ed.), *University of Ceylon – History of Ceylon*, vol. 3, Colombo
Schikele, R. (1970). *Land Settlement Policy in Ceylon, Ceylon Papers on Agricultural Development and Economic Progress (1967–70)*. Peradeniya
Tennent, J.E. (1860). *Ceylon*, 5th edn, London, Longman
Wanigaratne, R.W. (1979). *The Minipe Colonization Scheme – An Appraisal*. Research Study No. 29, Agrarian Research and Training Institute, Colombo

10 Agrarian structure and agricultural innovation in Bangladesh: Panimara village, Dhaka district

STEVE JONES

Over the past twenty years successive governments in what is now Bangladesh have made major efforts to increase agricultural production through the introduction of high-yielding varieties of paddy (HYVs), fertilisers, pesticides and modern irrigation technology such as low-lift pumps, which take water from rivers and creeks, and deep and shallow tubewells (Hossain & Jones, 1983). Between 1960 and 1980 the area irrigated by modern methods increased from zero to nearly 0.9 million hectares out of a net cropped area of 9 million hectares. The use of chemical fertilisers increased from nothing to over 100 kg per net cropped hectare, and the area under HYVs developed at the International Rice Research Institute (IRRI) and the Bangladesh Rice Research Institute (BRRI) reached over 20% of the total area under foodgrains. Foodgrain production which in the late 1950s averaged 8 million tonnes increased to 13 million tonnes by the late 1970s. Much of the increase was due to the cultivation of IR-8 and BR-3 under irrigation in the dry (*boro* or *rabi*) season, though the cultivation of the same varieties later on as an early monsoon (*aus* or early *kharif* season) crop, and other varieties such as IR-20 and BR-4 in the late monsoon (*aman* or late *kharif*), was also important.[1] In parts of the country, especially in the north and west, wheat cultivation has also increased rapidly since 1975.

Despite the significant success achieved in increasing agricultural production, however, Bangladesh paddy yields and input use are still amongst the lowest in Asia (Jones, 1979). Much more could be done. If full irrigation potential were realised food production could be doubled or trebled. With the development of flood control and drainage systems using existing, labour-intensive technology it could probably be quadrupled (World Bank, 1972).

What constrains agricultural development?

One factor commonly advanced by researchers and development agencies to explain the relatively low development of agriculture in the country is the nature of the agrarian structure (Islam, 1978; Stepanek, 1979; World Bank, 1979; Government of Bangladesh, 1980). Two aspects of this structure that are commonly held to constrain agricultural development are the preponderance of small farms and the widespread prevalence of sharecropping. The preponderance of small farms has been argued to limit agricultural development in two ways – by reducing the rate of adoption of HYVs, and by lowering the overall efficiency with which they are cultivated. The average operated holding in Bangladesh comprises 10 parcels totalling 1.4 ha, and it is argued that the owners of such holdings are poor, lack the resources to invest in improved agriculture, and are reluctant to take the increased risks associated with cultivating HYVs. Middle and large farmers who cultivate at most 40% of agricultural land on the other hand enjoy better access to credit and input markets, which, together with their better ability to bear risks, means that they are both bigger adopters of HYVs and cultivate them more productively. The well-documented negative relationship between farm size and productivity may hold for traditional varieties but, it is argued, is reversed in the case of HYVs.

The second way in which the agrarian structure is held to constrain agricultural development relates to sharecropping. About one quarter of agricultural land is cultivated by sharecroppers, most of it on terms which, it is argued, offer little incentive to the tenant to increase his productivity or to cultivate HYVs. Thus sharecropped land is thought to have lower yields than owner-cultivated land, and a smaller proportion of sharecropped land is thought to be under HYVs. If all sharecropped lands were owner-cultivated the area under HYVs would be greater and overall production higher.

The aim of this study is to empirically test this widely held view that the preponderance of small farms and sharecropping are serious impediments to agricultural development in Bangladesh. The analysis uses data collected by the author while living in northern Dhaka (Dacca) district in 1978 and during a second period of fieldwork in 1980. Additional data from other studies the author was engaged in, in Barisal (Centre for Social Studies, 1980) and Comilla (Bangladesh Unnayan Parishad, 1982) districts is also referred to, as is the work of other researchers who have examined the issue in Bangladesh (Asaduzzaman, 1977, 1980; Hossain, 1977, 1981; Rahman, 1979, 1981). The arguments put forward will be elaborated elsewhere (Jones, forthcoming).

Panimara village

Panimara, the village chosen for the study, is located in western Joydebpur *thana* ('county') about 55 km north-west of Dhaka, the capital. The village lies within the Kashimpur Agricultural Development Estate, an area of intensive agricultural development, and in 1980 had a population of 726 living in 125 households. It is located on one of the southern tips of the Madhupur Plateau, an area of uplifted alluvium probably of plio-miocene age. The village is not river flooded, but shallow rainwater flooding of bunded fields can occur. The area experiences a unimodal monsoonal distribution of rainfall typical of Bangladesh and neighbouring parts of the South Asian subcontinent. Over 70% of the annual rainfall of about 100 mm falls in the five months from June to October, and the water balance is negative from November to April (Fig. 10.1). Temperatures are favourable for plant growth throughout the year, though for a short period in December–January paddy growth is slow.

There are three main types of land in the village – *chala*, *ukhai* and *baid*. *Chala* is the local word given to higher plateau land at elevations of about 10 metres. The *chala* lands are dissected by narrow, flat-bottomed valleys 2–3 metres lower and up to 100 metres wide. The lower, broader part of a valley is referred to as *baid*, its upper reaches as *ukhai*. *Baid* and *ukhai* soils are silty and naturally porous but have generally well-developed plough pans, are only slowly permeable and therefore good for paddy cultivation. *Chala* soils are well- or moderately well-drained depending on the depth and extent of weathering. Where these soils are only shallowly weathered and overlie compact Madhupur clay at depths of about 0.3 to 0.9 metres, paddy can be successfully cultivated. Where deep weathering has taken place producing more permeable soils the land is better suited to vegetables and other *rabi* (non-paddy dry-season) crops. In Panimara *baid* land makes up about 40% of agricultural land, *chala* and *ukhai* about 30% each. Most land is good for paddy cultivation, which is grown on over 98% of the cropped area, though some *chala* lands are sufficiently permeable to make irrigated paddy cultivation prohibitively expensive and wet season paddy growing potentially risky. Yields on *baid* land are generally about 10% higher than those obtained on *ukhai* and 15–20% higher than on *chala* land. In addition to the

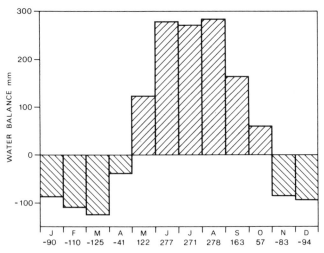

Fig. 10.1. Water balance by month at Dhaka. Water balance is defined as the balance of precipitation and potential evapotranspiration. Panimara is located about 30 km northwest of the Dhaka meteorological station. (Source: Manalo, 1978.)

three main land types there is also a small amount of high and very permeable land known as *tek*. Homesteads are sited on the higher land.

The distribution of land ownership and land operation in Panimara is, in common with the rest of Bangladesh, an unequal one, but the situation in the village differs from the national picture in two important respects. First, the average amount of land owned per household in the village, as in the rest of the 'minifundist' belt of Dhaka, Comilla and parts of neighbouring districts, is smaller than the national average (0.44 ha compared with 0.66 ha); and secondly, the proportion of land sharecropped (39% compared with 24%) is higher. The sharecropping system serves to make the pattern of land operation more equal than the pattern of land ownership, small farmers renting in about 70% of the land they cultivate. Farms are fragmented and comprise, on average, six separate plots.

The village of Panimara was opened up in the late nineteenth century when farmers from nearby low-lying and more densely populated areas were offered *raiyati* ('cultivators') rights by the Zamindars (revenue collectors-cum-landlords) in exchange for clearing the *sal* (*Shorea robusta*) forest. Since then there has been a continuing process of agricultural intensification culminating with the recent introduction of an irrigated HYV *boro* crop in the dry season (Table 10.1).

For the first decades after forest clearance began few cultivators actually lived in the village, most preferring to live in temporary huts (*bathan*) while cultivating the *aman* crop on the good *baid* lands and returning to their lowland villages after the harvest. Around 1920 the first cadastral survey recorded 82.1% of the total cultivated area under *aman* and a cropping intensity of only 105.8%. Slowly over the next 20–30 years poor peasants moved into the area and started sharecropping the land of the lowland *raiyats*. They began also to cultivate an additional broadcast paddy crop (*aus*) during the early *kharif* season. In the 1940s Naizershail, a better yielding, sharply photoperiod-sensitive 'locally improved' *aman* variety, was released by the colonial authorities. It proved particularly popular because it can be transplanted late in August or early September without significantly affecting the yield. Thus in years when the 'fixed period' *aus* crop is late because of the timing of the pre-monsoon rains needed for field preparation a good *aman* harvest can still be obtained. It became widely cultivated in the village in the 1950s and 1960s, and continues to be important today. Between 1900 and the early 1970s, when some farmers started to transplant the *aus* crop, paddy production probably increased by about 80%.

A Green Revolution in the 1970s?

During the 1970s there were marked increases in production following the introduction of deep tubewell irrigation and HYVs. Four deep tubewells of

Table 10.1. *Stages in the intensification of agriculture in Panimara, 1900–1980*

	Main cropping patterns			
Period	*Rabi* (*boro*)	Early *kharif* (*aus*)	Late *kharif* (*aman*)	Total yield[a] (mds/ac)
1900–1920s	Fallow	Fallow	LV[b] (transplanted)	20–22
1920s–1940s	Fallow	LV (broadcast)	LV (transplanted)	32–35
1950s–early 1970s	Fallow	LV (broadcast)	LV/LIV (transplanted)	35–40
Early 1970s–1980				
non-irrigated	Fallow	LV (broadcast/ transplanted)	LV/LIV[c] (transplanted)	40–45
irrigated	HYV (transplanted)	Fallow	LIV (transplanted)	65–70

Notes:
a. To convert maunds (mds) per acre to kg/ha multiply by 1.12. The yields given are for one acre of land cultivated with the dominant cropping pattern.
b. LV = local variety; LIV = locally improved variety; HYV = high yielding variety.
c. The proportion of LIV *aman* cultivated increased significantly in the 1970s.

55 litres/sec capacity were sunk, and by 1980 78% of the total cropped area was irrigated in the dry season. Production on the irrigated land probably increased by about 80% but the impact of the HYV package on the non-irrigated land and in other seasons was less pronounced. Overall production in the village in the 1970s probably increased by some 40 to 50%. Although such increases are certainly significant they should be seen as part of a continuing trend in agricultural intensification. The experience in Panimara supports B.H. Farmer's comment that

Contrary to a popular misapprehension, rice-growing in South Asia was not sunk in the primitive cultivation of low-yielding indigenous varieties until, suddenly, new high-yielding varieties (HYVs) became available . . . HYVs . . . are no revolutionary phenomenon. (Farmer, 1977, p. 13)

In Panimara, the introduction of irrigated HYV cultivation was not the only change that took place in the 1970s, and the present situation is by no means static. A number of changes have taken place over the past five to seven years and the dynamism of the last thirty years is continuing. These changes include the following:

(i) The replacement of IR-8 by BR-3 as the main irrigated HYV *boro* variety grown.

IR-8 while high yielding is coarse grained and susceptible to pests. BR-3 developed at the Bangladesh Rice Research Institute is equally high yielding but more pest-resistant. It is likely that recently released finer-grained HYVs suitable for the *boro* season such as BR-8 and BR-9 will become popular in the future as will other varieties being developed at BRRI. The new varieties should enable farmers to better match the HYVs they grow to the particular microecology of their farms.

(ii) The introduction of Padjam, a locally-improved variety (LIV), suitable as an *aman* crop. Generally higher-yielding than Naizershail, the finer-grained Padjam was initially confined to the *baid* land because farmers considered it less drought-resistant than Naizershail. In the last few years, however, Padjam has begun to supplant Naizershail and now covers about two-thirds of the LIV *aman* area.

(iii) The cultivation of rainfed HYVs on non-irrigated land in the *aus* season and in the *aman*, occasionally with supplementary irrigation. China (or Purbachi), a short duration variety, is the most widely grown HYV *aus* variety and BR-3 and BR-4 the most common HYV *aman* varieties. Although high-yielding varieties are only grown on 27% of the *aus* and 13% of the *aman* area compared with 99% for *boro*, both HYV *aman* and HYV *aus* acreages are increasing rapidly. They are likely to continue to do so with the introduction of new varieties such as BR-10 and BR-11 that can be transplanted later without significantly affecting yields.

The present cropping patterns on owner-cultivated land are shown in simplified form in Table 10.2. Triple cropping of paddy, though possible if two short duration HYVs are grown in the *boro* and *aus*, is only practised on about 2.5% of the net cropped area, farmers reporting lower overall yields possibly due to zinc or sulphur deficiency. Most of the remaining land is double cropped, the overall cropping intensity being 175.7. HYVs are grown on about 42% of the net cropped area, LIVs on 33% and LVs on 25%.

Costs and returns of alternative cropping patterns

The net returns to farmers from the irrigated cropping patterns made possible following the introduction of deep tubewells are considerably higher than those achieved under rainfed conditions (Table 10.3). The net returns from the most common irrigated cropping pattern (LIV *aman* – HYV *boro*) compared to the most common non-irrigated pattern (LV *aus* – LIV *aman*) are 58% higher on a 'full cost' and 49% higher on a 'cash cost' basis. While it is recognised that peasant farmers do not act purely on the basis of the relative profitability of alternative cropping patterns (Epstein, 1962; Rahman, 1979), other things being equal it is clear that such large differentials do offer an incentive to farmers to adopt irrigated HYV cultivation if they can afford the higher cash outlays. The irrigated cropping patterns are, moreover, more labour-intensive, requiring 68% more man-hours per hectare than the non-irrigated patterns.

Table 10.2. *Cropping patterns on owner-cultivated land in Panimara, 1980*

Rabi (*boro*) Dec/Jan–Apr/May	Early *kharif* (*aus*) Apr/May–Jul/Aug	Late *kharif* (*aman*) Jun/Sep–Nov/Dec	% Net cropped area[1]
HYV	Fallow	LIV	46.7
HYV	Fallow	Fallow	19.1
HYV	Fallow	LV/HYV	12.1
Fallow	LV/HYV	LIV	8.7
Fallow	Fallow	LV/LIV/HYV	5.6
Fallow	LV/HYV	LV/HYV	3.2
Triple cropped paddy, various LV/LIV/HYV combinations			
Fallow	LV/HYV	Fallow	1.6
LV	Fallow	LV/Fallow	0.5
			100.0

Total cropped area (A)	96.82 ha	
Net cropped area (B)	55.12 ha	
Cropping intensity (A/B)	175.7	

Note: 1. It is not possible to show the cropping pattern on tenanted land in the same way because land is often rented or sharecropped for one season only and tenants do not always know the land use in other seasons. The small amount of *tek* land cultivated with non-paddy crops has been omitted.

The adoption of HYVs

Early in the 1970s a number of analyses of the impact of the Green Revolution in different countries concluded that the benefits of the new technology were being monopolised by rich and middle farmers to the relative exclusion of small cultivators (e.g. Byres, 1972; Griffin, 1974). Although the new technology is 'scale-neutral' and in theory therefore capable of being cultivated equally productively by different classes of farmers, Byres, for example, argued that

The increase in working capital requirements brought about by the new seed-fertiliser-water-pesticide package is great and the new possibilities are, therefore, confined to those cultivators with large personal resources and/or access to credit on reasonable terms. Small peasants and sharecroppers . . . are thereby excluded, because of their lack of resources and lack of acceptable collateral. (Byres, 1972, p. 104)

Since that time there has been considerable debate as to whether small farmers are poorer adopters of HYVs than bigger farmers and, if so, whether this can be explained in terms of their relative lack of resources and their poor access to credit and other input markets.

In Bangladesh two important studies both concluded, based on data col-

Table 10.3. *Net returns of irrigated and non-irrigated cropping patterns, Panimara, 1980*

	Net returns (Taka/ha)		
	Irrigated[1]	Non-irrigated[2]	Increase with irrigation (%)
'Cash cost'[3] basis	13,434	8,986	+49.5
'Full cost'[4] basis	8,032	5,100	+57.5

Notes:
1. HYV *boro*–LIV *aman*
2. LV *aus*–LIV *aman*
3. Family labour and own cattle zero priced
4. Family labour and own cattle priced at market rates

lected in the mid-1970s, that bigger farmers adopted the new technology more frequently than smaller ones and that the proportion of their land under HYVs was greater (Rahman, 1979; Asaduzzaman, 1980). Rahman's study used data from Mymensingh and Comilla examined the adoption of HYVs in general without differentiating between different seasons. Asaduzzaman's data was collected in Rangpur and Noakhali and examined the adoption of HYVs in the late *kharif* (*aman*) season. Both authors note, as was done above, that the new technology is both more labour and capital intensive than traditional technology and discuss the possible impact of the differential opportunity costs of labour and capital to different classes of farmers on their adoption rates. Both conclude that the better access of richer farmers to capital and input markets and the risk-aversion behaviour of poor farmers are two of the most important factors explaining differential rates of adoption of the new technology by different classes of farmers.

Adoption in Panimara

The data for Panimara has been disaggregated for different landownership groups by season and for owner-cultivated and sharecropped land. Data for 1980 is compared with earlier data collected in 1978. The results, in contrast to the findings noted above, show that small farmers are the fastest adopters and have a consistently high proportion of their cultivated area under HYVs.

In Panimara there has been a rapid adoption of HYVs. HYVs were first introduced in the early 1970s and by 1978 were grown on 25.7% of the operated area. Between 1978 and 1980 the area covered expanded to 41.5% compared to 21% nationally (Government of Bangladesh, 1981). HYVs have made the greatest impact in the dry season (Fig. 10.2). They account for over 99% of the *boro* acreage but are also grown on 27.3% of the *aus* cultivated area (*aus* being the alternative to *boro* on non-irrigated land) and 12.7% of the *aman* land. The main reason for the low rate of HYV adoption in the late *kharif* (*aman*) is the widespread cultivation of locally-improved varieties (LIVs) such as Naizershail and Padjam which are grown on 73.4% of the area. As yet HYVs have not been introduced to compete with these varieties. The proportion of households adopting HYVs on at least part of their land increased from 85% to 95% between 1978 and 1980.

The pattern of HYV adoption on owner-cultivated land by different size classes of farmers followed in 1980 a roughly 'U-shaped' distribution, with the smallest farmers (group I) having the largest proportion of such land under HYVs followed by larger (groups IV and V) farmers and with groups II and III farmers having the smallest proportion of such land devoted to the new technology (Table 10.4). When the data are disaggregated by season the relationship becomes more complicated but these complications may be explained and the smallest farmers remain consistently high adopters (Fig. 10.3). In the *aman* season group I farmers are clearly the highest adopters but in *boro* and *aus* seasons they are not the group with the highest proportion of its land under HYVs. In the *boro* season this can be explained by the fact that the only farmers who own the type of low-lying, poorly drained land suitable for the cultivation of local *boro* without irrigation in the dry season come

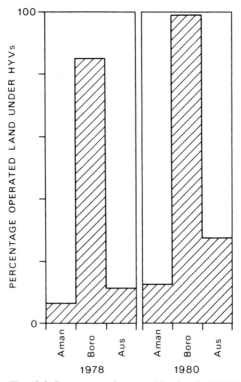

Fig. 10.2. Percentage of operated land under HYVs, Panimara 1978 and 1980.

Table 10.4. *Percentage of land under HYVs for different land ownership groups, Panimara 1978 and 1980*

Land-ownership group (ha)	Per cent under HYVs		
	Owner-cultivated land	All operated land	
	1980	1978	1980
I (0–0.39)	52.5	29.5	44.0
II (0.40–0.79)	43.1	30.3	40.4
III (0.80–1.19)	35.7	26.1	30.6
IV (1.20–1.59)	45.6	18.2	45.6
V (1.60 and above)	46.3	24.9	43.2
All groups	44.7	25.7	41.5

from this group. If this land were excluded group I and II farmers would, in common with all other groups, have 100% of their owner-cultivated land under HYVs. In respect to HYV *aus* cultivation group I farmers have a smaller proportion of their land under HYVs than group IV farmers but this can be explained by the fact that a disproportionately large amount of group IV's total land is not irrigable by the deep tubewells. Unable, therefore, to cultivate HYV *boro* farmers from this group put their resources into rainfed HYV *aus* cultivation.

If one examines the pattern of adoption on all operated land (i.e. owner-cultivated and sharecropped land), then the same 'U-shaped' distribution is apparent (Table 10.4), but whereas in 1978 the small farmers had been the greatest users of HYVs, by 1980 group IV farmers had a slightly larger proportion of their land under HYVs than the smallest (group I) farmers. The reason for this change is that the rate of adoption of HYVs on sharecropped land is lower than on owner-cultivated land – 36.7% compared with 44.7% in 1980. Because the smallest (group I) farmers are the biggest sharecroppers, the overall adoption of HYVs on their operated land fell somewhat relative to other groups. It is interesting, however, that these smallest farmers also showed the highest HYV adoption rate of any group on sharecropped land (40.7% compared to 27.9% for groups II–V). Were it not for this, the 'U-shaped' distribution would probably have disappeared.

Smaller farmers then are not lower adopters of HYVs than larger farmers. Rather it is the smallest farmers – often, perhaps inappropriately, called 'marginal' farmers – who are the highest and fastest adopters of the new technology both on owner-cultivated and sharecropped land. The 'U-shaped' relationship, however, is a dynamic one and showed some changes between 1978 and 1980. A further survey in 1982 will allow this dynamism to be examined over a four-year period (Jones, forthcoming).

Farm size and productivity

Another aspect of the argument that the preponderance of small farmers constrains agricultural development is that such farmers cultivate HYVs less productively than large farmers. In order to test this hypothesis for Panimara one could, in common with the approach adopted by many other authors, compare the yields obtained by different size classes of farmers in cultivating HYV paddy in given seasons. The problem with this approach, however, is that it ignores the fact that farmers do not try to maximise the yield of a single HYV grown in isolation, but rather try to maximise the return from the cropping *pattern* of which the crop would be a part (IRRI, 1977). The farmer's decision regarding the particular HYV to be cultivated, the date of planting and the inputs to be used all depend on production possibilities in other seasons.

In order to cultivate HYV *aman*, for example, the farmer must be able to transplant the crop by mid-August. If he does not do this the crop will not have flowered by early November at which time night temperatures are likely to be less than 21°C, the critical temperature below which the fertilisation of grain does not occur (Brammer, 1982). Photo-period sensitive local varieties may be transplanted as late as mid-September and still flower in time, but this is not the case for the 'fixed period' HYVs. To transplant HYV *aman* by mid-August, however, would mean that any preceding *aus* crop would have to be harvested by early August to allow time for field preparation. In most parts

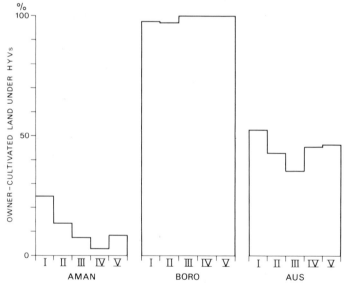

Fig. 10.3. Percentage of owner-cultivated land under HYVs by crop, Panimara 1980. (Land-ownership groups I–V are defined in Table 10.4.)

of Bangladesh this would preclude the possibility of cultivating a preceding HYV *aus* crop under rainfed conditions unless the variety grown is a lower-yielding, short-duration one such as Purbachi. Higher yielding HYVs such as BR-3 and IR-8 could not be grown. Moreover, if the farmer were to try to maximise the HYV *aman* yield by transplanting even earlier he would have to forgo the HYV *aus* crop all together and plant a lower yielding local variety. Maximising the yield of any one crop then may have a significant opportunity cost in that it constrains the farmer to make less than optimal decisions regarding the cropping pattern as a whole.

Because of this problem, in the following analysis, the annual value of production per hectare, a measure of the productivity of the farmers' entire cropping pattern, is used to compare the productivity of different size groups of farmers. The value of production is a better index than total production expressed in weight since it reflects the price differential which exists between the high-yielding but lower priced HYVs and the lower-yielding, finer-grained and generally higher priced local varieties.

Fig. 10.4 shows that on irrigated land on which HYV *boro* is grown in the dry season the hypothesised positive relationship between farm size and productivity is not found. Rather, a 'U-shaped' pattern similar to that noted above for the adoption of HYVs exists. Small farmers (groups I and II) are the most productive followed by large farmers (group V). Medium farmers (groups III and IV) are the least productive. On non-irrigated land, only

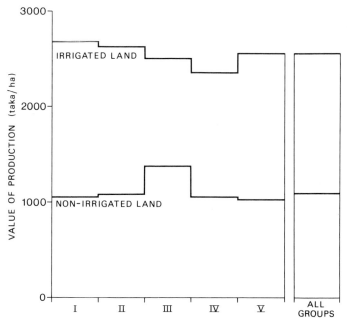

Fig. 10.4. Value of production on irrigated and non-irrigated land by farm size, Panimara 1980. (Land-ownership groups I–V are defined in Table 10.4.)

about 25% of the total cropped area of which is cultivated with HYVs (compared to 63% on irrigated land), there is a 'bell-shaped' distribution with small, larger medium and large farmers all showing low productivity per hectare and group III farmers being the most productive.

Contrary to much theoretical debate (see, e.g., Bhadwaraj, 1974; Sen, 1981) the Panimara data indicates that small farmers are not significantly more productive than large farmers when cultivating 'traditional', less intensive cropping patterns, but they are when practising irrigated HYV-based cropping patterns. Related to this, as might be expected, the smallest farmers use the highest amount of fertiliser per hectare though even they only use 40–60% of recommended levels and, in common with other farmers, use a disproportionate amount of urea relative to potash and phosphate. Similarly the smallest (group I) farmers take about 30% more credit per operated hectare than the average, mostly as interest-free loans from friends and relatives. Contrary to much theorising, then, small farmers do not appear to face severe enough resource constraints to seriously hamper their cultivation of HYVs.

The evidence from the Panimara case study then indicates that the preponderance of small farms in that area has led to a higher and faster rate of adoption of HYVs and higher overall land productivity under modern cropping patterns. The reasons underlying this will be elaborated elsewhere (Jones, forthcoming). Broadly similar findings have been found in two other relevant studies (CSS, 1980; BUP, 1982) in Barisal and Comilla districts.

Sharecropping and productivity

The other aspect of the agrarian structure commonly held to constrain agricultural development is the sharecropping system. In Panimara, as in Bangladesh in general, most sharecroppers also own some land, there being few pure sharecroppers. As noted earlier about 39% of cultivated land in Panimara is sharecropped compared to about one quarter nationally. About half of sharecropping contracts are on an annual basis and the remainder seasonal. Sharecropped land accounts for about 33% of land cultivated in the *aman* season, 34% of *boro* and 16% of *aus*. Over two-thirds of sharecropped land is cultivated in small parcels by farmers owning less than 0.4 ha of land. Most of the landlords are big farmers owning more than 1.6 ha of land and resident in nearby villages.

The main reasons for the widespread prevalence of sharecropping in Panimara, as in Bangladesh as a whole, are both economic and social (Hossain, 1981). For the landowner, the system is a way of having the land over and above that which he can farm himself with family labour and cattle cultivated in a way that is often cheaper than hiring and supervising additional labour. This is especially so if the opportunity cost of his time is taken into account. For the tenant, sharecropping similarly provides a way of

Table 10.5. *Cost-sharing and output-sharing practices in Panimara, 1980*

Crop	Proportion of costs borne by landlord (L) or sharecropper (S)		Proportion of output received by landlord (L) or sharecropper (S)		
	Irrigation	Fertiliser/ Pesticide	Harvest	Straw	Paddy
Boro	10L:90S[1]	100S	50L:50S	Seed[2] provider	50L:50S
Aus	Not needed[3]	100S	100S	100S	50L:50S
Aman	Not needed	100S	50L:50S	Seed provider	50L:50S

Notes:
1. 10L:90S means 10% paid by landlord, 90% by sharecropper
2. Tenant generally provides seed
3. If needed landlord normally pays one third cost

matching the land he cultivates to family labour and cattle numbers, and while the return to his family's labour may be less than could be gained working as a labourer, traditional social values regard sharecropping as less degrading. The system is also a way of overcoming the problem of fragmented and scattered landholdings resulting from the Muslim system of inheritance that splits a farm on the death of the owner equally between all sons with a half-share for daughters.

The impact of sharecropping on productivity depends on the terms and conditions of the sharecropping contract. Since in Panimara as elsewhere in Bangladesh landlords rarely stipulate what crops should be grown or what inputs used, the two main aspects of sharecropping contracts that could, in theory, affect resource allocation and productivity are (i) output and cost sharing practices, and (ii) the security of tenure enjoyed by tenants.

Output and cost-sharing practices in Panimara are shown in Table 10.5. In contrast to many other parts of the country, the terms of sharecropping contracts here differ little for HYVs compared with those for local and locally-improved varieties. In both the Barisal and Comilla studies mentioned above it was found normal for the output to be shared three ways: one third for the landowner, one third for the sharecropper, and one third for whichever of them provides the cost of irrigation, fertiliser and pesticide. In Panimara, however, the tenant bears all the costs except pump rent (about 10% of the total cost) when cultivating HYV *boro*, but splits the output 50:50 with the landowner. This results in much lower net returns and returns to labour for the sharecropper, as Table 10.6 shows, and a possible lower incentive for tenants to maximise production.

The other important aspect of sharecropping contracts that affects pro-

Table 10.6. *Net returns under different sharecropping contracts, 1980 full cost basis*

Sharecropping system	Net returns (Taka/ha)	
	Tenant	Landlord
Panimara system	− 337[1]	+ 4352
⅓ : ⅓ : ⅓ : system	+ 1048	+ 2967

Note: 1. Negative returns to tenant possible since on 'full cost' basis tenants' labour and bullock power valued at market prices.

ductivity and resource allocation is security of tenure. In Bangladesh in contrast to neighbouring West Bengal in India, there is no statutory protection for sharecroppers and almost all contracts are oral. In Panimara nearly 40% of such contracts are not renewed beyond one year. The risk of eviction then is high, and this risk is thought by some to give the sharecropper little incentive to invest in the long-term productivity of the land.

Studies that have been carried out of the impact of sharecropping on land productivity have come to confused and often contradictory conclusions. Some early studies (e.g. Raiquibuzzaman, 1973) found pure sharecroppers and owner-sharecroppers to be less productive than owner-cultivators while more recent work (e.g. Hossain, 1977) has found the productivity of sharecropped land to be higher than that of owner-cultivated land but argued that this was a reflection of the 'size effect', sharecroppers generally being small landowners who were more productive than bigger cultivators.

The problem with many of the studies that have been carried out is, as Hossain notes, that

the hypothesis that the sharecropping system induces some loss in production cannot be tested by comparing the performance between owner and tenant cultivators because . . . the latter are mostly part tenants who have both owned and rented land in the cultivated holding. Also . . . the resource position of owner cultivators and sharecroppers (are) different, and so the effect of this variable needs to be controlled for in estimating the effect of share tenancy. (Hossain, 1981, p. 66)

One way round this problem would be to compare the yields obtained by the same cultivator on his owner-cultivated and sharecropped land. This was attempted by Chaudhury (1981) and Hossain (1977) for villages in Mymensingh and Dinajpur districts. They found that the productivity on sharecropped land was 3–13% lower than on owner-cultivated land. However, while valuable, these studies do not make it clear whether land quality was also controlled. This is important because, *a priori*, it might be considered likely that sharecropped land would be of poorer quality than that retained

Table 10.7. *Comparison of average yields of same cultivators on own and sharecropped land, Panimara 1980*

Crop	Average yield (mds/ha)		Sharecropped yield as % own land yield
	Own land	Sharecropped land	
LIV *aman*	70.0	59.9	85.6
HYV *boro*	115.0	88.4	76.9

for self-cultivation and that this could account for the differences in yield found. The results obtained by comparing yields obtained by the same cultivator for the same crop on the same land type for owner-cultivated and sharecropped land in Panimara is shown in Table 10.7. On sharecropped land for LIV *aman* average yields are about 14% lower and for HYV *boro* about 23% less than on owned land.

The Panimara data then corroborates the findings mentioned above and indicates that the sharecropping system is a serious impediment to agricultural development in that both a smaller proportion of sharecropped land is cultivated with HYVs (see earlier) and that yields on sharecropped land are significantly lower than on owner-cultivated land.

Conclusion

This chapter has presented evidence from a village study in Dhaka district that indicates that while the predominance of small farms in rural Bangladesh is not a constraint to agricultural development, the sharecropping system is. One should obviously be cautious in generalising from a single village study, but other recent studies in Barisal (Centre for Social Studies, 1980) and Comilla (BUP, 1982) corroborate some of its findings.[2]

The policy implications of the study are that an effective tenancy reform including possibly the stipulation of cost and output sharing, and measures to give security of tenure, would lead to significant increases in productivity and to a more rapid diffusion of HYVs. However, although small farmers have managed to obtain the resources necessary to cultivate HYVs and to do so more productively than big farmers, there is little room for complacency. The deep tubewells in the village irrigate only 16–17 ha which is about 60% of potential and fertiliser use, while higher on small farms, is unbalanced and well below recommended levels. There is clearly a need for an improved extension effort and improved input delivery, especially of institutional credit, to enable all size classes of farmers to realise the full potential of HYV cultivation.

ACKNOWLEDGEMENTS

The author is grateful to B.H. Farmer for his patience and forbearance, and to A.K.M. Alamgir Chowdhury for his excellent field assistance.

NOTES

1. Strictly speaking the words *aus*, *aman* and *boro* refer to paddy crops, not to the seasons in which the crops are grown, i.e. the 'early kharif', 'late kharif' and 'rabi' seasons respectively. However, in common parlance, it is usual to refer to them as if they are seasons. A further complication is that the same paddy variety may often be grown in different seasons. *Aus* paddy is planted before the monsoon and harvested during the monsoon. *Aman* paddy is planted during the monsoon (except for deep-water varieties which are sown earlier) and harvested in the dry season after the monsoon. *Boro* paddy is planted and harvested in the dry season.
2. The findings of the paper on size variations and productivity are corroborated. A different methodology was followed in the Barisal and Comilla studies to assess the impact of sharecropping and the results are not comparable.

REFERENCES

Asaduzzaman, M. (1979). Adoption of HYV rice in Bangladesh. *Bangladesh Development Studies*, 7 (3), 23–52

(1980). An analysis of the adoption of HYV paddy in Bangladesh. Unpublished D.Phil. dissertation, University of Sussex

Bharadwaj, K. (1974). *Production Conditions in Indian Agriculture: a Study based on farm management surveys*. University of Cambridge, Department of Applied Economics/Cambridge University Press

Brammer, H. (1982). Characterisation of soils for non-irrigated rice cultivation in Bangladesh. Dhaka (mimeo)

BUP (1982). *Chandpur Irrigation Project: a Socioeconomic Evaluation*. Bangladesh Unnayan Parishad/World Bank

Byres, T.J. (1972). The dialectics of India's Green Revolution. *South Asian Review*, 5 (2)

Chaudhury, R.H. (1981). *Farm Size, tenurial relationship and productivity*. Bangladesh Institute of Development Studies, Dhaka (mimeo)

CSS (1980). *Barisal Area III Project – Report on Socioeconomic Survey*. Centre for Social Studies, Dhaka University/United Nations Development Programme

Epstein, T.S. (1962). *Economic development and social change in South India*. Manchester University Press

Farmer, B.H. (ed.) (1977). *Green Revolution?* Macmillan, London

Govt. of Bangladesh (1980). *The Second Five Year Plan, 1980–85*. Planning Commission, Dhaka

(1981). *Bangladesh Economic Survey 1980–81*. Ministry of Finance, Dhaka

Griffin, K. (1974). *The Political Economy of Agrarian Change*. Macmillan, London

Hossain, M. (1977). Agrarian structure and land productivity in Bangladesh – an analysis of farm level data. Unpublished Ph.D. dissertation, University of Cambridge

(1981). *Land Tenure and Agricultural Development in Bangladesh*. Institute of Developing Economies, Tokyo

Hossain, M. & Jones, S. (1983). Production, poverty and the co-operative ideal: contradictions in Bangladesh Rural Development Policy. In D.A.M. Lea & D.P. Chadhuri (eds.), *Rural Development and the State: Contradictions and Dilemmas in Developing Countries*. Methuen, London

IRRI (1977). *Cropping Systems Research and Development for the Asian Rice Farmer*. International Rice Research Institute, Manila

Islam, N. (1978). *Development Strategy of Bangladesh*. Pergamon, Oxford

Jones, S. (1979). A critical evaluation of Bangladesh Rural Development Policy. *Journal of Social Studies* (Dhaka), no. 6, 51–92

(forthcoming). *Agricultural Development and Agrarian Change in Bangladesh – a study of two villages in Dhaka District*. Ph.D. thesis, Cambridge University

Manalo, E.B. (1978). *Agro-Climatic Survey of Bangladesh*. BRRI/IRRI, Dacca

Rahman, A. (1979). Agrarian structure and capital formation: a study of Bangladesh agriculture with farm level data. Unpublished Ph.D. thesis, University of Cambridge

(1981). Adoption of new technology in Bangladesh agriculture: testing some hypotheses. In Wahiuddin Mahmud (ed.), *Develoment Issues in an Agrarian Economy – Bangladesh*, Centre for Administrative Studies, Dhaka University, pp. 55–75

Raquibuzzaman, M. (1973).Sharecropping and economic efficiency in Bangladesh. *The Bangladesh Economic Review*, 1 (2)

Sen, A. (1981). Market failure and control of labour power: towards an explanation of 'structure' and change in Indian agriculture. *Cambridge Journal of Economics*, 5, 201–28 and 327–50

Stepanek, J.F. (1979). *Bangladesh – Equitable Growth?* Pergamon Press, New York

World Bank (1972). *Bangladesh: Land and Water Sector Study* (7 vols), Washington DC

(1979). *Bangladesh – Current Trends and Development Issues*. South Asia Regional Office, The World Bank, Washington DC

11 A structural analysis of two farms in Bangladesh

GRAHAM P. CHAPMAN

This chapter examines the structure of two farms in Bangladesh, and the structure of knowledge associated with those farms, a structure which varies according to the perspective of the viewer. To do this, it uses a methodology which is as yet not well known – hence much of this chapter must be given to the technicalities of the methodology. Some readers might prefer less on the methodology and more on the case study, but I ask them to be patient, since some of the descriptive statements can only be understood if the methodology itself is grasped. But let it be stated emphatically that the motivation for developing new methodology comes from the desire to understand the world better, and in this case the great need to understand better the farmers and farms of Bangladesh, so that improvements can be introduced faster and less destructively.

The study in context

Within the field of agricultural studies this chapter falls within the focus of several themes. Firstly, although there is much talk of bottom-up development, most development is top-down, inevitably so, if one remembers that those that enounce bottom-up are in fact at the top. The methods of western science have been applied in the research stations of the developing countries, and the results transmitted down or out to the farmers. A bottom-up approach would have to begin with seeing how the farmers themselves see things, and by hearing their needs and priorities. Which citizens' advice bureau in the West begins by telling its prospective customers what their problems are?

A second focus, apparently unrelated to the first, but in fact part of its cause, is the damaging effect of the fragmentary and partitional knowledge which 'western' science has produced, and the subsequent fragmentation and partitioning of knowledge institutions. (The first question asked by one expert of another is 'What is your area of specialization?') Each specialist sees the farmers' problems from his particular expert viewpoint. Yet life for most Bangladeshi farmers is close to what it always has been, a well integrated whole, approaching sometimes a society-land gestalt. The needs of the farmers may be at a higher dimensional level than the expert observes. For example, high-yielding rice varieties demand the use of inputs purchased in the market, and also cut down the fodder produced (also reducing its storage quality) thus requiring the farmer both to sell output on the market and to buy extra fodder and inputs. One of the two farmers reported on in this study now uses HYV, now buys fodder for his cows, now has some increased pest problems on his non-HYV crops, and now purchases inputs. He sells vegetables and pulses to pay for his inputs, since his family consumes all the rice. His diet, a multi-dimensional concept involving proteins, carbohydrates, and vitamins, has probably changed. His original need had been identified in scientific terms as 'producing more grain per unit land area' – a singular unholistic aim, with subordinate consequences – seeking credit, buying fertilizers, having pests, using pesticides, changing diet, and buying fodder. It is similar to the subordination of labour to the production processes of large factories.

Research in Bangladesh is now beginning to shift away from the pursuit of singular products from singular crops, and is beginning to look at 'cropping systems' much more. This study is hopefully helping in this aim.

On hierarchies

The following examination of notions of hierarchy stems from the ideas of Q-analysis (see seminal works by Atkin, 1974 and 1977, and an introduction by Chapman, 1982) and draws considerably on the work of Johnson (1978; Johnson & Wanmali, 1981).

The notion of hierarchy commonly involves some idea of levels, some levels being higher than others, and also an idea of inclusion or subordination. In a hierarchy of social class, the superior is identified (e.g. 'upper class') and the subordination of the inferior ('lower class') commonly referenced – but in this case there is no notion of inclusion. The latter happens when, in the hierarchy of plants, for example, we recognize a mango tree as within the class of fruit trees, which is a class within the class 'trees'.

For reasons which are difficult to state briefly, there has in the West also been an assumption within formal intellectual debate that hierarchies should be partitional. This means that something at a lower level belongs to one and only one class at a higher level. Thus we would not allow, through dubious claims to scientific logic, the schema below for 'serious' study.

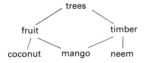

It represents an *intersecting* (coverset) *hierarchy*, and to the Bangladeshi not only is such a hierarchy 'true', it is the very essence of life – multiple categories and multiple uses of things. Before explaining how to make scientific sense out of these confusing situations, we need to look at hierarchies from basic principles. There are two approaches we need to consider – (i) aggregation, and (ii) combination (or arrangement).

(i) Aggregation

This, the usual approach, simply involves collecting elements into sets, and joining these sets into bigger sets. Suppose we have a set of trees G = {a, b, c, d, e, f}, being respectively mango, coconut, neem, bamboo,[1] banana, jackfruit. We can group these into fruit trees (*foler gas*) = FG, and non-fruit trees (*foler gas na*) = FGN. We can produce a *hierarchy by aggregation* as follows:

set of all trees = G =

types of trees

individual tree species

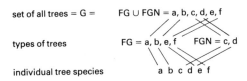

The only operation involved is set union, the addition or merging of sets. Therefore if a εFG and FG ⊂ G then a εG – e.g. a banana tree is a fruit tree, and a fruit tree is a tree, so therefore a banana tree is a tree. 'Normal' classifications are mostly like this, and are also partitional. They are used for classing individuals. The classifications are known as aggregations because only set union is involved.

A priori there appears to be no particular reason why we should not use these simple methods to make non-partitional hierarchies. Thus if K is the set of timber (*kat*) trees, and FGKN is the set of trees that is neither timber nor fruit trees, we could have:

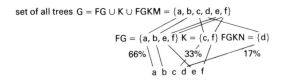

In the case of this *coverset hierarchy* how do we know what the levels are? We cannot find one 'superior' class which 'includes' lower classes as individuals. Johnson proposes a nested base rule, in which one set is below another if it is a proper subset of the other. According to this rule {a, b, e, f} is below {a, b, c, d, e, f} but {c, f} is not below {a, b, e, f} since it is not a subset of the latter. Partitionalists do not like this approach, because (i) at some points some sets overlap each other, so that the isolation of some problem or quality for study is impossible; (ii) at any one level numbers, for example the percentages of individuals in the classes of trees in the above example, do not add

Agrarian change at village level

up to a predetermined total; (iii) the problem of resolving levels is exceedingly tedious and gives rise to 'untidy' situations.

(ii) Orthogonal hierarchies

If two or more hierarchies do not intersect, they are called orthogonal. If an individual or set of individuals can be classed in all these hierarchies, then the hierarchies can be joined in a manner analogous to and sometimes directly equivalent to forming a cross-classified contingency table. Consider crop varieties a, b, c, d, e, f, g, h, and these three *orthogonal hierarchies*:

The contingency table will have dimensions $3 \times 3 \times 2$. Here we draw the 3×3 table, and indicate the third dimension by saying that 'e' is wheat and all others rice.

	Aus	Aman	Rabi
HYV	a	bc	e
LIV		g	
L	df	h	

Initially the discussion will be limited to the 3×3 table. We can derive a *two-level hierarchy* on one axis as follows:

and on the other axis as follows:

If we include the third dimension, the rice/wheat distinction, we can have any of six different arrangements of *three-level hierarchies*, two of which are:

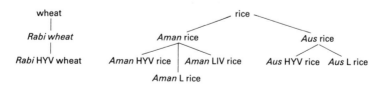

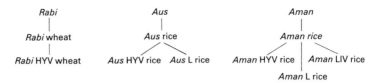

If there is any 'problem' it appears to be that we can use the major orthogonal axes to divide each other at arbitrary levels – e.g. divide plant type by season, or season by plant type.

These 'problems' are self-inflicted. The 'fact' that there are these different hierarchies *is an illusion* brought about by the unspoken assumption that the hierarchies must be partitional – as indeed the above ones are. All six of the 'possible' hierarchies, two of which are shown above, are in fact partitional subsets of the single coverset (i.e. intersecting) hierarchy which rises simultaneously on all three axes. This *simultaneous hierarchy* looks like this:

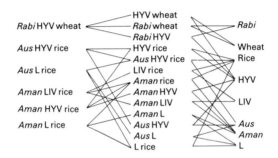

The major observation we can make as a result of this discovery is that partitioning is a highly selective filtering of the overall coverset classification system, which produces paltry subsets. If one uses such subsets one is always plagued by the nagging doubt that one should have done it the other way round – and indeed the first question at any seminar often is, 'Why did you not do it the other way round?'

In working with the farmers in Bangladesh I could not make any sense of their classification schemes until I adopted a 'simultaneous multiple' approach, since they would intuitively use any part of the overall coverset relevant to any discussion.

(iii) Hierarchies by combination

Combination methods require that we do not simply aggregate individuals qua individuals into sets, and then simply make unions of these sets, but that we make hierarchies by treating sets of things as wholes. To understand the distinctions involved it is necessary to introduce Bertrand Russell's famous Barber's Paradox, given here a colloquial setting:

In Ishurdi town, Pabna District, there is a man who is the barber, who shaves all those men and only those men who do not shave themselves. Does the barber shave himself?

If he does shave himself he is not shaved by the barber, since the barber shaves those men and only those men who do not shave themselves. But that can't be right, because he is the barber. On the other hand, if he does shave himself, he cannot be shaved by the barber, who shaves all those men and only those men who do not shave themselves. The resolution of this paradox lies in the fact that we are using two distinct meanings of the word 'barber'. The barber as an element, a man, is one meaning. The other is the barber as a set, a set of men defined by the shaving relation – i.e. the barber is the set of all those men who shave other men. Even if there is only one man in Ishurdi who shaves other men, say Md. Karim, the meaning of the barber as Md. Karim, an element, is a man, is different from the meaning of the barber as the set of those who shave others, which is B = {Md. Karim}. Suppose you have a friend Md. Riszvi who sits an examination with many other people. Suppose the set of all successful candidates is S = {Md. Riszvi}, it is quite clear that the concept of successful candidates and your friend Md. Riszvi are not the same.

Now of course there are many barbers in Ishurdi, as in any Bangladeshi town. But let us pretend there is only one. Does the barber, an element, a man, shave himself? The paradoxical answers given above can be resolved as follows. If he (first meaning, a man, an element) does, then he is not shaved by the barber (second meaning, the set of all men who shave those who do not shave themselves). So we find we are confusing two logically distinct meanings within one sentence, because both meanings are conveyed by one word. The solution is to restrict ourselves to one meaning when asking the question, say that of the element, and then simply to find out whether or not the barber does shave himself – it is a simple matter of data.

It is interesting to note, but not altogether surprising to discover, that in English the distinction is implicitly recognized in the sentence, 'I am going to the barber's shop today.' The noun is in the singular (genitive), implying an element, but the meaning is 'I will go to that barber's shop of all the barbers' shops, to which I normally go', or 'I will go to any barber's shop'. The singular and plural meanings are quite evident.

The consequences of the distinction between {b} and b are profound and far-reaching. Sets are distinct from elements, and sets of sets are distinct from sets, and so on up the hierarchy. At the bottom we have elements, say a, b, c, d, e, f. At the next level one can have any sets that one needs or finds useful, including non-partitional (i.e. intersecting) ones, providing that they are all members of the power set of the elements – that is the set of all possible subsets of the original set. If there are n original elements, then there are 2^n

members of the power set, any or which can be at the next hierarchical level above the elements. In this case we have 2^7 possible numbers = 128, such as {a, f, g} or {e, f, g} – all of them distinct. To go to the next level we need the power set of all of these sets. An example might make this clear.

Suppose a = *bhat* (cooked rice), b = *roti* (unleavened wheat bread), c = *moshor* (lentil), d = *mach* (fish), e = *narikel* (coconut), f = *roshun* (garlic), g = *moritch* (pepper). Let us now examine a *power set hierarchy* of these foods:

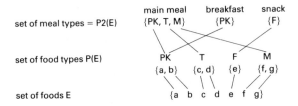

PK stands for *Prodhan Khaddyo* or staple food, T for *Trokari* which can best be translated as 'meats and vegetables', F is *fol* or fruit and M *mossla* or spices. Now, this time, note that a∈PK means that rice is an element of the staple foods and PK∈{PK, T, M} is an element of main meal, but this does not mean that rice is a main meal. That this is reasonable is obvious, and it stems from the fact that a main meal is a concept referring to the whole set {PK, T, M}. As we have defined it, PK is both rice and wheat – which then immediately opens up another series of questions about whether we define main meals in abstract terms, or in terms of the set of all acceptable meals (i.e. those which include rice or wheat but not necessarily both). I have used the latter approach in this second power set hierarchy, where for the sake of space I leave out *mossla* and *fol* (spice and fruit):

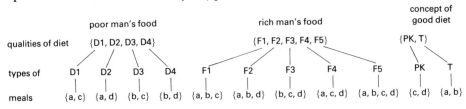

In this I have made the implicit definition that for a meal to be acceptable all the D and all the F satisfy both the conditions

$$D \cap PK \neq \emptyset \text{ and } D \cap T \neq \emptyset; F \cap PK \neq \emptyset \text{ and } F \cap T \neq \emptyset$$

There is a further distinction between this and the hierarchy by aggregation. In the latter, the name of a class is appropriate to a quality which can be applied individually to the elements in a class. Hence all members of the set TREES are trees. This is inseparable from the fact that we are using set unions as the only means of 'climbing' the hierarchy, the unions being defined for a property common to all elements at any 'level'. In the holistic combinatorial use of sets, since we aggregate by whole sets, the name is applied to the set in its entirety, and need not reflect any property common to all elements.

Consideration of this holistic definition of hierarchy is clearly most important. Regrettably I have not had sufficient time to include much by way of empirical example in the later parts of this chapter.

Relations between sets

A further part of the methodology is an analysis of the relations between sets. To understand this we must first define the idea of a relation, which we can do quite simply. A relation can be envisaged as a matrix of zeros and units – on one axis of the matrix are the elements of one set, and on the other axis of the matrix are the elements of the other (or sometimes the same) set. If a unit is recorded in the matrix, it means that the two elements defined by the row and column of that cell are related in a defined manner. Suppose we have six people and eight cats, we could define the owning relation iOj which means that person i owns cat j. We could define a liking relation – which need not of course be the same thing at all. One of the important points to notice is that these relations are found by observing something, and recording data. One could fill one of these matrices by imagination, but necessarily by theorizing.

Relations can of course be defined for the hierarchies of power sets which we discussed above. In this case we may have a relation iMj which means that i is a member of j.

The structure of a relation

Atkin's methodology gives a method for stating the structural characteristics of these relations. It is based on the idea that each element can be described by a polyhedron, whose vertices are the elements of the other set to which it is related.

Suppose we have four farms, Ashgar, Taher, Zia and Zaman, and that these four farms are related to eight crop types by the 'producing' relation: the eight types are rice, jute, spices, oil seed, dal, potatoes, radishes and fruit. Let us suppose the observed relation is as in Fig. 11.1.

It is easy to see that Ashgar has four things in common with Taher, and that Taher has four things in common with Zia. Because a point is represented by zero-dimensional space, a line by one-dimensional space, and a triangle by two-dimensional space, etc., we refer to such chains of connectivity as q-connectivity where q has a value 1 less than the number of vertices involved. In this case we are dealing with a chain of 3-connectivity. Notice that Zaman is 1-connected with both Zia and Ashgar, and via them with Taher. We can show these connectivities with a diagram such as Fig. 11.2. We can also carry out the analysis the other way round, and show how the crop types are connected via the farms that produce them, as in Fig. 11.3.

The significance of these multi-dimensional connectivities is that quite often change in one characteristic on one farm is not related to single characteristics elsewhere: instead we can think of cropping systems, where changes in a combination in one place induce changes in combinations elsewhere.

Note that these methods allow us to make statements about partitional and non-partitional classifications. The former lead to disconnected components. How often this is the result of the data, and how often it is forced on data by some dubious method, such as factor analysis, is of course very much open to debate.

Two farmers in Bangladesh

Let us at the outset comment on the different ways that the word 'farmer' can be used. The farmer as an element will mean a man – for example while visiting Taher's farm I may say, 'Where is the farmer?' – meaning Taher as a man. I can also conceive of the meaning of farmer as in the sentence, 'The Bangladeshi farmer is a patient fellow' – in which we do not know whether there is one farmer or there are many, but we know that he or they are that man or those men who are defined as a subset of all Bangladeshis by some-

FARM			CROPS				
Ashgar	A		C		E	F	G	H
Taher		B			E	F	G	H
Zia	A	B			E		G	H
Zaman	A			D			G	

Fig. 11.1. The relation between FARM and CROPS.

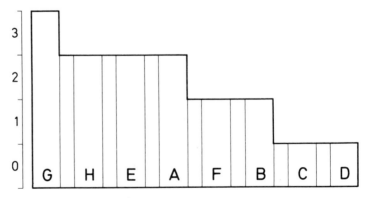

Fig. 11.2. The structure of FARMS ×CROPS.

Agrarian change at village level

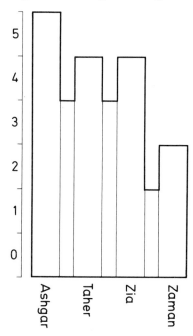

Fig. 11.3. The structure of CROPS × FARMS.

farming relation. I can also conceive of the meaning of farmer as the name of a relation. Observing a clever crop rotation I may say that Taher is a good farmer, by which I mean farmer as the name summarizing an interesting relation between sets of land and crops etc., which is a clever and useful one. These are not trivial observations. It is precisely because language is so ambiguous that we can be so creative in our thinking, but that is not the same as saying that we can tolerate the same ambiguities when attempting to use language for scientific description.

Ashgar Mia and Abul Taher are two farmers in Bangladesh,[2] whose ostensible circumstances seem similar, in that their holding sizes are not too different, their ages are not greatly dissimilar, and they live within three miles of each other in the same kind of terrain. But they have a different style of farming, and perhaps living, as a short description will make clear. My aim in this study is to describe them first in ordinary words, and then to begin to show how a description based on Atkin's methodology can force one to work much more consistently and less arbitrarily towards an understanding of major structural differences between them.

The farmers live in Pabna district, Bangladesh, not far from Ishurdi. The land is high enough not to suffer river flooding, but very small variations of a few feet in the micro-relief affect the moisture retention of the soil and the number of times it can be cropped. Additionally, some depressions may be flooded for much of the year.

Ashgar Mia lives in a house by the main road four miles east of Ishurdi. He is thirty, married with three children, none yet old enough to work on the farm. Recently he set up his own separate household – previously he had lived as part of his father's household. He, like his brothers, sharecrops some of his father's land, in his case three acres. He has built himself a house in his father's homestead area – known as the *bhithi*. He has done this by building on some of what was previously the kitchen garden – *baghan*. His father owns what little is left of the *baghan*, and all the trees, and the small pond – *khal*. Abul Taher lives three miles off the pukka road, but by *kutcha* track, up which it is possible to take a motorbike, or even a car during the dry season. He is forty years old, and has several children. The eldest boy already helps him on the farm. He has two acres which he sharecrops (although he is about to cash rent one small field) and he has a fair-sized homestead which includes a good kitchen garden, pond, and many trees. He does not keep a cow team, as Ashgar Mia does, which means that he does not have the same easy availability of draught power at ploughing time, nor the dung to spread on his fields.

Ashgar Mia uses HYV seeds, and fertilizer – although he thinks it is not as good as dung, and that it has increased the number of pest attacks. (He says it makes the plants fleshier and more attractive to pests. He also says it has had a depressing effect on the yields of ordinary varieties which might be grown without fertilizer subsequently on the same land.) Ashgar uses pesticide too, but he says this year[3] it had less effect than previously.

Taher would like to use dung – but has no cows to spread it. Sometimes he buys some and hires a team. Instead, he uses fertilizer, which he can broadcast by hand like he broadcasts seeds, but only if the crop has no pests, is well watered, and yet otherwise not doing well. He can only afford a small amount and anyway has to carry it on his head some miles.

Neither of the farmers has any concept which translates directly as 'fertility'. The nearest is Ashgar's concept of *shokti* – or power, strength. Mostly the land is referred to as *bhalo* – quite simply good – or not good. Good land is land which can be cropped more than once. The best is three-time land.

Neither farmer seems to have a concept for disease, other than those caused by a visible infestation of pests. Fungal and viral attacks which deplete the crops are classified along with storms, very much as acts of God. Interestingly, although both farmers had a concept of drought which they used to describe abnormally low rainfall in *Aus* and *Aman*, neither had a concept which applied to *Rabi*, the dry season. In the former case, drought could cause some grave loss of yield. In the latter case, yields could be good or bad, and bad could include nothing. This is part of the normal risk of the *Rabi* season.

In pursuit of my research interests I used the technique of classifying triples of words, taken from personal construct theory, to see if I could elicit coverset hierarchies of words. In this method the interviewer will give the farmer three words, for example wheat, rice and potatoes, and ask him to put any two on one side and the third on the other side, and then say how the two are similar, and why they are different from the third. A westerner would reply to these three that wheat and rice go together because they are grains, while potatoes are a root crop. A Bangladeshi might answer very differently, that rice is *Prodhan Khaddyo*, while wheat and potatoes are not, or that rice is a rainy season crop, whereas potatoes and wheat are a *Rabi* crop. The technique can be very useful in exploring someone's mental organization, but I encountered a problem here with Taher that I have encountered quite often before in Bangladesh. Quite simply, he could not take three words and group two together. To follow the previous example, the answer would always be, wheat is wheat, rice rice, and potatoes potatoes. In the UK children over the mental age of eleven should be able to manage the test quite easily. The fact that Taher cannot should not be taken to indicate a low mental age or any other kind of intellectual inferiority – his performance in naming weeds and crops varieties, simply listing them, was exceedingly good. The problem lies with a lack of education and a lack of literacy. He has never been taught to generalize, to think beyond his own horizons. The consequences for him are enormously restricting. He cannot have some new idea explained to him by appealing to high-level general concepts.

It might be tempting to think of Ashgar as the better off of the two. He lives by the road, has his own cows, has fewer children, and has more land. He also uses more modern farming methods. But it is interesting to note that the splitting of the *bhithi* among the sons has caused the loss of the kitchen garden and some of the trees. Additionally, his family and labour eat all the rice he produces, so that he cannot sell surplus HYV production to pay for the inputs he uses (this is not uncommon in this area). Instead he sells lentils and vegetables, which should be an important part of his diet. Taher has more children and no cow, but he buys and sells less, and above all has his kitchen garden and its extensive range of vegetable and tree crops.

A Structural description of Ashgar's and Taher's farms

A 'conventional' systems description

These two farms could be modelled using conventional systems techniques. The model of one might be something like Fig. 11.4. I have a profound distrust of such 'models'. My criticisms run as follows. Why are the boxes labelled at such arbitrary hierarchical levels? Why is the box labelled 'crops' not broken down into the actual crops? Why are the cows not shown individually? Why is the ecosystem shown as a box, rather than a whole complex of arrows relating components? In general these diagrams lack the discipline of

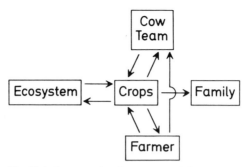

Fig. 11.4. A conventional systems model.

sorting out the sets and hierarchical levels properly, and of distinguishing between sets and relations between sets. Of course those who attempt to model such farms in actual rather than illustrative ways by writing computer programs to simulate the relationships do have to face these problems and give some kind of answer, but usually it is arbitrary.

Steps towards a structural description

The process reported on here has been evolving in the course of this research, and is not yet finished. Rather than go blandly to the latest results, I will go through some of the steps I have taken, because many of them are illuminating with respect to the problems confronted.

The process begins with defining the sets of things in which we are interested. To begin with I explored the ideas of CROPS and CROP DESCRIPTORS. The crops Ashgar currently grows and many that he does not grow were soon listed, but in a fashion which led to one complication within a short time. Rice, wheat and jute were named by him in varietal terms, whereas lentils, dals, mustard and oils were simply given by species name. This does not matter until one wants to climb the hierarchy by using names such as wheat and rice at the next level. What does one then do with those already described by species name? The idea of crop descriptors came from the use of triples which elicited ideas such as 'upland' or 'lowland' or 'HYV' as against 'local' (*deshi*). It soon became apparent that this collection of descriptors was a bit of a rag-bag, since it incorporated at least two kinds of ideas – 'the inherent descriptors' such as *Aus*, *Aman*, wheat, rice, etc., and 'the cultural descriptors' such as broadcast, transplant, needs no weeding, etc. This difference emerged when trying to make an incidence matrix of the relation between CROPS and CROP DESCRIPTORS. To do so it is necessary to specify what the relation is – e.g. owning, liking, touching, etc. The relation with the inherent descriptors is obviously 'genetically defined as' whereas the relation with the cultural descriptors is 'requires this kind of treatment'. Even then some of the distinctions are not obvious: upland and lowland were first put in the cultural descriptor set, but then shifted when it was realized that these words do not describe treatments. It emerges at the last stage of the analysis that these two kinds of sets have other meaningful distinctions. The inherent descriptors can be used to group the crops into types, but do not form part of an input-output relation describing the functional organization of the farm. The cultural descriptors such as 'requires weeding' are very much part of the activities involved in an input-output analysis.

The other sets used at the first stage included HAZARDS, HAZARD DESCRIPTORS, LAND, LAND DESCRIPTORS, FOOD, HOMESTEAD, SALES, PURCHASES, FAMILY. An investigation was made of the ways the elements in these sets aggregated up in different hierarchies, and it is from this stage that the above comments on the nature of simultaneous cross-classification were derived. To be specific, crops can be classified here according to their genetic history, such as High Yielding Variety, Local Improved Variety, or Local Variety; by their season, by their species type and category (oil seed, fibre, etc.) and by their preferred environment (lowland, upland, etc.). It would appear that we can endlessly divide either category by the other – but only if we insist that we use partitions. If we abandon that, then there is one complex simultaneous intersecting classification system. Here it starts with such categories as '*Aman*, lowland, HYV, rice, likes standing water' of which there are 14 categories. There are approximaitely 40 of the quadruple categories such as '*Aman*, lowland, HYV, rice' and 100 of the triple categories, 100 of the double categories, and finally 18 of the single categories. (These are: *Aus*, *Aman*, *Rabi*, HYV, LIV, L (local), Jute, Rice, Wheat, Mustard, Lowland, Upland, Likes-standing-water, Does-not-like-standing-water, *tishi* (an oil seed), *keshari* (a gram), *sola* (a gram, lentil.)

At the next stage it was realized that the level 'above' these sets would constitute the whole farm. Using the simple method of aggregating sets gives us a single set of many elements, which is the entire list of all the elements describing the whole farm at the bottom level (at least 'whole' in the sense of the totality of what one has chosen to observe). In the case of Taher the long list has 139 elements, and in the case of Ashgar 120. It is possible then to specify how this list of elements relates to itself in a large input-output matrix, in which a 1 is recorded whenever an element is an input to another element.

Ultimately of course everything is related to everything else, and it would be very tempting though not exactly professional to use the relation 'x is related to y'. The temptation to do so is very great. Here the relation did turn out to be general and compound. It was specified as 'is a work input to, or is a material input to, or is a necessary catalyst of'. This latter was necessary to include such items as a threshing floor, which is a necessary catalyst to the production of rice from paddy, but is neither a work input nor a material input. The stage of set union was itself extremely thought-provoking. For example, I have listed above a set called FOOD. Included in this set was the

226   UNDERSTANDING GREEN REVOLUTIONS

word 'rice'. Are the varieties such as BR4 inputs to 'rice' (that is to the horizontal axis in Fig. 11.5), or is 'rice' a class category for the rice varieties (that is the class word used on the vertical axis of Fig. 11.5)?

The answer, as with the barber, is that it is both, but we must never confuse the two meanings. Varieties as inputs to 'rice' mean that rice is a processed food derived from any number of rice varieties by means of threshing, parboiling, husking, etc. 'Rice' as a species of plant has none of these connotations, but merely a group genetic meaning. Further, is it right that we form a matrix in which the varieties are inputs to rice, and rice is an input to family, rather than a matrix in which the varieties are inputs to the family directly? The answer to this can only be found by being absolutely precise about the relation used, so that it never fails to discriminate.

Having formed this 139 × 139 matrix it is possible to:

(i) analyse its structure using the Q-analysis algorithm;
(ii) power this matrix so that second order indirect links are found, and to analyse this structure again using the Q-analysis algorithm;
(iii) 'reduce' either or both axes by whatever form is appropriate, coverset or otherwise;
(iv) analyse the structures of these matrices, again using the Q-analysis algorithm;
(v) and power these higher levels for indirect second order effects and analyse those structures too.

At a very high hierarchical level we can reduce the 139 × 139 matrix to a 1 × 1 matrix of the farm relating to the farm, a step which would of course lose

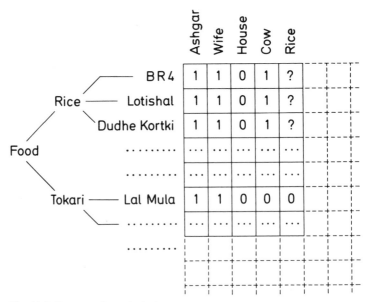

Fig. 11.5. Two meanings of 'rice'.

all the structure previously seen. We would in fact have the following relation:

The way that the combinatorial connectivities at higher hierarchical levels link the polyhedra together will be the result of two things: firstly, the elements defined at the bottom of the hierarchy and the data observed for defined relations; and secondly, the way in which the matrices are reduced by the aggregating procedures. These are the result of the researcher's hierarchical definitions, and these may be based on *either* his own ideas *or* on constructs elicited from the farmers. Since Atkin's algorithm has given us a method of displaying the structure of a relation, we can show how the changing definitions change the structure perceived, remembering always that this structure is the result of the interaction of data and our aggregating understanding of the data.

Stages in the analysis of the two farms

The above numbered stages are taken in the following analysis of Taher's and Ashgar's farms.

(i) Analysis of the basic 139 × 139 input-output matrix of Taher's farm. There are two distinct connectivity patterns to analyse – the connectivity of the sources via shared sinks is shown in Fig. 11.6 and the connectivity of sinks via shared sources in Fig. 11.7.

One interpretation we can give to the connectivity pattern of sources via shared sinks is that it shows the significance of these sources for a range of outputs, and also the extent to which these sources are not replaceable by other outputs. For example, the kitchen garden is the source of 20 outputs, but it is also what is known as highly 'eccentric' in that only three of its sinks are supplied as well by other sources, either directly or indirectly. This eccentricity is shown in the diagram by the fact that only at this low level is the garden connected. Bamboo is also eccentric, showing both its significance for a number of uses, and its irreplaceability. The *Aman* fields are well connected with each other – implying that they can be substitutes for each other – but as a group they are poorly connected with other groups, implying that there is no replacement possible for their function as suppliers to the farmer and his family. The two markets of Tebuiya and Dashuriya are also well connected with each other, but again as a group are poorly connected – again implying

```
                    DIMENSION
                    000000000011111111112
                    012345678901234567890

SHADA               ********************    GHUR                **********       KITCHEN GARDEN (BAGHAN)   ********************
                                  |                                  |                                                  |
KALAKORTKI          ********************    MANGSHO             **********       HIRED LABOUR PLOUGHING    **********
                                  |                                  |                                                  |
DUDHEKORTKI         ********************    MACH                **********       MALLET                    *******
                                  |                                  |                                                  |
TOSHA               ********************    MURGHIR DIM         **********       HIRED LABOUR HARVESTING   **
                                  |                                  |                                                  |
LALROPHAR           ********************    CLOTHES (CAPOR)     **********       POND (KHAL)               ***
                                  |                                  |                                                  |
KELEJAMLI           *******************     BANANA (KHOLA)      **********       WEEDING HOE               ***
                                  |                                  |                                                  |
KALIKARJARI (MASHKALAI) ******************  PESI SURISHA        ********         DAUGHTER 10               *
                                  |                                  |                                                  |
KOLOSHNGOR          ******************      PABNAIGAIRI         *****            TEBUUIYA                  ********
                                  |                                  |                                                  |
LALMULA             ******************      BETEL (SHUPARI)     *****            DASHURIYA                 ********
                                  |                                  |                                                  |
DINGLE              ****************        BROADCAST (BUNA)    **********       BAMBOO (BASH)             *********
                                  |                                  |                                                  |
DESHUL              ****************        RASHEED 40          ***********      PESTICIDE (POKA MARA OSHOD) ***
                                  |                                  |                                                  |
SONALIKA            ****************        SON 18              ***********      BABLA                     *
                                  |                                  |                                                  |
COCONUT (NARIKEL)   ****************        SON 12              ***********      FENCING (GHERA)           *
                                  |                                  |                                                  |
PALM (TAL)          ****************        SICKLES (CUTCH)     ***********      ROOFING (SAL)             *
                                  |                                  |                                                  |
JACKFRUIT (KATAL)   ***************         SPADES (KODOL)      ****************  WALLS (DERWAL)           *
                                  |                                  |                                                  |
NEEM                ***************         TRANSPLANT (ROWAR)  ***              PLINTHS                   *
                                  |                                  |                                                  |
PANGE               ***************         HIRED LABOUR GROWING *****           FURNITURE (ASBHAPPOTRA)   *
                                  |                                  |                                                  |
SUGAR (GHUR) PALM   ***************         BOROBHOI AUS        *********        FERTILIZER (RAISHANIC SHAR) ****
                                  |                                  |                                                  |
PAPAYA (PEPE)       ***************         SHUPORIGASBITE      **************   5 PLOUGHING               *****
                                  |                                  |                                                  |
POMEGRANATE (DALIM) **************          KUKURACAPAL AUS     **************   4 PLOUGHING               *********
                                  |                                  |                                                  |
LYCHEE (LICHU)      **************          BARIPALAN AUS       *********        PLOUGH TEAM (HAL GORU)    ***********
                                  |                                  |                                                  |
?NUT (BADAM)        **************          BOROBHOI AMAN       ***************  LADDERS (MOI)             ***********
                                  |                                  |                                                  |
SHORIFA             **************          BARIPALAN AMAN      ***************  3 WEEDING                 ****
                                  |                                  |                                                  |
BAMBOO BASKET (BASH DALI) *************     KUKURACAPAL AMAN    ***************  NO WEEDING                *******
                                  |                                  |                                                  |
JUTE BAG (BOSTA)    *************           SHUPORIGASBITE      ************     1 PLOUGHING               ***
                                  |                                  |                                                  |
HOUSE (BARI)        *************           BOROBHOI RABI       *********        6 PLOUGHING               **
                                  |                                  |                                                  |
ROAD: THRESHING YARD (KHOALA) *************  SHUPORIGASBITE     *********        1 WEEDING                 ***
                                  |                                  |                                                  |
COOK                *************           BARIPALAN RABI      *********        8–10 PLOUGHING            *
                                  |                                  |                                                  |
ROSHUN              *************           ADEPORPARBITE C     ********         3–4 PLOUGHING             *
                                  |                                  |                                                  |
PEPPER (MORITCH)    *************           ADEPORPARBITE U     ********         3 PLOUGHING               *
                                  |                                  |                                                  |
SALT (LABON)        *************           ADEPORPARBITE U     ********         NO PLOUGHING              *
                                  |                                  |                                                  |
FLOUR (MOIRDA)      *************           KUKURACAPAL RABI    ********         TEND BAGHAN               *
                                  |                                  |                                                  |
MANGO (AAM)         ***********             WIFE                *****            RAKE (NANGLA)             *
                                  |                                  |
```

Fig. 11.6. Analysis of basic matrix for Taher: connectivity of sources via sinks.

alternatives between the two, but a major significance of the markets for certain goods which cannot be obtained by alternative means on the farm.

The conjugate analysis of Fig. 11.7 shows how the outputs share common inputs, or are connected across a range of common inputs. As one might imagine, the demands of the family are paramount, and they share a considerable number of sources. But note that the markets are also connected with this group, so that in whole ranges of products the family is in competition with the markets, which are outputs sharing the same combinations of inputs. Were the farm to have a high cash crop component, this would show up here by disconnection. The connectivity also extends across many crops, to a group of weeds – *bhekini* to *dhela*. Clearly the weeds are also a competing set of outputs.

In the case of Ashgar, not shown here, the connectivity of the sources via the sinks shows a less continuous pattern – implying a more specialized

Agrarian change at village level

```
              DIMENSION
              0000000000111111111122222222223333333
              0123456789012345678901234567890123456678

RASHEED 40              **************************
WIFE                    **************************
GRANDMOTHER             **************************
SON 18                  **************************
SON 12                  **************************
SON 7                   **************************
SON 3                   **************************
DAUGHTER 10             **************************
DAUGHTER 5              **************************
DAUGHTER 1              **************************
TEBUIYA                 *************************
DASHURIYA               *************************
DEVOTURH                *************************
KHESHUR                 *************************
HIRED LABOUR PLOUGHING  ***************
HIRED LABOUR GROWING    ***************
HIRED LABOUR HARVESTING ***************
ZABAR POKA              *********
PLOUGH TEAM (HAL GORU)  ********
LADDERS (MOI)           ******        ATMUTI          ***************  LYCHEE (LICHU)       *       FLOUR (MOIRDA)         **
FURNITURE (ASBHAPPOTRA) ****          HOGATKURA       **************   ?NUT (BADAM)         *       SICKLES (CUTCH)        ***
GHUNDI POKA             ****          BAZARI          *******          SHORIFA              *       SPADES (KODOL)         ***
HOUSE (BARI)            ******        GHADI           *******          BAMBOO (BASH)        *       SHAMA                  **
FENCING (GHERA)         **            SHAELNAZAR      *******          BABLA                *       PERAGUSHI              **
WALLS (DERWAL)          **            ARELLI          *******          MAJRA POKA           **      8–10 PLOUGHING         **
KALAKORTKI              ******        MASHKATI        *****            BAMBOO BASKET (BASH DALI) ** 6 PLOUGHING            *
DUDHEKORTKI             ******        POSPHOSE        *****            ROOFING (SAL)        *       5 PLOUGHING            *
KELEJAMLI               ******        BHAGATA         ****             MALLET               *       4 PLOUGHING            *
TOSHA                   ***********   FESKE           ****             WEEDING HOE          *       3–4 PLOUGHING          **
SHADA                   ***********   BOGOMUTI        ****             RAKE (NANGLA)        *       3 PLOUGHING            **
LALROPHAR               **********    JHORA           ****             BOROBHUI AUS         ****    1 PLOUGHING            *
PESI SURISHA            *********     CHESE           ****             SHUPORIGASBITE       *****   3 WEEDING              **
SONALIKA                *******       BOLONGA         ****             BARIPALAN AUS        *****   1 WEEDING              *
KALIKARJARI (MASHKALAI) ********      PATASOLI        ****             KUKURACAPAL AUS      *****   COOK                   *
PABNAIGAITI             ********      KOLMI           ****             BOROBHOI AMAN        *****   COCONUT (NARIKEL)      **
KOLOSHNGOR              ******        ADAGASE         ****             KUKURACAPAL AMAN     *****   BETEL (SHUPARI)        *
DINGLE                  ***           SHANI           ****             BOROBHOI RABI        ****    MANGO (AAM)            *
DESHUL                  *****         DHELA           ***              SHUPORIGASBITE       *****   JACKFRUIT (KATAL)      *
LALMULA                 ****          BROADCAST (BUNA) **              BARIPALAN AMAN       *****   SUGAR (GHUR) PALM      *
TRANSPLANT (ROWAR)      ***           FERTILIZER (RAISHANIC SHAR) **** BARIPALAN RABI       *****   BANANA (KHOLA)         *
DROUGHT (SUKNA)         ****          TEND BAGHAN     ****             ADEPORPARBITE C      *****   PAPAYA (PEPE)          *
BHEKINI                 *****         MANGSHO         **               ADEPORPARBITE U      *       PALM (TAL)             *
DUBLE                   ******        MACH            **               ADEPORPARBITE U      *       POMEGRANATE (DALIM)    *
BADA                    ***********   PESTICIDE (POKA MARA OSHOD) **   KITCHEN GARDEN (BAGHAN) **** NEEM                   *
SHANI                   *************  CLOTHES (CAPOR) **              ROAD: THRESHING YARD (KHOALA) * PANGE
```

Fig. 11.7. Analysis of basic matrix for Taher: connectivity of sinks via sources.

relationship between sources and sinks. It is worth noting that in this original matrix the highest dimensional sources are the ladders for levelling the fields, and cow dung, which has many purposes, including fuel, preparing the threshing floor, making binding for the daub on wattle, and fertilizer. The ladders and the dung are not connected, since their outputs are for different purposes. Bamboo is eccentric, implying many uses but few alternative sources.

In the case of the conjugate analysis the family, labour and insects are competing for the same sets of sources, or connected sets of sources. The cow is highly eccentric, with many sources peculiar to itself.

(ii) Powering of the original matrices. The original matrices are powered to find the effects of one iteration of the input-output system. Figs. 11.8 and 11.9 show the two analyses made for Taher's farm.

In the analysis of the connectivity of sources via sinks the immediate contrast with Fig. 11.6 is provided by the increase in dimensionality of everything. This is to be expected, and simply says that after one iteration there are many indirect connections, such as fertilizer to field, and then field to crop. Interestingly, the relative importance of inputs has changed, and the prevailing connectivities and disconnectivities have also changed. Bamboo is still highly important and highly eccentric, but whereas Taher and his son were somewhat disconnected from the crops in Fig. 11.6, they are now well connected with the crops, and also slightly eccentric as a group of two. Their significance for a range of outputs is thereby stressed.

The conjugate is fascinating. Whereas in Fig. 11.7 the greatest dimensionality of sinks had been with Taher and his family, now we find the greatest dimensionality to be the crops themselves. This is the expression of work in ploughing, weeding, fertilizing, etc., at the previous stage, which now becomes translated into this large range of sources for the crops. The hired cow team is slightly eccentric.

Ashgar's case reveals some significant differences. In the analysis of the connectivities of the sinks via the sources, the family still remains the highest dimensioned consumer, and the crops are still fairly disconnected. The implication is that the sources for the crops are more specialized than Taher's.

(iii) Aggregation to higher level matrices. It is necessary to define a relation which specifies how the aggregation will occur. This can be written as a matrix of ones and zeros indicating which base level words are to be put in which classes at the next level. Usually these matrices would form a partitional classification scheme. Here we do not necessarily adopt the same restriction.

It is only possible here to give an example from Taher's case of the way in which the aggregating relation may be changed, and the consequent effects of that change on the input-output relation at the higher level. The initial classification is shown in Fig. 11.10, and it can be checked that the classification is very nearly partitional. This classification is examined for its combinatorial connectivities, as shown in Figs. 11.11 and 11.12. In the conjugate analysis it can be seen that everything except the first three rice types, one other rice type, and wheat, has been assigned to one class only. In the analysis

Agrarian change at village level

```
                              DIMENSION
                              000000000011111111112222222222333333333344444444445555
                              012345678901234567890123456789012345678901234567890012
```

BAMBOO (BASH)	··	BARIPALAN AUS	························
KALAKORTKI	······································	POND (KHAL)	························
DUDHEKORTKI	·······································	BOROBHOI AMAN	························
SHADA	·······································	SHUPORIGASBITE	························
LALROPHAR	··	BARIPALAN AMAN	························
TOSHA	·································	KUKURACAPAL AMAN	························
KELEJAMLI	································	MANGO (AAM)	······················
KALIKARJARI (MASHKALAI)	·································	PESI SURISHA	······················
KOLOSHNGOR	································	BARIPALAN RABI	······················
LALMULA	··································	GHUR	······················
RASHEED 40	·······································	MANGSHO	······················
SON 18	······································	MACH	······················
TEBUIYA	································	MURGHIR DIM	······················
DASHURIYA	··································	WIFE	······················
SONALIKA	·······························	CLOTHES (CAPOR)	······················
COOK	································	BANANA (KHOLA)	······················
ROSHUN	·······························	KITCHEN GARDEN (BAGHAN)	································
PEPPER (MORITCH)	······························	FENCING (GHERA)	····················
SALT (LABON)	······························	ROOFING (SAL)	····················
FLOUR (MOIRDA)	······························	WALLS (DERWAL)	····················
SPADES (KODOL)	·································	PLINTHS	····················
SON 12	······························	FURNITURE (ASBHAPOTTRA)	····················
COCONUT (NARIKEL)	······································	RAKE (NANGLA)	····················
PALM (TAL)	····································	HIRED LABOUR PLOUGHING	····················
SICKLES (CUTCH)	································	MALLET	····················
JACKFRUIT (KATAL)	·································	BABLA	············
NEEM	··································	FERTILIZER (RAISHANIC SHAR)	·························
PANGE	································	5 PLOUGHING	································
DINGLE	·······························	4 PLOUGHING	·····································
DESHUL	································	PLOUGH TEAM (HAL CORU)	··
SUGAR (GHUR) PALM	······························	LADDERS (MOI)	·····························
PAPAYA (PEPE)	·····························	1 PLOUGHING	·························
POMEGRANATE (DALIM)	······························	3 WEEDING	····················
LYCHEE (LICHU)	······························	8–10 PLOUGHING	····················
?NUT (BADAM)	······························	3–4 PLOUGHING	····················
SHORIFA	······························	3 PLOUGHING	····················
BAMBOO BASKET (BASH DALI)	······························	NO PLOUGHING	····················
JUTE BAG (BOSTA)	································	1 WEEDING	····················
HOUSE (BARI)	······························	NO WEEDING	····················
ROAD: THRESHING YARD (KHOALA)	······························	TEND BAGHAN	····················
BROADCAST (BUNA)	······························	6 PLOUGHING	··········
HIRED LABOUR GROWING	·································	PABNAIGAITI	········
SHUPORIGASBITE	··················	BOROBHOI RABI	·······
KUKURACAPAL AUS	··················	ADEPORPARBITE C	·······
BETEL (SHUPARI)	··················	WEEDING HOE	·······
TRANSPLANT (ROWAR)	··················	ADEPORPARBITE U	·····
HIRED LABOUR HARVESTING	··················	ADEPORPARBITE U	·····
BOROBHOI AUS	··················	DAUGHTER 10	·

Fig. 11.8. Analysis of the matrix in Fig. 11.6 at second power: connectivity of sources via sinks.

232 UNDERSTANDING GREEN REVOLUTIONS

```
              DIMENSION
              0000000000111111111122222222223333333333444444444455
              0123456789012345678901234567890123456789012345678901
```

LALROPHAR	·································			PALM (TAL)	·······
PESI SURISHA	·································			POMEGRANATE (DALIM)	·······
SONALIKA	·································			NEEM	·······
KALIKARJARI (MASHKALAI)	·································			PANGE	·······
KALAKORTKI	·································			LYCHEE (LICHU)	·······
DUDHEKORTKI	·································			?NUT (BADAM)	·······
KELEJAMLI	·································			SHORIFA	·······
TOSHA	·································			BAMBOO (BASH)	·······
SHADA	·································			BABLA	·······
KOLOSHNGOR	·································			ROOFING (SAL)	·······
DESHUL	·································			DROUGHT (SUKNA)	······
LALMULA	·································			BHEKINI	········
DINGLE	·································	8–10 PLOUGHING	················	DUBLE	········
PABNAIGAITI	·································	6 PLOUGHING	················	BADA	·········
TEND BAGHAN	·································	5 PLOUGHING	················	SHANI	·········
BROADCAST (BUNA)	·································	4 PLOUGHING	················	HOGATKURA	·········
TRANSPLANT (ROWAR)	·································	3–4 PLOUGHING	················	ATMUTI	········
FERTILIZER (RAISHANIC SHAR)	·································	3 PLOUGHING	················	MASHKATI	········
COOK	·································	1 PLOUGHING	················	ARELLI	········
MANGSHO	·································	3 WEEDING	················	POSPHOSE	·······
MACH	·································	1 WEEDING	················	BAZARI	·······
PESTICIDE (POKA MARA OSHOD)	·································	ZABAR POKA	················	GHADI	·······
CLOTHES (CAPOR)	·································	FENCING (GHERA)	··············	SHAELNAZAR	·······
FLOUR (MOIRDA)	·································	WALLS (DERWAL)	··············	BOGOMUTI	······
SICKLES (CUTCH)	·································	MAJRA POKA	·············	JHORA	······
SPADES (KODOL)	·································	GHUNDI POKA	············	CHESE	······
HIRED LABOUR PLOUGHING	·································	BOROBHOI AUS	············	BOLONGA	······
HIRED LABOUR GROWING	·································	BOROBHOI AMAN	···············	PATASOLI	······
HIRED LABOUR HARVESTING	·································	KUKURACAPAL AMAN	···············	KOLMI	······
RASHEED 40	·································	BARIPALAN AMAN	············	ADAGASE	······
WIFE	·································	ADEPORPARBITE C	············	SHAMA	·····
GRANDMOTHER	·································	SHUPORIGASBITE	············	BHAGATA	·····
SON 18	·································	BARIPALAN AUS	············	FESKE	·····
SON 12	·································	KUKURACAPAL AUS	············	PERAGUSHI	·····
SON 7	·································	BOROBHOI RABI	···········	DHELA	·····
SON 3	·································	SHUPORIGASBITE	··········	SHANI	·····
DAUGHTER 10	·································	BARIPALAN RABI	·········	KITCHEN GARDEN (BAGHAN)	·······
DAUGHTER 5	·································	HOUSE (BARI)	········	BAMBOO BASKET (BASH DALI)	···
DAUGHTER 1	·································	COCONUT (NARIKEL)	·······	ADEPORPARBITE U	··
TEBUIYA	·································	BETEL (SHUPARI)	·······	ADEPORPARBITE U	··
DASHURIYA	·································	MANGO (AAM)	·······	ROAD: THRESHING YARD (KHOALA)	·
DEVOTURH	·································	JACKFRUIT (KATAL)	·······	FURNITURE (ASBHAPOTTRA)	·
KHESHUR	·································	SUGAR (GHUR) PALM	·······	MALLET	·
PLOUGH TEAM (HAL GORU)	·································	BANANA (KHOLA)	·······	WEEDING HOE	·
LADDERS (MOI)	·································	PAPAYA (PEPE)	·······	RAKE (NANGLA)	·

Fig. 11.9. Analysis of the matrix in Fig. 11.7 at second power: connectivity of sinks via sources.

which shows the connectivities of the classes themselves, it can be seen that only *Aus* and *Prodhan Khaddyo* are connected with more than one element in common, and that there are some other connectivities where one element is in common. These may be checked by referring back to Fig. 11.10.

The initial aggregation was then changed, and a new one defined, which used a much more obviously non-partitional hierarchy. The listing is given in Fig. 11.13. It can be seen that here the seasonal class words *Aus*, *Aman*, and *Rabi* have been used not just to group crops of those seasons, but also the fields of those seasons too. If the farmer in using a seasonal word in his conceptualizing processes does so to include the various aspects of that season, then it would seem foolish to restrict its application to crops alone. The connectivities of this second definition of the aggregating relation are shown in Figs. 11.14 and 11.15. In the conjugate it can be seen that quite a few elements are now aggregated into more than one class, and it can be seen that there is an extensive pattern of connectivity between the various classes. The fact that fodder has such a high dimension, but also a connection to *Prodhan Khaddyo*, is because fodder comes from both a large number of weeds, and also from the straw of the various rices.

(iv) The analysis of the aggregated input-output matrices. The first comparison we will make is between the two cases of Taher's input-output matrix at the first power, based on the two aggregating definitions given in section (iii) above. It can be seen that the first definition (Fig. 11.6) gives rise to a matrix in which, by and large, the dimensions are less and the eccentricities greater than in the second case. (By definition all classes in a partitional hierarchy are infinitely eccentric.) In the second case (Figs. 11.17a and 11.17b) the cohesiveness of the input-output structure is clearly seen, both in the linkage of the sources via the sinks, and the sinks via the sources. In general, in the second case everything has a higher dimension, and is less eccentric than in the former case. In the conjugate analysis, the connectivity of the sinks via the sources, there is a slight distinction between the crops and seasons on the one hand, and the work, family, equipment, markets, homestead group on the other hand. This is because the inputs to the latter groups are the crops themselves, while to the former group it is the work and fields that are the inputs. Powering the matrix for one iteration will make most of these differences disappear. What is interesting is that even without such an iteration, the minimum level of connectivity between the two should be so great (between WORK and LIV it is dimension 6). This means that the farmer could see many connections between the concepts of Work and Local Improved Varieties, and through that, many other connections as well.

The second comparison we can make is between Taher (Fig. 11.6) and Ashgar (Figs. 11.18a and b) using in this case the simpler and more partitional aggregation. There are a number of similarities between the connectivities of

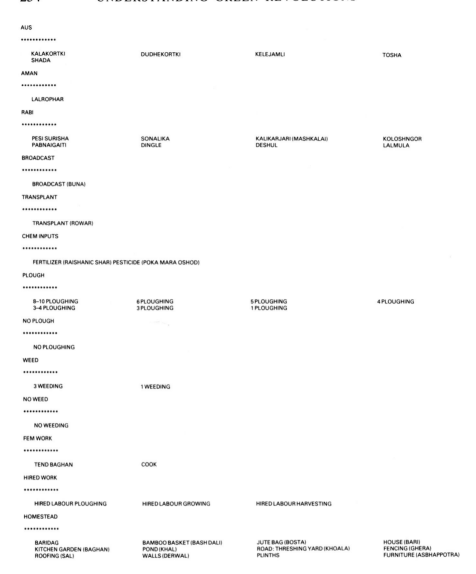

Fig. 11.10. First classification for aggregation of Taher.

Agrarian change at village level

FIELDS
....

BARIDAG
SHUPORIGASBITE AUS
BARIPALAN AMAN
ADEPORPARBITE CAPAL RABI
KUKURACAPAL AMAN

BOROBHOI AUS
SHUPORIGASBITE AMAN
BARIPALAN RABI
ADEPORPARBITE UCHU AMAN
KUKURACAPAL RABI

BOROBHOI AMAN
SHUPORIGASBITE RABI
ADEPORPARBITE CAPAL AUS
ADEPORPARBITE UCHU RABI

BOROBHOI RABI
BARIPALAN AUS
ADEPORPARBITE CAPAL AMAN
KUKURACAPAL AUS

TOKARI
....

PIAZ
MURGHIR DIM

ROSHUN

MANGSHO

MACH

MOSSLA
....

PEPPER (MORITCH)

SALT (LABON)

MISHTI
....

GHUR

PRODHAN KHADDYO
....

KALAKORTKI
SONALIKA

DUDHEKORTKI
FLOUR (MOIRDA)

KELEJAMLI

LALROPHAR

FAMILE MALE
....

RASHEED 40
SON 3

SON 18

SON 12

SON 7

FAMILY FEMALE
....

WIFE
DAUGHTER

GRANDMOTHER

DAUGHTER 10

DAUGHTER 5

MARKETS
....

TEBUIYA

DASHURIYA

DEVOTURH

KHESHUR

EQUIPMENT
....

SICKLES (CUTCH)
MALLET

SPADES (KODOL)
WEEDING HOE

PLOUGH TEAM (HAL GORU)
RAKE (NANGLA)

LADDERS (MOI)

TREES
....

COCONUT (NARIKEL)
JACKFRUIT (KATAL)
POMEGRANATE (DALIM)
?NUT (BADAM)

BETEL (SHUPARI)
BANANA (KHOLA)
NEEM
SHORIFA

MANGO (AAM)
PAPAYA (PEPE)
PANGE
BAMBOO (BASH)

JACKFRUIT (KATAL)
PALM (TAL)
LYCHEE (LICHU)
BABLA

POKA
....

MAJRA POKA

GHUNDI POKA

ZABAR POKA

WEEDS
....

SHAMA
DUBLE
PERAGUSHI
BOGOMUTI
CHESE
ADAGASE
SHAELNAZAR

BHEKINI
SHANI
DHELA
ARELLI
BOLONGA
BAZARI

BHAGATA
FESKE
ATMUTI
POSPHOSE
PATASOLI
GHADI

BADA
HOGATKURA
MASHKATI
JHORA
KOLMI
SHANI

```
                    DIMENSION
                    00000000001111111111122222
                    01234567890123456789 01234

WEEDS               **************************
AUS                 *****
                        |
PRODHAN KHADDYO     ******
                         |
AMAN                *
                    |
RABI                ********
BROADCAST           *
TRANSPLANT          *
CHEM INPUTS         **
PLOUGH              *******
NO PLOUGH           *
WEED                **
NO WEED             *
FEM WORK            **
HIRED WORK          ***
HOMESTEAD           ************
                    |
FIELDS              ******************
TOKARI              *****
MOSSLA              **
MISHTI              *
FAMILY MALE         *****
FAMILY FEMALE       *****
MARKETS             ****
EQUIPMENT           *******
TREES               ****************
POKA                ***
```

Fig. 11.11. Analysis of the classification in Fig. 11.10: connectivity of aggregation.

the sources via the sinks, and a few differences such as the greater eccentricity of the homestead in the case of Taher, and the greater eccentricity of the markets in the case of Ashgar. In the former case it means that for a variety of outputs there is no alternative to the homestead, and in the second case that there are few alternatives for the inputs brought from market. (This partly reflects Ashgar's greater reliance on fertilizer and pesticide.)

(v) Powering of the aggregated input-output matrices. By the second power (first iteration), Taher's analysis (Figs. 11.19a and 11.19b) shows little eccentricity, except that the pests and weeds remain disconnected. In general the whole structure is cohesive and interlinked. In Ashgar's case (Figs. 11.20a and 11.20b) there is again little eccentricity, and considerable cohesiveness. Interestingly, the cow and equipment have now become the highest dimensioned sources, i.e. the sources with the highest number of outputs by the end of the first iteration, but since neither is eccentric with respect to the other, they must naturally be supplying the same outputs. In the conjugate analysis in Ashgar's case there is a slight distinction between the family and work as one group, and the crops as another group of outputs, i.e. they are dependent on slightly distinguishable input sources. This is similar to Taher's case in the second form of aggregation.

	DIMENSION 00 01							
KALAKORTKI	**	1 WEEDING	*	HOUSE (BARI)	*	TEBUIY	*	GHUNDI POKA *
DUDHEKORTKI	**	NO WEEDING	*	KITCHEN GARDEN (BAGHAN)	*	DASHURIYA	*	ZABAR POKA *
KELEJAMLI	**	TEND BAGHAN	*	POND (KHAL)	*	DEVOTURH	*	SHAMA *
TOSHA	*	COOK	*	ROAD: THRESHING YARD (KHOALA)	*	KHESHUR	*	BHEKINI *
SHADA	*	HIRED LABOUR PLOUGHING	*	FENCING (GHERA)	*	SICKLES (CUTCH)	*	BHAGATA *
LALROPHAR	**	HIRED LABOUR GROWING	*	ROOFING (SAL)	*	SPADES (KODOL)	*	DUBLE *
PESI SURISHA	*	HIRED LABOUR HARVESTING	*	WALLS (DERWAL)	*	PLOUGH TEAM (HAL GORU)	*	BADA *
SONALIKA	**	BARIDAG	**	PLINTHS	*	LADDERS (MOI)	*	SHANI *
KALIKARJARI (MASHKALAI)	*	BOROBHOI AUS	*	FURNITURE (ASBHAPOTTRA)	*	MALLET	*	FESKE *
KOLOSHNGOR	*	BOROBHOI AMAN	*	PIAZ	*	WEEDING HOE	*	HOGATKURA *
PABNAIGAITI	*	BOROBHOI RABI	*	ROSHUN	*	RAKE (NANGLA)	*	PERAGUSHI *
DINGLE	*	SHUPORIGASBITE A	*	MANGSHO	*	COCONUT (NARIKEL)	*	DHELA *
DESHUL	*	SHUPORIGASBITE A	*	MACH	*	BETEL (SHUPARI)	*	ATMUTI *
LALMULA	*	SHUPORIGASBITE R	*	MURGHIR DIM	*	MANGO (AAM)	*	MASHKATI *
FLOUR (MOIRDA)	*	BARIPALAN AUS	*	GHUR	*	JACKFRUIT (KATAL)	*	BOGOMUTI *
BROADCAST (BUNA)	*	BARIPALAN AMAN	*	PEPPER (MORITCH)	*	BABANA (KHOLA)	*	ARELLI *
TRANSPLANT (ROWAR)	*	BARIPALAN RABI	*	SALT (LABON)	*	PAPAYA (PEPE)	*	POSPHOSE *
FERTILIZER (RAISHANIC SHAR)	*	ADEPORPARBITE CA	*	RASHEED 40	*	PALM (TAL)	*	JHORA *
PESTICIDE (POKA MARA OSHOD)	*	ADEPORPARBITE CA	*	SON 18	*	POMEGRANATE (DALIM)	*	CHESE *
8–10 PLOUGHING	*	ADEPORPARBITE CA	*	SON 12	*	NEEM	*	BOLONGA *
6 PLOUGHING	*	ADEPORPARBITE UC	*	SON 7	*	PANGE	*	PATASOLI *
5 PLOUGHING	*	ADEPORPARBITE UC	*	SON 3	*	LYCHEE (LICHU)	*	KOLMI *
4 PLOUGHING	*	KUKURACAPAL AUS	*	WIFE	*	?NUT (BADAM)	*	ADAGASE *
3–4 PLOUGHING	*	KUKURACAPAL AMAN	*	GRANDMOTHER	*	SHORIFA	*	BAZARI *
3 PLOUGHING	*	KUKURACAPAL RABI	*	DAUGHTER 10	*	BAMBOO (BASH)	*	GHADI *
1 PLOUGHING	*	BAMBOO BASKET (BASH DALI)	*	DAUGHTER 5	*	BABLA	*	SHANI *
NO PLOUGHING	*	JUTE BAG (BOSTA)	*	DAUGHTER 1	*	MAJRA POKA	*	SHAELNAZAR *
3 WEEDING	*							

Fig. 11.12. Analysis of the classification in Fig. 11.10: conjugate analysis of connectivity.

As the iterations are repeated, naturally the dimensions and cohesiveness of the structures increase. Totally disconnected components obviously remain so – in the case of Taher the pests and weeds remain as sources not connected through their outputs to anything else, since Taher does not consume them. In the case of Ashgar the weeds become as significant a source as any other, because via the cow they are connected throughout the farm.

This last observation leads one to speculate on the effects that a weed control programme would have (there is no such programme at present). Clearly it would have ramifications in the whole farm economy. This does not mean that a weed control programme would necessarily be bad, but it does mean that its costs would have to be calculated against the costs of replacing fodder, and the loss or gain of work opportunities in the new pattern of farming.

Structure and change (traffic and backcloth)

A central part of Q-analysis is the belief that there is a multi-dimensional geometry which affects the way in which forces can be transmitted in a struc-

FODDER
••••••••••••

KALAKORTKI	DUDHEKORTKI	KELEJAMLI	LALROPHAR
SHAMA	BHEKINI	BHAGATA	DUBLE
BADA	SHANI	FESKE	HOGATKURA
PERAGUSHI	DHELA	ATMUTI	MASHKATI
BOGOMUTI	ARELLI	POSPHOSE	JHORA
CHESE	BOLONGA	PATASOLI	KOLMI
ADAGASE	BAZARI	GHADI	SHANI
SHAELNAZAR			

PRODHAN KHADDYO
••••••••••••

| KALAKORTKI | DUDHEKORTKI | KELEJAMLI | LALROPHAR |
| SONALIKA | FLOUR (MOIRDA) | | |

AUS
••••••••••••

KALAKORTKI	DUDHEKORTKI	KELEJAMLI	TOSHA
SHADA	BOROBHOI AUS	SHUPORIGASBITE AUS	BARIPALAN AUS
ADEPORPARBITE CAPAL AUS	KUKURACAPAL AUS	KITCHEN GARDEN (BAGHAN)	

AMAN
••••••••••••

| LALROPHAR | BOROBHOI AMAN | SHUPORIGASBITE AMAN | BARIPALAN AMAN |
| ADEPORPARBITE CAPAL AMAN | ADEPORPARBITE UCHU AMAN | KUKURACAPAL AMAN | KITCHEN GARDEN (BAGHAN) |

RABI
••••••••••••

PESI SURISHA	SONALIKA	KALIKARJARI (MASHKALAI)	KOLOSHNGOR
PABNAIGAITI	DINGLE	DESHUL	LALMULA
BOROBHOI RABI	SHUPORIGASBITE RABI	BARIPALAN RABI	ADEPORPARBITE CAPAL RABI
ADEPORPARBITE UCHU RABI	KUKURACAPAL RABI	KITCHEN GARDEN (BAGHAN)	

TOKARI
••••••••••••

TOSHA	SHADA	KALIKARJARI (MASHKALAI)	KOLOSHNGOR
PABNAIGAITI	DINGLE	DESHUL	LALMULA
ROSHUN	GHUR	MANGSHO	MACH
MURGHIR DIM	PEPPER (MORITCH)	SALT (LABON)	COCONUT (NARIKEL)
MANGO (AAM)	JACKFRUIT (KATAL)	SUGAR (GHUR) PALM (KHEZUR)	BANANA (KHOLA)
PAPAYA (PEPE)	PALM (TAL)	POMEGRANATE (DALIM)	LYCHEE (LICHU)
?NUT (BADAM)			

WORK
••••••••••••

RASHEED 40	WIFE	SON 18	SON 12
HIRED LABOUR PLOUGHING	HIRED LABOUR HARVESTING	TEND BAGHAN	COOK
PLOUGH TEAM (HAL GORU)			

BROADCAST
••••••••••••

BROADCAST (BUNA)

TRANSPLANT
••••••••••••

TRANSPLANT (ROWAR)

DESHI
••••••••••••

KALAKORTKI	DUDHEKORTKI	KELEJAMLI	TOSHA
LALROPHAR	PESI SURISHA	KALIKARJARI (MASHKALAI)	KOLOSHNGOR
PABNAIGAITI	DINGLE	DESHUL	LALMULA

Fig. 11.13. Revised aggregation for Taher.

LIV
****
    SHADA   SONALIKA

UPLAND (UCHU)
****
    SHUPORIGASBITE AUS   SHUPORIGASBITE AMAN   SHUPORIGASBITE RABI   ADEPORPARBITE UCHU AMAN
    ADEPORPARBITE UCHU RABI

LOWLAND (CAPAL)
****
    ADEPORPARBITE CAPAL AUS   ADEPORPARBITE CAPAL AMAN   ADEPORPARBITE CAPAL RABI   KUKURACAPAL AUS
    KUKURACAPAL AMAN   KUKURACAPAL RABI

MAZARI
****
    BARIPALAN AUS   BARIPALAN AMAN   BARIPALAN RABI   BOROBHOI AUS
    BOROBHOI AMAN   BOROBHOI RABI

CHEM INPUTS
****
    PESTICIDE (POKA MARA OSHOD) FERTILIZER (RAISHANIC SHAR)

FIELD PREPARATION
****
    8–10 PLOUGHING   6 PLOUGHING   5 PLOUGHING   4 PLOUGHING
    3–4 PLOUGHING   3 PLOUGHING   1 PLOUGHING   3 WEEDING
    1 WEEDING

HOMESTEAD
****
    BAMBOO BASKET (BASH DALI) JUTE BAG (BOSTA)   HOUSE (BARI)   KITCHEN GARDEN (BAGHAN)
    POND (KHAL)   ROAD: THRESHING YARD (KHOALA) FENCING (GHERA)   ROOFING (SAL)
    WALLS (DERWAL)   PLINTHS   FURNITURE (ASBHAPPOTRA)

FAMILY
****
    RASHEED 40   WIFE   GRANDMOTHER   SON 18
    SON 12   SON 7   SON 3   DAUGHTER 10
    DAUGHTER 5   DAUGHTER 1

MARKETS
****
    TEBUIYA   DASHURIYA   DEVOTURH   KHESHUR

EQUIPMENT
****
    SICKLES (CUTCH)   SPADES (KODOL)   PLOUGH TEAM (HAL GORU)   LADDERS (MOI)
    MALLET   WEEDING HOE   RAKE (NANGLA)   ROAD: THRESHING YARD (KHOALA)
    BAMBOO BASKET (BASH DALI) JUTE BAG (BOSTA)

POKA
****
    MAJRA POKA   GHUNDI POKA   ZABAR POKA

```
                    DIMENSION
                    0000000000111111111 2
                    0123456789012345678 90
FODDER              ************************
                    I
PRODHAN KHADDYO     ******
                    I
AUS                 *************
                    I
RABI                ****************
                    I
TOKARU              ************************
                    I
DESHI               *************
                    I
AMAN                *********
                    I
UPLAND (UCHU)       *****
                    I
LOWLAND (CAPAL)     ******
                    I
MAZARI              ******
                    I
WORK                *********
                    I
FAMILY              **********
                    I
LIV                 **
                    I
HOMESTEAD           ***********
                    I
EQUIPMENT           **********
BROADCAST           *
TRANSPLANT          *
CHEM INPUTS         **
FIELD PREPARATION   *********
MARKETS             ****
POKA                ***
```

Fig. 11.14. Analysis of revised classification: connectivity of aggregation.

ture – indeed the structure is the multi-dimensional geometry. The structure is called the backcloth, and the phenomena that 'live' and move on the backcloth are the traffic. In the case of roads it is obvious that there is a structure of connection and alternative routes, and that traffic is confined to the backcloth. If a road network is highly connected, then obstruction in one part may easily be transmitted over the whole. For that reason more and more roads are built now as limited access roads.

The same ideas prevail at a more abstract level about any backcloth and traffic. Taking an example from farming, it is quite common for trial analyses of different outputs to be conducted combinatorially. For example, output may be tested under varying combinations of N, P, K and Water. In general, it is quite common to see an output expression in polynomial form – for simplicity's sake we will use just N and Water and state that output $O = xN + yW + zNW$, i.e. it is a function of Water alone, N alone, and the all-important interaction effects of N and W together. Let us then imagine a relation between Fields and Inputs as follows:

	P	F	I	H	O	D
f1					1	
f2	1	1	1	1		
f3		1	1		1	
f4		1	1	1		
f5	1				1	1

where f1–f5 are fields and P is pesticide, F fertilizer, I irrigation, H high yielding varieties, O ordinary varieties, and D dung.

Fig. 11.15. Analysis of revised classification: conjugate analysis of connectivity (conjugate of Fig. 11.14).

(a) AGGREGATED MATRIX CONNECTIVITY OF SOURCES VIA SINKS

```
                    DIMENSION
                    0000000000
                    0123456789
EQUIPMENT           **********
                             |
HIRED WORK          ******
                         |
FIELDS              *****
                        |
FAMILY MALE         *******
                          |
AUS                 *******
                          |
RABI                *******
                          |
PRODHAN KHADDYO     *******
                          |
AMAN                ******
                         |
HOMESTEAD           ********
                           |
TREES               ******
                         |
FEM WORK            ****
                       |
BROADCAST           ***
                      |
TRANSPLANT          ***
                      |
TOKARI              ***
                      |
MOSSLA              ***
                      |
PLOUGH              **
                     |
WEED                **
                     |
NO WEED             **
                     |
MISHTI              **
                     |
FAMILY FEMALE       **
                     |
MARKETS             ****
                       |
CHEM INPUTS         **
                     |
NO PLOUGH           *
                    |
PESTS               *
                    |
WEEDS               *
```

(b) AGGREGATED MATRIX CONNECTIVITY OF SINKS VIA SOURCES

```
                    DIMENSION
                    00000000001
                    01234567890
HOMESTEAD           ***********
                              |
HIRED WORK          ********
                           |
FAMILY MALE         **********
                             |
FAMILY FEMALE       **********
                             |
MARKETS             ******
                         |
EQUIPMENT           *******
                          |
FIELDS              *****
                        |
POKA                *****
                        |
AUS                 ******
                         |
AMAN                *****
                        |
RABI                *******
                          |
PRODHAN KHADDYO     *******
                          |
CHEM INPUTS         **
                     |
PLOUGH              **
                     |
WEED                **
                     |
FEM WORK            **
                     |
TREES               **
                     |
BROADCAST           *
                    |
TRANSPLANT          *
                    |
TOKARI              **
                     |
WEEDS               *
                    |
NO PLOUGH           *
                    |
NO WEED             *
                    |
MISHTI              *
                    |
MOSSLA              *
```

Fig. 11.16. Structure of Taher's aggregated matrix by first aggregation: (a) connectivity of sources via sinks; (b) connectivity of sinks via sources.

This relation between Fields and Inputs is shown as an analysis of the connectivities in Fig. 11.21. Remembering that the dimensionality is always one less than the number of vertices, we can see that field 1 is represented by a zero-dimensional point, field 2 by a three-dimensional tetrahedron, etc. We can also see that field 5, which is a two-dimensional triangle, shares an edge of one dimension (a line) with field 2, because they have the two vertices P and H in common. Now, production in f5 is a function of D, P and H, in all combinations. It does not share the total DPH with f2, but it does share PH with f2. In turn PH is a subset of the tetrahedron PFIH, and that in turn is linked via the subset FI to f3 (FIO). Hence f3 and f5 are linked at the one-dimensional level. It follows that any change in either at a two-dimensional level (i.e. involving interaction effects dependent on all three vertices in each case) could not be transmitted from one to the other, but changes involving one dimension could. If any change involves fertilizer and irrigation at f3, this clearly can affect f2 which uses FIPH, and changes in that can affect PH in f5. The geometry does not *require* that changes will occur, nor does it say that there will necessarily be changes at the highest dimensional level of connec-

Agrarian change at village level

```
        (a)                                    (b)
        DIMENSION                              DIMENSION
        00000000001111111111                   000000000001111
        01234567890123456789                   01234567890123

WORK              ********************   RABI              ***************
                                     |                                   |
EQUIPMENT         ******************     PRODHAN KHADDYO   **************
                                   |                                   |
AUS               **************         TOKARI            **************
                               |                                      |
RABI              *************          DESHI             *************
                              |                                      |
FAMILY            ************           FODDER            ************
                             |                                     |
AMAN              ************           AUS               ***********
                             |                                    |
HOMESTEAD         ***********            AMAN              **********
                            |                                    |
MAZARI            *********              LIV               *********
                          |                                     |
BROADCAST         *******                WORK              ************
                        |                                          |
LOWLAND (CAPAL)   *******                FAMILY            ***********
                        |                                         |
FIELD PREPARATION *******                EQUIPMENT         ************
                        |                                          |
PRODHAN KHADDYO   ******                 MARKETS           **********
                       |                                         |
TOKARI            ******                 HOMESTEAD         **********
                       |                                         |
TRANSPLANT        ******                 POKA              *********
                       |                                        |
DESHI             ******                 LOWLAND (CAPAL)   ****
                       |                                    |
LIV               ******                 MAZARI            ****
                       |                                    |
UPLAND (UCHU)     ******                 UPLAND (UCHU)     ***
                       |                                   |
FODDER            *****                  CHEM INPUTS       ***
                      |                                    |
CHEM INPUTS       *****                  BROADCAST         **
                      |                                   |
MARKETS           ****                   TRANSPLANT        **
                     |                                    |
POKA                                     FIELD PREPARATION **
```

Fig. 11.17. Structure of Taher's aggregated matrix by second aggregation: (a) connectivity of sources via sinks; and (b) connectivity of sinks via sources.

tivity possible. But it certainly does say what cannot occur, what cannot be transmitted. In this case interaction effects DPH could not effect FIO.

The relationship between backcloth and traffic is one well worth pursuing, although it is difficult ground. Quite clearly diet can be seen as a complex high-dimensional traffic on some complex backcloth. It is also clear that in Bangladesh diet is being degraded as population pressure forces a simplification of the backcloth, with fewer kitchen gardens and orchards remaining to provide vitamin sources.

Another way in which we can consider backcloth and traffic is with regard to mental traffic, the traffic of ideas on a backcloth of established mental attributes. Taking an academic example, someone who is skilled in statistical analysis, historical demography and Bengali might be able to hold an interesting conversation with someone with the same range of attributes on a project for the quantitative analysis of Bengali migration in the nineteenth century. With someone who lacked the statistical side, he may be able to discuss the general hypotheses of the project, but not the execution of it. So, with the farmers, it is clear to me that their mental traffic flows on a backcloth of connected combinations of things, whereas the scientific community is only just beginning to realize the significance of this.

It also follows that changes in the geometry can cause major changes in what can be transmitted. Adding an element may release a whole new set of effects through a system, or deleting something may inhibit transmissions. Whether these changes are good or bad obviously depends upon other qualities. I have not yet had the time to explore these avenues properly with regard to these two farmers, but it is clear that given the fairly high levels of physical connectivity on the farms, in general complex effects can be transmitted through them fairly easily. This is a reflection of the high level of integration that they exhibit. It is for this reason, I think as yet dimly felt, that research in Bangladesh is beginning to turn away from single crop research, into cropping system research. This latter avowedly needs a combinatorial approach, but so far proper methodologies for such analyses have not been forthcoming. I hope this study has shown some of the ways in which some progress may be made.

On the mental side, one hardly needs to add more than to say that literacy and numeracy are skills which permit a better managerial traffic on the farm in contemporary trading situations.

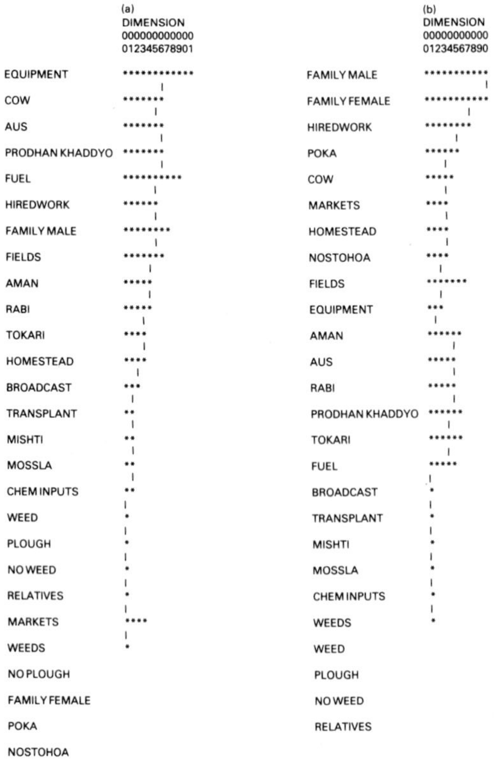

(a) DIMENSION 000000000000 012345678901		(b) DIMENSION 00000000000 01234567890	
EQUIPMENT	*************	FAMILY MALE	***********
COW	*******	FAMILY FEMALE	***********
AUS	*******	HIREDWORK	********
PRODHAN KHADDYO	*******	POKA	*******
FUEL	**********	COW	*****
HIREDWORK	******	MARKETS	****
FAMILY MALE	********	HOMESTEAD	****
FIELDS	********	NOSTOHOA	****
AMAN	*****	FIELDS	*******
RABI	*****	EQUIPMENT	***
TOKARI	****	AMAN	******
HOMESTEAD	****	AUS	*****
BROADCAST	***	RABI	*****
TRANSPLANT	**	PRODHAN KHADDYO	******
MISHTI	**	TOKARI	******
MOSSLA	**	FUEL	*****
CHEM INPUTS	**	BROADCAST	*
WEED	*	TRANSPLANT	*
PLOUGH	*	MISHTI	*
NO WEED	*	MOSSLA	*
RELATIVES	*	CHEM INPUTS	*
MARKETS	****	WEEDS	*
WEEDS	*	WEED	
NO PLOUGH		PLOUGH	
FAMILY FEMALE		NO WEED	
POKA		RELATIVES	
NOSTOHOA			

Fig. 11.18. Structure of Ashgar's aggregated matrix: (a) connectivity of sources via sinks; and (b) connectivity of sinks via sources.

Agrarian change at village level

Conclusion

This chapter has tried to do the following:

(i) begin to describe the complexities and subtleties of farms in Bangladesh;
(ii) demonstrate how the structure that is seen is the result of both the real world data relations, and how we aggregate these afterwards using our own definitions;
(iii) hint at how the aggregated pictures can vary according to the observer;
(iv) hint at how important it is to understand the structure from the farmers' point of view. Otherwise, changes that are made to it from an alternative perspective may cause damaging unintended complex effects.

The task of pursuing these ideas in detail and with rigour is continuing.

ACKNOWLEDGEMENTS

I wish to acknowledge the help of the following for financial or other help in the conduct of the research reported on here: the Bangladesh Agricultural Research Council, particularly Dr M.M. Rahman; the Ford Foundation, Dacca, particularly Dr Martin Hanratty; the Bangladesh Agricultural Research Institute at Ishurdii; and the

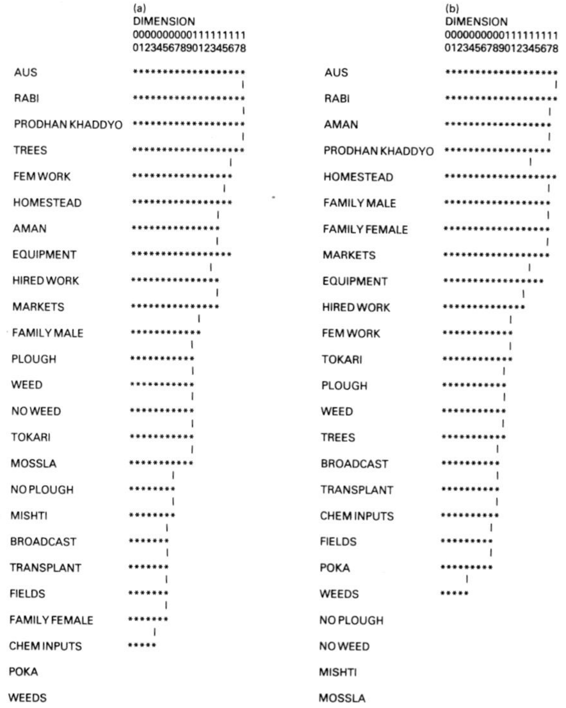

Fig. 11.19. Structure of Taher's aggregated matrix (first definition) at second power: (a) connectivity of sources via sinks; and (b) connectivity of sinks via sources.

```
                    (a)                              (b)
                    DIMENSION                        DIMENSION
                    00000000001111111                00000000001111111
                    01234567890123456 78             01234567890123456

COW                 *******************    AMAN     *****************
                                    I                               I
EQUIPMENT           ******************     AUS      *****************
                                   I                                I
FUEL                *****************      RABI     *****************
                                  I                                 I
AUS                 ****************       PRODHAN KHADDYO *****************
                                 I                                  I
PRODHAN KHADDYO     ****************       TOKARI   *****************
                                 I                                  I
HOMESTEAD           ***************        FUEL     *****************
                                I                                   I
FAMILY MALE         ***************        BROADCAST **********
                                I                             I
CHEM INPUTS         *************          TRANSPLANT **********
                              I                               I
RABI                ************           COW      **********
                             I                               I
HIREDWORK           **********             HIREDWORK **************
                           I                                   I
FIELDS              **********             FAMILY MALE ****************
                           I                                    I
AMAN                **********             FAMILY FEMALE ****************
                           I                                    I
TOKARI              ********               HOMESTEAD  **********
                         I                                   I
MISHTI              ********               POKA      **********
                         I                                   I
MOSSLA              ********               FIELDS    *********
                         I                                  I
BROADCAST           *******                EQUIPMENT ********
                        I                                  I
TRANSPLANT          *******                NOSTOHOA  ********
                        I                                  I
WEED                *******                MARKETS   *******
                        I                                 I
PLOUGH              *******                WEEDS     *******
                        I                                 I
NO WEEDING          *******                MISHTI    ****
                        I                              I
WEEDS               *******                MOSSLA    ****
                        I                              I
MARKETS             ******                 CHEM INPUTS ****
                       I                                I
RELATIVES           ****                   WEED
NO PLOUGH                                  PLOUGH
FAMILY FEMALE                              NO WEED
POKA                                       RELATIVES
NOSTOHOA
```

Fig. 11.20. Structure of Taher's aggregated matrix (first definition) at second power: (a) connectivity of sinks via sources; (b) connectivity of sources via sinks.

```
        DIMENSION
        0000
        0123

F2      ****
          I
F4      ***
          I
F3      ***
          I
F5      ***
          I
F1      *
```

Fig. 11.21. Structure of fields and inputs.

Smuts Fund, Cambridge. But above all I wish to thank W.A. Shah of BARI at Ishurdi, for his unceasing help in the field work, and finally Ashgar and Taher, the two farmers who spent hours talking about their farms with Shah and I.

NOTES

1. Any 'scientist' who objects that bamboo (or banana) is not a tree will probably not understand this paper.
2. These names are pseudonyms to protect the privacy of the two individuals concerned.
3. The field work for this paper was conducted in November and December 1982.

GLOSSARY

aam mango
adagase a weed
Adeporparbite a named field
Aman main rainy season
arelli a weed
asbhappotra furniture
atmuti a weed
Aus early rainy season
babla a kind of tree
badai a weed
badam groundnut
baghan (kitchen) garden
Banisphor a named field
bantuphan storm
bari house
Baridag a named field
Baripalan a named field
bash bamboo
bazari a weed
bhagata a weed
bhalo good
bhat cooked rice
bhekini a weed
bhithi a homestead
bil low swamp land
bis seed
bogomuti a weed
bolonga a weed
bonna flood
Borobhoi a named field
bosta jute bag
buna broadcast
capal low land
capor clothes
chese a weed
chicon mati fine soil
chini sugar
Choitali a name for Rabi
dal pulse
dalim pomegranate tree
Dashuriya a named market
deki rice husker
derwal wall
deshi country (local, rustic)
Devoturh a named market
dhela a weed
Dhophirbite a named field
dim egg
dingle a variety of gourd
duble a weed
dudhekortki a variety of Local Aus rice
dudhli a weed
feske a weed
fol, *phol* fruit
ghadi a weed
ghash weeds, grass, fodder
ghera fencing
ghundi a pest
ghur crude sugar
goam wheat
gobar dung
gola godown (store)
goru cow
gorughor cowshed
hal goru plough cow
halud turmeric
hengti a weed
hogatkura a weed
HYV High Yielding Variety
jhora a weed
kaishe a weed
kalabori a Local Aus Rice
kalakortki a Local Aus Rice
kalikajari a variety of mashkalai (blackgram)
kat timber
katal a jackfruit tree
kelejamli a local Aus Rice
keshari a kind of pulse
Keshur a named market
khal a pond
kher rice straw
khet a field
khoala threshing floor
khola banana
khora a drought
khezur sugar palm tree
khura bran
kodol a spade
koloshnogor a variety of onion
kolmi a spinach
kori fuel

Kukuracapal   a named field
kus ghash   a grass
kutcha   not proper (unmetalled road, unbaked brick)
L   Local (deshi)
labon   salt
lakri   wood (for fire, fuel)
lal   red
lalrophar   local Aman rice variety for transplant
lalmula   a variety of radish
lau   a gourd
lichu   lychee tree
LIV   Local Improved Variety
lotishal   LIV Aman Rice Variety
mach   fish
majra poka   stem-borer pest
mangsho   flesh, meat
mara oshod   pesticide
mashkalai   black gram
mashkati   a weed
mazari   middle (e.g. middle level ground)
mishti   sweets
moi   ladder
moirda   flour
moritch   pepper
moshor   a lentil
mossla   spices
mota mati   thick (clay) soil
mula   radish
murghir   hen
nangla   rake
narikel   coconut tree
neem   a variety of tree
nostohoa   calamity
pabnaigaiti   a variety of onion
pange   a variety of tree
papaya   pawpaw tree
pat   jute
pata   leaves
patasoli   a weed
pat nara   jute stumps
peraghushi   a weed
pesi surisha   a variety of mustard
phol   fruit
phoreng   grasshopper
piaz   onion

poel pala   haystack
poka   bug-pest
poka mara oshod   pesticide
poroshi   neighbour
posphose   a weed
prodhan khaddyo   staple food
pukka   proper (e.g. metalled road, tiled roof)
Rabi   dry (winter) season
rhaishanic shar   fertilizer
Reherderboi   a named field
rog   disease
rophar (*rowar*)   transplant
rosh   juice-sap
roshun   garlic
roti   bread
Runaphor   a named field
sabse   vegetable
sag   green vegetable-leaves
sal   roofing
shada pat   a variety of jute
shaelnazar   a weed
shama   a weed
shani   a weed
Shemegato   a named field
shokti   power, strength (fertility)
shorifa   a tree
shupari   betel nut tree
Shuporigasbite   a named field
sola   a black gram
sonalika   a variety of LIV wheat
sukna   drought
surisha   mustard
tal   palm tree
Tebuniya   a named market
Tetultala   a named field
tishi   an oil seed
tori surisha   a variety of mustard
torkari   non-staple food, vegetable and animal protein sources
tosha pat   a jute variety
toshi surisha   a variety of mustard
tursh   rice husk
uchu   upper (higher level, of land)
zab   a pest
zabapoka   a pest
Zularoypar   a named field

REFERENCES

Atkin, R.H. (1974). *Mathematical Structure in Human Affairs*. Heinemann, London

Atkin, R.H. (1977). *Combinatorial Connectivities in Social Systems*. Birkhäuser Verlag, Basle

Chapman, G.P. (1982). Q-analysis. In N. Wrigley & R.J. Bennett (eds.), *Quantitative Geography: A British View*. Routledge & Kegan Paul, London, Boston and Henley, pp. 235–47

Johnson, J.H. (1978). Describing and classifying TV programmes: a mathematical summary. International Television Flows Project, Department of Geography, University of Cambridge (mimeo)

Johnson, J.H. & Wanmali, Sudhir (1981). A Q-analysis of periodic market systems. *Geographical Analysis*, 13, 262–75

PART III
Development planning and agrarian change

12 Rural-based models for rural development: the Indian experience

SUDHIR WANMALI

Urban bias in Indian planning has now become an accepted feature of all academic, and to some extent even policy, debates on rural development in that part of the world. This urban bias manifests itself in many ways and is found even in the 'unconscious assumptions of the planners themselves' (Lipton, 1968). B.H. Farmer in his work has analysed several instances of such assumed, and indeed real, urban bias in the macro-planning of rural development in India. It was at the end of this fieldwork for his project *Green Revolution?* (1977) that Farmer became convinced of the incomplete understanding of countryside in existing literature on Indian rural development. He noted in a paper presented to the Second Indo-British Geography Seminar that the urban-rural relationships in India are between towns and agriculturalists and not between towns and commuters/holiday-makers/retired townspeople (Farmer, 1975). With a characteristic humility, Farmer described this statement as 'so trite as to be unworthy of a paper intended for an intelligent and informed readership'. Yet what he had to say on this aspect is not insignificant. There are examples of studies on urban-rural relationships which completely lack the rural view; which demonstrate unwillingness to discuss rural attitudes and problems in anything but a rather 'general and unrealistic way' (Lipton, 1968); and which recommend imposition of urban (or western) ideas for the solution of Indian problems. Farmer strongly recommended that nothing short of a complete reversal of the current angle of view (which is urban based) is likely to rectify the situation (Farmer, 1975).

In this chapter an attempt is made to examine critically the underlying assumptions, and realities, of the current macro-economic-geographical models of rural development in India, as advanced by Indian policymakers and academics; and to suggest an alternative which takes into consideration the economic-geographical realities in rural India.

In India, rural development and planning have meant different things to different people. To some, amongst whom are a large number of government organisations and an equally large number of the Indian academic community, it means nothing but urban and industrial development. To others, and amongst these are a few government organisations and only a few of the Indian academic community, it also means development of agriculture, irrigation facilities and provision of services in rural areas.

If we examine service provision in rural India not only in relation to the urban, and industrial, based models of rural development, but also in the light of more recent attempts to view the process from the angle of the villages, then a number of issues must be considered. This study notes first of all the features of government policy, with its explicit, and implicit, emphasis on theories of regional development; it then examines the models of rural development in India as suggested by development administrators and planners; it offers a critique of these models; and, finally, based on the empirical evidence from rural India, it suggests a rural-based model for service provision in that part of the world.

National Plans and spatial policies

Indian planning is characterised by heavy reliance on budgetary allocations for the development of various sectors of the national economy. It is also characterised by the existence of a time dimension in all its plans where each plan lasts for five years. So far, the country has had three uninterrupted plans until 1966; then for two years the Government of India went on a 'plan holiday'; and from 1969 onwards there were two more plans. There appears to be a greater concern for formulating a plan in India than for its implementation. This is underlined by the fact that the implementing authority, and its structure, has remained unchanged during the years 1951–81. This authority is still the State Government which executes the programmes of the Plan in the districts. The process of plan formulation is based on a series of discussions between the State Governments and the Government of India; but while formulating a Plan little attention is paid to the problems of its implementation.

The objectives of National Plans

The objectives of the National Plans, first set out in the Second Five Year Plan, and repeated in the subsequent plans, are: (a) a sizeable increase in the national income so as to raise the standards of living, (b) rapid industrialisation with particular emphasis on the development of heavy industry, (c) a large expansion of employment opportunities, and (d) a reduction of inequalities in income and wealth and a more even distribution of economic power. These objectives are not unrelated and it is possible to derive two policy statements from them. These are that economic growth will be achieved and that a more equitable distribution of wealth and income will also be achieved but through a planned development of both urban and rural sectors (Government of India, 1956).

The objectives, or the statements related to the objectives, make no mention of space or spatial policies; this is more curious since all activity takes place within geographical space. Economic growth was to have been achieved through full employment, higher national output and by an improvement in the general standards of living. In the First Five Year Plan (1951–56) the vehicle for achieving economic growth was overall rural development; in the Second Five Year Plan (1956–61) it was heavy industry; in the Third Five Year Plan (1961–66) it was application of science and technology to agriculture with an emphasis on the development of medium scale industries. The subsequent plans (Fourth, 1969–74 and Fifth, 1974–79) have used these vehicles although with differing emphasis; some of the effort is concentrated in the backward areas and for the benefit of the weaker sections of the society (as is evident from the many special area, and target group, programmes which tended to form a part of the planning process from 1969). But the early Indian plans rarely contained specific locational suggestions, or spatial policies, for rural/regional development (Lewis, 1962).

Spatial impact of urban and industrial development

Although there was no direct mention of spatial policies in the Indian Plans, this was not synonymous with a complete lack of awareness of this aspect of planning. The spatial aspect tended to crop up in the deliberations of the departments, or the ministries, whose development programmes had a definite spatial angle (Govt. of India, 1952, 1956, 1961, 1970, 1976). Notable amongst these, at least until the Fourth Five Year Plan period, were the Department of Urban Development in the Ministry of Works and Housing and the Ministry of Industrial Development (Govt. of India, 1969, 1969a, 1969b). In addition, the National Council of Applied Economic Research (NCAER), the Town and Country Planning Organisation (TCPO) and the Office of the Registrar General of India were also deeply aware of the spatial implications of the National Plans (NCAER, 1965; TCPO, 1968, 1971, 1971a; Census of India, 1968). The literature which is produced by these ministries and organisations, no doubt based on an extensive survey of the secondary data, came up with the following recommendations regarding the spatial nature of the Indian economy: (i) that there are differences in the levels of economic development in India, (ii) that these levels of development mainly reflect the levels of urbanisation and industrialisation, (iii) that the urban centres (which include metropolitan cities, urban agglomerations and towns of various sizes) need to be strengthened by investing in the improvement of their overall infrastructure which, when completed, would facilitate a smooth urban-rural integration, (iv) that the industrial centres, primarily established to manufacture goods, are capable of integrating their rural hinterlands, and (v) that the existing 'gaps' in the geographical distribution of urban and industrial centres need to be filled in quickly in order to achieve the twin objectives of economic growth and social justice.

Since these recommendations tended to be followed up sectorally, the National Plans note the budgetary allocations for the development of metropolitan regions, urban agglomerations, market towns and heavy and medium-sized industries. With each plan period, the emphasis tended to shift; from the metropolitan cities and the heavy industries in the Second and the Third Plans to the urban agglomerations, market towns and industrial estates of the subsequent plans. It must be borne in mind that these attempts do not amount to a policy of rural development. The characteristic features of the spatial impact of these urban and industrial development programmes are noted below.

Metropolitan cities and urban agglomerations

Metropolitan cities, urban agglomerations and large-sized towns have been described in Indian planning literature as agents of transformation of the rural countryside. The Registrar General of India has published a detailed account of the levels of economic development in India in which it is noted that large areas of India are near such urban centres and yet are devoid of basic civic amenities (Census of India, 1961, 1968). It was assumed by early planners, and by others who followed them, that if these urban centres had the necessary industrial and socio-economic infrastructure, then the surrounding countryside would benefit from it. Thus, the strengthening of the urban core, or the urban system, or both, with adequate socio-economic facilities was considered as a viable strategy (NCAER, 1965; Johnson, 1970; TCPO, 1968, 1971, 1971a; Misra, Sundaram & Rao, 1974; Sundaram, 1977; Misra, 1978).

Generally, it can be said that a few metropolitan plans have been able to distinguish, at the stage of formulation, between the problems of the core and those of the region. Thus, the Delhi Development Plan talks of the metropolitan area and the National Capital Region (TCPO, 1971b). Even this recognition, of local and regional problems of metropolitan planning, is missing from other plans (Chakraborty, 1972; Wanmali & Khan, 1970). At the stage of implementation, however, there are spectacular failures. In the case of Delhi, this was due to the lack of coordination between the objectives of the development of the metropolitan area and its ring towns. In the case of Calcutta, the idea to link the development with the hierarchy of towns throughout the Calcutta Metropolitan District appears to have been abandoned in favour of area development plans for some towns only, notably Howrah; but these are town plans rather than regional plans, and they do not solve any regional or rural problems. In addition, it was not recognised that metropolitan areas, and their problems, differ from one metropolitan region to another; that urban agglomerations are not the same as the metropolitan regions; and that the objectives of metropolitan planning in India are not identical all over the country (Misra, 1978).

There were problems of coordination between urban and rural sectors of a metropolitan plan; betwen the local and regional aspects of development; between inter-district, and sometimes inter-state, administration; and between state and national governments. These problems mostly related to the matters of administrative control and financial authority. In many cases, an easy way out was sought by making the urban local government responsible for the development of urban areas within a metropolitan region and by leaving the rural areas in the jurisdiction of the district development administration. The more radical solution of the establishment of an independent metropolitan development authority, with adequate financial and administrative powers, was always avoided. It is a consequence of this lack of coordination that the metropolitan areas have not always been able to solve even the basic regional (rural) problems. A number of studies have demonstrated that many of the basic amenities such as education, health, communications, trade, banking, transport, agricultural inputs, retail services and animal husbandry services are physically inaccessible to most of the villages in a typical metropolitan region (Wanmali, 1970, 1976; Wanmali & Khan, 1970; Alam & Khan, 1972). Further, no efforts are made to improve this situation. On the other hand, urban amenities such as roads (within towns), water supply, electricity, parking facilities, shopping centres, residential areas, recreational facilities, health, education and transport are being continually improved within the urban municipal limits of the same metropolitan region (Alam & Khan, 1972; Misra, 1978).

Industrial centres

Industrialisation was also considered as a means of transformation of rural India (Govt. of India, 1963, 1964, 1969, 1969a, 1969b, 1969c). The exercise on the levels of development in India noted that there existed some areas in India which were rich in resources but were very poor industrially (Census of India, 1961). It was in these areas that the new basic and heavy industries were located. New industrial towns such as Bhilai, Rourkela, Bokaro, Durgapur, Korba, Sindri, Bongaigaon, Haldia, Ramagundem, Neyveli and Koradih; and new townships near Hardwar, Rishikesh, Pinjore, Bhopal, Ranchi, Ghatsila, Hyderabad, Cochin, Trivandrum, Bangalore, Vishakapatnam, Pune, Bombay, Baroda, Nagpur, Bhusaval and Mathura, were established for manufacturing of steel, copper, coal, chemicals, aluminium, electricals, heavy engineering products, machine tools, rare earths, uranium, defence products, atomic energy and consumer goods. The ease with which factor and product links were identified, and established, in these industries added to the myth that these units are also capable of integrating their geographical regions quickly (Misra, Sundaram & Rao, 1974).

What these industries did achieve, by way of regional development (apart from a spectacular growth in the overall industrial production), was only a rudimentary form of integration with the surrounding geographical regions. First, during the period of construction of these industrial centres, a large rural population was employed as labourers on the building sites; second, the rural areas provided, and are continuing to provide, the inhabitants of these new industrial centres with vegetables, fruits, milk and milk products, meat, poultry and foodgrains (Wanmali, 1980, 1981). The non-food-producing population of the industrial centres was a sitting, and captured, demand for these goods.

But in other ways the industrial centres have effectively prevented the rural areas from being integrated with them. These centres are good 'company towns' with excellent facilities in education, health, communication, transport, banking, wholesale and retail trade, facilities which are rarely, if at all, used by anyone except the employees of the industrial unit (Wanmali, 1981). Now, these are indeed some of the very services which could effect a quick integration of a centre and its rural hinterland. The industrial centres, however, have tended on the whole to keep these services to themselves. Perhaps it is incorrect to assume that the industrial centres were supposed to integrate the surrounding countryside, so that one should not necessarily anticipate any regional implications of industrial development. Perhaps the time scale which the planners have adopted is the wrong one. Whatever the underlying reason, although their own product and factor links were established efficiently, with some minor exceptions (Wanmali, 1981; Wanmali & Ghosh, 1975), the industrial centres have so far done little to serve their rural hinterlands.

Agro-based industries, on the other hand, were fairly evenly distributed throughout rural India. These ranged from small processing units rooted firmly in their agricultural regions to complex finished products units in big cities. The links between the small and large units, wherever these existed, date back to the turn of the current century. The new agro-processing units were encouraged to locate themselves in large and medium-sized towns with the help of a policy of establishing industrial estates and, more recently, of district industrial centres. The trading and commercial links of these towns with their immediate rural hinterlands are very strong.

A critique of urban and industrial models

The ad hoc attempts, from the Second Plan to the Fourth Plan period, at urban and industrial development did not achieve their implied spatial objectives. There is awareness now that even the more limited objectives, of a non-spatial nature, were also not fully achieved. This becomes clear when one reads the resolution of the expert committee on National Urbanisation Policy (Govt. of India, 1975). This committee met in 1975 to review the progress made by the policy of urban-based spatial development in India. The committee was seriously concerned by the lack of attention given to such models of spatial planning; this despite almost two decades of adherence to urban-based models only. The committee, however, recognised that the problems of urban planning are also related to those of the rural areas and that in the future the urban-based spatial development can not afford to ignore the rural areas. This was a very salutary change in the attitude of the Government of India; it was the acknowledging that the rural areas existed, not just incidentally, but in their own right. Thus, for the first time in Indian planning the planning space was viewed in its totality. But the rural problems continued to be viewed from the urban angle.

In the analysis of the spatial impact of urban and industrial develoment and, indeed, in the declarations of the National Urbanisation Policy, the urban centres, the urban hierarchies and the urban-rural relationships tend to play an important part. It was assumed by the exponents of the urban based models of rural/regional development that there exists in India an interconnected system of metropolitan cities which is supported by a similar system of large and medium-sized towns. Rural areas in these two systems were assumed to be geographically 'disorganised' (NCAER, 1965; Johnson, 1970). It was felt, therefore, that if all the growth and development inputs are located in metropolitan, and other urban, areas, their interconnected nature would help the distribution, and diffusion, of these inputs to the rural areas (NCAER, 1965; Johnson, 1970; Misra, Sundaram & Rao, 1974; Sundaram, 1977). This distribution, and diffusion, was to have been achieved as follows: (i) within a metropolitan, and urban, region from the metropolis, and the town, outwards and downwards to their respective rural hinterlands in a hierarchical manner; and (ii) between a system of metropolitan, and urban, regions, from higher order regions downwards to lower order regions.

There is enough empirical evidence in India to suggest that the urban based process of rural/regional development will not follow the pattern noted in the previous paragraph for the following reasons:

(i) There exist demographic, functional and spatial gaps in the urban system of India (Wanmali, 1967, 1975, 1981; Khan & Wanmali, 1972; Chapman & Wanmali, 1981);
(ii) These gaps effectively prevent the outward and downward spread of development inputs;
(iii) There is a greater degree of 'functional friction' within the metropolitan areas which has prevented the rural hinterland from deriving benefits of a metropolitan economy (Wanmali, 1970, 1976; Wanmali & Khan, 1970; Alam & Khan, 1972; Sundaram, 1977; Harris, 1978; Misra, 1978);

(iv) The growth in heavy and basic industries does not diffuse to all the centres in the surrounding rural region but primarily to those where the factors of production are located (Wanmali & Ghosh, 1975);
(v) The types of development inputs which are in high demand in the rural areas tend to be such services as education, health, transport, communications, trade, agricultural input distribution, retail outlets and animal husbandry services (Wanmali, 1970; Wanmali & Khan, 1970; Sen et al., 1971; Alam & Khan, 1972; Bhat, 1976; Misra, Sundaram & Rao, 1974); but these appear overwhelmingly to be located in urban centres which are inaccessible to the rural areas (Wanmali & Khan, 1970; Sen et al., 1971);
(vi) There do not exist interconnected systems of metropolitan and urban regions in India (Chapman & Wanmali, 1981).

It is significant to note here, however, that there do exist metropolitan centres and *their* rural hinterlands; large and medium sized towns and *their* hinterlands and small towns and *their* rural hinterlands; each functions in its own peculiar way and maintains, no doubt, some kind of product and/or commodity links with other regions.

Spatial impact of rural development

Policies of rural development also exhibit a heavy reliance on budgetary allocations and time horizons as major means of achieving the planned objectives in rural development (Govt. of India, 1952, 1956, 1961, 1970, 1976). Insofar as there exist differences between States, and districts within States, in budget allocations, the spatial impact of the programmes of development tends to differ between, and within, States. It will not be out of place to describe briefly the spatial impact of the various programmes of rural development.

Community development programme

The First Five Year Plan saw the introduction of the community development programme in rural India. It was the first comprehensive attempt to solve the problems of rural India since Independence. The programme itself was a mere listing of priorities of rural development. It was launched in October 1952, but on a pilot scale, to cover 52 blocks in the country. By the end of the Plan period, however, the entire country was covered by a network of the community development blocks. The programme was aimed at changing the attitudes of the people in rural areas and it hoped to prepare them for an era of rural development and planning (Mukherjee, 1967).

At the end of the First Five Year Plan period, it was realised that the community development programme was not providing the necessary impetus to the one major national objective which was increased food production. Thus, from the position of giving equal importance to all aspects of rural development, as in the First Plan, the Government chose to give a higher priority to the development of agriculture in the Second Five Year Plan period. This also meant a change in the administrative and organisational structure of the community development programme, through whose network it was hoped to achieve higher agricultural production. Changes of the former type gave a more direct role to various technical departments at the district level.

In the Third Five Year Plan period, a further element of selectivity was introduced in the agricultural development programme. This was achieved by choosing some districts, and some crops within the districts, for preferential assistance in the overall drive for higher agricultural production (Hunter & Bottrall, 1974). The hybrid, and high yielding, varieties of such crops as wheat, paddy, jowar, bajra, cotton, groundnuts, castor and sugarcane were released to the farmers during this and the subsequent plan periods. By the end of the Fourth Plan, the rural areas in India had experienced a selective regional transformation; once again based on the districts. This also meant that other districts were experiencing imbalanced development. The scheme, therefore, tended to become more localised, and specialised, with heavy reliance on pilot projects which got located in areas (districts) where the returns on investment were not only higher but also quicker. It was believed that this would give rise to demonstration effects at least in the districts which were geographically adjacent to the locations of the pilot projects. Even this belief was not fulfilled; the expected spread of demonstration effects did not take place and this further accentuated the imbalanced development. The community development blocks and the districts continue, however, to provide the administrative framework for various schemes of rural development. The spatial impact of these schemes is thus felt at the level of the district.

Panchayati Raj programme

Along with the community development programme, the Government of India was busy establishing a structure of rural local government. The process was started in 1958 and was completed in 1962 (Parikh, 1960; Naik, 1961; Ali, 1964; Pai, 1964; Raju, 1964). The Panchayati Raj programme now covers about 98% of the rural population through a network of about 210,000 *gram panchayats* (at the village level), 3550 *panchayat samitis* (at the community development block level) and about 240 *zilla parishads* (at the district level). The members of these bodies are elected by the people; and these elected representatives of the people confer with the administrative and technical experts, who are also based at the same three tiers within a district noted above, to arrive at the priorities of development within their respective areas of jurisdiction.

The perception of the Panchayati Raj institutions varied from one group of people to another. For the development administrators, these institutions were the instruments by which the fruits of science and technology were brought to the rural areas; the rural elite considered them as a means of legitimising their traditional power base; and the weaker sections of the society tended to see them as necessary vehicles to voice their fears and grievances (Hoffsomer & Dube, 1961; Sen, Gaikwad & Verma, 1967), or they were simply sceptical about these institutions (Farmer, 1977).

There are inter-state variations in the working of the Panchayati Raj institutions. These variations tend to reflect not merely the nature of adjustment to the local conditions but also the commitment of the State Government to the idea of popular participation in the process of planning (Appleby, 1962; Jacob, 1962; Chaturvedi, 1969). Thus, a definite pattern of spatial impact in rural areas, and within districts, was identified by the end of the Third Five Year Plan period. By then the district was not only a unit of revenue administration but also that of development administration (as in the community development programme) and of local government (as in the Panchayati Raj programme). In this respect, at least, the States which had effectively devolved administrative and financial powers to these local government institutions have shown a remarkable progress in rural development.

By 1969, as in the case of urban, and industrial, based models of rural/regional development, the Government of India had become aware that the programmes of rural development have accentuated the regional imbalances. In other words, the normal channels of distribution of programmed funds were not delivering goods effectively; for the reasons of lack of policy, or coordination, or both. In order to correct these imbalances, the Government of India launched centrally sponsored projects for hill areas, tribal areas and the drought-prone areas as well as for the small farmers, marginal farmers and agricultural labourers, in the post-1969 plan periods. More significantly, an attempt was also made to identify the characteristic features of the spatial organisation in rural India by initiating a pilot research project on rural growth centres (Govt. of India, 1970).

The pilot research project on rural growth centres

The first to be introduced in India as a matter of spatial policy, although on a pilot basis, the project on rural growth centres was also unique in its approach to rural development (Govt. of India, 1970). It viewed rural India from the angle of villages and not from that of the urban centres only. The aims of the pilot project were to develop a broad research methodology for identifying emerging growth centres in rural areas, and to indicate how these centres could be meaningfully woven into the framework of district plans and thus help the process of planning from below (Govt. of India, 1970; Sen et al., 1971). The reports from the twenty-odd pilot project areas all over India are unanimous in their findings that in a rural region it is possible to use some form of locational analysis, together with the studies of resource endowments and of commodity flows, to identify spatial relations between villages. The results were used for recommending certain policy planning measures for the development of rural areas which were covered by the pilot projects. The findings of the project, which are not unique to the Indian rural scene, are listed below; these indicate that the rural settlements in India are distributed, and function, along certain well-known principles of spatial organisation.

The project categorised services in rural areas into those provided by the government and those which were provided by the non-government agencies. From the list of those provided by the government, services for which no spatial interaction takes place were not considered. The services provided by the non-government agencies were also not considered. An analysis of the services included in the exercise revealed that these are available in a few settlements and are availed of by a number of settlements (the latter being those which do not have the services in question); from this interaction a spatial pattern was obtained. This resulted in the categorisation of settlements into those which were functioning as service centres and those which were dependent upon the service centres for the satisfaction of a particular type, and level, of service. A four-tier hierarchy of service centres, which tended to serve all the settlements, was identified in a district. ('Rural growth centres' was a misnomer from the beginning: what the settlements were functioning as was more akin to service centres. The incorrect terminology of the pilot project was responsible for much academic discussions within, and outside, India during the late sixties and early seventies.)

In all the studies of the pilot project, there was a clear indication that certain services tended to cluster within definite population size groups; as one went up the scale of population size, more complex services were encountered. The higher order service centres tended to have extensive service areas and the service areas of the lower order service centres tended to nest under those of the higher order service centres. For individual services such as branch post office, centre for medical checkup, secondary school, branch of a nationalised bank, centre for distribution of agricultural inputs (such as fertilisers, seeds and pesticides) and for trade there existed definite zones of population size as well as ranges of service areas. The villages which had less population than the zones did not have that particular service whereas villages with more population than the zones always possessed the service. Although, as is to be expected, the exact values of either population or area varied from one region to another in India, the concepts as such held good (Wanmali, 1973). All the pilot project studies noted that there were serious gaps in the provision of services in rural areas. All made recommendations, based on the analyses of gaps, to reduce the degree of their imbalanced provision.

The Government of India, and the State Governments, were justifiably pleased with the results of the pilot project. The exercise could be conducted with the help of planned funds and could be adjusted to the existing time horizons of the Five Year Plans. Further, it could be viewed in the context of local, and relevant, spatial relationships rather than as a part of some distant urban system. At the end of the Fourth Five Year Plan period, the project was 'handed over' to the State Governments with the recommendation that they should initiate similar exercises in other districts. It is very sad to note that with the exception of Andhra Pradesh no other State has followed up this recommendation seriously.

Critique of the programmes of rural development

In the theoretical exposition of the community development programme, and the Panchayati Raj programme, it was assumed by the government that all people are equal. It was implicitly also assumed that they will be equally mobile. The Government then went about setting up a structure of rural development institutions expecting that these will be equally accessible to all the people. When this expected pattern is viewed against the reality, it becomes clear that the rural people are not equal, that the mobility of the rural people is influenced by their socio-economic status, and that, therefore, the people tend to have differential mobility to the same set of services (Wanmali, 1976). Further, the services themselves are not adequately distributed and the socio-economic disadvantage and distance from such services together can prevent the services being used by all people.

The policy of spatial development through rural growth centres can be criticised for assuming that when the gaps in the service provision are filled, these service centres, or services, will be used by all people with uniform frequency; that the services provided by the government are the only types which can organise rural space (by this also assuming that other systems of service provision are of no significance or that these do not exist); and that the spatially fixed services alone can fill the gaps in service provision. There is enough evidence from rural India to suggest that frequency of use of services is not uniform throughout the year (Wanmali, 1975a); that the services are not uniformly accessible to people just because these are provided in a uniform manner (Wanmali, 1976); that the services provided by the non-government agencies from spatially fixed locations (Wanmali & Ghosh, 1975), or from spatially fixed but temporally mobile locations (Wanmali, 1980, 1981), are also capable of organising rural space; that in some service provision, such as regulated marketing of agricultural produce, the government has created, rather than solved, more problems (Wanmali, 1980); and that there is room to look at the concept of mobile service provision in rural India (Wanmali, 1981).

There are, however, some positive aspects of rural-based models of service provision in India. In a recent resurvey of the study area in Andhra Pradesh (of the pilot research project on rural growth centres), it has been observed that the introduction of spatial planning to the total planning process, which hitherto included budgetary allocations and time horizons only, was responsible for a remarkable improvement in the level of provision of both rural (controlled by the government sector) and retail (controlled by the private sector) services. The study area has two structurally different regional economies, canal-irrigated tract and dry tract. The improvement in service provision is more spectacular in the irrigated tract than in the dry tract; and more in rural services than in retail services. There is, however, a clear indication that the retail services are better provided in the irrigated tract (where the returns on investment are high) than in the dry tract (Wanmali, 1983, 1983a).

One of the more important consequences of this spatial planning exercise is that the settlement system of the study area has become less primate. This means that, demographically, the two towns of the study area (both less than 20,000 population each) are now at the apex of a settlement system which is fast becoming log-normal in its distribution. Functionally, the system has shown evidence of 'strengthening' in a hierarchical fashion; both rural and retail services are spreading outward from a major centre and downward along the settlement system. The rural services are providing the framework within which the retail services are being located. Spatially, the impact of this service provision is such that it had made the services (both rural and retail) more accessible to the people. The extent of service area and service population has dropped considerably; although more in the irrigated tract than in the dry tract (Wanmali, 1983, 1983a).

Rural-based models for rural development

It becomes clear from the foregoing discussion that the current approach to rural development in India, which consists of budgetary allocations and time horizons, can be usefully complemented by the studies of spatial organisation. What is significant about this approach is that it views the development plans and processes from the grassroots level. After almost five Five Year Plans, the planners in India appear to have got bogged down in the confusion of their own creation. This is basically a consequence of their unwillingness to look at other policy options which could help deliver the goods to rural India. The urban, and industrial, based models of rural development have had a very limited impact on service provision in the Indian countryside.

There is enough evidence in rural India today which points to a well-organised entity. The service centres; their service areas; the thresholds of services; clustering of services; the hierarchy of service centres; the interconnected nature of this hierarchy; the overlap of government, private and traditional systems of service provision; and the progressive strengthening of the spatial features of a settlement system are all elements of a well-organised entity. All these elements exist in a politico-administrative unit in rural India such as the district which, in addition, has also become a unit of planning. The district has both executive and financial powers to implement the programmes of rural development. The process of sectoral and spatial integration at the district level has been described elsewhere (Wanmali, 1983, 1983a); but suffice it to say here that development in agriculture in a district is linked to, and was a consequence of, other sectoral developments in irrigation, transport, service provision, electrification and agro-processing.

When viewed in the temporal scale of Five Year Plans, the process of service provision in a typical district can be described as follows: in the first stage, the services were based entirely in towns; if the towns did not have the requisite services, these were made available under the programmed funds during the first three Five Year Plans (1951–66); it was hoped that once the process of filling the gaps in the service provision is completed, the towns will be able to act as service centres for the surrounding rural areas. In the second stage, a set of less complex services was located in what were described as central villages (these central villages were identified on the basis of studies conducted during the Fourth and Fifth Plan periods, 1969–79). For reasons of differences in the socio-economig status of villagers, the services provided both in towns and in central villages were differentially accessible to people at large. The next stage (post-Fifth Five Year Plan period), perhaps, would involve provision of services through a locationally fixed (at either the periodic markets or the central villages) but temporally mobile system; this would reduce the cost of maintaining the system of service provision by not investing in buildings to house services whose frequency of use is very low. Such services, which can be provided in a mobile fashion, are health, communication (postal services), banking, credit, input distribution, sale of urban consumer goods and purchase of rural produce (the last two are already being provided in this manner through the periodic markets in rural India).

The line of argument in this future scenario can still be criticised for not considering adequately the social impact of service provision. But this is, perhaps, because spatial planning by itself is incapable of ensuring the establishment of a socially acceptable or just pattern of service provision. It can be said, however, that spatial planning is one of the tools in the hands of the development administrators with which it is possible to bring the services nearer to the people than ever before, thereby making these services physically more accessible.

ACKNOWLEDGEMENTS

The author is grateful to Deryke Belshaw, Charles Gore and Raymond Apthorpe for their helpful comments on an earlier draft.

REFERENCES

Alam, S.M. & Khan, W. (1972). *Metropolitan Hyderabad and Its Region: A Strategy for Development*. Bombay
Ali, Sadiq (1964). *Report of the Study Team on Panchayati Raj*. Jaipur
Appleby, P.H. (1962). Some thoughts on decentralised democracy. *Indian Journal of Public Administration*, 18, 443–55
Bhat, L.S. (1976). *Micro-Level Planning: A Case Study of Karnal Area, Haryana, India*. New Delhi
Census of India (1961). *Levels of Regional Development in India*. New Delhi
   (1968). *Economic Regionalisation of India: Problems and Approaches*. New Delhi
Chakraborty, S. (1972). Delineation of planning areas: an experiment on Calcutta 1961. Paper presented to the First Indo-British Seminar on Geography, New Delhi
Chapman, G.P. & Wanmali, Sudhir (1981). Urban-rural relationships in India: A macro-scale approach using population potentials. *Geoforum*, 12, 19–44
Chaturvedi, T.N. (1969). Case for change in the pattern of development at panchayati raj level. Seminar on Community Development and Panchayati Raj in India, Jaipur
Farmer, B.H. (1975). Urban bias in urban geography. Paper presented to the Second Indo-British Geography Seminar on Urban-Rural Relations, St John's College, Cambridge
   (ed.) (1977). *Green Revolution? Technology and Change in Rice Growing Areas of Tamilnadu and Sri Lanka*. London, Macmillan
Govt. of India (1952). *The First Five Year Plan*. Planning Commission, New Delhi
   (1956). *The Second Five Year Plan*. Planning Commission, New Delhi
   (1961). *The Third Five Year Plan*. Planning Commission, New Delhi
   (1963). *Report on Industrial Townships Committee on Plan Projects*. New Delhi
   (1964). *Notes on Perspectives of Development in India: 1960–61 to 1975–76*. New Delhi
   (1969). *Report of the Industrial Licensing Policy Inquiry Committee*. New Delhi
   (1969a). *Report of the Working Group on the Identification of Backward Areas*. Planning Commission, New Delhi
   (1969b). *Report of the Working Group to Recommend Fiscal and Financial Incentives for Starting Industries in Backward Areas*. New Delhi
   (1969c). *Report of the Rural-Urban Relations Committee*. New Delhi
   (1970). *The Fourth Five Year Plan*. Planning Commission, New Delhi
   (1975). *National Urbanisation Policy*. New Delhi
   (1976). *The Fifth Five Year Plan*. Planning Commission, New Delhi

Harris, N. (1978). *Economic Development, Cities and Planning: The Case of Bombay*. Bombay
Hoffsomer, H. & Dube, S.C. (1961). *A Sociological Study of Panchayati Raj*. Hyderabad
Hunter, G. & Bottrall, A. (eds.) (1974). *Serving the Small Farmer: Policy Choices in Indian Agriculture*. Hyderabad
Jacob, G. (ed.) (1967). *Readings on Panchayati Raj*. Hyderabad
Johnson, E.A.J. (1970). *The Organisation of Space in Developing Countries*. Cambridge, Mass., Harvard University Press
Khan, W. & Wanmali, Sudhir (1972). Impact of linguistic reorganisation of states on city-size distribution in peninsular India. In V.V. Pokshenshivsky & B.K. Roy-Burman (eds.), *Economic and Socio-Cultural Dimensions of Regionalisation*. New Delhi
Lewis, John P. (1962). *Quiet Crisis in India*. Washington
Lipton, M. (1978). Strategy for agriculture: urban bias and rural planning. In P. Stretton & M. Lipton (eds.), *The Crisis of Indian Planning*. London, Oxford University Press, pp. 83–148
Misra, R.P., Sundaram, K.V. & Rao, V.L.S.P. (1974). *Regional Development Planning in India: A New Strategy*. New Delhi
 (ed.) (1978). *Million Cities of India*. New Delhi
Mukherjee, B. (1967). *Community Development in India*. Bombay
NCAER (1965). *Market Towns and Spatial Development in India*. New Delhi
Naik,V.P. (1963). *Report of the Committee on Democratic Decentralisation*. Bombay
Pai, P. (1964). *Report of the High Power Committee on the Reorganisation of Panchayat Samiti Blocks and Allied Matters*. Hyderabad
Parikh, Rasiklal (1960). *Report of the Committee on Democratic Decentralisation*. Ahmedabad
Raju, M.T. (1964). *Report of the Committee Constituted to Examine the Question of Organisation of the District Administration*. Hyderabad
Sen, L.K., Gaikwad, V.R. & Verma, G.L. (1967). *People's Image of Community Development and Panchayati Raj*. Hyderabad
Sen, L.K. et al. (1971). *Planning Rural Growth Centres for Integrated Area Development: A Study in Miryalguda Taluka*. Hyderabad
Sundaram, K.V. (1977). *Urban and Regional Planning in India*. New Delhi
TCPO (1968). *Planning Regions of India*. New Delhi
 (1971). *Report on Damodar Subarnarekha Sub-Region*. New Delhi
 (1971a). *Regional Imbalances in India: Some Policy Issues and Problems*. New Delhi
 (1971b). *Role of Growth Foci in Regional Development Strategy*. New Delhi
Wanmali, Sudhir (1967). Regional development, regional planning and the hierarchy of towns. *Bombay Geographical Magazine*,15, 1–30
 (1970). *Regional Planning for Social Facilities: An Examination of Central Place Concepts and Their Application: A Case Study of Eastern Maharashtra*. Hyderabad
 (1973). Lessons of work on growth centres for micro-level planning. *Indian*

Journal of Public Administration. Special Volume on Multi-Level Planning, 19, 308–19

(1975). Urbanisation and regional policy. *Management and Labour Studies*, 1, 6–15

(1975a). Rural service centres in India: present identification and acceptance of extension. *Area*, 7, 167–70

(1976). Popular participation and organisation, distribution and consumption of social services and facilities in rural human settlements: an Indian experience. United Nations, New York (mimeo)

(1980). The regulated and periodic markets and rural development in India. *Transactions of the Institute of British Geographers*, n.s. 5, 466–86

(1981). *Periodic Markets and Rural Development in India.* New Delhi

(1983). *Service Centre in Rural India: Policy, Theory and Practice.* New Delhi

(1983a). *Service provision and rural development in India: a study of Miryalguda Taluka.* Research Report No. 37, International Ford Policy Research Institute. Washington D.C.

Wanmali, Sudhir & Khan, W. (1970). Role of location in regional planning with particular reference to the provision of social facilities. *Behavioural Sciences and Community Development*, 4, 65–91

Wanmali, Sudhir & Ghosh, A. (1975). Pattern of distribution of consumer goods in rural India. *Management and Labour Studies*, 1, 79–94

13 Planning and agrarian change in East Africa: appropriate and inappropriate models for land settlement schemes

DERYKE G.R. BELSHAW

Land settlement schemes have been defined by B.H. Farmer as 'the establishment of people on wasteland by government organisations for agricultural purposes and in groups large enough to require completely new villages' (Farmer, 1974, p. 1). In South Asia schemes of this sort are often termed 'agricultural colonisation'. They appear to provide particularly favourable conditions for the introduction of new technology such as that associated with the Green Revolution, for innovations in the provision of social services, and for land tenure reform.

Unfortunately, experience in a range of countries has shown that land settlement does not necessarily provide any simple answer to problems of development planning. The design of land settlement schemes and land tenure policies is still not an exact science, and although research in this area has expanded, our capacity to design successfully is not noticeably more advanced today than when B.H. Farmer (1957) conducted his pioneer study of *Pioneer Peasant Colonization in Ceylon* thirty years ago. The model which I am proposing in this chapter aims to provide a context in which planning interventions in this area can be viewed. My intention is to appraise alternative policy options for problems of land and population in land-surplus rural sectors. Such conditions are typical of large areas of tropical Africa and south-east Asia, and are not altogether absent even in more densely populated regions. The discussion is illustrated with examples drawn mainly from East African experience.

Analytical framework

The following initial conditions are assumed to obtain:

(i) The presence of large areas, relative to demand, of fertile land for cultivation or grazing use within the rural sector;
(ii) A continuing growth in rural population, with the non-rural employment opportunities increasing less rapidly than the labour force;
(iii) The presence of a simple exchange system offering a range of consumer goods desired by the rural population in return for surplus food or non-food output;
(iv) The presence of a simple social service infrastructure providing a set of desired functions in return for direct (cash) or indirect (tax) payment;

(v) The presence of a dualistic land-use pattern in the form of alienated holdings reserved for public and/or private use (forest reserves, state or parastatal farms or ranches, private plantations or estates, etc.) occupying a relatively small if well-favoured total land area. These exist alongside traditional and transitional farms where the system of production is either pastoral or based on cultivation, and either family-based or kinship-based;

(vi) The existence of ethnic, cultural or religious divisions in the rural population strongly associated with spatial distribution, i.e. social territoriality is a pervasive factor;

(vii) The non-existence of rural indebtedness and 'landlordism', i.e. unencumbered peasant proprietorship is the dominant mode of production.

The major dynamic element in the model is assumed to be rural population growth; it causes 'better' – in terms of all its attributes – land to become increasingly scarce. The scale and location of the exchange and social service systems are assumed to reach equilibrium positions relative to population after a short time-lag. The sectoral terms of trade, the set of rural production activities and production technology are three other key system variables; in the initial analysis these are assumed to remain constant. The policy instruments on which attention is focussed are (i) investment in infrastructure and/or production projects intended to assist or accelerate population relocation (and thereby improve access to productive land and water resources) and (ii) changes to traditional systems of land tenure.

The criteria relevant for the identification, design and selection of appropriate strategies are to be derived from two objective functions: (i) maximising the present value of the associated stream of net social benefits, and (ii) attaining a specified reduction in absolute and/or relative poverty within the rural population. The relative weights given to these two objectives is assumed to vary between different political systems to produce a range of appropriate sets of policies and projects which lie along a strategy continuum running from equity-constrained growth to growth-constrained equity. The extreme ideological positions of economic laissez-faire and deterministic blueprint planning lie outside the concern of this study, because in neither case is there a concern with informed and rational choice.

A three phase analysis of population, land and settlement

The essential feature of the model, therefore, is the movement over time of the rural sector along a continuum with land resources becoming increasingly scarce in relation to rural population. This continuum is explored by arbitrarily distinguishing three consecutive phases. It is predicated that different efficiency and equity effects will result from the application of the same strategy in different time phases. If this assumption is correct, the identification, design and selection of appropriate strategies for a specific rural sector will be assisted by the prior specification of its position on the relative factor-endowment continuum.

Phase I

In Phase I it is assumed that population growth can be accommodated by short-distance intra-rural migration. Land of similar natural potential is available nearby so that intangible costs arising from the disruption of social networks are minimised. Higher costs in terms of reduced access to exchange and social infrastructure, however, will be incurred even over distances of a few miles as long as roads are absent. Where land is virtually a free good, customary communal tenure systems will typically prevail. The associated usufructuary rights, however, may gradually convert to *de facto* freehold as land becomes scarcer in the original 'heartlands', particularly if perennial cash crops are planted over time and other land-saving capital formation occurs (drainage, terracing, etc.).

Whilst the spontaneous settlement mechanism can cope with the population problem, both efficiency and equity gains can often be secured from low-cost, pump-priming public investment in physical infrastructure, e.g. roads, domestic water supply and basic health facilities. By reducing the pioneering costs for low income families on the settlement frontier, these can accelerate the rate of relocation of population (with corresponding gains in the exodus area) and the growth of marketed surplus from the settlement area.

Examples of successful low-cost assisted resettlement schemes can be found in the northern Kigezi area, between 1946 and 1953 in Uganda (Belshaw, 1968) and in the Sukumaland Scheme of the 1950s in Tanganyika (de Wilde, 1967; McLoughlin, 1970). These were small, intra-regional projects designed and executed at the local level. A case for similar prior investment in infrastructure at numerous new village sites has been identified in the less densely populated parts of rural Tanzania in the current post-villagisation period (Coleman et al., 1978). Whilst clarification and modification of customary rights in land may be beneficial in reducing elements of uncertainty and social friction, only limited effort in this direction is popularly desired or socially justified given continuing access to an open land frontier nearby (cf. the failure of land registration schemes in Uganda in the early 1960s, Brock, 1969).

Large-scale production units and areas of forest reserve pose no major efficiency or equity problems, rather permitting land-extensive, management-intensive, high-risk monoculture (buffered by state or multinational joint-stock institutions) on otherwise unutilised resources and providing the labour-force entrant with a period of wage earning prior to 'investing' in a wife and new farm – and, later probably, cattle or perennial crops.

Except where a feudal social structure exists, wealth inequalities between families can usually be explained by a cyclical capital accumulation process, the older generations becoming increasingly wealthy prior to, on their death, the subdivision of assets to members of younger generations according to the particular inheritance system (Chayanov, 1925).

Phase II

The onset of Phase II is defined by the closing-off of short-distance (i.e. within the jurisdiction of the local ethnic or kinship group) settlement opportunities. Movement is entailed to surplus land areas under the traditional political control of other communities. The transcending and unifying power of the nation-state is required to create an inter-regional planning framework for the transfer and absorption of newcomers into what is often perceived as a socially, as well as physically, hostile environment. Once successfully demonstrating the gains to be obtained, however, these formal projects may lead to a second period of spontaneous settlement.

An interesting example is provided by the tsetse-fly barrier settlement schemes in Bunyoro in western Uganda in the late 1950s. These were originally settled by Maragoli people from western Kenya; these were later joined by Bakiga from the overcrowded Kigezi District some 200 kilometres to the south. Although the schemes were terminated in 1963, spontaneous migration of Bakiga in large numbers continued into other unsettled parts of Bunyoro over the next dozen years directly as a result of the original abandoned national strategy. Rational relocation of population across strong ethnic boundaries may be politically difficult to achieve where central government politics is strongly influenced by territorial interest groups. For example, in Tanzania, despite the presence of machinery for multi-regional planning and specific proposals for large-scale resettlement projects (Belshaw, 1975), long-distance movements currently occur only on a tolerated or 'blind-eye' basis, e.g. Chagga moving southwards from Kilimanjaro to Morogoro Region and Wasukuma and Masai southwards from Mwanza, Shinyanga and Arusha Regions to Mbeya Region (pers. comm., Prime Minister's Office, Tanzania, 1981). Larger numbers could be moved at lower net cost, with more immediate returns from quite low expenditure, if a sound multi-regional settlement strategy had been designed and approved.

In the regional economies where the open land frontier no longer exists, extensive forms of land use inevitably come under increasing attack, politically and also physically. Forest areas and game reserves are particularly vulnerable; illegal clearing, burning and hunting on an increasing scale can be expected unless significant intensification of land use is achieved in both the settled and the reserved areas. In the latter case, technical opportunities for multi-purpose land use are often present, for example agro-forestry and multi-storey cropping in the case of forest land, pastoralism and game tourism in the case of savanna reserves. On the other hand the vested interests of single-purpose public sector institutions in retaining their exclusive control prevents desirable changes from being effected (delays in establishing multi-purpose land use planning machinery in Kenya along the lines envisaged by the Third Five-year Plan are a case in point; see Govt. of Kenya, 1978).

Increasing land scarcity relative to population and increasing monetarisation of rural production systems is usually accompanied by the spread of a market in land, whether land is held under *de jure* freehold title or not. It is frequently held that this process leads to the creation of a *rural* landless class (see e.g. Ghai, 1981). Where landlordism and rural indebtedness are absent, as is the case in most of Tropical Africa, it seems doubtful if either theoretically or empirically much support can be found for this view. Theoretically, small subsistence plots tend to generate a higher stream of income than as an addition to a large farm because of both the usual greater use intensity with decreasing plot size (Dorner, 1972) and the higher value of output valued at retail price opportunity cost than at producer prices. In practice, small plot accumulation is difficult on the ground, private investment funds find more lucrative returns outside agriculture (Sharpley, 1978) and the observably landless, who are found in the urban areas, usually retain residual, if small, rights in land in their rural ethnic homelands.

Phase III

Phase III is defined as marking the closing-off of a frontier of fertile land anywhere in the rural sector. Spontaneous settlement, where it still occurs, is into low-potential and often ecologically fragile areas, and becomes more a part of the problem than its solution. More generally, intensification of existing small-scale activity is accelerated. Land settlement may have a role to play, however, in the intensification of land use on previously extensively used land resources. The commonest examples are land reform projects and irrigation schemes.

Usually an influx of additional settlers must be accommodated. The future livelihoods of the large-farm labour force (in the case of land reform), or rainfed cultivators or pastoralists (in the case of irrigation schemes) should be (but often are not) given priority attention at the design stage. Also in Phase III, the location of any remaining land-extensive and low employment-generating activities on high-potential land should be critically examined, with a view to intensification or relocation. A good case may be made, for example, to move forestry from high rainfall areas to less favourable ecological zones such as semi-arid areas, replacing it with perennial food and cash crops or other soil and water conserving agricultural systems, such as annual crops grown with minimum tillage techniques and inter- and relay-cropping practices.

In high-density settlement and irrigation projects the desire to retain management control over land and water use often results in the adoption of short-term tenancy arrangements. The disincentives for investment and continued commitment to scheme participation, however, are well known. On the other hand, freehold title may lead to undesirable levels of land accumulation more readily than with unplanned land ownership patterns because it is easier for the purchaser to ensure plot contiguity. As a compromise tenurial system the combination of limited freehold and medium-term leasehold appears to have much to commend it. The 'core' plot would be held on freehold, but the remainder of the holding on 5–15 year leasehold. (In Zambia, for example, fourteen-year leaseholds are in operation on a farming settlement scheme, see Farrington, 1978.) The leasehold rents reflect a charge for project capital investment and recurrent costs. Plot sizes can be adjusted to reflect changing land scarcity and relative income levels when leaseholds expire, probably with priority for new leaseholds given to adult offspring of existing settlers.

Finally, in Phase III we should note that difficult trade-offs between efficiency and equity objectives are likely to become more frequent. Widespread rural unemployment, for example, may indicate that maximum labour absorption is desirable, with plot sizes reduced to provide a low target income per family; this will usually include a large element of non-marketed food output. Marketed surplus, on the other hand, would be larger per unit area if farm sizes were somewhat larger, although not so large that it is offset by falling average product per unit area as farm-size rises. A technical solution to this problem is to replace food crops by a cash crop which requires immediate processing, such as tea, sugar or cotton. But even if such schemes are attractive to settlers, other social problems have been reported, particularly reductions in the part of the family income reaching wives and children (e.g. UNICEF, 1979, reporting a nutrition survey in Kenya).

The ability to achieve both efficiency and equity objectives along the changing factor-endowment continuum can be badly frustrated if fundamental structural disequilibria are allowed to dominate the rural sector. These commonly arise with the emergence of socio-economic dualism either between the urban and rural sector ('urban bias'; Lipton, 1971) or within agriculture between a modern and a traditional sector. In the former case, declining net barter sectoral terms of trade cause increasing rural-urban migration and in the extreme case stagnation or decline in surplus rural production; Uganda after 1975 provides a particularly vivid example (Commonwealth Secretariat, 1979). In the case of intra-rural dualism, concentration of either modern production inputs, especially if these are labour-saving, or lucrative market opportunities in the hands of a minority of farmers will deprive the majority of the rural population of opportunities to earn comparable, or even marginally improved, incomes. At the level of the general development literature these dangers are well recognised, if less so in public decision-making bodies. In the design of settlement schemes, a particular danger rises from the concern with achieving adequate settler incomes and project viability; this can too easily be achieved by utilising an undue share of scarce inputs or by producing for a limited domestic market at the expense of existing suppliers or potential spontaneous entrants to that activity. In general, project resources should be allocated to expand output of products with high price and income elasticities of demand.

Inappropriate land settlement and tenure strategies

In principle it would seem that land settlement schemes are bound to satisfy both efficiency and equity objectives: (i) they combine under-utilised land and labour resources to raise production at what should be, therefore, low unit costs; and (ii) they provide new self-employment opportunities either to new entrants to the labour force or to under-employed families, both these groups being probably among the poorest of the poor.

The African experience

In practice, however, inappropriate designs relative to the factor-endowment continuum have led to a plethora of disappointing experiences in this area (see Chambers, 1969, for a wide-ranging view of African experience in the 1950s and 1960s). Brief consideration of a small number of specific instances can help to illustrate this general theme. Firstly, two attempts at establishing relatively high-income farm settlements in Tanganyika in the 1950s and 1960s when it was probably nearing the Phase I–Phase II interface, ran into insoluble problems. Both approaches emphasised mechanised techniques and high-value cash cropping. The first approach – tenant farms under supervision of Tanganyika Agricultural Corporation management on land originally cleared for the Groundnuts Scheme – ran into efficiency problems exemplified by the high rates of settler turnover (Lord, 1964). Non-supervised farming opportunities elsewhere, and the risky nature of annual tenancies and rain-fed agriculture in the scheme area, meant that tenants left when they had accumulated either a savings target or large debts.

In the second approach, the Village Settlement Agency programme for 170 settlement schemes was the main component of the agricultural strategy in the post-independence First Five-year Development Plan. The VSA programme incorporated a number of features derived from the *moshav*, following an Israeli technical assistance mission shortly after Independence. Very high levels of capital investment and technical assistance were provided to overcome the settler turnover problem. The resulting allocation of T£ 1000–1500 per family, compared with agricultural services costing an average of T£ 40–50 per family outside, drew heavy criticism on both equity grounds, for obvious reasons, and also efficiency grounds because higher returns to scarce resources could be obtained from the improvement of productivity on existing small-scale farms (Ross Report, 1965). The later emphasis on low-cost, communal agriculture using divisible inputs (*ujamaa* farming: see Nyerere, 1968) is exemplary in terms of equity but has foundered on grounds of efficiency (see e.g. UNDP/FAO, 1976; Belshaw, 1981a). The basic problem was that the communal activity was identical to that already preferred on family farms – which receive priority in terms of seasonal labour inputs – instead of concentrating on areas where communal operations could supplement or be more efficient than individually organised ones (village irrigation schemes, agricultural processing operations, plant nurseries and seed multiplication plots, etc.). In the current post-villagisation situation in Tanzania, now clearly in Phase II, concentration of population into compact village settlements has in many areas made land, water, fuel and grazing prematurely scarce resources (Belshaw, 1981b; von Freyhold, 1979). The stability of some villages is now open to question.

A different illustration of the same principle of appropriate timing can be made for land tenure policy, through reference to the successive modifications of the 1900 Agreement in Uganda. This act conferred a form of freehold title on 3700 notables and unprotected tenancy status on the great majority of Buganda peasants (Wrigley, 1959). After popular unrest, a rent restriction act was passed in 1927 (with no revision clause to cope with inflation). Meanwhile the original 3700 holdings with freehold title had increased to 58 000 by 1953 (Richards, 1963) and an estimated 170 000 in the late 1960s. West (1972) estimated that less than 200 individuals owned more than 1000 acres of land at the time of writing. Initial land accumulation (or seizure), therefore, has been dispersed in an equitable manner rather than leading to continued concentration as structuralist theories of development suggest would inevitably happen. Clearly the original land settlement of tenurial rights was inconsistent with the predominant family farming orientation in Buganda society which continued across eighty years of increased cash cropping, wage labour inputs and general commercialisation of agriculture.

Conclusion

There are purely pragmatic arguments that suggest the development planner should avoid too heavy-handed an involvement in land settlement schemes. The reasons are best summarised by Robert Chambers:

Where a settlement scheme is unavoidable, and where there is a choice of type to be adopted, there is much to be said on organizational grounds for the simplest type of scheme that is compatible with the circumstances of settlement. The simpler approaches are relatively undemanding of scarce administrative and technical capacity, and engage it for shorter periods. They involve relatively low risk and low commitment. Moreover, schemes with individual holdings exploit the drives of property ownership and individual incentive which can make productive the labour which is the most abundant unused resource in much of the third world. The simpler schemes also require intermediate levels of organization corresponding with the intermediate technology which may also be appropriate. If the beginning is ambitious, a complex organization may collapse and find equilibrium at a lower level; but if the beginning is modest, a more complex technology and organization can grow up organically and gradually. (Chambers, 1969, p. 261)

The theoretical arguments proposed in this study and empirical evidence also suggest that there are advantages to a lightly-planned and administered approach to land settlement and tenurial reforms. Such caution appears to be particularly desirable in Phases I and II of the agrarian transition.

REFERENCES

Belshaw, D.G.R. (1968). An outline of resettlement policy in Uganda, 1945–63. In R.J. Apthorpe (ed.), *Land Settlement and Rural Development in Eastern Africa*, Nkanga Editions 3, pp. 14–23

(1975). The national and inter-regional policy context of regional-level planning in Tanzania. *Bureau of Resource Assessment and Land Use Planning, University of Dar es Salaam, Joint Working Party on Regional Planning Methodologies, Working Paper* No. 4. Pp. 18 (mimeo)

(1981a). Rural development policy and experience in Tanzania, 1967–79. Development Studies Association Annual Conference, Keble College, Oxford (mimeo)

(1981b). Village viability assessment procedures in Tanzania: decision-making with curtailed information requirements. *Public Administration and Development*, 1, 1

Brock, Beverley (1969). Customary land tenure, 'individualisation' and agricultural development in Uganda, *East African Journal of Rural Development*, 2 (2), 1–27

Chambers, Robert (1969). *Settlement Schemes in Tropical Africa: A Study of Organisations and Development*. London, Routledge

Chayanov, A.V. (1925; ed. D. Thorner, 1966). *The Theory of Peasant Economy*. Homewood, Illinois, Irwin

Coleman, G., A. Pain & D.G.R. Belshaw (1978). *Village Viability Assessment in the Context of Regional Planning in Tanzania*. Norwich, Overseas Development Group for UNDP/FAO

Commonwealth Secretariat (1979). *The Rehabilitation of the Economy of Uganda: A Report by a Commonwealth Team of Experts*. 2 vols. London

de Wilde, J.C. et al. (1967). *Experiences with Agricultural Development in Tropical Africa*, vol. 2. Baltimore, Johns Hopkins University Press for the World Bank
Dorner, Peter (1972). *Land Reform and Economic Development*. Harmondsworth, Penguin
Farmer, B.H. (1957). *Pioneer Peasant Colonization in Ceylon*. London, Oxford University Press for Royal Institute of International Affairs
  (1974). *Agricultural Colonization in India since Independence*. London, Oxford University Press for Royal Institute of International Affairs
Farrington, T. (1978). 'Family Farms Ltd': a study in the establishment of settlement schemes, Southern Province, Zambia. London, Ministry of Overseas Development (mimeo)
Ghai, Dharam (ed.) (1981). *The Agrarian Crisis in Africa*. Geneva, International Labour Office
Govt. of Kenya (1978). *Development Plan: 1979–1983*, 2 vols. Nairobi, Government Printer
Lipton, M. (1977). *Why Poor People Stay Poor: A Study of Urban Bias in World Development*. London, Temple Smith
Lord, R.F. (1964). *Mechanised Farming at Nachingwea, Southern Tanganyika*. London, HMSO
McLoughlin, P.F.M. (1970). Regional rural development in Sukumaland, Tanzania, 1946–65. In A.H. Bunting (ed.), *Change in Agriculture*, London, Duckworth, pp. 411–18
Nyerere, J. (1968). Socialism and rural development. In *Freedom and Socialism: Uhuru na Ujamaa: A Selection from Writings and Speeches 1965–67*. Dar es Salaam, Oxford University Press
Richards, Audrey I. (1963). Some effects of the introduction of individual freehold into Buganda. In D. Biebuyck (ed.), *African Agrarian Systems*, London, International African Institute, pp. 267–80
Ross Report (1965). Report of the British Economic Mission on the Tanzania Five-year Development Plan (Confidential)
Sharpley, J. (1977). Inter-sectoral capital flows: evidence from Kenya. *Harvard Institute for International Development, Development Discussion Paper* No. 32
UNDP/FAO (1976). *Iringa Region, Tanzania: Integrated Rural Development Proposals for the Third Five-year Plan, 1976–81*. 2 vols. Overseas Development Group for FAO, Rome
von Freyhold, M. (1979). *Ujamaa Villages in Tanzania: Analysis of a Social Experiment*. London, Heinemann
West, H.W. (1972). *Land Policy in Buganda*. Cambridge University Press
Vrigley, C.C. (1959). *Crops and Wealth in Uganda: A Short Agrarian History*. East African Studies No. 12, London, EAISR

14 Metropolitan expansion in India: spatial dynamics and rural transformation

K.V. SUNDARAM and V.L.S. PRAKASA RAO

As urban population grows, the urban settlements also grow in area. In the case of smaller urban settlements, the patterns of urban sprawl are simple; first by infilling in the left-over spaces in the core of the settlement, and then by extension of built-up area and urban land use into the adjoining rural areas. In the core, both population and housing density increase with consequent increase in both ground and house congestion. In the initial stages, the pattern of sprawl is concentric, if the nucleus of the core (wholesale market or a temple or an industry) has a centripetal pull. Even here the converging arterial transport routes or the transit main routes passing through the town promote growth, and then the lateral or secondary routes pull the growth toward them. The pattern of growth is one of axial sprawl and then lateral (interstital) spread. Growth of factories, and residential colonisation in the periphery of the town initiate extensive growth along with intensive infilling in the core. With the extensive and outward growth, the villages in the periphery get drawn into the town area by its extension, and get finally absorbed into the town, transforming both rural land-use and occupations into urban land-use and urban occupations. During this phase, the sprawl takes place in a haphazard manner along and across the road and/or rail routes leaving out or thinly filling interstices. Infilling is intermittent and sprawl is haphazard. In the case of a smaller town, the sprawl is limited to the rural periphery of the town.

The sprawl of cities

In the case of cities, the sprawl takes on the scale of haphazard physical explosion. Residential colonies, industries and public and semi-public institutions promote urban sprawl in the rural periphery. One of the consequences of urban sprawl into the rural periphery is a considerable loss of cultivated lands which seems inevitable. For example, during the period 1920–1950 the loss of cultivated land in some Karnataka towns in South India varied from 20% of the town area in Chikballapur, a market town, to 63% in Nelamangala, a satellite of Bangalore. A number of adjoining villages become incorporated for the extension of conservancy services or protected water supply, a process which enlarges the urban service zone. It is at this stage and scale that the urban settlement starts to acquire its regional or metropolitan function by developing a city-region.

The pattern of growth is basically influenced by the character of a city's site and situation. For instance, the form and pattern of urban sprawl differ in the case of a port city, a city at the foot of the lateritic plateau, or a city in the deltaic plain with its dense network of canals and braided streams. The different physical landscape elements have the potential either to enhance or mar the beauty of city landscape. The canals in a deltaic city for instance can be lined with green avenues or with slums polluting the canal water.

The characteristic patterns of sprawl also differ with different phases and scales of growth and specific development thrusts consequent upon developments in transport networks, or location of industries, or extension of residential layouts. In contrast to the simple patterns of infilling in the core and outward spill and incorporation of the adjoining village or villages that are characteristic of small and medium-size towns, the patterns of sprawl of a large city such as a metropolitan or a million city are more complex both in structure and scale.

The impact of urban growth and physical expansion of the city on the rural area is varied, and it depends upon factors such as the relative location of the village, its accessibility to the city, and the extent of rural-urban interaction. The urban-induced changes may be *economic*, such as changes in land-use, occupational structure, technology transfer etc.; *social*, for example changes in value systems, behavioural patterns, life styles, etc.; or *physical*, for instance changes in house-types and other structures, change in the form of settlement, etc. The physical explosion of the city tends to draw the rural areas within its fold by expansion of city municipal boundaries from time to time. The dynamics of change in the incorporated areas is extremely complex and interesting. There are often lags both in social-economic transformation as well as in physical transformation between the early urbanised parts of the metropolis and the newly incorporated area, giving rise to a core-periphery structure, marked by problems of adjustment and by confrontations among people.

Stages in metropolitanisation

Studies in the fringes of Indian metropolitan cities show that the process of metropolitanisation is accompanied by a certain sequential transformation in the rural tract and in the rural settlements in the vicinity of the growing metropolis. Bina Srivastava (1976) has hypothesised that each village in the metropolitan fringe passes through six stages of transformation:

Stage I	Rural stage;
Stage II	Development of rural-urban linkages;

Stage III   Transformation of occupations;
Stage IV   Changes in land-use;
Stage V   Incorporation of the rural settlement into the metropolis and its transformation into urban village with its deterioration into slum.
Stage VI   Redevelopment of the urban village and its physical integration into the metropolis.

Metropolitan development is thus a continuing process requiring long time periods for the assimilation and integration of its parts. This chapter discusses both the physical process of urban growth as well as the social process of its transformation from the rural to the urban. Bangalore and Delhi, where field studies have been conducted by the authors, have been chosen to illustrate how these processes operate.

A number of classical approaches have been used by geographers to the investigation of the urban spatial growth process (Bogue, 1950; Clark, 1951; Schnore, 1957; Hoover & Vernon, 1959; Garrison, 1962; Berry et al., 1963; Griffin, 1965; Hudson, 1969; Newling, 1969). Some leading approaches are:

(i) The ecological school of urban studies which has contributed the model of wave-like spread.
(ii) The suburbanisation school which emphasises the ascendancy of the dispersive over the cohesive forces, resulting in the peripheral development and a simultaneous decline of the city centre.
(iii) The sequent occupancy concept which interprets the growth process in terms of a sequence of distinct stages.
(iv) Urban population density models which consider the evolution of the urban density pattern in a dynamic framework interpreting it as a cyclic process.
(v) The diffusion-type model of urban growth which may be also interpreted in the framework of the wave-like analogue model.

In the context of Indian cities, there are few systematic studies that have analysed the urban spatial process (but see Srivastava, 1976; and Prakasa Rao et al., 1980).

Bangalore: a case study of the physical process of urban growth

During the period 1901–71, the city area of Bangalore increased from 54 sq. km with a population of 159 000 to 155 sq. km with a population of 1.42 million.[1] Population growth was greater in proportion than increase in the city area; consequently there was an increase in population density from 30 to 92 persons per hectare (Table 14.2). Within this overall population density of 92 persons per hectare the intra-urban densities vary from 5 to 882 persons per hectare.

The pattern of urban growth from 1537 onwards is shown in Fig. 14.1, and is summarised in Table 14.1. An examination of the pattern and structure of growth from the initial pre-urban nucleus, the fort, reveals three types of

Table 14.1. *The process of city growth, Bangalore, 1537 to 1976*

Phase period	Pattern of growth	Range (km)	Examples			
I 1537–1939	Residential leapfrogging, residential infilling	1.5–6.5	to the north	Seshadripuram Malleswarum Gamdhinagar Kumarapark	1882 1898 1930 1938	} Leapfrogging infilling
			to the south	Basavanagudi Shankarapuram Visveswarapuram	1898 1908 1918	} Leapfrogging infilling
II 1940–1959	Industrial leapfrogging (along axial routes)	10–13	Hindustan Aeronautics Bharat Electronics Hindustan Machine Tools		1940 1948 1949	} Leapfrogging
	Residential infilling (interstitial areas)		Sadashivanagar Indiramagar Rajajinagar			} Infilling
III 1960 onwards	Institutional leapfrogging (along axial routes)	13–19	University of Agricultural Sciences at Hebbal Bangalore University Campus at Kengeri			} Leapfrogging
	CITB Labour infilling (interstitial areas)		CITB Layouts			} Infilling

sprawl. The earliest was mainly in the nature of residential *leapfrogging* and residential *infilling*, together with ribbon development of shopping and commercial land-uses although the expansion induced by the establishment of the Indian Institute of Science was an exception. The distance range involved was 3–6 km from the fort. The second type, from 1940 onwards, was characterised by leapfrogging of large-scale industrial complexes such as HAL, ITI, HMT and BHEL,[2] located about 13 km from the nucleus. This process was followed by residential infilling along major transport routes and in the interstitial area, along with growth of residential areas in the vicinity of the industries, and near the then edge of the city's built-up area.

The third type of growth, since about 1960, has been characterised by the leapfrogging of institutional complexes, such as Bangalore University and the new extensions of industrial complexes. There has also been an infilling of residential layouts promoted by the City Improvement Trust Board, around the circumference of the built-up area in order to gain benefits of proximity to the city centre. The result is that the city shape is tending to become increasingly oval and compact with only the residential corridors along the arterial roads contributing to some distortion in shape.

In the process of leapfrogging and infilling that was induced by the expansion of residential, industrial, and institutional land-uses, the main determinants were: (i) the axial transport routes, particularly for industries; (ii) proximity to the city core; (iii) preference for location near the outward-moving edge of the city, to avoid congestion; and (iv) the availability of space at the city's edge. The one common denominator in the spread of the city was the haphazard mix of the land uses in spite of the city Master Plan. This is attributed to the multiplicity of jurisdictions involved in the city development, and the uncoordinated and individual decisions of the private developers. Nearer the outward-moving city boundary, within a distance of 13 km from the city centre, the steep slopes of the distance-decay curves, the interlacing of boundaries, the urban-industrial growth in isolated clusters and along the corridors, all indicate the irregular and leapfrogging nature of urban-industrial and institutional growth. Residential and retail shopping centres contributed their share to this haphazard and ribbon growth.

The Bangalore Development Plan made a pointed reference to the chaotic and haphazard growth of the city particularly in the adjoining countryside. The city corporation area, the conurbation area (using the term conurbation loosely), and the metropolitan area are the three officially designated areas in the plan to accommodate the expanding metropolis. The Corporation had to shift its boundary in 1965 from the one in 1949, following the sprawl of the city. The conurbation boundary includes most of the built-up area. The rapid growth of the non-agricultural population during 1961–71 and industrial development, further induced urban spread and the transformation of the area into rural/urban transformation. Urban growth in the adjoining villages outside the Corporation boundary tended to be haphazard. This situation forced the State Government to take decision to extend the Corporation boundary. This led to the inclusion of about 110 villages within its limits, thus adding 210 sq. km of area and a population of about 200 000. The urbanisable area of the city is now estimated at 320 sq. km.

Thus the urban spatial growth process analysed here shows three distinct time phases (1537–1939, 1940–59, and since 1960). During each period, the growth was brought about first by a leapfrogging process and then followed by an infilling process. While the first phase of growth involved a distance range of 1.5–6.5 km and was a long drawn-out process extending over a period of about 400 years, the other two phases of growth involved comparatively longer distance ranges (10–13 km and 13–19 km respectively) but were squeezed into a shorter time span of about 20 years. Thus, the growth shows

Development planning and agrarian change 285

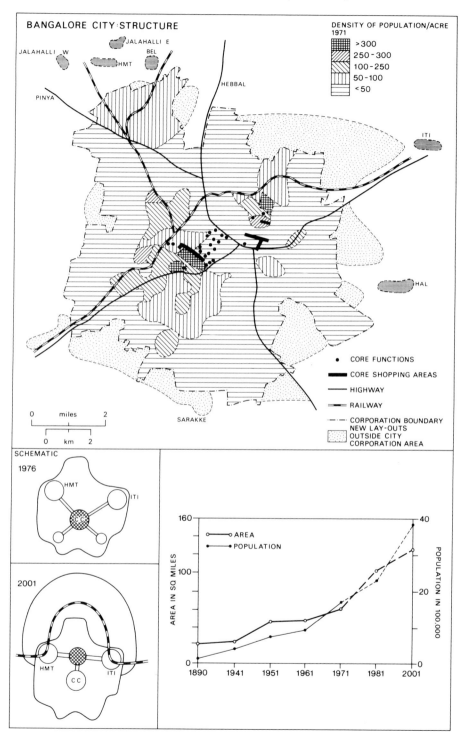

Fig. 14.1. Patterns of urban growth in Bangalore.

low frequency and longer periods initially, followed by greater frequency and shorter periods since 1940. In the absence of a more rigorous analysis of population growth and redistribution within each zone and study of the evolution in types of occupancy, it would be difficult to make further generalisations about the growth pattern of the city.

Metropolitan Delhi: a case of rural and social transformation in the urban fringe

As a metropolitan city grows in population and space, it tends to absorb a number of rural settlements that were once on its periphery. In the urbanisation context in India, these rural settlements cannot be quickly assimilated and adapted to their new urban environments. The qualitative change which one associates with urbanisation tends in these circumstances to be a slow and long drawn-out process, and its pace depends on the intensity of rural-urban interaction. The term 'urban village' is used to designate such 'villages' transported into the urban setting. In 1971, there were about 48 such urban villages in Metropolitan Delhi. A case study of one such village, Kotla Mubarakpur in South Delhi, is presented here to illustrate the nature and rate of rural transformation that accompany urban growth (see also Sundaram, 1977, pp. 88–114).

Kotla Mubarakpur today is surrounded on all sides by developed residential colonies which stand in sharp contrast to the village both in physical form as well as in the endowment of basic urban services and amenities. It has neither the quiet charm and pleasantness associated with the traditional Indian village, nor the advantages and facilities that one expects to find in an urban setting. To its east and south, the urban village is sharply differentiated from 'posh' (upper- and middle-class) residential colonies. Indeed the social distance which separates this village from these colonies is many times its geographical distance. Kotla Mubarakpur must beseen really as the result of an intermittent growth process spread over a period of more than 400 years. In its physical pattern of growth and social groupings, four distinct settlement units may be seen (Fig. 14.2):

(i) Kotla, the oldest settlement which originated in the 15th century;
(ii) The Aliganj and Pilanji group of settlements, formed by families rehabilitated after eviction from areas which were acquired for the New Delhi capital project;
(iii) Areas inhabited by groups of migrants who came to Delhi mainly as labourers during the different phases of the capital construction project (1911–47);
(iv) Areas which are post-partition developments consisting of displaced persons from West Pakistan (after 1947).

In the case of Kotla Mubarakpur, rural transformation may be said to have started almost immediately after 1911, when some of its land was acquired for

Table 14.2. *Variation in the area and population of Bangalore City, Bangalore Metropolitan Area, 1901–2001*

Year	Urban area	Area (sq. km)	Population	Decadal increase (%)	Gross density per hectare
1901	City + cantonment	53.6	159 000	–	29.7
1941	City + cantonment	63.2	407 000	39	64.4
1951	Corporation area	119.1	779 000	91	65.4
1961	Corporation area	119.1	905 000	16	76.0
1971	Corporation area	155.4	1 422 000	57	91.5
1981	Metropolitan area	246.2	2 300 000	62	87.1
2001	Metropolitan area	321.2	3 800 000	33	118.3

Source: 1901–1907 – Prakasa Rao et al., 1980.
1981, 2001 – projections by Town Planning Department, Bangalore.

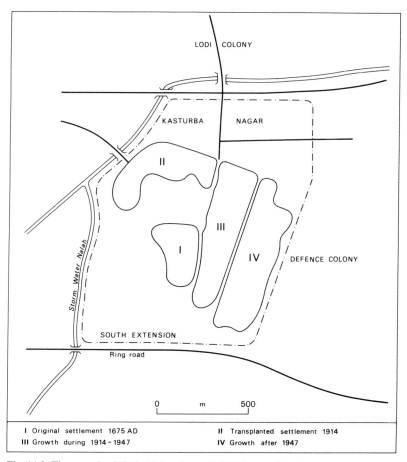

Fig. 14.2. The growth of Kotla Mubarakpur, Delhi Metropolitan Area.

resettling the displaced villages of Aliganj and Pilanji. Following this event, for almost a period of 25 to 30 years, the village remained a 'fringe village', a rural outpost of urban Delhi, transforming its economy into an urban-oriented one. Its transformation leading to the present position as a 'rural enclave' within the metropolis, started in the late 1940s and was almost complete in the early 1960s. The physical growth of the metropolis in the southern part of Delhi gained considerable momentum during the 1950s and 1960s. The Defence Colony and South Extension Residential Schemes were completed between 1956–60 and with these developments Kotla Mubarakpur became a rural enclave surrounded by urban developments. Thus it may be noted that till the 1950s, Kotla Mubarakpur was only a fringe village, but since then its interaction with urban Delhi has been increasing.

Land-use changes

The several changes that took place when this 'fringe village' was transformed into an urban village can now be considered. Among these, the land-use changes are the most important. The village Kotla Mubarakpur had originally 486 holdings under cultivation, and 81 of them went out of cultivation by 1921. This change was due to the shifting of the villages of Aliganj and Pilanji around 1914 which were affected by the Capital Project. During the next two decades (1921–41) the changes that took place were small, and the agricultural lands of the village, by and large, remained intact. Between 1941 and 1951, however, the changes that occurred were of a sweeping nature, as they eliminated the majority of the agricultural lands of the village (481 holdings), and converted them into urban use. Table 14.3 brings out these changes clearly.

We can note from Table 14.3 that Kotla Mubarakpur retained a considerable proportion of its cultivated lands till the 1950s. The slow change in its traditional economy reflected in the land-use changes may be attributed to the fact that the urban economy of Delhi, till then, did not generate many demands. Although the planning of the Capital project commenced as early as 1912, the first phase of construction lasted till 1930 or so. During this period, Kotla Mubarakpur was serving only a limited urban market. Further, it must be noted that New Delhi grew mainly as a governmental city, notably lacking in industrial employment. This is reflected in the occupational structure of the village which has only a small proportion of population engaged in industries and a considerable proportion engaged in service occupations.

Changes in occupational structure

Following the disappearance of cultivated lands, important changes in the occupational structure of the population took place. The traditional economy

Table 14.3. *Land-use changes in Kotla Mubarakpur, 1901–1971*

Land use	Number of land holdings in each land use category							
	1901	1911	1921	1931	1941	1951	1961	1971
Built-up area	–	–	81	87	89	481	486	486
Waste land	34	33	30	30	30	–	–	–
Cultivated land	432	435	357	352	351	–	–	–
Well	8	7	7	6	6	–	–	–
Drain	3	3	3	3	3	2	–	–
Pathways	5	5	5	5	4	3	–	–
Garden	2	2	2	2	2	–	–	–
Ponds	1	1	1	1	1	–	–	–
Total:	486	486	486	486	486	486	486	486

Source: Sundaram, 1977.

of the village underwent significant changes from time to time, largely as a result of urban influences during the British rule and post-independence period. The growth of New Delhi, particularly in the 1930s, encouraged cultivators to start growing vegetables and other crops for the city market. Some villagers also made considerable profit from the sale of fowls, eggs, milk and butter. A few also sought employment in the city. This resulted not only in a diversification of occupations in the village, but also brought in an element of mobility in occupations, as the persons who went out from the village for work were mostly unskilled workers who had to face some insecurity in their jobs in the beginning. The preponderance of unskilled and manual workers in the occupational structure of the village was a characteristic feature, even as late at 1958.

According to the 1961 Census count, the proportion of workers engaged in various industrial categories of employment was as follows:

Cultivators and agricultural labourers	1.3%
Livestock and allied activities	9.5%
Manufacturing and household industries	15.5%
Construction	12.9%
Trade and commerce	16.8%
Transport	3.2%
Services	40.8%

It may be seen from the above figures that by 1961 the agricultural element was almost absent in the village. Even the small agricultural component that was present consisted of either persons who were working as gardeners in the

Table 14.4. *Frequency of shifts in employment, by families*

Number of changes	Number of families	First occupation of the family
None	7	S1, S2, S3, S4, S5
Once	8	A1, B1, E, C1, S4
Twice	15	A1, A2, B2, E, S2, S3, C1
Three times	12	A1, A2, C2, D, E, S2, C1
Four times	6	A1, A2
Five times or more	2	A1, A2

Note: A1 – farming   E – labourer
A2 – gardener   S1 – washerman
B1 – trade   S2 – barber
B2 – business   S3 – potter
C1 – customary service   S4 – sweeper
C2 – shop   S5 – carpenter
D – weaving

Source: authors' sample survey.

city or persons who owned land outside the city and cultivated it. A significant proportion (about 10%) of the population constituted the Gujars, a pastoral caste who are engaged in livestock and allied activities. Service occupations, however, constituted the biggest group among the employment categories. A study of the inter- and intra-generational mobility of occupations shows that while some occupational groups stagnated, others showed greater mobility. Table 14.4 brings out the major features of occupational mobility.

Thus it is clear that the traditional service castes have shown the least tendency to change. Among them, however, the barber caste appears to be little more mobile than the rest. As is to be expected, the farming community has shown the greatest mobility in occupations. Among the significant recurrent patterns of mobility are:

Farmer–Gardener/Labourer–Dairy–Service
Farmer–Business
Labourer–Contractor
Labour–Service
Customary service–Service

The data on occupational mobility also reveals the struggle that has been undergone in making adjustments to the new jobs and therefore to new roles and situations. There are cases where we find a person shifting to a new occupation like business, failing in the venture, taking to service, rehabilitating himself and later, returning to the same venture once again. Another interesting feature in the shifts of occupations is the pursuit of a traditional calling in a modern urban setting.[3] Thus the barber of the village who was previously performing his function under the Jajmani system[4] has now opened a hair-cutting shop in the bazaar street. Similar is the case of the village potter who is now manufacturing and selling flower pots on contract to foreigners and upper-class residents in Defence Colony and South Extension residential colonies. These provide interesting instances of adaptation in which persons have acquired new skills connected to their old profession.

Cultural change

Flows constitute an important element in any study of interaction. Such flows may be of people from the rural to the urban area for employment, shopping, credit facilities, recreation or higher educational and cultural facilities. There may be also flows of people from urban to rural in order to take advantage of any specialities which the village may offer.

A commodity which moves out of the village to the adjacent residential colonies is milk. But this does not bring the urban residents of these colonies to the village, as the supply is usually arranged through delivery by the producer. But there are certain other attractions which an 'urban village' of this type offers to people in the city. Among these may be mentioned the attraction provided by it as a low rent neighbourhood, to persons in the low income groups who are unable to find cheap accommodation in the city, or to new immigrants from the village or town who find in it like situations, and people of similar tastes with whom they find easy rapport. Shop-owners in the city who are unable to afford cheap godowns also rent space for their godowns in the village and one may see a large number of such godowns in this village. All these bring urban contacts into the village. As a result of such contacts, the rural houses have undergone some degree of transformation and adaptation to new circumstances. An intangible element in these flows is, however, the flow of ideas, which brings about changes in life styles and in the traditional rural structure. The constant and continuous contact with the city, through which the villager participates in a different social and cultural milieu, transforms the behaviour and values characteristic of the village life. This process, identified as the 'feed-back' process of urbanisation, must be recognised as an important aspect in the context of Indian urbanisation. Here the daily commuter from the village is an important agent of change.

An interesting aspect of the urban village is the preservation of some relict features of the rural areas in the present urbanised lay out. These include: (i) the persistence in the settlement of the village squares or *chopal* with their shady tree and little platform; (ii) the continued existence of the village well, which is still a meeting place for women; (iii) the preservation of the old street plan with its narrow and winding streets and with its numerous small dead-end streets or alleys; and (iv) the presence of typical mud houses with flat roofs. To these elements, we may also perhaps add the neatly and even elegantly constructed piles of cowdung cakes known as *bitauras*, which are found in all Indian villages and which give to the village scene its characteristic appearance and smell.

Thus it may be seen that the physical transformation of the 'fringe village' into an urban village has not erased the essentials of village form and appearance; nevertheless it has reduced the open space available in the village and has led to great residential congestion and environmental deterioration.

Conflicts between rural and urban values

An important aspect of rural transformation is the degree of social change that has taken place in the community. The most striking among these is the remarkable loosening of the rigidity of the caste system in the village. The 'caste neighbourhoods' which existed in the village in earlier times, with the dominant caste occupying the centre of the village and the lower castes living in the peripheries, have disappeared, owing to a considerable degree of mingling of castes in the village, particularly after the infiltration of immigrants. But even today, the higher castes do not dine or smoke with the lower castes. The distinction between the castes appears to have been more or less obliterated among the younger age group.

Another important change that has occurred is the disappearance of the Jajmani system of service relations. As mentioned above, many of the service castes have adapted themselves to their new roles. The joint family system has more or less broken down in a number of cases; where it exists, it does so with some changes, e.g. the joint families living under the same roof, but separately with their independent kitchens; or a clear apportionment of space existing within the house for the different families. Thus while the traditional ways of living, beliefs and norms are undergoing some changes, there are attempts to retain some of the old social values. Even a casual observation of the community reveals the flux of their cultures and the inconsistencies of their efforts to combine the rural and urban ways of living.

The rural and urban value systems now and then come into open conflict. This is particularly so, when redevelopment issues come to the forefront. Redevelopment efforts made so far constitute an interesting study. An ambitious redevelopment plan prepared in the 1960s which sought to bring about a substantial demolition of the village was rejected. Subsequently, a more modest plan also could not get off the ground, as it was in conflict with the value systems of the community. An important point of conflict was with reference to the use conversion, suggested in the plan for the little vacant space available in the village for providing certain civic amenities like parks, playgrounds, schools and shopping centres. This space is important to the villagers for keeping cattle which (despite the many restrictions placed on this activity by the city government) still constitutes an important occupation in the village. Thus, an important dimension of the integration of the incorporated rural areas into cities relates to the implications that such development has on the living patterns of the people.

Implications for urban planning

The case study of an urban village in a metropolitan periphery brings into sharp focus the problems of a hybrid urban society which has 'rural nostalgias' as well as 'urban appetites'. To what extent do newcomers to this society become enculturated into the urban community? What are their satisfactions and irritations with their physical surroundings? How important are the living qualities of the city as compared to opportunities to find employment and the opportunities for social participation? Does the area have a high career mobility, and under what conditions are changes in inter-generational career patterns in particular evidence? These questions reflect upon the value systems held by the area's residents, their behaviour patterns and how emotionally prepared they are for growth problems ahead, and to what extent they will tend to identify themselves with action programmes aimed at solving these problems.

In this situation both the physical integration of the village with the urban area, and its social assimilation with the urban community, have to be secured in stages. These stages of transformation should be brought about with great understanding of the people whom it is intended to integrate and assimilate. This needs some real input of thought and effort. Highly ambitious programmes aiming at rapid and total transformation may be impossible to attain in the Indian context, for various reasons. The annexed rural areas represent a complex situation in social, economic and physical terms. The most appropriate method seems to be to move *progressively* towards the goal of redevelopment. In this, as well as in many other aspects of development, it should be emphasised that the best is the enemy of the good. The integration problem must also be seen in the totality of all urban problems and not in isolation. A certain time-bound effort for the development of the incorporated areas is needed, linking the physical, economic and social programmes for these areas with those of the city as a whole.

Since the usual run of city governments are dominated by urban elites, they are unable to comprehend the problems of the incorporated rural areas and are not responsive to the value systems of the incorporated community, who constitute a very large segment of the urban poor. Therefore, some special devices in metropolitan cities to protect the interests of the incorporated rural areas seem to be called for.

At present, in the Indian context, there are no specific policies or guidelines or provisions in the Municipal Acts to guide the local governments as to how the processes of transformation in the newly incorporated areas of cities should take place. Herein lies an inherent injustice. There is a need to fill in this policy vacuum by adding specific provisions to the Municipal Acts specifying the commitment of local governments as well as the role of public agencies and private parties to bridge the gap between the incorporated rural areas and the rest of the city area within a defined time-frame.

The pattern of redevelopment for such areas itself demands a new approach. More than physical redevelopment and opening up the rural enclaves, some immediate infrastructural improvement programmes and some anti-poverty policies are essential. These may include provision of water supply, sewerage and latrines along with sanitation on the physical improvement side, and measures for ensuring an adequate income maintenance among the urban poor by the provision of certain incentives and subsidies to them and encouraging the build-up of an economy geared to lower unemployment and providing guaranteed job opportunities for every able worker. The positive uplift that such policies will have on the low-income-group households in the incorporated rural areas will more than justify the costs and effort put in this direction. In our view, such policies are of higher priority.

Conclusion

The general purpose of this study has been to describe and to explain the urban growth and transformation processes that operate when a metropolis extends its corporate limits and annexes the adjacent rural territories. The inquiry is stimulated by the shortcomings that have been noticed in the metropolitan cities in India experiencing rapid physical expansion of their boundaries. A basic conviction underlying this study is that all metropolitan programmes must be based upon an accurate understanding of facts, relationships and processes. For the rural enclaves in metropolitan areas, which are really in the nature of 'underdeveloped pockets', mere physical development programmes alone will not do; these have to be supplemented by effective economic and social programmes. We may therefore emphasise that at least in the urban areas of metropolitan cities, physical and social planning should be brought together around a set of rather basic goals common to, and meaningful for, both these activities.

Urban-growth dynamics is indeed a complex phenomenon. While the two case studies reported here do not provide complete answers to several questions that may be raised, they do shed light on a wide range of processes of physical growth, social change, and the integration of 'rural areas' into the main city. These are processes which must be taken into account by policy-makers.

NOTES

1. Bangalore City (population in 1971, 1.54 million) was ranked in India seventh in city size in 1971 and fourth in rate of city growth during 1951–71. During the decade 1961–71 the population increase in the outer area (townships) was 92%. In contrast to this, the increase in the inner city area was 35%. The two nuclei in the metropolis are the city market area and the Russel Market area.
2. HAL: Hindustan Aircraft Ltd; ITI: Indian Telephone Industries; HMT: Hindustan Machine Tools Ltd; BHEL: Bharat Heavy Electricals Ltd.
3. The significance of this change is the difference between employment in the traditional society and employment in a modern urban society. In the latter category, the employment is based on certain terms and conditions which are highly impersonal, while in the former, the employee has hereditary service relations with his patrons.
4. This refers to the institutionalised service relationships existing in the Indian village. The castes usually participating in the Jajmani system are the smiths, barbers, potters and sweepers. They are usually paid in kind for their services. The rights of service are hereditary.

REFERENCES

Berry, B.J.L., Simmons, P.W. & Tennant, R.J. (1963). Urban population densities: structure and change. *Geographical Review*, 53, 389–405

Bogue, D.J. (1950). *Metropolitan decentralization: a study in differential growth.* Scripps Foundation Series in Population Distribution, No. 2

Clark, C. (1951). Urban population densities. *Journal of the Royal Statistical Society*, ser. A, 114, 490–6

Garrison, W.L. (1962). Towards simulation models of urban growth and development. *Lund Studies in Geography*, ser. B, 24, 91–108

Griffin, T.L.C. (1965). The evolution and duplication of a pattern of urban growth. *Economic Geography*, 41, 133–56

Hoover, E.M. & Vernon, R. (1959). *Anatomy of a Metropolis: The Changing Distribution of People and Jobs within the New York Metropolitan Region.* Harvard University Press, Cambridge, Mass.

Hudson, J.C. (1969). A location theory for rural settlement. *Annals of the Association of American Geographers*, 50, 365–81

Newling, B. (1969). The spatial variation of urban population densities. *Geographical Review*, 59, 242–52

Prakasa Rao, V.L.S. et al. (1980). *Bangalore, An Emerging Metropolis.* Allied Publishers, Delhi

Schnore, L. (1957). Metropolitan growth and decentralization. *American Journal of Sociology*, 63, 171–80

Srivastava, Bina (1976). The rural-urban fringe of Delhi: structural and functional patterns. Ph.D. thesis, Department of Human Geography, Delhi School of Economics, University of Delhi

Sundaram, K.V. (1977). *Urban and Regional Planning in India.* Vikas, New Delhi

15 Green Revolution and water demand: irrigation and ground water in Sri Lanka and Tamil Nadu

C.M. MADDUMA BANDARA

The subject of irrigation and ground-water supply in South Asia has remained close to the heart of B.H. Farmer since the 1950s. In particular, his early contributions on rainfall and water supply in the Dry Zone of Sri Lanka (Farmer, 1951, 1954, 1956a) and on 'Land use lessons learnt in Madras applicable to the Dry Zone of Ceylon' (Farmer, 1956b) stand unparalleled in this field even today, not only for their academic content, but also because of the vistas they opened for further research and for actual water resources development in the areas concerned. The intention of the writer in presenting this chapter, as one who has had the privilege of direct access to the wealth of Farmer's academic experience, is to review and update the knowledge on this important subject in relation to those lands where Farmer made his pioneering studies, namely, the Dry Zone of Sri Lanka, and the Tamil Nadu of South India. The essay also focusses attention on rice fields and Green Revolutions which have represented Farmer's most recent research interests.

History of Sri Lankan irrigation

For centuries irrigation had been an art, a science, and a way of life to the people living in the drier areas of South Asia. Many cities and settlements emerged and flourished in irrigated hinterlands. In some cases the dependence of communities on irrigation was so heavy as to warrant the use of the term 'hydraulic societies' by certain scholars to describe such civilizations (Leach, 1959; Gunawardhana, 1979). On the other hand highly developed civilizations have collapsed and disintegrated due to the decay of these stupendous irrigation systems (Murphy, 1957). Like their counterparts in South India, the ancient Sinhalese mastered the art of irrigation, and at the height of its development around 8th century AD it is believed that Sinhalese technologists were even working in consultative capacities in other countries of the region.

There is evidence to suggest that irrigation existed in Sri Lanka even before the legendary King Vijaya landed in the island in the 6th century BC.[1] Nevertheless, the actual expansion of irrigation and water supply schemes commenced around the 3rd century BC with the development of the City of Anuradhapura, the ancient capital of Sri Lanka. The Abhayawewa reservoir

(Basawakklulama tank) which is believed to be the oldest of the ancient tanks in Sri Lanka was the first city tank to serve Anuradhapura. With the growth of the city, which reached the size of a metropolis at one stage covering an area of land as large as that of the Greater London area today, two more tanks, namely Tissawewa and Nuwarawewa, had to be constructed. The development of this reservoir-based gravity irrigation technology, continued with the building of more and more reservoirs such as Nachchaduwa, Kalawewa, Minneriya, Parakrama Samudra, and many hundreds of smaller irrigation tanks. Up to about the 12th century AD these irrigation systems flourished in the Dry Zone of Sri Lanka under the patronage of great Sinhalese kings who believed that the construction of irrigation reservoirs was the most meritorious and benevolent contribution that they could make to the country, so that their names would go down to posterity. However, due to reasons which are still not properly understood this great hydraulic civilization began to collapse around the 12th century AD (Paranavitana, 1960), and the centres of population which thrived on these irrigation systems migrated to other parts of the island.

When the European colonial powers arrived in the 15th century AD, the ruins of many ancient irrigation systems remained under forest cover in the Dry Zone areas. Since both the Portuguese and the Dutch occupied only the maritime provinces they were not too concerned with the renovation of ancient irrigation works. However, the British who conquered the entire island after the fall of the Kandyan kingdom, rediscovered the ancient irrigation works in the process of their explorations and mapping of the interior of the country. Brohier's *Ancient Irrigation Works* (1935) outlines the wealth of information gathered mainly in the process of topographical surveying.

The magnificent size and nature of ancient irrigation reservoirs aroused the interest of many British colonial administrators. The scarcities of rice particularly during the times of world war compelled the colonial government to develop irrigated agriculture. Thus with the gradual eradication of malaria began a phase of restoring ancient irrigation works and pioneer peasant colonization in Sri Lanka, which continued even after independence (Farmer, 1957). It was evident that the period of renovating major irrigation works was coming to an end by the late 1960s. By 1970 almost all major ancient reservoirs had been renovated although many minor irrigation tanks remained abandoned.

Thus, by the late 1950s, a deviation from the old policy of bringing new land under irrigation was becoming clearly discernible. There were some attempts by the state to increase the productivity of existing paddy lands through crop diversification, through the use of improved seeds, and by an increased use of fertilizer and agrochemicals (Govt. of Ceylon, 1966). Moreover, by the early 1960s Agricultural Research Stations at Gannoruwa, Maha Illuppallama, Batalagoda, Labuduwa, etc., were already functioning as centres of agricultural innovations. These research stations later became the centres from which Green Revolution technologies were taken to the country at large.

The Green Revolution and irrigation development

Table 15.1 shows the development of irrigation in Sri Lanka during the fifteen years 1965–79. This period may be taken to represent the period in which the Green Revolution in Sri Lanka reached its peak development, then declined in the wake of the energy crisis, and subsequently achieved some stabilization.

It is clear from Table 15.1 that the irrigable area as well as the irrigated area under major irrigation schemes had a steady increase up to 1979. However, the irrigation intensity[2] fluctuated between 1.05 and 1.47. The situation in the areas under minor irrigation was somewhat different from that under major irrigation. The increase in the irrigable area under minor irrigation was not as rapid as that under major irrigation. In fact in 1979 this had dropped from 185 000 to 171 000 ha. One reason for this was the incorporation of minor irrigation areas under major irrigation schemes. Furthermore, the irrigation intensity under minor irrigation schemes fluctuated between 0.91 and 1.24 indicating a greater unreliability of irrigation water than under major schemes.

Table 15.2 shows the cultivated area, production and average yield of paddy for the same period, i.e. 1965–79. A cursory examination of Table 15.2 indicates that while the *asweddumized* area increased steadily over the years, the sown area and harvested area fluctuated markedly. This fluctuation is reflected to a considerable extent in the production and yields of paddy.

An examination of national paddy production statistics for the last 50 years (1930–80) clearly indicates that there had been a significant rise in the yield as well as in the production since 1950. However, a closer scrutiny shows that, up to the 1950s, the year-to-year fluctuation in paddy production was not very marked. On the other hand in spite of the rapid increase in production after the 1950s, the annual production level appears to have fluctuated very widely. One possible explanation for this state of affairs is that in years of adequate rainfall the production goes up quite significantly, particularly in the *maha* season, and in years of poor rainfall it falls very rapidly (Domroes, 1976). Thus it appears that the success or failure of the Green Revolution technology was determined more by the vagaries of *maha* rainfall in the last two decades than ever before. The increased minimum levels of production were, however, due to the expansion of irrigation facilities during the same period.

It should be noted that the national statistics which are given in Tables 15.1 and 15.2 include information from all agro-ecological regions and of all culti-

Table 15.1. *Irrigation of paddy lands in Sri Lanka (in 1000 hectares)*

	Major irrigation schemes		Irrigation intensity %	Minor irrigation schemes		Irrigation intensity %	Total irrigable area	Total irrigated area	Irrigation intensity %
	Irrigable area	Irrigated area		Irrigable area	Irrigated area				
1965	154	187	1.21	157	154	0.98	311	341	1.09
1966	163	226	1.39	158	172	1.09	321	398	1.23
1967	162	215	1.33	156	175	1.12	318	390	1.22
1968	168	236	1.40	154	177	1.15	322	413	1.28
1969	174	222	1.27	160	181	1.13	334	403	1.20
1970	179	263	1.47	162	201	1.24	341	464	1.36
1971	181	354	1.40	163	184	1.13	344	438	1.27
1972	184	245	1.33	166	184	1.11	350	429	1.22
1973	188	246	1.30	164	181	1.10	352	427	1.21
1974	196	273	1.39	168	203	1.21	364	376	1.30
1975	203	213	1.05	173	157	0.91	376	370	0.98
1976	206	237	1.15	178	165	0.93	384	402	1.04
1977	208	283	1.36	181	203	1.12	389	486	1.24
1978	217	320	1.47	185	216	1.17	402	536	1.33
1979	228	328	1.44	171	195	1.14	399	523	1.31

Source: Department of Census and Statistics, Colombo.

Table 15.2. *Area (in 1000 hectares) and yield of paddy in Sri Lanka, 1964–79*

Agricultural year	*Asweddumized* area	Sown area	Harvested area	Production (in '000 tonnes)	Yield (kg/ha)
1964/65	515	588	503	757	1773
1965/66	536	654	611	953	2137
1966/67	539	662	634	1145	2137
1967/68	546	705	661	1337	2400
1968/69	561	692	623	1373	2563
1969/70	570	759	718	1916	2629
1970/71	574	725	694	1396	2386
1971/72	586	726	639	1312	2388
1972/73	583	725	672	1312	2277
1973/74	606	824	797	1602	2306
1974/75	621	695	597	1154	2245
1975/76	621	724	636	1252	2255
1976/77	643	828	782	1677	2463
1977/78	658	875	840	1871	2568
1978/79	653	846	790	1917	2697

Source: Department of Census and Statistics, Colombo.

vation seasons. In spite of this fact, the importance of the expansion of the irrigated area over and above any other factor in paddy production is brought out most strikingly. This correlation is further illustrated by Fig. 15.1 which shows how paddy production had been a function of the irrigated area even when aggregate national statistics are used. Only the 1970 paddy production figure shows some significant deviation from the general trend. The Green Revolution technology which led to significant increases in paddy yields, particularly in 1970, has undoubtedly contributed to the increases in national paddy production in recent years. Nevertheless, one cannot overlook the fact that the expansion of the irrigated area stands out as the most important factor that has contributed to the increase in paddy production in Sri Lanka in the last fifteen years, as has been the case throughout her history.

The benefits of irrigation development

The expansion of irrigation has been observed to bring several potential benefits. In the first place it leads to an increase in the area under cultivation. Water is necessarily land-augmenting under Dry Zone conditions, and some writers (e.g. Chambers, 1974) have suggested that paddy production should

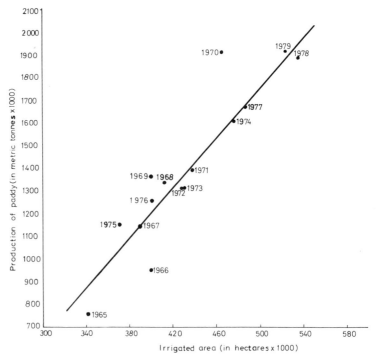

Fig. 15.1. Relationship between irrigation and paddy production in Sri Lanka, 1965–1979.

Table 15.3. *Major reservoirs in the Accelerated Mahaweli Programme*

Reservoir	Net storage capacity (m cu-m)	Extent of land benefited (ha)	Hydropower potential (MW)	Cost in Rs (mill.) (at 1978)	Source of foreign assistance
Kotmale	408	16,194	200	9000	Sweden
Victoria	690	29,555	420	8000	UK
Maduru Oya	430	46,750	10	2150	Canada
Randenigala	860	24,291	122	4500	FRG
Moragahakanda	686	22,200	40	1750	Japan

be expressed not in terms of yield per unit of land but in terms of yield per unit of water, i.e. not in bushels per acre but in bushels per acrefoot of water. Secondly, irrigation can lead to an increase in yield when it is combined with other practices such as the use of improved seed varieties and other modern technologies. In fact in most parts of South India irrigation has been a necessary vehicle for the progress of the Green Revolution. Thirdly, irrigation can increase crop production by making it possible to grow more than one crop per year on a given tract of land. This is indicated by the irrigation intensity, an increase of which can have the same effect on paddy production as an increase of area under cultivation. Thus the irrigation intensity is always higher on lands under major irrigation where the supply of water is more dependable than those under minor irrigation schemes. Irrigation can also enhance the security for the farmer by relieving him at least partly from the adverse effects of the vagaries of rainfall. Thus irrigation can make a farmer more confident to adopt the technologies which eventually contribute to greater crop production.

The Mahaweli Project

Since 1976 with the diversion of Mahaweli waters to the North Central Dry Zone the total irrigated area and the irrigation intensity has increased considerably. Thus due to Mahaweli waters 53 500 ha of existing lands are now double-cropped and some 28 800 ha of new lands are now irrigated in the Kandalama and Kalawewa areas (Govt. of Sri Lanka, 1981b). Perhaps the greatest benefit that Mahaweli diversion has brought is that the national paddy production does not now fall below a certain minimum level. With the Accelerated Mahaweli Development Programme now in progress the irrigated area will increase significantly during the next few years. At the completion of the five major reservoirs under the Accelerated Mahaweli Development Programme, over 130 000 ha of new land will be brought under irrigation (Table 15.3). Some 12 000 ha of existing lands will benefit from the

Project, together with 130 000 ha of new lands, of which 113 000 ha are on the right bank of Mahaweli and some 16 000 ha are on the left bank in the Polonnaruwa District (Govt. of Sri Lanka, 1981a). Thus the Mahaweli Accelerated Programme will increase the irrigated area by at least 30% before the end of this decade, bringing the total area under irrigation to over 550 000 ha. In other words, the Mahaweli Project if continued at its present rate of progress is bound to change the geography of irrigation development in Sri Lanka in a substantial way.

New irrigation projects

Apart from the Mahaweli Project, one of the major features of irrigation expansion in Sri Lanka in the recent past has been the development of irrigation facilities with foreign assistance (Govt. of Sri Lanka, 1981c). This includes village irrigation rehabilitation projects, modernization of major irrigation schemes and the undertaking of new major irrigation projects. Among these activities is the Village Irrigation Rehabilitation Programme which envisages the rehabilitation of some 1200 village works at a cost of Rs. 800 million with the assistance of the IDA. Under the Major Irrigation Modernization project five major tanks in the North and North Central Provinces, including Maha Villachchiya and Mahakahadarawa, are now being modernized with assistance from IDA and UK. Here the existing irrigation facilities are to be improved with the aim of increasing the irrigated area as well as the efficiency of water management.

At least five major irrigation projects were undertaken for development with foreign assistance during the last four years. Some information on these five projects is given in Table 15.4.

Impact of Green Revolution

It has been mentioned that studies of the adoption of Green Revolution technologies have mostly been concentrated in the deltaic areas of assured irrigation water supply (Harriss, 1977). It could be assumed that as far as rice is concerned the Green Revolution itself had more success stories in such areas. On the other hand the higher yields due to improved seed and other methods have induced the farmers to grow more paddy in at least two ways: (i) by expanding the cultivated area wherever possible, and (ii) by double-cropping of existing lands. These methods ultimately lead to increased demands for irrigation water, from minor irrigation tanks as well as from major irrigation schemes.

As indicated in Table 15.5 the Register of Irrigation Projects lists more than 3000 minor irrigation tanks spread out in the twelve districts of the Dry Zone. Kurunegala District has the largest number, while Anuradhapura

Development planning and agrarian change

Table 15.4. *New irrigation projects in Sri Lanka*

Project	Extent of land benefited (ha)	Source of foreign assistance
Mahadiulwewa	486	EEC
Muthukandiya	810	Australia
Ginganga	4858	China
Kirindi Oya	13289	ADB, IFAD and German KFW
Inginimitiya	2643	Japan

Table 15.5. *Minor irrigation tanks in the Dry Zone Districts*

District	No. of minor irrigation tanks	Average capacity (HM)*	Average irrigable area (ha)	Capacity per hectare (HM)*
1. Amparai	10	58.48	56.72	1.03
2. Anuradhapura	1047	49.03	40.92	1.20
3. Batticoloa	82	68.45	65.74	1.04
4. Hambantota	100	18.10	26.11	0.69
5. Jaffna	36	41.40	41.36	1.00
6. Kurunegala	1298	17.93	21.67	0.82
7. Mannar	80	22.04	31.99	0.69
8. Moneragala	25	27.99	25.79	1.08
9. Polonnaruwa	29	88.19	68.99	1.28
10. Puttalam	86	46.60	56.92	0.82
11. Trincomalee	158	22.88	27.35	0.84
12. Vavuniya	168	35.96	38.99	0.92
Total	3119	$\bar{x} = 41.39$	$\bar{x} = 41.88$	$\bar{x} = 0.95$

Note: *HM = hectare metres.
Source: Based on information given in The Register of Irrigation Projects, Irrigation Department, Colombo, 1975.

comes a close second. These two Districts together account for more than 75% of all minor irrigation reservoirs in the country. The average capacity of minor irrigation tanks range from 17.93 HM (hectare-metres) in the Kurunegala District to 88.19 HM for the Polonnaruwa District with an average of 41.39 HM for the Dry Zone. The average irrigable area also ranges between 21.67 ha and 65.64 ha with a Dry Zone average of 41.88 ha. The ratio of tank capacity to irrigable area varies between 0.69 (Hambantota and Mannar Districts) and 1.28 (Polonnaruwa District).

In many Dry Zone areas where land was cultivated under minor irrigation tanks and where additional land was available for *asweddumization*, more irrigable land has been added in recent times to LDO blocks located at the margin of the old paddy fields. Earlier this land was either under *chenas* or under rainfed paddy. Because of the increased yields and attractive market prices, attempts were made by many farmers to expand the acreage under minor irrigation tanks while the capacity of the tanks remained often unchanged. This has been most conspicuous in the areas with higher population density and smaller tanks.

Figs. 15.2 and 15.3 show the relationship between the capacity of the tanks and their irrigable areas in two districts of the Dry Zone where minor irrigation tanks dominate the agricultural landscape. Closer examination of the two scatter diagrams indicate that the relationship between storage capacity and irrigable acreage is slightly different in the two districts. In the Kurunegala District, which has the largest number of minor irrigation tanks in the island (see Table 15.5), the tanks are much smaller in capacity. However the acreage under their command is much bigger in proportion to their size. This could be due to several reasons: in some parts of the Kurunegala District the climate is wetter with intermediate conditions, and therefore does not need as large tanks as in the Anuradhapura District for irrigation.

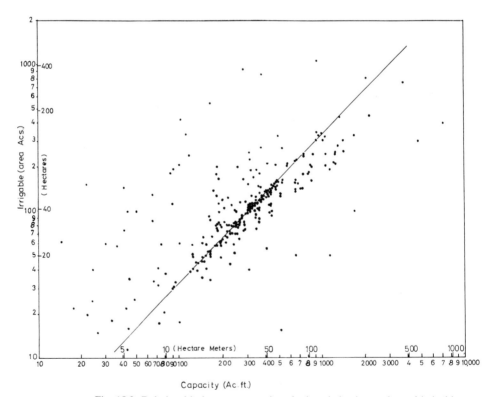

Fig. 15.2. Relationship between capacity of minor irrigation tanks and irrigable area under their command, Anuradhapura District.

Furthermore, due to the greater pressure of population on land in the Kurunegala District, the tendency for increasing the *asweddumized* area is much greater than in the Anuradhapura District. In both districts, however, there had been an increase of *asweddumized* lands below the minor irrigation tanks in the recent past. Although reasons for this expansion of *asweddumized* acreage are difficult to disentangle, it is likely that the recent agrarian changes, particularly those due to the Green Revolution, have contributed at least indirectly to this phenomenon. It is possible that the higher yields and the increasing price of paddy during the late 1960s encouraged many farmers to cultivate larger and larger blocks of land under the same tank.

An increase in the double-cropping of existing lands has also created greater demands for irrigation water particularly in the major irrigation areas. As can be seen from Table 15.1 irrigation intensity increased from less than 1.10 in 1965 to more than 1.30 in the recent years. It is interesting to note that the highest irrigation intensity on record was 1.36 in 1970, the year which recorded the highest yield and the highest paddy production in the period between 1965 and 1976. It has been claimed that the year 1970 marked the highest achievement of the Green Revolution strategy. However, there is hardly any doubt that the high level of paddy production in that year was also the outcome of many other favourable conditions.

The increase in the irrigation intensity was most conspicuous under major

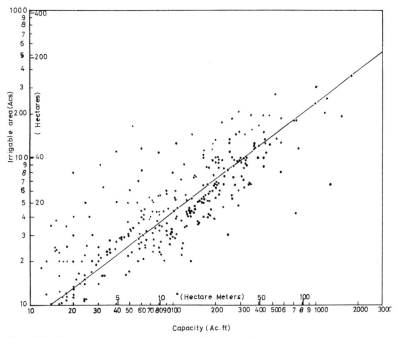

Fig. 15.3. Relationship between capacity of minor irrigation tanks and irrigable area under their command, Kurunegala District.

irrigation schemes where it ranged between 1.05 and 1.47. As already noted, under minor irrigation it varied between 0.91 and 1.24. The highest irrigation intensities under both minor and major irrigation schemes were recorded in the year 1970. Thus it is obvious that the peak production of paddy in 1970 was also due to the increased intensity of irrigation. This shows that if irrigation intensities, which did not exceed 1.50 during the period under consideration, could be increased further, then national paddy production would almost certainly be enhanced. Although double-cropping of all irrigated lands is a difficult proposition for Sri Lanka, it is clear that there is much scope for this kind of development particularly in the fields under minor irrigation.

Irrigation water management

The increased irrigable acreage and the increased intensity of irrigation due to double-cropping have obviously created greater demands for scarce irrigation water in many Dry Zone areas. Thus the management of existing water resources began to surface, first as a serious research concern and later as a prominent administrative and political issue. Up to the early part of the 1970s water management was hardly heard as a subject of discussion in the academic or agrarian development planning circles. One writer summarized this situation lucidly:

Water management in the Dry Zone is a neglected subject. It is not a major focus of attention in any of the books and reports which have been consulted. The UNDP/FAO Final Report on Mahaweli Ganga is remarkable for the attention paid to other agricultural inputs and their management to the neglect of water. (Chambers, 1974)

Since Chambers' work in 1974, there have been more than a dozen research and development projects devoted to the management of irrigation water in the Dry Zone. Some of the most well-known projects include: the Rajangana and Mahakanadarawa water management studies conducted by the Irrigation Department; the Walagambahuwa Project conducted by the Maha Illuppallama Agricultural Research Station (Mahendrarajah, 1979); and the USAID water management project at Galoya (Govt. of Sri Lanka, 1981c). As an outcome of one of these projects, an attempt is now being made by the agricultural extension services to replicate the Walagambahuwa model in a few other Dry Zone districts.

Several academic studies centred on water management have been conducted during recent years: (Moore, 1980; Tilakasiri, 1979; Harriss, 1977; Chambers, 1979; Karunanayake, 1979; Madduma Bandara, 1980). There have also been several on-farm water management experiments such as those at Maha Illuppallama and at Kalankuttiya in the Mahaweli 'H' area. As a result of these studies there is now a deeper understanding and a growing concern for the issues involved in irrigation water management in the Dry Zone. The Government, recognizing the need for improved water management, has created several administrative arms and planning and policy-making authorities to achieve this purpose. The most recent of them is the proposal to set up a Water Management Board (Govt. of Sri Lanka, 1981a). The recent droughts in the upper catchment of Mahaweli and Dry Zone areas have also created a new interest and a greater public awareness of the importance of better irrigation water management practices (Madduma Bandara, 1981).

Ground-water irrigation

Nearly thirty years ago, Farmer (1951, 1956) had the geographical vision to recognize the fact that there are certain important land use lessons that the Dry Zone farmers in Sri Lanka could learn from the *ryots* in Tamil Nadu. The most important of these was the use of ground water for irrigation, a practice by which Madras Tamils manage to cultivate particularly their high lands in perpetuity. Farmer attempted to explain the differences between the landuse system of Tamil Nadu and that of the Dry Zone of Sri Lanka – two areas which are geographical analogues in many respects. Thus he drew attention to the climatic, pedological and hydrological factors and to the differences in manuring practices. However, he emphasized that 'probably the most important factor of all in many villages . . . is the use of well-irrigation.'

Even today the major difference between irrigation in South India and that in Sri Lanka lies in the area of ground-water use. As suggested elsewhere (Madduma Bandara, 1977), the extent of land under well-irrigation in Tamil Nadu surpassed the extent under tank irrigation in the 1967–8 period. By 1974 in many parts of South India ground-water irrigation was beginning to show symptoms of overextraction (Madduma Bandara, 1977b). In contrast the use of ground water for irrigation in the Dry Zone of Sri Lanka has been extremely slow, and is still virtually non-existent in many areas.

It is interesting to examine here the reasons adduced by Farmer for the differences in the levels of ground-water development in Tamil Nadu and the Dry Zone of Sri Lanka. He noted that 'Tamil Nadu had a greater proportion of its rain in the South West monsoon and to that extent does not suffer the extreme seasonal reversal which is so characteristic of the Dry Zone.' The greater availability of perennial surface water in Tamil Nadu due to construction of tanks for water table preservation, and technological factors related to the well design, were some of the other reasons given. Above all, Farmer thought there was 'a more fundamental factor rooted in geomorphology', namely the more mature landscapes in Tamil Nadu resulting in a greater availability of ground water in those areas than in the Dry Zone of Sri Lanka (Farmer, 1956).[3]

Looking back on the developments that have taken place during the last three decades it is clear that most of Farmer's early thoughts on the Dry Zone of Sri Lanka have withstood the test of time. If the land use lessons enunciated by Farmer had been properly followed by agricultural planners in Sri Lanka there is little doubt that Sri Lanka could have progressed much faster in her food production and rural development programmes. If ground-water irrigation in Sri Lanka had been given the same attention it received in Tamil Nadu, a Green Revolution would have reached many remote villages in the Dry Zone of Sri Lanka where its impact so far has been feebly felt or not felt at all.

In my own work I have been able to add more detail and information to this important subject even though I have not always kept to the path mapped out by the pioneer (see Madduma Bandara, 1973, 1977a, 1977b and 1980). In particular, the more recent developments in ground-water irrigation tend to confirm the view that the slow rate of ground-water development in the Dry Zone of Sri Lanka is more due to 'human factors' than due to geological or other 'natural factors'. Observations of water levels made simultaneously on the wells of North Arcot District in Tamil Nadu and those in the Hambontota and Moneragala Districts of Sri Lanka have indicated that the behaviour of the water table in the two areas is not as significantly different as Farmer surmised (Figs. 15.4 and 15.5). For example, in south-eastern Sri Lanka the mean depth of the water table was much closer to the surface than in the North Arcot District of Tamil Nadu in spite of the fact that Sri Lankan observations show a greater standard deviation. One reason for higher water table levels in Sri Lanka is the artificial recharge from the tanks and irrigation channels where they are found in close proximity to irrigation wells. Fernando (1974) estimated that recharge from major and medium-scale irrigation works in Sri Lanka alone would be around 49 716 HM per annum. This is in addition to the 795 825 HM per annum he estimated to be due to direct recharge from rainfall. Similarly, de Mel and Sumanasekera (1973) estimated by means of statistical analysis that recharge could be in the region of 20% of rainfall in *Yala*, while Dharmasiri and Dharmawardhana (1980) arrived at the same conclusion for the Dry Zone hard-rock areas on the basis of isotopic studies. In the light of this information it can be assumed that the prospects of using ground water for irrigation in the Dry Zone, at least for supplemental purposes, are not as poor as were supposed twenty-five years ago (Madduma Bandara, 1977).

A recent study on the impact of drought on peasant communities in the Dry Zone indicated that the most damaging droughts occur in the Dry Zone in the months of January or February (Madduma Bandara, 1981). This is a season in which the availability of ground water in the Dry Zone is definitely greater, as indicated in Figs. 15.4 and 15.5. Therefore, any programme to use

Development planning and agrarian change

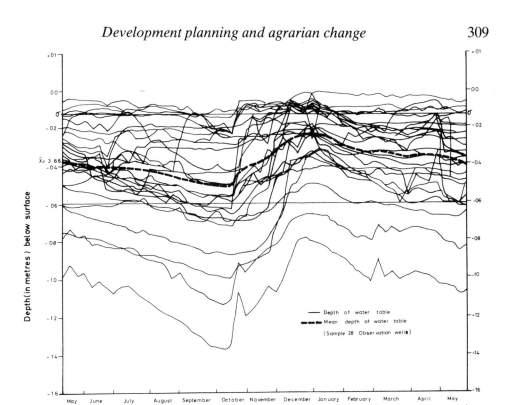

Fig. 15.4. The seasonal behaviour of the water table in southeastern Sri Lanka.

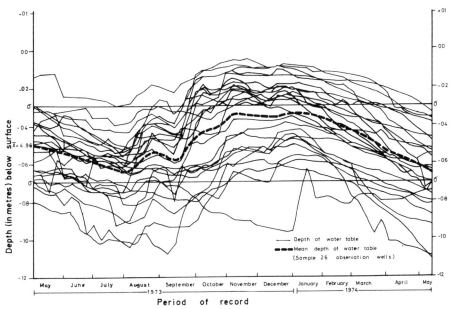

Fig. 15.5. The seasonal behaviour of the water table in North Arcot District of Tamil Nadu, South India.

ground water for supplemental irrigation during this period is bound to increase agricultural production, particularly in the minor irrigation areas.

Vavuniya District – a case study[4]

It has already been pointed out that the reasons for lack of ground-water development in the Dry Zone hard-rock areas are not entirely hydrogeological, but rather cultural and organizational. Some of these reasons have been discussed elsewhere (Madduma Bandara, 1977a). We can illustrate this finding by reference to some recent developments in ground-water irrigation, particularly those in the Vavuniya District in the North Central plains of Sri Lanka. In 1974 and 1975 alone about 2000 irrigation wells were constructed in the Vavuniya District (Govt. Agent, Vavuniya, 1976) and it was estimated that there were some 3000 irrigation wells in the District by 1976. It was also estimated that there were 4119 ha of irrigated highlands growing subsidiary food crops by 1977. These irrigated highlands were mostly dependent on Indian-type large diameter irrigation wells, and the major crops on them were chillies, red onions and ground nut. In addition to highland wells there were also some wells (about 4%) located in the paddy lands.

The Vavuniya experience indicates that nearly 96% of the farmers who practised well-irrigation were farmers without paddy lands, the great majority of them Tamils (Madduma Bandara, 1980). A large proportion of the highland blocks (68%) were lands granted by the Land Development Ordinance on the usual 99-year lease. The difference between the attitudes of Tamil and Sinhalese farmers to well irrigation was more striking than any known climatological or geological factor. About 81% of the wells had water during all seasons of the year indicating a rate of success comparable to that of the North Arcot District of Tamil Nadu. In spite of the haphazard siting of wells, 61% of the farmers thought that their investment was worthwhile. The increasing use of oil pumpsets (61% at the time of the survey) exhibited a general resemblance to the situation which existed in Tamil Nadu ten to fifteen years ago. An ODM research team (Foster, Yearwood & Carruthers, 1976) found that well yields in the Vavuniya District range from 10000 to 50000 litres per day, and their computations indicated that chilli cultivation was economically viable under the conditions prevailing in the District. Although the oil-price increases and the recent government policy of importing chillies has adversely affected the practice of well-irrigation, the introduction of windmill pumps by the Water Resources Board during the last five years is bound to make well-irrigation economically attractive to Dry Zone farmers (Buch-Larsen, 1979). Several governmental as well as non-governmental organizations are now actively engaged in the extraction of ground water for irrigation and domestic supply in the Dry Zone. The work done by voluntary organizations such as Redd-Barna as well as by the UN agencies such as

UNICEF deserve special mention in this regard. The latter organization in collaboration with the Water Supply and Drainage Board has successfully introduced tube-wells to many Dry Zone villages for domestic supplies. It is interesting to recollect how introduction of tube-wells in hard-rock areas was considered an impossible task 25 years ago when Farmer started writing on ground water.[5]

It was also interesting to find that nearly 96% of the farmers in the Vavuniya survey recommended that well-irrigation should be taken to the other parts of the Dry Zone. The question remains, however, as to how the practice of ground-water irrigation could be introduced to Sinhalese farmers who are living in parts of the Dry Zone not benefiting from large irrigation projects.

The future

Any projection of present trends to the future would show that in Sri Lanka the irrigable area and the irrigated area particularly under major irrigation schemes is bound to increase by at least 30% by the end of this decade. The result of this expansion of the irrigated area would be a significant increase in national paddy production, whether or not the various Green Revolution technologies continue to improve yields. The irrigation intensity has been gradually increasing over the years particularly in the areas under major irrigation, and this will create increased demands for the available irrigation water. The result will be an even greater need for better water management practices aimed at optimizing the use of available water resources.

Similarly, in Tamil Nadu it is estimated that the area under irrigation today will expand to 5.06 million ha by 2000 AD – representing an increase of about 44%. The corresponding water requirement is estimated to be in the region of 4.42 MHM which is more than the supply available for agricultural purposes, i.e. 3.98 MHM (Sivanappan & Palanisami, 1981). Thus both in Sri Lanka and in Tamil Nadu there is an increasing need for improved water management practices. In the Dry Zone of Sri Lanka, under minor irrigation schemes the *asweddumized* acreage will continue to expand where additional land is available, creating greater demands for available tank water. Here lies an area where ground-water irrigation may be successfully utilized as in South india. Nevertheless, every precaution has to be taken to avoid over-extraction which is beginning to appear as an ecological problem in Tamil Nadu today. In other words, the latest lesson that the farmers in the Dry Zone of Sri Lanka can learn from their counterparts in South India is to avoid the mistakes made in India and to base any future ground-water extraction programmes on sound ecological planning.

NOTES

1. The folk lore maintains that Kuweni the Queen of Lanka at the time of Vijaya's landing was spinning cotton on the bund of a tank when Vijaya visited her. Some recent scholars such as A.D.N. Fernando maintains that the ancient Bisōkotuwa (sluice outlet) discovered at the Maduru Oya dam site in 1980 was constructed by the Yakkas or the pre-Vijayan settlers of the island.
2. Irrigation intensity is the ratio of irrigated area to the irrigable area expressed as a percentage. Thus if the full extent of an irrigable area is cultivated once a year the irrigation intensity is 100%. If the same extent is double-cropped irrigation intensity would be 200%.
3. Farmer went on to use this example in defending the role of genetic geomorphology within the discipline of geography.
4. This section is based partly on unpublished data obtained as part of the project directed by B.H. Farmer on agrarian change in Tamil Nadu and Sri Lanka, in the period 1973–5.
5. The writer vividly remembers how Farmer related the story about a proposal to sink tube-wells in the Anuradhapura District in the early 1950s by some Indian experts. When this suggestion was made, Farmer had jokingly took up the challenge to drink all the water that would issue from any tube-well sunk into the Dry Zone hard rocks.

REFERENCES

Brohier, R.L. (1935). *Ancient Irrigation Works of Ceylon*. Govt. Press, Colombo

Buch-Larsen, B. (1977). *Economics of Windmills in Sri Lanka: Four case studies*. Wind Energy Unit, Water Resources Board, Colombo

Chambers, R. (1974). *Water Management and Paddy Production in the Dry Zone of Sri Lanka*. Agrarian Research and Training Institute, Occasional Publication

    (1979). In search of a Water Revolution: Priorities for Irrigation Management in the 1980s. Paper presented at the Institute of Development Studies Workshop on Irrigation Bureaucracy and Performance

Domroes, M. (1976). Aspects of recent rainfall fluctuations with regard to land utilization in Sri Lanka. In K. Takahashi and M.M. Yoshino (eds.), *Climatic Change and Food Production*. University of Tokyo Press

Farmer, B.H. (1951). Some thoughts on the Dry Zone. *Bulletin of the Ceylon Geographical Society*, 6, 3–16

    (1954). Problems of landuse in the Dry Zone of Ceylon. *Geographical Journal*, 120, 21–33

    (1956a). Rainfall and water supply in the Dry Zone of Ceylon. In R.W. Steel & C.A. Fisher (eds.), *Geographical Essays on British Tropical Lands*, Philip, London

    (1956b). Land use lessons learnt in Madras and applicable to the Dry Zone of Ceylon. *Bulletin of the Ceylon Geographical Society*, 10, 9–19

    (1957). *Pioneer Peasant Colonization in Ceylon*. Oxford University Press, London

Fernando, A.D.N. (1973). *The Groundwater Resources of Sri Lanka.* Planning Division, Ministry of Irrigation, Power and Highways, Colombo
  (1974). Artificial groundwater recharge from surface water issues in the major irrigation schemes of Sri Lanka. 30th Annual Session of the Ceylon Association for the Advancement of Science
  (1982). The ancient Hydraulic Civilization in relation to its natural resources. Unpublished Address to the Royal Asiatic Society on 26 February 1982
Foster, S.S.D., Yearwood, Y.D.F. & Carruthers, I.D. (1976). *Groundwater for Agricultural Development in Sri Lanka: Resources and Economics.* Ministry of Overseas Development, United Kingdom
Govt. Agent, Vavuniya (1976). *Agricultural Development Proposals: 1977 Implementation Programme.* Kachcheri, Vavuniya
Govt. of Ceylon (1966). *Ministry of Land, Irrigation and Power, Plan of Development 1966–70.* Ministry of Planning and Economic Affairs, Colombo
Govt. of Sri Lanka (1981a). *Mahaveli Projects and Programme.* Information Service of the Ministry of Mahaweli Development, Colombo
  (1981b). *Mahaweli Ganga.* Information Service of the Ministry of Mahaweli Development, Colombo
  (1981c). *Resource Development.* Information Service of the Ministry of Lands and Land Development, Colombo
Gunawardhena, R.A.L.H. (1971). Irrigation and hydraulic society in early medieval Ceylon. *Past and Present*, 53, 3–27
Harriss, J. (1977). Bias in perception of agrarian change in India. In B.H. Farmer (ed.), *Green Revolution?* Macmillan, London, pp. 30–6
Leach, E.R. (1959). Hydraulic society in Ceylon. *Past and Present*, 15, 2–26
Karunanayake, M.M. (1977). Irrigation research possibilities in Sri Lanka: a challenge to the social sciences. *Vidyodaya Journal of Arts and Science*, 7
Madduma Bandara, C.M. (1973). Groundwater in the hard rock areas. *Ceylon Association for the Advancement of Science Annual Sessions* (Abstract)
  (1977a). The prospects of recycling sub-surface water for supplementary irrigation in the Dry Zone. In S.W.R. de A. Samarasinghe (ed.), *Agriculture in the Peasant Sector of Sri Lanka*, Wesley Press, Colombo, pp. 85–99
  (1977b). Hydrological consequences of agrarian change. In B.H. Farmer (ed.), *Green Revolution?* Macmillan, London, pp. 323–39
  (1979). A study of the practice of well irrigation in the country around Vavuniya in northern Sri Lanka. *Sri Lanka Journal of Social Sciences*, 2 (2), 65–88
  (1980a). Challenge of groundwater development in the Dry Zone hard rock areas. Sri Lanka Association for the Advancement of Science, Symposium on Groundwater Development (mimeo)
  (1980b). Some aspects of the behaviour of the water table in the vicinity of selected major irrigation reservoirs in the Dry Zone of Sri Lanka. *24th International Geographical Congress, Hydrology Section (Abstracts).* Tokyo, Japan
  (1980c). Water management under minor irrigation schemes in the Dry Zone of Sri Lanka. *24th International Geographical Congress, Main Session (Abstracts)*, vol. 1. Tokyo, Japan
  (1981). The effect of drought on the livelihood of peasant families in the Dry Zone

of Sri Lanka: a study of the Mahapotana Korale in the North Central Province. Paper presented to the International Geographical Union Working Group Meeting of International Hydrological Programme and Tropical Climatology and Human Settlements, Sri Lanka

Mahendrarajah, S. (1979). Economic evaluation of cropping systems under minor tanks. Agricultural Research Station, Maha Illuppallama (mimeo)

Moore, M.P. (1979). The management of irrigation systems in Sri Lanka: a study in practical sociology. *Sri Lanka Journal of Social Sciences*, 2 (2), 89–112

Murphy, R. (1957). The ruin of ancient Ceylon. *Journal of Asian Studies*, 16 (2), 181–200

Paranavitana, S. (1960). The withdrawal of the Sinhalese from the ancient capitals. In K. Indrapala (ed.), *The Collapse of the Rajarata Civilization*, Peradeniya

Sivanappan, R.K. & Palanisami, K. (1981). *Demand for Water in Tamilnadu in 2000 A.D. – Future Focus and Policy Issues*. Tamilnadu Agricultural University, Coimbatore

Tilakasiri, S.L. (1979). *Water Rights and Irrigation Practices: A Study of a Thoranegama Hamlet in the Mahaveli Development Area*. People's Bank, Colombo

16 Social organisation and irrigation: ideology, planning and practice in Sri Lanka's settlement schemes

JOHN C. HARRISS

Benny Farmer's book *Pioneer Peasant Colonisation in Ceylon* (1957) is a classic of agrarian studies; and its synthesis of environmental, economic and social analyses in explaining the pattern of development that has taken place in the settlement schemes of Sri Lanka's Dry Zone, represents an instance of the holism of the geographical tradition at its best. This study is intended as a small tribute to that book, which – though Farmer himself modestly describes it as 'widely quoted and little read' – comes to conclusions which are still of relevance today, while many of its practical recommendations have come gradually to be implemented.

This study is based on short periods of fieldwork in four of the older Dry Zone settlements, in the 'H' area of the new Mahaweli Project, and on Uda Walawe, all carried out in 1978, as well as on my earlier research in Hambantota District in 1974, which formed part of the Cambridge 'Green Revolution' Project that B.H. Farmer directed. The concern about water management which the essay reflects is one that Farmer himself identified in 'Pioneer Peasants' when he wrote: 'One of the most urgent tasks if Ceylon's water resources are to be used to best advantage is to arrive at more economical use of irrigation water.' This advice was largely ignored, however, until the recent past. Robert Chambers' work, in particular, in the 'Green Revolution' Project, contributed much to increasing awareness of the importance of water management issues in official circles in Sri Lanka, and in development agencies. And at the time of writing (late 1981) there is a great deal of experimenting going on in Sri Lanka, with the design and operation of irrigation systems and with institutions for water management (these have been admirably reviewed by Moore, 1980a). The practical point at which this study is directed has by now been widely recognised, therefore, but the implications of the social conditions of production in settlement schemes, analysed here, have not been examined hitherto, and they were somewhat glossed over in B.H. Farmer's early work. I also show the impact of ideologies on the practice of settlement planning and organisation. In these ways I hope that the essay complements the masterly analysis of Farmer's book.

Background to Dry Zone colonisation

It is well known that Sri Lanka contains within itself two broad geographical regions: the so-called 'Wet Zone' in the south-western quadrant of the country, and the 'Dry Zone'. Although the Dry Zone was the base of the great kingdoms of medieval Ceylon, founded on highly developed irrigation systems, for reasons which are still not fully understood these kingdoms rapidly declined after the fourteenth century, and the political and economic centre of gravity of the country shifted to the Wet Zone. The colonial period confirmed the dominance of the Wet Zone in terms of population density and in the economic and political life of the country, while the Dry Zone saw continuing decline. In the early part of this century large parts of the Dry Zone were almost uninhabited, there was scarcely any commodity production and only a very limited development of economic infrastructure (conditions which still prevail in some pockets within the region). Some very tentative efforts were made at organised land settlement in the Dry Zone in the nineteenth century, but it was not until the 1930s that a consistent policy for such settlement was formulated, under the State Council elected on the franchise extended under constitutional reforms after 1931.

The drive to 'colonise' the Dry Zone came from a complex of objectives, including the aims of relieving overcrowding in parts of the Wet Zone and of increasing food production within the country, but also for the purpose of protecting Sinhalese peasant agriculture – which was believed to have been adversely affected by the growth of the plantation economy in the nineteenth century. The policy of colonisation was further intimately bound up with the political objectives of the nationalist movement, which linked the colonisation of the Dry Zone with the idea of a return to the old heart of the country and a recovery of the lost greatness of the Sinhalese people.

A number of 'colonies' (as settlement schemes used to be called), based on irrigated paddy cultivation, had been established by the time of Independence in 1948, and thereafter 'colonisation' remained a major plank of the development policies of successive governments at least until the later 1960s when efforts to intensify agricultural production became more important. Latterly the policy of developing the agricultural economy by means of the extension of irrigated settlement has taken on renewed significance with ambitious plans for making greater use of the water of the country's largest river, the Mahaweli Ganga. Assistance has been obtained from international donor agencies and from individual governments for the construction of a number of interconnected irrigation and power projects, and some of these are already under way. The rapid implementation of the Mahaweli Development Project has a major part to play in the proposals of the government elected in 1977 for solving the country's unemployment problem and its food problem.

Objectives of this study

Irrigated settlement schemes have played, and continue to play a most important role in the economic development of Sri Lanka. This study examines four propositions about irrigated settlements in the Dry Zone:

(i) In explanations of the failure of Sri Lanka's irrigated settlements to achieve the economic objectives set for them, the very poor standards of water management which prevail – low levels of efficiency in water use and conditions approaching anarchy in irrigation management – must have an important part. The same factors will seriously affect the implementation of the Mahaweli Development Project.
(ii) The social conditions of production and related features of the social structures of the settlements largely determine standards of water management. These conditions are the result of the way in which the settlements have been organised.
(iii) Poor water management for which both cultivators and government staff share responsibility actually reinforces the social conditions referred to in the second proposition.
(iv) The determinants of social organisation and of water management practice in the Dry Zone settlements have been obscured by the ideologies which have influenced settlement policy. Thus policies, often contrary to the values and the stated objectives by which they have been guided, have probably contributed to the perpetuation of the social conditions referred to in the foregoing propositions.

The record of land settlement in the Dry Zone

Government policy on land settlement has reflected a variety of objectives, different objectives having been given greater or lesser emphasis at different times. They have included, principally, (1) the relief of poverty resulting from landlessness; (2) increasing food production and thereby enhancing national self-sufficiency; (3) the protection of peasant farmers; (4) employment creation; (5) increasing GNP; and (6) the establishment of growth centres. While these objectives need not necessarily be in conflict with one another there has been some conflict between the broader social objectives of settlement, and production goals – a conflict reflected, in the opinion of several writers, in differing policies over the selection of settlers. There has undoubtedly been some success in terms of the first four objectives distinguished (though probably at an unnecessarily high cost), but very little success at all in regard to the last two. This was the conclusion of the IBRD Agricultural Sector Survey of 1973.

Economic evaluations of settlements have given rise to considerable criticism of the levels of productivity achieved upon them. This was, indeed, the main subject of an IBRD Mission in 1966, as a result of which a number of special projects were set up in some of the schemes in an effort to improve productivity (these projects principally involved the expansion of existing agricultural extension services). Those who studied settlements drew attention to the low levels of adoption of intensive practices in paddy cultivation, to low levels of utilisation of 'highland' (that is, 'dryland') plots and the lack of attention to crops other than paddy (see Farmer, 1957; Barnabas, 1969). Farmer emphasised the urgent need to develop cultivation systems for highland, but this has remained an area in which little progress has been made. To balance against these observations we must note, however, the high paddy yields and efficient cultivation practices found in colonisation schemes in Polonnaruwa District in the early 1970s by the ARTI in surveys of paddy production, and the high yields recorded by Amerasinghe in his surveys at Minipe (reported in Hameed, 1977), so that there has been progress in some areas since the time at which Farmer (1957) reported his findings.

Comprehensive cost-benefit evaluations of settlements have not been carried out to any great extent. A high level committee, chaired by B.H. Farmer, did undertake a detailed evaluation of the Gal Oya Scheme, however, and demonstrated an adverse cost/benefit ratio (project discounted costs were found to have exceeded discounted benefits by Rs. 277 M). Gal Oya and the Uda Walawe Scheme are the two most important projects to have been implemented before Mahaweli. While Uda Walawe has not been the subject of the same kind of evaluation there can be little doubt that it too has failed to realise more than a fraction of the benefits it was designed to achieve when one considers that the area actually irrigated there is only about one-third of what was planned.

Problems of irrigation management

Explanations for this record of generally low achievement, for low levels of productivity and high costs have included, variously, the personal characteristics of settlers, the lack of incentives working through the land tenure system, the nature of the bureaucratic management of settlement, and the absence of cooperation between people and the lack of 'social cohesion' in the settlements. I will discuss all these explanations later in the chapter.

The factors mentioned are obviously not all of the same status as explanations, and it is accepted too, that a combination of them is involved. A further problem, noted by Farmer in 1957 but not given much attention thereafter, at least until the mid 1970s, is that of the efficiency of water use in relation both to productivity and to the social goals of settlement. It is *not* the claim of this study that the standard of water management is the 'x' factor which explains the failures of the policy of establishing irrigated settlements in the Dry Zone, but it is suggested that water management is a *crucial* problem both because of its importance in itself, and because it may be seen as underlying some of the other factors listed earlier. It is a pivotal problem, as a determinant and as the result of the structural problems in the political economy of Sri Lanka's settlement schemes. It is of pivotal importance in the sense that attempts to 'correct' other problems referred to earlier will be confounded by continuing inefficiency in water management – again both because of its importance in itself and because the persistence of current practices would mean that any efforts to create 'social cohesion', for example, or to increase commercial production would be seriously impaired.

Mahaweli Development Programme

An impression of the critical importance of water management may be derived from a brief consideration of the Mahaweli Development Programme. The economic appraisal of any irrigation project is very sensitive to assumptions made about water use; and up to 1978 plans for Mahaweli had been based on water duties lower than almost any ever actually recorded under field (as opposed to experimental) conditions in Sri Lanka. Even under tighter management achieved on pilot projects run by the Irrigation Department the low water duties that were assumed for Mahaweli had not been attained. The UNDP/FAO Report of 1969 adopted an estimated 'irrigation duty' of 8.3 feet for two crops of paddy; while the IBRD Appraisal for Mahaweli Project Two of 1977 estimated that an average of about 7.5 feet of water would be available annually for irrigation over the entire Project area. These figures must be compared with estimates for actual water use over both seasons on Dry Zone tanks of about 12 feet (5 feet for *maha* and 7 feet for *yala*), and with average annual duties achieved on the Irrigation Department's Special Projects of between 8.4 and 10.2 feet. It should further be noted that these duties were recorded on pilot projects much smaller in scale than the various sub-systems of the Mahaweli Project, and that it may not be correct to assume that the management innovations introduced would be as effective when implemented on a wider scale. Given these observations, and having in mind the history of the Uda Walawe Project, where so much less land has actually been irrigated than was planned, it appears that for the Mahaweli Project to succeed in terms of the production and employment objectives set for it, almost a revolution would be required in existing standards of water management.

These few comments demonstrate the importance of water management: for if it is assumed that the water available in an irrigation scheme will irrigate a certain acreage, and that acreage is not realised, then the cost/benefit ratios will be substantially altered, and the impact of the project on people's livelihoods will be much less than it might have been. In addition to these concerns regarding the productivity of water use, poor irrigation design, wasteful water practices and the tampering with structures associated with these, often lead to tail-end problems. Tail-enders receive less water and are thus exposed to higher levels of risk, have little incentive to apply inputs such as fertilisers and frequently obtain lower yields. In particular many of them have to forego the possibility of cultivating a *yala* crop. The harmful effects of the deprivation of the tail-enders in terms of productivity also make for their relative impoverishment (see Chambers, 1976).

Reasons for water waste

The proximate causes of wasteful water practices include combinations of the following factors:

(i) *Poor irrigation design.* Michael Moore writes:

Existing irrigation systems, excluding only those built in recent years, were designed and constructed in such a fashion as to make efficient water management almost impossible. The central physical features of the older schemes are: very long distributory and field channels designed to command as large an area as cheaply as possible; lack of clear distinction between the various levels of channels . . . relatively few control structures on channels, and, above all, scarcely any cross-regulation structures. (Moore, 1980a, p. 3)

These design characteristics are closely related to the problems of water management, including the difficulties of getting water to the tail-ends of systems, those of designing fair rotational schedules, ' . . . and the impossibility of controlling water flows without cross-regulators and intermediate storage between the main reservoir and the field' (Moore, 1980a, p. 4).

(ii) *Inadequate structures and lack of suitable measuring devices.* On the great majority of irrigation systems in Sri Lanka there are very few devices for measuring the flow of water, so that it is actually extremely difficult for irrigation staff to monitor how much water is flowing into different parts of the system. There are few control structures, and the quality of construction and of installation of minor irrigation structures is often poor (this was even true of the 'H' area of Mahaweli, in 1978). Further, maintenance budgets are small and there are, anyway, acute difficulties over getting maintenance done.

(iii) *The rationality of high water use for individual farmers.* This is because continuous flooding checks the growth of weeds and therefore reduces labour demands; and because it makes the whole cultivation operation less demanding than systems which involve any form of rotational water issues. Too often planners like to assume that cultivators work in the national interest; and here is a clear case where there may be conflict between individual interest and social interest.

(iv) *Cultivation delays*. Delayed cultivation of fields leads to staggering of cultivation periods. Surveys carried out by a team from the Geography Department of Colombo Campus in the *maha* season of 1977–78 showed that in a sample of 120 farmers in a part of system 'H' of Mahaweli, the first to begin cultivating his fields did so in the first week of October, and the last in the first week of January. The effects of such differences in timing between the farmers within a small area may be evened out if they are cultivating varieties of different duration, but even so the overall effect on the total water demand may be considerable.

The reasons for these delays include principally shortages of farm power (or so it has been suggested), and also the apparently traditional practice in the Dry Zone of waiting until the reservoir is full instead of beginning cultivation with the first rains. This practice is documented in studies of two settlement schemes conducted by the Agrarian Research and Training Institute (ARTI, 1979a, 1979b), and it is explained as a response to uncertainty over rainfall. Traditionally Dry Zone cultivators have also delayed operations in their paddy fields until after the completion of the sowing and clearing of *chenas*, and this has also been documented in the ARTI surveys, from which it has been concluded that '[the] key explanatory factors for the predominance of *chena* farming . . . can be summed up as the farmer's poor liquidity position, his subsistence level of production and lack of other alternative means of resource application, along with a remarkably high rainfall uncertainty' (ARTI, 1979a, p. 100).[1]

(v) *Cultivation of wet rice on permeable soils*. This practice has been a major cause of the very high water duties obtaining in tracts 2–7 at Uda Walawe, for example, where it was intended that much of the land should be put under sugarcane. Even a meeting presided over by Mrs Bandaranaike, then the Prime Minister, in May 1974, when it was decided that the growing of paddy in the *yala* season in these tracts should be banned, had no effect on the cultivation pattern. An exactly comparable situation appeared to be developing in the 'H' area of Mahaweli by mid-1978. The Project design rested on the proposition that crops other than wet rice should be grown on permeable soils, but in practice almost all the areas with those soils had gone under rice in the *yala*. The reasons for the farmers' preferences, according to my interviews, include their familiarity with wet rice and lack of familiarity with other crops proposed; the unproven profitability of some of the other crops given the pricing policies then existing and the absence of marketing structure, and their relatively high labour demands – and the advantages of rice because of its fairly good storage properties (as farmers said, 'It is like money in the bank', for them).

(vi) *The lack of water management and the absence of 'discipline'*. The circumstances considered hitherto are all associated with the kind of 'anarchy' over access to water which has been observed on irrigated tracts in Sri Lanka (for one example, see Harriss, 1977). A vicious circle has often been established. The design of systems is such as to make it difficult, anyway, for the irrigation staff to control the delivery of water; they lack the means to monitor flows; and farmers have demands which are sensible from their individual points of view, but which may bring them into conflict with one another. In these circumstances it is not surprising that they resort to tapping channels and damaging structures, when the irrigation bureaucracy often cannot meet their legitimate needs. Then once these actions have gone uncontrolled other farmers are encouraged to take the same course. Disorder in irrigation thus tends to be self-reproducing and self-reinforcing.

Although there has been legislation for a long time – in the various Irrigation Ordinances – laying down water charges and penalties for offences such as the illegal tapping of a channel, damaging a structure, or even for delayed cultivation, it is widely recognised that these provisions have hardly ever been implemented. Even if they are motivated to do so, which is not often the case, it is generally difficult for irrigation staff to catch those who are responsible for structural damage. Prosecutions have to be carried out by the police, who have usually treated water offences as trivial, and who do not have the same incentives to tackle them as in other cases. Further, delays over court proceedings and the very light fines which have been imposed on those who have been found guilty of irrigation offences, have made the legal sanctions ineffectual. Because of this situation and because of the physical dangers to which, as a result, junior irrigation staff may be exposed when they attempt to reduce or to cut off water supplies, it is hardly surprising that it is commonly observed on irrigation systems that gates are missing, structures damaged, channels tapped by encroachers and others – and in general that the state of the physical systems of irrigation is such as to make them hardly manageable. Again, the situation observed in the 'H' area of Mahaweli in 1978 was not encouraging. Even the spindle gates at the heads of distribution channels had sometimes been broken or tampered with so that it was impossible for the flow to be cut off completely; and two young Technical Assistants, when asked why they did not attempt to prevent blatant water poaching, replied that they were afraid to because of the fear of being assaulted.

A corollary of these points concerning the absence of effective discipline (either of a collective kind, or imposed from without) is that in many cases routine maintenance work is not carried out, or cannot be carried out fully. Parts of the irrigation system of Uda Walawe are said never to have had maintenance work carried out on them.

The essential point here is not that farmers are stupid or irrational, or utterly selfish, or that the irrigation bureaucracy is incompetent, but that both groups act in the context of physical and organisational structures which tend to set up the circle of actions described. The context of the organisational structure of the bureaucracy has been analysed by Moore, who shows how the structure does not encourage attention to water management (1980b). It follows that action to change the way in which irrigation systems are operated will have to involve *both* farmers and bureaucrats, and to improve the communication between the two groups (as I emphasised in an abstract way elsewhere: Harriss, 1976; and as Moore has argued more practically: Moore, 1980a).

(vii) *Political interventions*. Further underlying the weakness of water discipline in Sri Lanka is the extent of partisan political interference in the operation of irrigation systems. One important reason for the resigned cynicism even of other otherwise zealous officers is that actions taken against encroachers (of whom there were already substantial numbers in the 'H' area in 1978), or against those guilty of other irrigation offences, prompts interventions by politicians who have to respond to appeals from groups of their local supporters in order to maintain their own positions. Such interference is of course frequently a response to short-term political needs and takes no account whatsoever of the overall demands of water management, quite apart from its insidious effects on the morale and efficiency of officials. There is no question here of denying the right, or the duty indeed of a politician to represent the interests of his constituents, or of placing any part of the administration beyond political scrutiny, but the point is that interventions which are partial, motivated by short-term and partisan considerations, cannot be described as 'democratic', and can damage the interests of the mass of the people.

Here we examine especially the issue of 'water discipline' since it concerns both settlers and the staff who manage the settlements, and because any action on the other problems to which we have drawn attention calls for a greater degree of control over water than exists at present.

The organisation of Dry Zone settlement

In order to understand the determinants of the problems of water management we must know something of the way in which the Dry Zone settlements have been organised.

The Land Development Ordinance of 1935 established the principle of government initiative in selecting settlers and alienating Crown land to landless people. Subsequent land settlement policy has continued to be guided to a great extent by this Ordinance, the main principle of which was to lease land to settlers with conditions guarding its use, and with limitations preventing transfer, mortgage, sale or the sub-division of holdings. The Ordinance permitted the conversion of permits to grants after some years, but restrictions on leasing, transfer and sub-division remained, the object of these provisions being to protect the settlers from middlemen to whom they might otherwise mortgage their land and become indebted, and to protect the holdings from what were seen as the dangers of fragmentation and misuse. It is well known, however, that levels of indebtedness amongst settlers have often been high, and that there has been pledging of both crops and land to moneylenders. It is also known that both hidden tenancy and hidden fragmentation of lands has occurred quite widely. There has been a continuing debate on the principle of unitary succession laid down by the Land Development Ordinance, and over the desirability or not, of allowing freehold purchase of holdings within the settlements. The general trend has indeed been towards individual freehold tenure of the land, though there have been some experiments with collective forms of tenure (especially under the United Front government between 1970 and 1977).

The size of holdings alienated to settlers in the schemes under the Land Development Ordinance have varied from five acres of wetland and three acres of highland, which was general on the earlier schemes, to three acres of wetland and two acres of highland, which became the generally adopted norm by the later 1950s. Other sizes of holdings have been alienated at different times, however, such as the two acres of paddy land and two acres of highland alienated at the Mapakada Colonisation Scheme in 1956. In the first areas settled under the Mahaweli Development Project the norm adopted has been two-and-a-half acres of wetland and half an acre of highland.

It is most important to note that, in strong contrast with many irrigated settlement schemes in other parts of the world, settlers are not the tenants of a project authority to which they are liable to supply a commercial crop (as in the Gezira Scheme for instance; see Barnett, 1977), nor are they required to pay high rents. A small land rent was supposed to be levied under the Land Development Ordinance, and a water rate could be imposed under the Irrigation Ordinance, but these have rarely been collected. It has been the deliberate object of settlement policy in Sri Lanka to establish a large number of small private holdings which are quite near, in terms of their area, to being subsistence units. It has been a policy of perpetuating, or of creating, relatively small-scale and largely independent peasant production. Such production has been largely independent, in spite of the appearance of quite close supervision which might be deduced from the Land Development Ordinance, because the provisions of the Ordinance have rarely been strictly enforced.

Recruitment of settlers

Other aspects of settlement organisation which we must note include: the processes whereby settlers have been recruited and selected; the level of and the kind of provision which has been made for new settlers; features of the physical planning of settlements; and their management and administration. Others have discussed these procedures in detail (Farmer, 1957; Ellman et al., 1976) and we need note only some salient points.

The way in which the selection and recruitment of settlers has been carried out has undoubtedly, and not surprisingly, been subject to political influence both at the 'macro' level of the source areas chosen and at the 'micro' level of individual selection. But the main qualification for selection has always been landlessness, together with having a large family (so as to provide for labour on the allotment). The result of this emphasis has been that many of those who moved to the early Dry Zone settlements lacked agricultural experience and skills, and by the 1960s more attention began to be paid to the agricultural abilities of the applicants, at least in official statements of policy. It is doubtful how far it has been possible in practice to assess the abilities of applicants (according to land officers I have interviewed), and the social demands of landlessness appear to have remained a powerful influence on selection. Another consequence of the process of settler selection employed in the older settlement schemes was the creation of socially heterogeneous groups, in which people of different localities and castes were mixed together. It has been felt by some observers that this has accounted to a great extent for the lack of cooperation amongst settlers, and the low level of 'social cohesion' which they believed to characterise the settlements. Conflicts between people of different castes were reported, as well as between settlers and local people.

Planning controls

Until recently at least, there has been a policy of subsidising the settlers quite highly, by providing them with housing, agricultural inputs, and subsistence allowances as well as with social infrastructure. This policy probably stemmed from the need which was felt at first, to offer strong inducements for people to move to the malarial and inhospitable Dry Zone. But as it developed it resulted in high costs and the lack of cost consciousness which was noted in the Gal Oya Evaluation. More recently efforts have been made to reduce costs by such measures as asking farmers to clear their own holdings, and by building cheaper houses. In spite of heavy subsidisation, as we have already remarked, levels of indebtedness amongst settlers have commonly been high. It is thought that heavy subsidisation has at the same time encouraged an attitude of 'dependence' upon government.

The physical planning of settlement and planning of agricultural development were at first non-existent, and even in the more recent period it has been felt by many observers that engineering considerations have been allowed to dominate agricultural and social concerns to rather too great an extent. Settlements have been allowed to develop, ribbon-like, along the banks of canals and beside roads, and it has been thought that this has contributed to the lack of 'social cohesion' in the colonies.

The management of the Dry Zone settlements, to this day, has been carried out by Colonisation Officers from the Land Commissioner's Department. These men have usually had a training in agriculture, but not invariably so, and their lack of suitable training has sometimes been commented upon in evaluation studies. The management of the settlements has also frequently been criticised as being top-heavy and paternalistic, and as being marked by 'departmentalism', with quite inadequate coordination between the various departments involved (those of the Land Commissioner, under whose general authority the process of settlement has been carried out, and the departments of Agriculture, of Irrigation, and later of Cooperation and Agrarian Services). It has been felt that the management of the settlements has suppressed the settlers' initiative, and that more participation in policy making and administration is desirable (these views were expressed in the IBRD Agricultural Sector Survey of 1973, and they exercised a powerful influence on the proposals made by SOGREAH for the development of Mahaweli). It was partly in response to concerns about 'departmentalism' that a special authority, the Gal Oya Development Board, was set up to manage the Gal Oya River Valley Development, which later became the River Valleys Development Board – the organisation responsible in particular for Uda Walawe. Mahaweli has a unitary development authority also; but it is a matter for discussion as to whether the creation of such authorities has entirely overcome the problems of coordination of services. Impressions gleaned in the 'H' area of Mahaweli in 1978 suggested that departmental loyalties remain strong amongst irrigation engineers, agriculturalists and community development workers – and that the first mentioned are usually most powerful.

The process of social and economic differentiation

The social conditions of production established by the policies which have just been outlined are those of small-scale production, and of the processes of social and economic differentiation associated with it. As we have already had occasion to remark, a characteristic of the economic conditions prevailing in the Dry Zone settlements, observed by virtually all of those who have studied them, is the high level of indebtedness of the settlers, and the very high rates of interest which they pay. Interest rates on borrowings in the informal money market reported to me were commonly 10% per month; and Abayaratne in his study (1972) found both that 70% of settlers' borrowings were obtained from moneylenders and boutique keepers and that the average interest rates on these loans were 14% per month. Tambiah (1958) and

Amunugama (1965) both commented upon the emergence of a class of money-lending middlemen; and while there is no doubt that there has been a substantial expansion of cheap credit from official institutions over the last ten years or so, recent studies at Minipe and elsewhere have shown that there is still considerable reliance on informal credit and that the class of middlemen and wealthier farmers, who also lend money, remains firmly entrenched (see the work of Amerasinghe, reported in Hameed, 1977). The very high level of interest rates remains inadequately explained, though one factor is probably the very peaked demand that seems to characterise major irrigation schemes.

The levels of indebtedness recorded are both indicative of the social and economic differentiation that occurs in the settlements, and also are instruments of it. What seems to happen is this: the settler households start off with more or less the same resources, but differences in family size and in the stage in the developmental cycle of the household (which determines the ratio between the numbers of consumers and the number of workers on the family farm); differences in access to resources from outside and to cheap credit; and differences resulting from what may initially be random factors like variations in soil fertility or differences in access to water; as well, perhaps, as differences in individual ability, soon begin to create disparities of wealth between households which tend to become accentuated over time, and particularly as the second generation takes over.[2] Then, as is well known, there is effective fragmentation of land, and large numbers of people end up with very small holdings, and some of them will be operated on *ande* (by sharecropping) which can have the effect of reducing the cultivators' margins drastically. At this stage a great deal may depend upon the extent to which the original allottee's holding of land and other resources has to be divided up between his children.

In this process of differentiation between households some people are forced to take loans from private moneylenders and the indebtedness which often results (given the very high interest rates payable) further intensifies differentiation. Such indebtedness plays a large part in accounting for the low levels of productivity on some farms, as has become particularly apparent following the introduction of high-yielding varieties of paddy and the inputs required for their cultivation (on this see Amerasinghe, reported in Hameed, 1977). It should be noted, finally, that the process of differentiation referred to here may be partly cyclical in character.

The problem of 'social cohesion'

The kinds of societies which have developed on settlement schemes in Sri Lanka have often been characterised as lacking 'social cohesion'; low levels of cooperation between people have been noted; absence of 'effective leadership' and a strong tendency towards dependence upon officials have been described, combined with strongly individualistic attitudes. Farmer, Tambiah, Amunugama, Barnabas, and the French engineering consultants SOGREAH (1972) reporting on the 'H' area under Kalawewa, have all made very similar observations on these points; and I found them to be substantiated in my own interviews with settlers. It has been considered that these characteristics reflect undesirable tendencies in settlement societies – undesirable both in themselves, and in terms of their effects upon productivity. A constant theme is the one: 'If only settlers would cooperate together more, they would use water less wastefully, they would not fall so much into debt (etc.).' Sociologists have been intrigued by the problems of 'leadership', and a number of them have proposed methods for identifying and promoting a suitable set of leaders in settlement society.

Explanations of settlement society

The characteristics described have been explained as being the result of a combination of the following factors: the fact that people have been settled as individuals in heterogeneous groups where they have been cut off from friends and relations in the tightly knit kinship and neighbourhood groups of their old villages; the fact that these heterogeneous groups have often been divided by caste and other social differences; the fact that the ribbon-like settlement patterns of the schemes work to reduce social interactions (though Farmer at least observed that this was certainly not a sufficient explanation); and the fact that both the high level of government subsidisation and the attitudes of government officers have encouraged dependence upon them.

It has further been suggested (Farmer, Tambiah, Barnabas) that the restrictions on the division of holdings and the other provisions in the Land Development Ordinance, which contrast so much with traditional land tenure systems anywhere in Sri Lanka, have fostered the development of serious tensions within families. Because of the requirement of unitary succession, strong sibling rivalries are believed to have developed, and the unity which might have existed within families, to have been dissipated. One consequence of this may be the tendency, that certainly exists, for sons not to work with their fathers very much, but to go off as soon as they can to cultivate their own highland or *chena* plots and to secure their own independent sources of income. People whom I interviewed on several settlements in 1978 reported that only 10–15% of the young men remain working with their fathers on the family farm – an observation which may explain the phenomenon which has puzzled students of the costs of paddy production, the relatively low level of utilisation of family labour and the apparently uneconomic employment of wage labour. Anthropologists (Yalman, 1967; Harriss, 1977) have observed the same tendency amongst Dry Zone farmers outside colonisation schemes too; and it has been suggested that the general availability of some land for cultivation in the form of highland, or *chena* plots, has been one condition of the egalitarian, individualistic ethos of Dry Zone people. (I remember vividly the statement of one Dry Zone cultivator: 'It is our *chena* which makes us free.')

All of these factors do appear to be relevant to the explanation of the social characteristics of settlement schemes, but it is important to examine whether or not they provide a *sufficient* explanation because of the policy prescriptions which follow from them. If the settlement pattern, or the practice of settling people in heterogeneous groups explain the 'lack of social cohesion' in settlements, then it should be possible to put it right. But to what extent has the problem been diagnosed correctly?

The reality of peasant communities

Several observations may be made on this point; and it is here that, in my view, ideological views of the nature of Sinhalese village society have entered in, to obscure an important part of the social process of settlement societies. The result has been policy prescriptions which fail to cope with fundamental problems, and which may have results which are the reverse of what was intended. Specifically, the kinds of proposals to which I refer have argued for democratisation and the encouragement of participatory forms of management. I think that it is possible, because these proposals have failed to establish the conditions for the kind of democratic management which they envisage, that they may in the end have results which are the reverse of their intentions – and actually encourage the oppression of the mass of cultivators, for their failure encourages belief in the view that farmers are irresponsible.[3]

The first observation is this: that the idea of a 'socially cohesive community' is hard to define, and it is in any case an ideal. The political ideologies and the practical policies of many countries have been guided by ideas about harmonious and socially cohesive rural communities – as for example in the *ujamaa* villages and African socialism of Tanzania, or the idea of the 'village republic' in the community development approach to rural development adopted in India in the 1950s.

Such ideas have ignored the reality that peasant societies are usually not homogeneous and undifferentiated, but contain within themselves substantial inequalities and processes of differentiation, as well as being divided by ideological differences such as those of caste and kinship, by factions and by differences in political power. In so far as these societies have appeared harmonious and cohesive, it has frequently been because of a strong social hierarchy. (Evidence on these points may be found in a large number of monographs and studies; on their impact on community development programmes in India, see Etienne, 1968.) Policies which have followed from these myths about village communities have invariably foundered because they have ignored these facts, or they have succeeded in enhancing the power of those who were already powerful, who have usually been able to manipulate the 'community' institutions that have been established, to their own advantage. There is evidence for this from Sri Lanka (Weerawardena, 1975).

The need for social distance

A second observation is that the idea of a 'socially cohesive community' ignores the fact that the maintenance of social distance can be very important in the circumstances of village society. It may seem paradoxical, but it is the case that it is precisely *because* people do have to rely upon one another for their security, when the chips are finally down, that they may seek to avoid close ties with others. It has often seemed to outsiders that if only village cultivators would share their resources more than they do, then all would benefit. Sometimes the benefits seem to be so obvious that it has appeared to observers that farmers are behaving irrationally in not cooperating. But, from the farmers' point of view, sharing resources involves a large amount of risk for two reasons. One is that the act of sharing will increase the likelihood of tensions and conflict arising between themselves and others, which they try to avoid because they need to be able to call upon one another's help in real emergencies; the second is that the act of sharing involves a careful calculation, for in order to realise benefits it is necessary to surrender some part of their independent control of the resources on which the livelihoods of their families depend.

In one way and another these ideas were frequently expressed in the interviews which I held with settlers, and they often came up in the context of discussing settlement patterns. People almost universally disliked the ideas of the clustered hamlets so much favoured by the planners. The planners like clustered hamlets, partly because they are supposed to overcome the problem of the lack of social interaction in ribbon-settlement. But people disliked the idea of settlement clusters, because they feared that such settlements would give rise to conflicts because of cattle straying, or children fighting, and because of the jealousies which would arise. One woman argued that in a clustered hamlet people would be more jealous of those who were a little richer than the majority, with the result that these richer people would tend to cut themselves off from others, and would not, for example, lend food or money to their neighbours: 'And then where should we be?' she said.

Social differentiation and collective action

Thirdly, following on from the last two points, it is argued here that it is the conditions of small-scale production, with its inherent susceptibility to risk and uncertainty, and based on the small-scale property holding on which the whole settlement policy of Sri Lanka has always rested, which accounts for the general absence of collective action. It has been argued that these conditions give rise to processes of differentiation, and these restrict the possibilities of collective action. People simply do not have the same interests. Clashes of interest are further created and exacerbated by the circumstances of canal irrigation, which in the absence of strong controls (whether resulting from collective self-discipline, or from imposition from outside), very easily gives rise to conflicts between individuals and groups (see discussion of literature and bibliography in Harriss, 1979). These conditions are likely to be of much more fundamental importance than the fact that settlers have been put together in heterogeneous groups, or than any of the other factors proposed in the existing literature. People may be settled in kinship groups, but the conditions of risk which underlie the attitudes described in the last paragraph will still apply; and they may be set against one another if the irrigation system operates in such a way as to make them compete for access to water.

Conclusion: a powerful myth

The conclusion which is drawn from this discussion is *not* that the kinds of groups in which people are settled are *entirely* irrelevant, but that they do not provide the kind of key to the establishment of 'socially cohesive communities' which some other writers have seen. Further the whole idea of the 'socially cohesive community' is something of a myth, and one which would certainly be very difficult of realisation in the conditions of small-scale property holding and small-scale production of Sri Lanka's settlement schemes. These have created a peasantry which might aptly be described in terms of Marx's famous metaphor of 'the sack of potatoes'. It is a powerful myth however, and it appears that the quest for the realisation of the myth has drawn attention away from the fundamental problems of water management.

My argument, then, is that the way in which the Dry Zone settlements have been organised has set up conditions in which a high level of cooperation and collective action is inherently unlikely. This is the fragile foundation on which there weigh the demands for organisation, coordination and cooperation, of large-scale irrigation and it is hardly surprising that there is disorder – especially when we consider, too, that there has been a persistent tendency in practice to weaken the administration which might have created a stable frame. Another fact that has been ignored by those who have pursued the chimaera of the 'socially cohesive community' is that a large-scale irrigation system links together a 'community' of people (of a kind) far exceeding in scale the communities linked by multiplex relationships, which have informed their models.

Ideology and planning in Dry Zone settlements

In spite of the social conditions which have been described here, ideas concerning Dry Zone settlement have placed considerable faith in the virtues of self-help and cooperative, collective self-management, while the context of agricultural institutions in the country as a whole has seen a series of attempts to build up local organisations to manage all aspects of rural development, outside the bureaucracy, at least since the passing of the Paddy Lands Act of 1958 and until the regime of the government elected in 1977. That Act, it will be remembered, abolished the old system of irrigation headmen and replaced it with elected 'Cultivation Committees'. These committees, like the cooperative societies and the rural development societies, were often ineffective and frequently dominated by an elite of relatively wealthy people. Under this leadership the institutions were either ineffective and non-operational, or in some cases they were manipulated by the leadership for their own purposes.

These statements, though sweeping, have been strongly substantiated (Weerawardna, 1975; and in relation to irrigation in particular; Chambers, 1976 and Harriss, 1977). The following statement, in one of the ARTI studies on 'The Role of Local Groups in Rural Development', is typical: 'In Mawegama it was amply demonstrated that the existing inequalities of the power structure . . . resulted in the control and manipulation of rural institutions by the more powerful groups.' The policy of establishing these institutions has been influenced by (broadly) socialist ideas. Their record in practice serves to make the point that *elements* of a socialist sytstem of planning and administration do not work, or worse, may strengthen social forces which are reactionary, when they are set up outside the context of a socialist society.

Planning for Mahaweli

Amongst those who have planned for Mahaweli, Barnabas at least argued that it would not be possible to recreate traditional societies in the conditions of the settlement schemes, and that the emphasis in social planning for Mahaweli should accordingly be on the creation of new communities. For this reason he argued the advantages of *heterogeneity* amongst the settlers and the breaking of old social ties. But he believed also in the necessity of developing a new 'leadership' – and he failed to consider the problems of managing the irrigation system at all.

The SOGREAH team of French consultants and Sri Lankan co-workers produced policy proposals for Mahaweli in 1972, on the basis of a number of surveys and in-depth studies using participant observation. They came to rather more optimistic conclusions concerning the inherent potential of settler initiative and leadership. Central problems were identified as being the attitudes of 'dependence' upon the administration in existing settlements, and the distrust which existed between people and officials; together with the lack of coordination and compartmentalisation between government departments involved in settlement planning and management.

The SOGREAH recommendations were based, therefore, on the view that it would be possible to develop a system of self-management by the settlers themselves, through a system of farmers' organisations to which officials should act in an advisory capacity. Management should rest on a contract between people and staff, in which both parties would accept obligations as well as certain rights. An active programme of community development should be the cornerstone of the project, served by a new kind of official trained to work with and to encourage the initiative of the settlers, rather than either to dictate to them or to treat them in a paternalistic fashion. These main planks of the SOGREAH proposals – farmers' organisations, a contract between people and staff, community development and the creation of a 'new' cadre of officials – would be supported by a selection procedure which would recruit settlers for their *social* as well as for their agricultural skills. The SOGREAH team did not make any specific proposals concerning the management of the irrigation system, but treated it as one of several subjects which would be handled within the framework of the farmers' organisations.

Thus SOGREAH argued that by the settlement of people in group that would preferably be self-selected, and which would be naturally homogeneous, in small clusters of dwellings resembling as far as possible the old *purana* villages; and by changing the attitudes of government staff (though how this would be done was never spelled out) it would be possible to release the capacities of the people for self-development. This would also create a situation in which high agricultural productivity would be encouraged.

One may sympathise entirely with the values contained in these proposals, and have no less faith in the inherent capacities of the people, and yet still find this argument quite unsatisfactory. The problem is that in its pursuit of the community and of collective organisation, the SOGREAH team ignored the social conditions of production set up by the land system of the settlements, and the particular organisational demands of a large-scale irrigation system (though to be fair to the SOGREAH team, they did also advocate a movement towards collective ownership). The danger is that by ignoring these conditions the proposals would go off at half-cock. Such a result could lead to the reverse tendency, for it would appear to confirm the view that peasants are reactionary, and need to be 'modernised' – and dragooned if necessary. But it is perhaps more likely that such a result would simply favour the persistence of existing structures of power and economic relations.

An alternative model

It has been argued here that the establishment of a large number of individual households on private holdings the size of a 'viable' farm, first of all encourages individualistic attitudes (which many of the settlers – certainly if they come from the Dry Zone – probably bring with them in any case), and strong jealousies develop between people (I observed this on system 'H' in 1978). Thereafter a process of differentiation begins to occur – on the lines which were described earlier. Given such differentiation, and the persistence of small-scale property, the development of collective action is, to say the least, problematical. This kind of differentiation both supports, and is in turn supported by, alliances between members of the bureaucracy and wealthier individuals amongst the settlers, because they have interests in common. Members of the bureaucracy may benefit by having particular friends amongst the settlers, on whom they can rely for help (this is true, for example, of the lowly agricultural extension worker, who needs to be able to get information in a hurry, or to find 'volunteers' for a new extension programme); and their friends in turn can call upon them for help in raising money or obtaining agricultural inputs – including water.

SOGREAH did not explain how the measures which they proposed would help to overcome these tendencies, or the problems of irrigation management which are intimately related to them – and in the last analysis reliance was placed on changing people's attitudes. Thus it was that SOGREAH argued that community development should be ' . . . the core of the strategy of implementation'. We must note, though here because of constraints of space it can only be in passing, that concepts of 'community development' rest on ideas of 'community' like those which have already been subjected to criticism in this paper, and that the record of 'CD' in Asia is mainly one of failure. The way in which 'CD' was being organised in the 'H' area of Mahaweli in 1978 did not suggest that it was likely to succeed in meeting up to the expectations of it in the SOGREAH proposals – and it seemed rather to justify the conclusion of one expert on rural development: 'Community Development . . . is a holistic (and valid) concept which is however, not administratively helpful. Rivalries between Community Development and other departments have done much harm' (Guy Hunter).

It should be clear that I believe very firmly that the attitude and values which people hold *are* important in explaining how and why they behave as they do, but that I also believe that the circumstances – or the 'structural conditions' – in which they live have to be taken into account in explaining the persistence of their values. As long as the conditions of small-scale production and the tendencies towards differentiation to which it gives rise in the market economy prevailing in settlement schemes, then it is unlikely that efforts to change attitudes towards more collective modes of action, will be successful. Supposing that farmers' organisations like those proposed by SOGREAH had been set up, what would have prevented them from passing into the control of the same class of people who were identified in the SOGREAH studies as having taken over earlier institutions such as the Cultivation Committee? No answer was given to this question.

To those who would object that the conditions of production of the settlement schemes are much like those in the old *purana* villages, and that these old villages *were* characterised by extensive collective action, a word of caution has already been sounded here. It is most important to distinguish between myth and reality, and something of a myth is still heard about 'the *purana* village' in Sri Lanka. There is at least as much evidence that *purana* villages were, as they still are, places in which people did not always cooperate together. Administrative reports of the nineteenth century contain accounts by Government Agents expressing their concern about the collapse of *purana* village tanks, and commenting on the fact that the reasons for these collapses were often that people would not work together. There is much evidence, too, of the under-utilisation of agricultural land in the old villages, with land being left uncultivated sometimes because of the lack of cooperation between shareholders in the land. The idea that the old villages were effective communities in which people worked together, should not be taken uncritically – as it appeared to be by some in 1978, when it was being argued that *purana* villages should be 'recreated' in the Mahaweli Settlements.

In the end then, the ideologies which have influenced settlement policy are distracting, and they have certainly failed to direct attention to one central problem – that of the operation of the irrigation systems themselves. These ideologies accurately reflect the attitudes of the Sri Lankan ruling classes towards small rural producers over a long period, combining as they have done, paternalism – aimed sometimes at pre-empting possible unrest and resistance – and a certain romanticism about the peasantry. The results of such attitudes, when translated into public policy towards smallholder agriculture, have rather been to subsidise such producers than to encourage productivity through material incentives (see the important discussion of public policy by Moore, 1981). The lack of attention to the use of irrigation water, at least until the very recent past, is of a piece with this broader pattern of relations between state and peasantry.

A final word, on what can be done

This study has a critical and analytical purpose rather than a prescriptive one. Still, it would not be surprising if some readers – especially Sri Lankans – were to retort that having disposed of some favourite 'myths', and poured cold water on the idea of management through participative organisations, I have failed to mention any other possible modes of operation. In order to respond adequately to this reaction, I would have to write another paper – though its theme would be one which I mentioned, rather in passing, in the course of this study. This is the view that action to change the way in which irrigation systems are operated must involve *both* farmers and bureaucrats. A workable system of management would necessarily involve cultivators, for the bureaucracy cannot extend its control down to every field. But the involvement of the farmers depends upon the establishment of suitable conditions – which include, perhaps crucially, the setting up of a framework which cannot easily be disrupted by self-interested individuals and groups. And that, in turn, implies that the physical systems of irrigation should be capable of being operated more flexibly than those that have been constructed in the past. It is necessary to reverse the vicious circles referred to earlier.

The implication of the argument of this study, therefore, is *not* that farmers' organisations have no role to play, but only that too much must not be expected of them. There is a good deal to be done in irrigation design, and system operation, as well as in bureaucratic reform, in order to set up conditions in which participative modes of operation of irrigation and settlement will have a good chance of working well – in the cultivators' interest as well as in the broader social interest (on all these areas for action see Moore, 1980a, 1980b). Design and operation, and the irrigation and settlement bureaucracies, all pose difficult problems for reform, but they are less intractable than those posed by attempts at massive social engineering in Sri Lanka's irrigated settlements.

ACKNOWLEDGEMENTS

I would like to thank Percy Silva for his kindness in sharing with me some of the results of his research in the 'H' area of Mahaweli; Robert Chambers for making available to me some of the data included here, and for offering so much encouragement when I undertook research in Sri Lanka in 1978; and Mick Moore for discussion of the problems that I have dealt with. None of these friends is at all responsible, however, for the content of my essay.

NOTES

1. There is still some debate about the extent of conflict between the demands for labour of *chena*, and of paddy farming, in Sri Lanka. Silva, in his work on this question in the 'Cambridge Project', concluded that there was not much conflict in Hambantota District at least (Silva, 1977); but this conclusion should not be generalised. It is part of the subject of a research project currently being carried out on *chena* cultivation in Sri Lanka, directed by B.H. Farmer.

2. Barnett (1977) offers a detailed analysis of such a cyclical process of differentiation on the Sudanese Gezira Scheme.
3. The present government, indeed – that formed by the United National Party after the general election in 1977 – has already replaced many of the formally democratic institutions involved in rural development since the 1950s, by appointed officials and official committees. (This does not mean, of course, that 'oppression' has thereby been increased.)

REFERENCES

Abayaratne, G.M. (1972). Economic aspects of some peasant colonisations in Ceylon. D.Phil. thesis, Oxford University

Amunugama, S. (1965). Chandrikawewa: a recent attempt at colonisation in a peasant framework. *Ceylon Journal of Historical and Social Studies*, 7, 130–62

ARTI (1979a). *A study of five settlement schemes prior to irrigation modernisation. Vol. 1, Mahawilachohiya*. Research Study No. 28. Colombo, Agrarian Research and Training Institute

(1979b). *A study of five settlement schemes prior to irrigation modernisation. Vol. II, Mahakandarawa*. Research Study No. 31. Colombo, ARTI

Barnabas, A.P. (1969). Sociological aspects. *FAO/UNDP Report on Mahaweli Project*, vol. XI. Colombo

Barnett, T. (1977). *The Gezira Scheme: an illusion of development*. London, Cass

Chambers, R. (1976). *Water management and paddy production in the Dry Zone of Sri Lanka*. Occasional Publication No. 9. Colombo, ARTI

Ellman, A.O., et al. (1976). *Land Settlement in Sri Lanka 1840–1975*. Research Study No. 16. Colombo, ARTI

Etienne, G. (1968). *Indian Agriculture: the art of the possible*. Berkeley, University of California Press

Farmer, B.H. (1957). *Pioneer Peasant Colonisation in Ceylon*. London, Oxford University Press, for Royal Institute of International Affairs

Hameed, N.D. Abdul, et al. (1977). *Rice Revolution in Sri Lanka*. Geneva, United Nations Research Institute for Social Development

Harriss, J.C. (1976). Problems of water management policy and objectives. Paper D3, ODI Workshop on Choices in Irrigation Management, London (mimeo)

(1977). Problems of water management in Hambantota District. In B.H. Farmer (ed.), *Green Revolution?* London, Macmillan, pp. 246–55

(1979). *The use of documentary and historical evidence in irrigation studies*. Discussion Paper. Norwich, University of East Anglia, School of Development Studies

Moore, M.P. (1980a). *Approaches to improving water management on large-scale irrigation schemes in Sri Lanka*. Occasional Publication No. 20. Colombo, ARTI

(1980b). The management of irrigation systems in Sri Lanka: a study in practical sociology. *Sri Lanka Journal of Social Sciences*, 2 (2), 89–112

(1981). The State and the Peasantry in Sri Lanka. D.Phil. thesis, University of Sussex

Silva, W.P.T. (1977). Chena-Paddy Relationships. In B.H. Farmer (ed.), *Green Revolution?* London, Macmillan, pp. 85–91

SOGREAH (1972). *Feasibility study for Stage II of the Mahaweli Ganga development.* Vol. VII, Mahaweli Development Board, Colombo

Tambiah, S.J. (1958). Some sociological problems of colonisation in a peasant framework. *The Ceylon Economist*

Weerawardena, I.K. (1975). *Lessons of an experiment: the Paddy Lands Act of 1958.* Evaluation Studies No. 3. Colombo, Division of Rural Institutions and Productivity Laws

Yalman, N. (1967). *Under the Bo Tree.* Berkeley, University of California Press

17 Environmental hazard and coastal reclamation: problems and prospects in Bangladesh

DAVID R. STODDART and JOHN S. PETHICK

The area

Geomorphology

Bangladesh occupies the delta area of the Ganges and Brahmaputra Rivers at the head of the Bay of Bengal (Fig. 17.1). The whole area consists of low-lying deltaic sediments, mainly silts and clays, nowhere higher than 1 m above mean water level. The surface consists of older, raised and dissected deposits inland, with more actively accreting areas to seaward (Morgan & McIntire, 1959). Over recent centuries the locus of maximum discharge has shifted from west to east. The active tidal delta consists of a maze of tidal channels, chief of which are the rivers Meghna, Shahbazpur and Tetulia. These vary in width from 3 to more than 30 km and are usually less than 5 m deep; they are separated by the large estuarine islands of Bhola, Hatia and Sandwip, with innumerable smaller ephemeral islands and shoals. The land area surrounding these channels comprises the *thanas* of Barisal, Patuakhali and Noakhali.

The mean annual discharge of the Ganges–Brahmaputra system is 30.9×10^3 cumecs (of which the Brahmaputra contributes 62%), a discharge second only to that of the Amazon among the world's rivers (Meybeck, 1976). Because of the monsoonal rainfall the discharge is highly seasonal, with the extreme high flow being twenty times the low flow in the Ganges and over sixty times in the Brahmaputra. The average suspended sediment load of 2.18×10^9 tons/year (67% delivered by the Ganges) is the largest of any river system in the world (Holeman, 1968).

The western part of the delta, still largely occupied by the mangrove forests of the Sunderbans, is now almost completely without freshwater fluvial inputs, and its soils have become progressively more saline and depleted in soil nutrients. Thus for reasons of soil fertility and water availability agriculture is largely confined to the active eastern part of the delta, where high discharge, rapid flow velocities (which can average 4 m/sec in the main channels), massive sediment loads, and easily erodible bank materials combine with high astronomical tides and cyclonic storm surges to give a dangerously unstable environment for human activity.

Immediately seaward of the delta shoreline is a delta-front platform

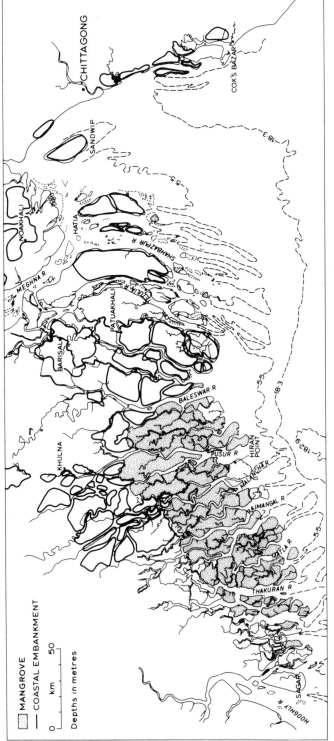

Fig. 17.1. Deltaic coastlands of Bangladesh, showing the distribution of mangroves and coastal embankments.

5–10 m deep and 50–100 km wide, terminating in a delta-front slope where the bottom falls to more than 60 m depth in a distance of 12–27 km. A submarine canyon (Swatch of No Ground) leads to the deeper floor of the Bay of Bengal. Surveys since that of Rennell in 1779 indicate that the shoreline of the western part of the delta has been remarkably stable, while in spite of considerable local variability that of the eastern delta does not show the progradation that might be expected given the heavy sediment loads. Much of the sediment must therefore be used in building the delta-front platform, or is lost to the deep ocean floor, rather than being added to the subaerial delta surface. A comparatively small proportion is held in temporary storage in ephemeral banks and islands, known as *charlands*, in the channels. The Bangladesh Landsat Programme identifies the total area of charlands as 486,000 ha. The fact that more are not converted into dry land may result from the progressive removal of mangrove forest for agriculture over many centuries.

A further reason why little coastal aggradation is taking place is undoubtedly the high-energy environment at the head of the Bay of Bengal. It is estimated that the root mean square wave height in this area is 1.41 m, the nearshore wave energy 0.585×10^7 ergs/sec, and the wave power at the 10 m isobath 732.3×10^7 ergs/sec (Wright et al., 1974). Tidal ranges are also high and complex, and subject to considerable seasonal variation with river discharge. Extreme tidal ranges on the Bangladesh coast vary from 4.2 to 8.9 m, reaching a maximum in the flaring channels of the eastern delta, and mean sea level shows a variation of up to 1 m through the year (Ghulam Kibria, 1978).

Under these conditions coastlines are highly unstable. Comparison of the 1940 topographic survey of East Pakistan with 1978 aerial photographs shows that bank erosion may be as high as 200 m/yr in some localities, a rate that must be amongst the highest in the world. Rates of erosion are very variable, however, in both space and time: the average annual rate of erosion during the 1940–78 period was 90 m/yr, with some areas showing progradation. It is of particular interest that in the major channels of the Shahbazpur and Meghna both banks are eroding simultaneously. This may be a consequence of the eastward shift in discharge in the delta as a whole: Rennell's map of 1779 suggests that over the past two centuries, for example, the channel of the Tetulia has shrunk to one quarter of its former width while that of the Shahbazpur is twice its eighteenth-century dimension. If this trend continues it is probable that the Shahbazpur itself will be progressively abandoned, and the channel of the Meghna widened by bank erosion in the future. It is also likely that human activities, in particular the reclamation of estuarine marsh, will cause channel constriction, changes in velocity, and consequent bank erosion. Clearly human settlement and agricultural activity must adapt to this environmental instability on a variety of time scales.

Mangrove forests

Although most of the eastern delta is now cleared for agriculture, stratigraphic evidence indicates that it was formerly occupied by mangrove woodland. The western part of the delta, in India and Bangladesh, constitutes the largest continuous mangrove area in the world. This forest, known as the Sunderbans, has an area of over 420,000 ha (Blasco, 1975, 1977; Blasco et al., 1975; Mukherjee & Mukherjee, 1978; Vaclav & Skoupy, 1973). By contrast the two main areas of mangrove in eastern Bangladesh have areas of only 3,400 and 6,500 ha. The Sunderbans mangroves consist of a tall woodland, often reaching 20–25 m, of *Heritiera minor* (*sundri*), *Excoecaria agallocha* (*gewa*), *Ceriops decandra* (*goran*) and *Sonneratia apetala* (*keora*). The first two species are characteristic of the higher inland mangals, with decreased frequency and depth of inundation; both are intensively managed for forest products. *Sonneratia* forms the pioneer community on muddy intertidal substrates. It is noteworthy that genera which are elsewhere common components of mangals, notably *Rhizophora* and to a lesser extent *Bruguiera*, are comparatively rare in Bangladesh. In addition to the mangrove woodland, large areas in the low intertidal are colonised by a monospecific salt marsh of the stoloniferous grass *Porteresia* (*Oryza*) *coarctata*. This is the dominant cover of many treeless chars, and also often forms a narrow band to seaward of pioneer mangroves.

It is highly likely that the removal of mangroves in the eastern delta has contributed to shoreline destabilisation (cf. Savage, 1972). It is possible too that mangroves may have acted in the past in that area as a protection against storm surges and cyclonic winds and waves, and that their removal may have exacerbated the catastrophic consequences of recent storms (Fosberg, 1971). Present environmental conditions are so different in the old and in the active delta, however, that it is not really possible to extrapolate from experience in the Sunderbans to make predictions about the likely consequences of mangrove growth further east. Certainly, without human intervention, it is unlikely that mangroves will naturally re-establish themselves in the active delta. Not only is there intense competition with other modes of land use, notably for rice and grazing, but there is now no local source of propagules and the river discharge is such that any which do reach the area are rapidly flushed away.

The problem of population and food

Population dilemma

Of all third-world nations, probably no other exhibits so acutely the classical Malthusian dilemma as does Bangladesh. Ranked 126th by the World Bank

Development planning and agrarian change

(1980) among the world's nations in terms of per caput GNP (US$ 80 in 1977), it is a country where almost every index of physical and social well-being has declined over the last decade, in spite of large food imports and massive amounts of external aid.

It is undoubtedly true that with a population of 10 millions Bangladesh would be a very pleasant place to live in (Faaland & Parkinson, 1976, p. 1). In the seventeenth century and earlier the population was stable at about 17 millions. But towards the end of the nineteenth century, with at least partial control of famine and disease, numbers began to grow: to 29 m. in 1901, 51 m. in 1961, and approximately 93 m. in 1982 (see Table 17.1 and Fig. 17.2). This increase results from the combination of a stable birth rate (45–50 per 1,000) throughout this century, and a rapidly falling death rate (from 40–45 per 1,000 ca 1920 to 23.0 in 1960 and 18.0 in 1977). The present annual growth rate of nearly 3% per annum (compared with less than 1% before 1950: Duza, 1974) indicates a doubling period for the entire population of less than 25 years. Government forecasts envisage a population of 109 m. in 1990, 128 m. in 2000, 148 m. in 2010, and 167 m. in 2020 (SYBB, 1979, p. 60), though without effective fertility control the totals could be higher.

The present age distribution of the population is very broadly based (Fig. 17.2). 16% of the population is less than 4 years old, 42% less than 14 years, and 53% less than 19 years. Such numbers (45 million people aged 19 or younger) place a heavy burden of support on the adult population, and also represent an inevitable future increment to the reproductive age groups. At present, 13% of live births do not survive to the first birthday and 23% do not

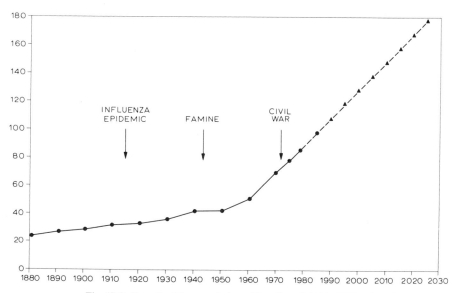

Fig. 17.2. Growth of the population of Bangladesh 1880–1980 and projections 1980–2020 (source of data: SYBB, 1979).

Table 17.1. *Population of coastal districts, Bangladesh, 1901–1979*

	Area sq km	1901	1911	1921	1931	1941	1951	1961	1970*	1974	1979*	Density per sq km 1901	Density per sq km 1979	Ratio of 1979:1901 densities
Bangladesh	134,615	28.93	31.56	33.26	35.60	42.00	41.90	50.80	68.12	76.40	86.64	215	644	3.00
Khulna	10,417	1.27	1.38	1.47	1.63	1.94	2.08	2.45	3.40	3.84	4.40	122	422	3.46
Barisal	6,501	2.49	2.61	2.84	3.19	3.81	2.64	3.07	3.81	4.18	4.60		708	
Patuakhali	3,553						1.01	1.19	1.46	1.60	1.78	248	501	2.55
Noakhali	3,973	1.14	1.30	1.47	1.70	2.22	2.27	2.38	3.10	3.44	3.86	287	972	3.39
Chittagong	6,568	1.35	1.51	1.61	1.80	2.15	2.31	2.98	4.09	4.65	5.48	206	834	4.05

Population figures are in millions and are derived from census data, except for years marked * which are estimates.
Source: Statistical Yearbook of Bangladesh 1979.

Development planning and agrarian change

reach their fifth: any improvement in life expectancy can only worsen the demographic situation. Population projections indicate a modification in age-sex distributions over the coming decades (Fig. 17.3), but nonetheless absolute numbers of people in the reproductive age bracket 20–49 years will treble by the year 2000.

This enormous population is supported almost entirely by the land. 90% of the total is classified as rural, and 80% (60 millions) is directly employed in agriculture. The overall population density in Bangladesh has trebled from 215 per sq km in 1901 to 644 per sq km in 1979. It is projected to increase to 950 per sq km in 2000 and to 1243 per sq km in 2020 (SYBB, 1979, p. 60). With a cultivated area of 9.1 million ha, the present density per cultivated hectare is 9.5, and unless the cultivated area can be substantially expanded this too will double within the next forty years.

What options are available to cope with this progressive and foreseeable catastrophe? Given the paucity of natural resources, the industrialisation strategy of the initial Indian Five Year Plans can be excluded. This leaves

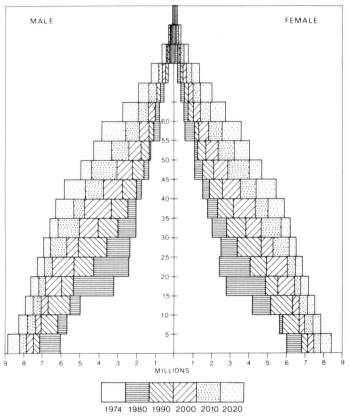

Fig. 17.3. Age-sex pyramids for the population of Bangladesh 1974 and 1980 and projections for 1990–2020 (source of data: SYBB, 1979).

three possibilities, which are of course not exclusive: population control; increase in agricultural output; and international subsidy.

Population control

Given the present demographic structure and the fact that the reproducers of the next several decades are already born, the prospect of adequate population control is remote. This situation is reinforced by complex social, economic and religious attitudes. In Bangladesh women traditionally marry earlier than do men: in 1974 32% of women aged 10–14 were married and 89% of those aged 15–19, compared with 2% and 12% of men in these age groups (SYBB, 1979, p. 91). Such early marriage of women not only increases their reproductive span, but also renders them liable to a prolonged widowhood in which they will need to be supported by their children (21% of women aged 35–44 and 46% aged 45–54 are widows, compared with 3% and 5% of men in these age brackets who are widowers). Given the high infant mortality and constant risk of death of children from malnutrition, disease and natural disaster, it is not surprising that most women bear 6–7 children each. Any woman who voluntarily limited herself to one or two children would face the prospect of penurious and unsupported old age.

The acceptance of techniques of birth control is subject to many constraints, especially to those of education and literacy which apply to women more than they do to men and to rural more than to urban areas. It must be recalled that only one person in five in Bangladesh has any formal education at all, and only 6% have completed secondary school. Stoeckel and Choudhury (1973) in a sample study found that 80% of Hindu women were aware of contraceptive practices, 70% approved them, but only 15% used them; while the figures for Muslim women were, respectively, 40%, 40% and 3%. Recent data show that women receptive to contraception are those who already have several children. Ominously, Stoeckel and Choudhury (1977) also showed that the number of children desired by women increased with the number they already had: from 4 when they had none, to 7 with four, and to 8 or 9 with more than four.

Given the explicit emphasis on the magnitude of the population problem in the Bangladesh First Five Year Plan, the resources devoted to the population control programme (Taka 700 m. or US$ 90 m.; 1.8% of total expenditure) seem inadequate with an at-risk population approaching 40 million people (thus providing less than 50 cents per person per year). Planned investment increased to 2.7% in the Two Year Plan, but fell back to 2.4% in the Third Plan (with provision for an increase to 2.8% if the money could in fact be spent). This latter figure is equivalent to approximately US$ 2 per person at risk per year. The success of the control programme has been limited by structural rather than technical difficulties, however. The allocation of funds was underused in every year of the First Five Year Plan. In 1978–79 the underexpenditure amounted to 27% of the allocation. Provision of cash incentives to acceptors also led to substantial abuse. The major achievement of the First Plan was to move away from surgical methods of control to the use of condoms (which increased from 11.2 m. in 1973–74 to 65.7 m. in 1977–78) and pills (from 0.44 m. cycles in 1973–74 to 7.5 m. in 1977–78). But even these totals are inadequate, amounting in the final year to 3.8 condoms per head of the male population aged 20–54 (with some districts such as Barisal, Patuakhali and Chittagong having well under 0.5 per head) and 0.34 pill cycles per head per annum for the female population aged 10–45. (Indian experience has indicated a condom requirement of 72 per head per year for significant population control.) In spite of this weak performance, the Second Five Year Plan envisages reducing the crude birth rate from 43.25 to 31.56 per 1,000 and the crude death rate from 16.75 to 13.78 per 1,000 by 1984–85: it is difficult to see any realistic prospect of these targets being achieved.

Not surprisingly it has been concluded that the only effective check to population growth in the short term will be famine (Faaland & Parkinson, 1976, p. 123). This is scarcely an available policy option for the Government, however, and were it to occur the international agencies would undoubtedly do their best to alleviate it.

Increasing food production

Rice provides 93% of the cereal consumption of Bangladesh, with a total cropped area of 10 m. ha and yield of 18.5 m. metric tons. The main crop (54% of the total area) is *aman*, a wet-season crop usually transplanted in July–August and harvested in November–January. *Boro* (20% of the total) is an irrigated dry season crop, transplanted in November–February and harvested in March–May. The *aus* crop (24%) is transplanted in March–April and harvested in July–September. In spite of double-cropping of large areas and the country's dependence on the crop rice yields are mediocre: the average of 1,850 kg/ha compares with averages of 2,897 in the Philippines, 3,294 in China and 5,563 in Japan. This is usually ascribed to defective agricultural technology and lack of adequate water control, and to the extent that these can be improved the supply of rice could presumably be substantially increased. Some indeed have seen the introduction of new high-yielding varieties as of greater importance for the alleviation of Bangladesh's problems than population control: according to Stepanek (1979, p. 33) 'rapid growth of a modern rice culture can be the foundation for Bangladesh's development'.

Nevertheless, after a decade of experimentation with HYV rice, the overall effect has been minimal. Average yields in both Bangladesh and eastern

India have remained static since 1960 (Fig. 17.4), in contrast to the situation in north and south India, Pakistan and Sri Lanka, where average yields have increased by one-third. The problem lies less in the new technology itself than in its adoption. The average yield of HYV rice in Bangladesh is 2.3–2.6 t/ha compared with 0.8–1.5 t/ha for local varieties, but HYV rice occupied only 12% of the total rice area in 1977–78 (compared with 62% in the Philippines and 67% in Sri Lanka), producing 21% of the crop.

The impact of HYV has been variable between crops and thus between areas. The greatest impact has been on *boro* crops in areas irrigated by lowlift pumps: HYV now exceeds local varieties in both area and production for this crop. Adoption of HYV in *aus* and *aman* crops has been comparatively small, though IR20 is increasing in *aman* areas. Except for Barisal District the delta areas lag significantly in adoption of HYV, with only 6–7% of the rice area in new varieties in Khulna and Patuakhali by 1977–78. Moreover, after initial rapid expansion in the early seventies, the area under HYV has substantially contracted, from 1.55 m. ha in 1973–74 to 1.20 m. ha in 1977–78 (or from 15.7% to 12% of the total) (SYBB, 1979, p. 167). Similarly the distribution of improved seed by the Bangladesh Agricultural Development Corporation

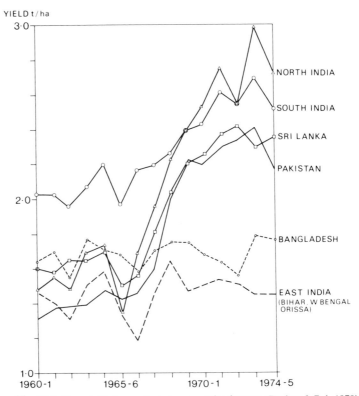

Fig. 17.4. Rice yields for south Asian countries (source: Barker & Pal, 1979).

declined from 8,900 metric tons in 1973–74 to 1,780 metric tons in 1977–78 (Saleh Uddin, 1980, p. 20) and its price increased sharply.

Taking a longer view, it is apparent that the major expansion of cropped area in Bangladesh occurred before HYV was introduced, and that while output has increased steadily over the past 25 years the new varieties have made no dramatic impact. Only with the *boro* crop have yields been such as to justify early optimism. Achievement with HYV lagged desperately behind targets during the First Five Year Plan (the area planted to HYV in 1977–78 was only one-third of the First Plan target). The Second Five Year Plan aims to increase HYV area by 2.5 and to treble HYV production, but in the light of recent experience this seems to be no more realistic than optimistic population control forecasts. Perhaps not surprisingly, the treatment of rice goals in the Second Plan is markedly less explicit than in previous planning documents. This dismal record has many causes (problems of storm and flood, small farm size, poor water control, civil unrest). At present prices, exacerbated by massive inflation in the mid-1970s, use of chemical fertiliser gives little economic advantage (Barker & Pal, 1979). Moreover, as Salah Uddin (1979) points out, 'most of the environmental and socio-economic constraints are beyond the capacity of an average farmer to overcome without assistance', and Government agencies themselves have failed to act as successful agents of change – 'the present institutional arrangements . . . [being] characterised by a multiplicity of agencies resulting in a confusion over functions and responsibilities, duplication of work and lack of coordination'.

Our purpose in this discussion is simply to indicate that early optimism about raising rice yields from 1.0 to 2.5–3.0 t/ha by introducing new varieties and thus producing at least a temporary respite in the Malthusian dilemma has proved illusory. Nor is it in the least practicable or useful (even faced with an extra 1.75 m. people to feed every year) that they could eat water lilies, water hyacinths and banana leaves in order simply to survive (Thorner, in Robinson & Griffin, 1974, p. 285).

International aid

The last immediate option, of postponing disaster by massive international aid, is to a large extent an alleviation rather than a solution of the problem. Total foreign aid commitment has increased through the last decade from less than US$ 0.5 billion to more than US$ 1.2 billion by 1977–78, and disbursements per annum from US$ 0.14 to US$ 0.8 billion. The sums are equivalent to 5% of GNP in the early 1970s and over 10% in the late 1970s (World Bank, 1980). Already nearly 20% of the population is fed by imported food. Faaland and Parkinson (1976) see continued international aid at the level of US$ 1.5 billion per annum as the only way to prevent national and social disintegration. But even if such aid were to be efficiently and productively utilised, it could not in the intermediate or short term change the problem starkly posed by the equation of population and food here outlined.

Environmental hazards

Cyclones

The coastline of Bangladesh is one of the most cyclone-prone in the world (Sadler & Gidley, 1973). Some 69 major storms have been recorded since 1793, and exceptional storms (such as that of 1584) are recorded even earlier. They occur mainly during October–December, with a small secondary maximum in May. Wind speeds rarely exceed 160 km/hr; the highest recorded is 225 km/hr during the catastrophic storm of 12 November 1970. Because of the shallow offshore topography of the delta-front platform and the funnel-shaped delta distributary channels, sea surges associated with cyclones are particularly well developed along the Bangladesh coast. In 1970 the maximum surge height reached 10 m, and resulted in widespread inundation and an estimated death toll of 280,000 (Frank & Husain, 1971).

Existing surge prediction studies unfortunately apply only to the open Bay of Bengal (Flierl & Robinson, 1972; Das, 1972; Das et al., 1974; Johns & Ali, 1980; Johns, 1981), and do not take into account the non-linear enhancement of the surge where it interacts with local shoreline topography. Fig. 17.5

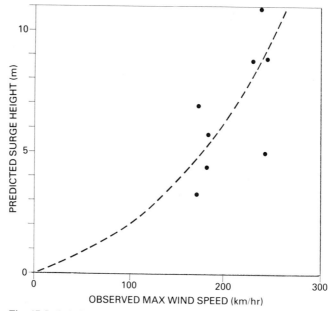

Fig. 17.5. Relationship between surge height and wind speed for the storms listed in Table 17.2. The equation for the curve is Y (surge height in m) = $0.0022 \, X^{1.5}$ (maximum wind velocity, km/hr).

shows the relationship between surge height and maximum wind speed for cyclones during 1960–70 listed in Table 17.2. Based on existing and admittedly inadequate records, the 25 yr storm will have a wind speed of 85 km/hr and will produce a surge of 3.5 m in deep and 5.25 m in shallow water. A storm of magnitude comparable to that of 1970 has a recurrence interval of 300 years (Figs. 17.6 and 17.7).

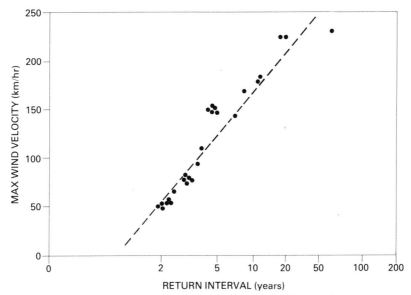

Fig. 17.6. Return interval of storms with different maximum wind speeds.

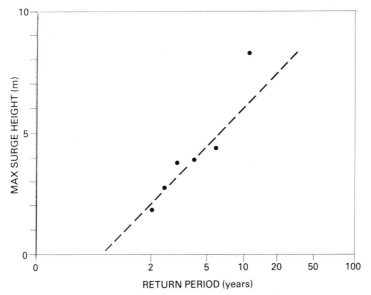

Fig. 17.7. Return inverval of storm surges with different heights.

Table 17.2. *Characteristics of recent cyclones, coastal Bangladesh*

Date	Maximum wind speed, km/hr	Height of storm surge, m
9 October 1960	160	3.0
31 October 1960	209	6.1
9 May 1961	145	2.4–3.0
30 May 1961	145	4.6
28–29 May 1963	200	5.2
11 May 1965	160	3.7
15 December 1965	210	3.7
1 October 1966	145	6.1
12 November 1970	220	10.1

Source: Mawla, 1976.

It needs to be emphasised that the consequences of such storms are not simply a function of their physical characteristics. The degree of death and destruction is to a very considerable degree related to the social and occupational characteristics of the population at risk, its perception of the hazards, and its willingness to take appropriate action (Islam, 1971a, 1971b, 1974; Islam & Kunreuther, 1973; Khan, 1974). Such disasters also have considerable long-term effects, especially on health and well-being (Chen, 1973).

Water availability and salinity

Paradoxically, in an area where river discharge is so high and where mean annual rainfall varies from over 3,000 mm at the coast to 1,500 mm inland, the pressures to increase agricultural production to feed the rising population are such that cultivation is now being forced into areas where water availability is a limiting factor. The extension of agriculture in the delta can take two forms. Areas previously regarded as too hazardous for settled cultivation, because of cyclone, storm surge and coast erosion, may be brought into use; or attempts may be made to increase the number of crops taken from the same land each year.

Traditional agriculture in the delta concentrates on the wet monsoon *aman* rice crop, using seasonal floods to provide water for the paddy fields. The dry season, from November to March, has not been used for cultivation except in the landward limits of the delta. The rainfall during this period averages less than 100 mm for the entire five months, while rice crops require at least 200 mm during the same period. The dry season or *boro* crop thus depends on irrigation. With new technology *boro* crops have increased markedly in the central delta region, but conditions in the tidal delta are quite different.

The main obstacle to such extension in the tidal delta is presented by salinity levels. Sea-water incursion in the estuaries means that both monsoon flooding and dry-season irrigation may be rendered unfit for agricultural use. Rice is moderately tolerant of saline conditions, growing in soils with electrical conductivities of 2,000 micromhos or less and tolerating water salinities or 1,300 micromhos. However soil salinities in excess of 4,000 micromhos and dry season water salinities of 10,000 micromhos are common in the tidal delta, so that rice cultivation is severely restricted unless measures are taken to reduce these salinities. The problem is rendered more acute by the variability of salinity over time and space. Penetration of saline waters in the estuaries varies with season and channel morphology, and until this can be accurately predicted salinity must be viewed as a hazard rather than simply as a problem.

Saline incursion in an estuary takes place by the incursion of a salt 'wedge' along the channel floor, giving a density stratification with fresh water overlying salt. In areas with a high tidal range and high velocities, however, mixing takes place at the salt-fresh interface, to give either a 'partially-mixed' or in extreme cases a 'fully-mixed' estuary (Dyer, 1973). The estuaries of the active tidal delta are partially mixed, so that a salinity gradient with depth is found and the saline intrusion extends inland for about 50 km. Salinity levels and their landward extension depend on the level of freshwater outflow: in the dry season the intrusion may reach as far as the confluence of the Meghna and the Shahbazpur, but during the monsoon it is forced seaward to the south of Bhola and Hatia islands. The application of theoretical models of saline intrusion to the Bangladesh delta is made difficult by the existence of numerous interconnections between the major channels. One such is the Ilsha River between the Shahbazpur and the Tetulia north of Bhola. The Shahbazpur has a larger and more efficient channel than the Tetulia, and this allows the flood tide to propagate inland more rapidly and with smaller decrease in amplitude. As a result the saline intrusion extends further inland in the Shahbazpur, the water levels in that channel may be up to 1 m higher than in the Tetulia, and when the flood tide along the Shahbazpur reaches the Ilsha it spills through into the Tetulia. Hence agriculture must utilise Tetulia rather than Shahbazpur water for irrigation, but must avoid the high salinity pulse which ebbs down the Tetulia after flowing into it through the Ilsha. Detailed considerations such as these, combined with the more obvious hazards of cyclone and storm surge, constrain the strategies available to the population in the delta for making an adequate living from the land.

Strategies

Agriculture

The basic strategy employed to meet the demand for increased agricultural output involved an extension of the agricultural area and a diversification of cropping methods to ensure at least two rice crops each year. Traditional monsoon-based agriculture relies on long-stemmed 'floating' varieties of rice which can tolerate depths of flooding up to 4 m. This *aman* crop is broadcast in the riverine parts of the delta, but in the tidal delta it is necessary to transplant seedlings from a prepared seedbed since soil salinities in the fields are too high in the early monsoon to allow direct seeding. Closer to the sea and major channels soil salinities may be too high for even the monsoon rains to reduce them below the critical salinity level for cultivation. Extension of the *aman* crop thus depends on reducing salinity in the coastal areas, and also on the replacement of long-stemmed varieties by HYV short-stemmed varieties, though the latter require careful water management during the monsoon to prevent overdeep flooding. The dry season *boro* crop demands more water than is available from rainfall during its growing season, and thus requires irrigation. If suitable irrigation water can be found then considerable increases in yield are possible, since the *boro* crop is particularly suited to high-yielding varieties. Thus increasing agricultural production in the delta requires both control of salinity and also control of fresh water for irrigation.

Coastal embankments

Desalination of soils in the coastal zone requires the exclusion of tidal floods which occur during the period of high monsoon discharges. During this period low tide levels are higher than the level of dry-season high tides: thus at Barisal during the monsoon low water is approximately 1 m above mean sea level. Land drainage is thus impeded, and this together with the high-tide salt water increment causes extensive flooding with salinity levels exceeding the critical levels for rice cultivation near major channels.

Exclusion of saline tidal flooding has been largely achieved in the delta by the system of coastal embankments. These are earth embankments, 4.8 m high in the most exposed coastal areas and along the banks of the Shahbazpur and Meghna, but reduced to 1–2 m high along tributary creeks. The total length of embankments is 3,650 km (2,267 miles), enclosing 86 polders with a total area of 810,000 ha. The cost of the embankment has been extremely high (estimated in 1976 at US$ 16,000/km) but the effect on soil salinities has been remarkable. Thus in the eastern part of Bhola in 1967 soil salinities were measured at over 4,000 micromhos, whereas in 1981, three years after the completion of embankments, the level had fallen to below 1,000 micromhos.

Erosion of channel banks leads to undermining and breaching of embankments, and in some more vulnerable areas a series of additional embankments has had to be constructed inland of the main embankment. Difficulties have also been experienced with the maintenance of sluices which permit fresh water outflow but prevent saline inflow. Particularly damaging was the psychological impact of the 1970 storm surge which overtopped the embankments, which were not designed to cope with surges of such magnitude. The cost of proper maintenance of over 3,500 km of embankments is more than most rural communities can support.

Irrigation

One of the most ambitious irrigation projects within the tidal delta is the Barisal–Patuakhali scheme, which provides for the irrigation of more than 280,000 ha or 40% of the total agricultural land. The scheme was implemented in areas identified as possessing optimum physical conditions in terms of soil, land elevation, and availability of low salinity water. The main aim of the scheme is to allow an extension of the *boro* crop from its previous 5,200 ha to a final 45,000 ha with a parallel shift to HYV rice. A secondary aim is to allow sufficient control over wet-season water levels so that long-stemmed traditional varieties of rice can be replaced by short-stemmed HYV strains in the *aman* crop. The *aman* crop area amounts to 35,000 ha within the area of the irrigation scheme. Pumps are used to extract low salinity water at high tide and store it in large creeks sluiced off from the main channel. The water in these reservoir creeks is then pumped onto paddy fields using low-lift secondary pumps.

Boro rice requires standing water of about 5 cm throughout the growing season. The field efficiency of the crop varies from 25% on loams to 45% on clays, the average for silty-clay soils being 40%. This requires a weekly water input of 8 cm in order to maintain required levels; the total water requirement for the growing season thus amounts to 152–177 mm. Provision of adequate irrigation facilities to meet this need requires careful planning. Secondary pumps are rated at 0.057 cumecs and are capable of commanding an area of 10–20 ha to give the required 8 cm/week, assuming that pumping is only carried on during daylight. Care must be taken to avoid overpumping (which can lead to bank erosion) and also underpumping (which can lead to creek-bed accretion or eutrophication).

Silviculture and reclamation

An important contribution to resource development in coastal Bangladesh would be made if the present seasonally submerged charlands could be stabilised and brought under permanent cultivation. The total area of chars estimated by the Bangladesh Landsat Programme is 486,000 ha. If only half of this could be brought under paddy it could yield 450,000 tons of rice, an increase in national production of 4.5%. A programme to reclaim the chars has been begun by the Forestry Department through the planting of mangroves, especially the pioneer species *Sonneratia apetala* (Hasan &

Howlader, 1970; Das, 1971, 1973; Atawor Rahman, 1977). Seeds from the Sunderbans are raised in seedbeds and then transplanted onto bare mud flats. In spite of high initial losses of seedlings growth is rapid, and once established the mangroves encourage rapid vertical accretion. While the plantations were first established to act as shelter belts against cyclones and surges and to stabilise the chars, this vertical accretion raises the possibility of the land surface reaching levels at which the mangroves could be felled for timber and the land used for rice.

Mangroves can be planted at the level of approximately mean low water neaps. At known rates of sedimentation in the lower delta it is reasonable to expect the land surface to be raised to approximately the level of mean high water springs in 10–25 years. Above this level the depth, duration and frequency of inundation decline rapidly, and accretion rates also diminish. Areas at the mean high water spring level are, however, still liable to flood during equinoctial spring tides, and they would need to be protected by embankments if agriculture is to be possible on them. Once an area is reclaimed and embanked it is likely that accretion will continue at peripheral lower levels, which can in turn then be reclaimed; the pattern of accretion will of course depend on the discharge and tidal velocities in the channels.

The planting programme began in 1966, initially on a small scale. By 1970 the total area planted was 1,600 ha. By 1978 this had risen to 25,500 ha, and it was planned to plant a further 4,000 ha in 1979. During the Second Five Year Plan 1980–85 it is proposed to increase the area planted each year from 4,000 to 12,200 ha, and if this is achieved it will give a total afforested area of 70,000 ha (15% of the total available charlands) by 1985. The cost of the programme during the Second Plan is put at Taka 9,700 lakh (US$ 64 m.). It is the largest mangrove planting programme ever undertaken (though it is said that in 1934 an area of 38,000 ha was planted in South Vietnam). Most existing mangrove planting programmes are on an experimental basis, and are scarcely applicable to Bangladesh conditions (Carlton, 1974; Pulver, 1976; Teas, 1977): thus in one programme in Florida *Rhizophora* seedlings have been planted by dropping them from a helicopter (Teas, 1979). Elsewhere, especially in Thailand, mangrove planting is carried out to re-establish mangrove forest in logged areas, rather than to reclaim new land.

Several problems arise in the successful prosecution of the Bangladesh programme. One is that the rate of landform development through accretion is more rapid than the growth of the mangroves themselves. Pioneer species such as *Sonneratia apetala* soon find themselves growing in conditions more appropriate to *Bruguiera*, *Xylocarpus* or *Excoecaria*. It will probably be necessary to replace the first plantings by species more appropriate to the newer and higher conditions. It is also quite possible that when reclamation of the mangrove areas for agriculture is attempted acid sulphate soils will develop. This is a common phenomenon in reclaimed *Avicennia* mangals, where free sulphuric acid in the soils inhibits the growth of crops (Tomlinson, 1967; Hesse, 1959, 1961; Bloomfield and Coulter, 1973; Jordan, 1964; Moormann & Pons, 1975). Such soils do not appear to be recorded in reclaimed *Sonneratia* swamp, but the risk is certainly present and proper soil management procedures will need to be applied to avoid it.

More serious is the risk of continued inundation. It has already been noted that extreme astronomical tides will flood the highest accreted areas to depths of up to 1.5 m, and that these will have to be protected by embankments. There is, however, no real possibility that such embankments could be constructed to exclude storm surges. The existing coastal embankments have a design elevation equal to maximum recorded tidal stage plus 1–1.5 m. It has been estimated that to contain a 7 m storm surge the embankments in the eastern delta would need to be 15–17 m high. If the land cannot be safeguarded from such surges, then measures must necessarily be taken to safeguard the people attracted to such new coastal lands, through efficient warning systems and adequate and secure cyclone shelters.

The incidental benefits of the mangrove plantation programme are likely to be considerable, in terms of yield of timber, firewood, other forest products and fish (cf. Ahmed & Karim Khan, 1959; Mohan Jana & Chatterjee, 1975). Table 17.3 shows the yield of mangrove products in the Bangladesh Sunderbans over a 20-year period. The fish yield alone approximates 5.04 kg per ha or 12.08 kg per km of channel. The average yield of prawns in Asian mangroves has also been estimated at 4 tons/sq km/year.

Land tenure

Land-holding systems in the delta are extremely complex and have long been a major impediment to the establishment of irrigation schemes and their associated new crop varieties. The share-cropping system has been particularly restrictive, with up to half a crop being given by a tenant to his landlord, a system which does not encourage investment in new methods.

Conclusion

This essay began with a stark portrayal of the problem posed by a inexorably increasing population and a largely static agricultural resource base in Bangladesh. We then considered in some detail the environmental problems faced in the coastal deltaic areas of the country, where nearly one quarter of the total population lives. Massive river discharges and repeated natural disasters combine to reduce the options available for agricultural improvement, and in consequence there has been progressive degradation of the environment, largely through deforestation, extending over many centuries.

Strategies of water control through empoldering have had considerable

Table 17.3. *Output of natural products from the Sundarbans mangroves, 1957–1977*

Year	Timber ('000 m^3)	Firewood ('000 m^3)	Thatch ('000 ton)	Honey (m ton)	Wax (m ton)	Fish (m ton)
1957	217.9	337.4	108.3	224.0	52.3	2,351.8
1958	317.0	366.6	119.5	261.3	63.5	2,426.5
1959	444.3	521.7	115.7	410.6	104.5	2,575.8
1960	291.5	516.6	119.4	261.3	63.5	2,874.4
1962	373.6	543.7	89.6	112.0	29.9	2,538.4
1963	421.7	499.9	85.9	186.7	52.3	2,650.4
1964	444.3	527.0	89.6	149.3	44.8	2,277.1
1965	489.6	552.0	108.3	149.3	48.5	1,978.5
1966	489.1	343.7	74.7	149.3	22.4	2,015.8
1967	532.0	372.9	74.7	149.3	3.7	2,090.5
1968	418.8	383.3	67.2	112.0	29.9	2,314.5
1969	467.0	243.7	63.5	186.7	52.3	2,314.5
1970	433.0	262.5	67.2	186.7	52.3	2,351.8
1971	350.9	191.6	56.0	37.3	37.3	1,791.8
1972	107.5	25.0	41.1	149.3	48.5	634.6
1973	118.7	104.2	70.9	149.3	48.5	1,343.9
1974	162.5	85.4	70.9	112.0	33.6	1,007.9
1975	87.5	83.3	67.2	186.7	52.3	597.3
1976	85.4	116.6	70.9	149.3	37.3	1,194.6
1977	89.6	145.8	67.2	224.0	59.7	3,733.0
Mean	327.3	423.6	81.4	177.3	46.8	2,053.2
	(m^3/ha)	(m^3/ha)	(kg/ha)	(kg/ha)	(kg/ha)	(kg/ha)
Mean per forest ha	0.804	1.04	199.9	0.44	0.115	5.04

Source: Bangladesh Country Report, UNESCO Mangrove Symposium, Dacca, 1978.

success, and emphasis is now being placed on the reclamation of low-lying charlands through afforestation by mangroves and ultimately conversion to agriculture. This is the largest such programme attempted anywhere in the world, and if the 70,000 ha planted by 1985 can be converted to paddy it will make a significant contribution to relieving population pressure and food shortages in the coastal areas.

Sadly, we must conclude that against the general background of a rapidly expanding population, these achievements can only offer a temporary respite. Small wonder that, in this beautiful but wretched land, the Minister for Planning ended his introduction to *The Two Year Plan 1978–80* with the words 'So help us God'.

Fragmentation of holdings is another major difficulty, especially in the case of irrigation schemes which ideally require land to be managed in 10 ha blocks. The majority of holdings in the delta are less than 2 ha and many are less than 0.2 ha. Many of the smallest holdings are also tenant-farmed, which increases resistance to innovation.

One benefit of the coastal embankment and coastal reclamation schemes has been to create areas of land suitable for agriculture which previously were useless. In these new areas the problems of tenure and fragmentation are less acute than in the traditional farming areas. Moreover the new areas have attracted farmers who show more enterprise and who are more willing to adopt innovative technologies. Consequently investment in these areas is capable of achieving a far greater increase in agricultural production and justifies the capital expenditure on the embankments and reclamation projects.

REFERENCES

Ahmad, N. & Karim Khan, F. (1959). The Sunderban forests of East Pakistan: a resource appraisal. *Oriental Geographer*, 3 (2),13–32

Al-Mamun Khan, A. 1974. Perception of the cyclone hazard and community response in the Chittagong coastal area. *Oriental Geographer*, 18, 1–25

Atawor Rahman, M. 1977.Irrigation and coastal afforestation. *Proc. 1st Bangladesh Nat. Conf. Forestry*, 148–50

Barker, R. & Pal, T.K. (1979). Barriers to increased rice production in eastern India. *Int. Rice Res. Inst. Res. Paper Ser.* 25, 1–23

Blasco, F. (1975). The mangroves of India. *Trav. Sect. Sci. Tech., Inst. Fr. Pondichery*, 14, 1–175

(1977). Outlines of ecology, botany and forestry of the mangals of the Indian subcontinent. *Wet coastal ecosystems*, ed. V.J. Chapman. Amsterdam, Elsevier, 241–60.

Blasco, F., Caratini, C. & Thanikaimoni, G. (1975). Main characteristics of Indian mangroves. *Proc. Int. Symp. Biol. Management Mangroves*, 1, 71–87

Bloomfield, C. & Coulter, J.K. (1973). Genesis and management of acid sulphate soils. *Advances in Agronomy*, 25, 265–326

Carlton, J.M. (1974). Land-building and stabilization by mangroves. *Envir. Conserv.*, 1, 285–94

Chen, L.C. (ed.) (1973). *Disaster in Bangladesh*. London, Oxford University Press, xxviii, 290 pp.

Das, P.K. (1971). Afforestation of coastal belt and offshore island. *Forestdale News*, 3 (4), 28–34

(1972). Prediction model for storm surges in the Bay of Bengal. *Nature, Lond.*, 239, 211–13

(1973). Artificial regeneration of mangroves in Bangladesh. *Bano Biggyan Patrika*, 5 (2), 70–82

Das, P.K., Sinha, M.C. & Balasubramanyam, V. (1974). Storm surges in the Bay of Bengal. *Quart. J. R. Met. Soc.*, 100, 437–9

Duza, B. (1974). Population policy in Bangladesh. In E.A.G. Robinson and K.

Griffin (eds.), *The economic development of Bangladesh within a socialist framework*. London, Macmillan, pp. 260–82

Dyer, K.R. (1973). *Estuaries: a physical introduction*. London, John Wiley

Faaland, J. & Parkinson, J.R. (1976). *Bangladesh: the test case of development*. London, Hurst, xi, 203 pp.

Flierl, G.R. & Robinson, A.R. (1972). Deadly surges in the Bay of Bengal: dynamics and storm-tide tables. *Nature, Lond.*, 239, 213–14

Fosberg, F.R. (1971). Mangroves v. tidal waves. *Biol. Conserv.*, 4, 38–9

Frank, N.L. & Husain, S.A. (1971). The deadliest tropical cyclone in history? *Bull. Am. Met. Soc.*, 52, 438–44

Ghulam Kibria, A.M.M. (1978). A short note on the hydrology of Bangladesh with special reference to the tidal and coastal areas. *XVI Conv. Idraulica e Costazzioni idrauliche (Torino 1978)*, paper B18, 1–12

Hart, M.G.R. (1959). Sulphur oxidation in tidal mangrove soils of Sierra Leone. *Pl. Soil*, 14, 215–36

Hasan, S.M. & Howlander, N.I. (1970). Coastal afforestation in Noakhali District. *Forestdale News*, 2 (3), 41–9

Hesse, P.R. (1961). Some differences between the soils of *Rhizophora* and *Avicennia* mangrove swamps in Sierra Leone. *Pl. Soil*, 14, 335–46

Holeman, J.N. (1968). The sediment yield of major rivers of the world. *Water Resources Research*, 4, 737–47

Islam, M.A. (1971a). Human adjustment to cyclone hazards: a case study of Char Jabbar. *Natural Hazard Research Working Paper* 18, 1–34

(1971b). Cyclone hazard and the strategy of human occupance in the coastal areas of Bangladesh. *Oriental Geographer*, 15 (1–2), 37–45

(1974). Tropical cyclones: coastal Bangladesh. In G.F. White (ed.), *Natural hazards, local, national, global*. New York, Oxford University Press, pp. 19–25

Islam, M.A. & Kunreuther, H. (1973). The challenge of long-term recovery from natural disasters: implications for Bangladesh. *Oriental Geographer*, 17 (2), 51–63

Johns, B. (1981). Numerical simulation of storm surges in the Bay of Bengal. In J. Lighthill and R.P. Pearce (eds.), *Monsoon dynamics*. Cambridge University Press, pp. 689–97

Johns, B. & Ali, M.A. (1980). The numerical modelling of storm surges in the Bay of Bengal. *Quart. J. R. Met. Soc.*, 106, 1–18

Jordan, H.D. (1964). The relation of vegetation and soil to development of mangrove swamps for rice growing in Sierra Leone. *J. Appl. Ecol.*, 1, 209–12

Mawla, M.S. (1976). Statement at the third session of Tropical Cyclone Panel held at Madras from 20th to 26th April 1976 (mimeo)

Meybeck, M. (1976). Total mineral dissolved transport by major world rivers. *Hydrol. Sci. Bull.*, 21, 265–84

Mohan Jana, M. & Chatterjee, S. (1975). Some aspects of fishing in Sunderbans: its problem and future development. *Geogrl. Rev. India*, 36, 76–82

Moormann, F.R. & Pons, L.J. (1975). Characteristics of mangrove soils in relation to their agricultural use and potential. *Proc. Int. Symp. Biol. Management Mangroves*, 2, 529–47

Morgan, J.P. & McIntire, W.G. (1959). Quaternary geology of the Bengal basin, East Pakistan and India. *Bull. Geol. Soc. Am.*, 70, 319–42

Pulver, R.R. (1976). Transplant techniques for sapling mangrove trees *Rhizophora mangle*, *Laguncularia racemosa*, and *Avicennia germinans*, in Florida. *Florida Mar. Res. Publs.*, 22, 1–14

Robinson, E.A.G. & Griffin, K. (eds.) (1974). *The economic development of Bangladesh within a socialist framework*. London, Macmillan, xxii, 330 pp.

Sadler, J.C. & Gidley, R.E. (1973). Tropical cyclones of the north Indian Ocean. Naval Postgraduate School Environmental Prediction Facility (Monterey), *Tech. Pap.* 2–73, i–viii, 1–60

Saleh Uddin, M. (1980). *High-yielding varieties of rice and fertilizer supply in Bangladesh*. Thammasat University, Bangkok, M.Econ. thesis, 147 pp.

Savage, T. (1972). Florida mangroves as shoreline stabilizers. *Prof. Pap. Florida Dept. Nat. Res.*, 19, 1–46

Stepanek, J.F. (1979). *Bangladesh – equitable growth?* New York, Pergamon, xvi, 191 pp.

Stoeckel, J. & Choudhury, M.A. (1973). *Fertility, infant mortality and family planning in Bangladesh*. London, Oxford University Press

SYBB (1979). *Statistical yearbook of Bangladesh 1979*. Dacca, Bangladesh Bureau of Statistics

Teas, H.J. (1977). Ecology and restoration of mangrove shorelines in Florida. *Env. Conserv.*, 4, 51–8

  (1979). Silviculture with saline water. In A. Honaender (ed.), *The biosaline concept*. New York, Plenum, pp. 117–61

Tomlinson, T.E. (1957). Relationship between mangrove vegetation, soil texture and reaction of surface soil after empoldering saline swamps in Sierra Leone. *Trop. Agric., Trin.*, 34, 41–50

Vaclav, E. & Skoupy, J. (1973). Sunderbans – the mangrove forests of Bangladesh. *Silvaecultura Tropica et Subtropica*, 3, 41–52

World Bank (1980). *Statistical Yearbook*. New York, World Bank

Wright, L.D., Coleman, J.M. & Erickson, M.W. (1974). Analysis of major river systems and their deltas: morphologic and process comparisons. *Cstl. Stud. Inst. Louisiana State Univ. Tech. Rept.* 156, 1–114

18 Beyond the Green Revolution: a selective essay

ROBERT CHAMBERS

'The Green Revolution' is used so loosely to cover so much technological, agrarian and social change, in so many countries and zones, with so many ecological and social differences, that generalisations are precarious and subject to exceptions. Even if we focus on India, and on small farmers and labourers, as this essay does, almost every statement still deserves a paragraph of qualification. Even if the Green Revolution is narrowed to changes linked with new agricultural technology, taking the rapid rise in wheat production in Northwest India in the later 1960s as a classic case, there is still much room for debate and disagreement.

Views of the Green Revolution

Discussion is not made easier by the passionate assertion to which the Green Revolution has given rise. Little attention has been paid to the psychology and sociology of ignorance, prejudice and the selective use of evidence in analysing the Green Revolution; yet one obvious feature, with which it is salutary to start, has been the polarisation between those who have taken views which are positive and optimistic, and those whose views have been negative and pessimistic.

Those who have been positive and optimistic have included biological scientists involved in creating the new technologies. In the early days of the Green Revolution some of them saw an enormous potential for increased production. They were fired with enthusiasm and faith, excited at the way in which the new dwarf wheats and rices shifted yield potentials to new high levels. Attention was concentrated on geographical areas which were well endowed with irrigation water and infrastructure, most notably the Punjab and Haryana in India where the new seed-fertiliser-water technology was exploited very quickly. The spectacular trebling of wheat production in the Indian Punjab during the decade of the 1960s encouraged optimism. As the Green Revolution spread to other crops, some saw the prospect of banishing hunger from the world.

Those who took negative and pessimistic views included social scientists concerned with political economy, and with who gained and who lost from the Green Revolution. Many studies showed that the new technologies were captured by and benefited the rural elites and those in the more favoured regions.[1] Social scientists' attention was drawn especially to the new high-yielding varieties of foodgrains, which they found being planted, fertilised, and protected by pesticides, most where there was irrigation, and most on the fields of the larger and more prosperous farmers. Biplab Dasgupta concluded from his study of the Green Revolution in India that some of the major social and economic consequences of the new technology included 'proletarianization of the peasantry and a consequent increase in the number and proportion of landless households, growing concentration of land and assets in fewer hands, and widening disparity between the rich and poor households . . . ' (1977, p. 372). Evidence was accumulated of tenants displaced by landlords as agriculture became more profitable, of landless labourers deprived of employment through mechanisation, and of women whose post-harvest employment was destroyed as hand-processing was replaced by mechanical methods. In their negative assessments, some social scientists saw the Green Revolution sharpening social tensions, and some spoke of it turning red.

The positive optimists

With hindsight, errors can be seen in both points of view. The positive optimists made two main mistakes. The first was to suppose that the dramatic rises in wheat output of the early Green Revolution in Northwestern India, and the high-yielding potential of early rice HYVs like IR8, could be realised on a much wider scale. This belief was sustained by misleading statistics for the adoption of HYVs elsewhere. Agricultural extension staff were given ambitious targets, and reported these achieved when the reality lagged far behind: in part of South India, the area under HYVs according to official reports was over three times the actual (Chinnappa, 1977, p. 98) and in part of Bangladesh five times (pers. comm., Hugh Brammer). Moreover, as is now recognised, wheat in Northwest India was a special case. Agricultural production there had been held back because the application of nitrogenous fertiliser led to lodging, a problem which the short-strawed HYVs overcame at a stroke. A generally uniform environment and fertile soil, good groundwater, good infrastructure, land consolidation, and commercially-minded farmers, provided the preconditions for rapid adoption of the HYV package once it was available. But elsewhere, and with other crops, conditions were not as favourable. For rice, in particular, there were many problems of environment, water control, pests, and diseases which inhibited rapid spread (Farmer, 1979; Barker & Pal, 1979).

The second major error of the positive optimists was to see poverty as a problem of food production. Technical scientists and macro-economists have frequently fallen into this error. Calculations are made of world or country food requirements, and of per capita food production. Targets for food production are set, with the assumption that if the food is there, people will be able to eat it. But as Amartya Sen (1981) and others have shown, malnutrition is much less the result of lack of food grown, and much more the result of poor people lacking the means to obtain it; in short, a problem of poverty more than a problem of food supply.

The negative pessimists

For their part, the negative pessimists also made two main errors. Both concern the selection and analysis of evidence. In the first place, attention was drawn to geographical areas and to incidents which generated and sustained conclusions about the Green Revolution turning red. As John Harriss (1977) pointed out for India, published studies were biased towards the better-irrigated districts selected for the Intensive Agricultural District Programme (IADP), especially around the Punjab Agricultural University in Ludhiana, leaving vast areas of central India largely unreported. In concluding his own carefully documented study of a village in North Arcot District in Tamil Nadu, he notes (1982, p. 300) that 'widely expressed expectations of "social change" as a consequence of the "green revolution", have generally been simplistic', and attributes this in part to these expectations being based on areas in which the agrarian structures have been dominated by landlords and where movements of agrarian protest may be more likely. In his village, and in contrast to some common views, he found the intensification of agriculture increasing the demand for labour, probably raising agricultural wages, and strengthening not weakening the relations of dependency between poor peasants and labourers, and rich farmers.

There are, of course, the usual dangers of over-generalising from one village or one incident. Others have fallen, perhaps willingly, into this trap with the notorious Kilvenmanai incident in Thanjavur District in Tamil Nadu in 1968 when 43 Harijans were killed. The incident involved larger landowners, local labourers, and immigrant labourers. Repeatedly quoted by non-Indian observers (e.g. Wharton, 1969; Frankel, 1971; Vallianatos, 1976), Kilvenmanai was interpreted as a sign that the Green Revolution was turning red; yet as Harriss notes, there had been a history of such conflicts in Thanjavur. But those who were looking for evidence of this sort seized on the incident, and reinforced each other by repetition. In the early 1980s both the reality and the interpretations have shifted: violence against Harijans and landless labourers appears more common now but both less noticed than it deserves and less interpreted to be a result of technological change.

Second, there was a tendency towards a rather narrow analysis of cause. Changes which occurred were sometimes attributed to the new technology and its monopoly by rural elites to the neglect of other causes, such as population pressures on resources, subdivision of land on inheritance, and contingencies which forced land sales. The counterfactual tended to be overlooked – what would have happened without the new technology. A further problem faced by negative assessments which found the poorer people worse off (e.g. Rajaraman, 1977) was population movements. Technological change could certainly displace labour through capital-intensive methods; but it could also draw in labour, as it did in a South Indian village, Kalpattu, where a good aquifer, numerous electric pumpsets, and cultivation round the year attracted immigration and was associated with higher wage rates than nearby (Chambers & Harriss, 1977). Similarly, it can be asked for the Indian Punjab whether the slight declines in consumption levels of the poorest three deciles identified by Rajaraman may not have been associated with inmigration from other, poorer areas (eastern Uttar Pradesh and Bihar) where people would have been much worse off if they had not moved. As much care is needed in negative as in positive assessments of technological change.

Finally, most observers, of whatever discipline, were misled into giving excessive prominence to the new varieties of foodgrain as against other conditions and changes. The summary of findings of the major study by UNRISD (1974) was entitled *The Social and Economic Implications of the Introduction of the new Varieties of Foodgrains*. Lester Brown wrote *Seeds of Change* (1970), Andrew Pearse *Seeds of Plenty, Seeds of Want* (1980), and P.R. Mooney *Seeds of the Earth* (1980). The Nobel Prize went to Norman Borlaug who was involved in the seed-breeding work with wheat and maize. Seed-breeders rode high, and the seeds were the most dramatic new input. Now it is true that seed-breeding, and also the conservation of genetic resources, are crucial activities; and it is also vital to look ahead, as M.S. Swaminathan (1981) has done, to see how breeding priorities should be modified for future conditions and needs. But in many past and future changes in agriculture, new varieties are only one element, and may sometimes not feature at all. Earlier, the rapid spread of the use of chemical fertilisers, especially before 1973, led some to speak of a fertiliser rather than a seed revolution. But above all, in the Indian subcontinent at least, it is water that has been the least recognised yet most important factor in rural agricultural change. The irrigated potential said to have been created in India has more than trebled since independence: in 1947 it was 19 million hectares, and in 1981 some 60 million. Irrigation has raised yields, reduced risks, provided preconditions for using high-yielding packages, generated employment, and made wages higher than they would have been. But water is an odd subject which somehow slips between the disciplines. Seeds can be created, displayed, and held in the hand; water is dispersed and elusive and slides out of sight. Only in the 1980s is its true significance in rural development in South Asia beginning to be recognised.

Pluralist realism

The lesson to be drawn is that caution is needed in assessments of the social effects of technological change. Unless interpretations are empirically based, tested for selective perception, and open to qualification, they are liable to serious error. More broadly, the history of ideas about rural poverty and rural development in the 1960s and 1970s is sobering. So many insights have become available so late; so many professions and professionals have been so wrong so much of the time, and yet so sure they were right. There have been many false turnings and blind alleys: the earlier orthodoxy that elevated industrialisation and neglected agriculture in development strategies; the belief that two-thirds of the rural people in the third world were malnourished, whereas a better understanding of nutrition and more careful analysis suggest much lower figures (Sukhatme, 1977; Edmundson, 1980; Seckler, 1980; Poleman, 1981); the belief that malnutrition was primarily a protein problem, not, as now generally held, largely a problem of calorie deficiency; the belief that village-level post-harvest losses were very high, of the order of 10 to 40% (with 30% often loosely stated), not as now established by meticulous research, almost always less than 10% (e.g. 6.9% for post-harvest rice operations in Bangladesh (Greeley, 1982)); the belief that failure to adopt new agricultural practices was the result of cultural constraints and ignorance, not, as now recognised, much more a function of rational risk-aversion and defects in the practices recommended; and the belief that modern scientific knowledge was inherently superior to what rural people know, whereas the richness and validity of indigenous technical knowledge is now much better recognised (IDS, 1979; Brokensha et al., 1980). The list could be lengthened with other insights such as urban bias (Lipton, 1977) and seasonal dimensions to rural poverty, but the point is made. Professionals have often been wrong.

The most obvious implication of these changes in development beliefs is that whatever is believed now may in its turn be proved wrong. A much humbler attitude is called for from the development professions. Perhaps the best that one can do at any one time is to try to summarise current clusterings of ideas, recognising that they will be superseded.

One such clustering in the early 1980s could be described as pluralist realism in approaches to rural poverty. This entails taking insights freely from different disciplines and ideologies. One normative version of a pluralist contemporary view might run as follows. Development should be about the poorer people, and their livelihoods, basic needs, and quality of life. Development policy which focusses on this must emphasise command over resources and the ability to make effective demands. Those who are assetless must be enabled to obtain more employment and more assets both for their own production and as buffers against contingencies. But most redistributive

Development planning and agrarian change

reform of existing resources, notably land, has failed. Moreover, rural elites tend to capture programmes intended for those who are poorer. Professionals concerned with rural development should therefore concentrate more of their attention on resources which local elites are less likely or able to capture, and to which the poorer people have a realistic chance of establishing lasting rights.

This requires a new sort of analysis and search for which three guiding principles can be suggested. The first is to seek changes in which the poor can gain while those who are less poor do not lose and may even gain overall. For the landless an example is the introduction of year-round irrigation which gives them more work and which may generate labour shortages and raise daily wages. Others include physical and biological research and development which is based on and fits the needs and resources of the poor. The second is to concentrate attention on common property resources of land, water, grassland, forests, fisheries and so on, and explore ways in which their productivity can be increased and the poor can control and benefit from that increase. The third is to examine the scope and concerns of existing disciplines, professions and departments, and ask what potentials in rural development they systematically overlook. Programmes based on their traditional scope and concerns have already been implemented, and have already all too often been captured by rural elites. But in the gaps which they have left, there may be major potentials yet to be realised, and from which the poor might disproportionately benefit. Where all three of these guiding principles apply, the opportunities for this approach may be greatest.

Resources for the rural poor

Analysis on these lines can indicate many potentials, some of them not yet well recognised, to help small farmers and landless labourers to gain command over more resources. Five illustrations can suffice:

(i) Water reform for canal irrigation

On canal irrigation systems in India, as also elsewhere in South and Southeast Asia and in North Africa (Egypt and Sudan), there is a disciplinary, professional and departmental gap between the major irrigation works which are the concern of civil engineers and Departments of Irrigation, and crops on farmers fields which are the concern of agriculturalists and soil scientists and of Departments of Agriculture and of Soil Conservation. Analysis and procedures for scheduling and distributing water on main irrigation systems, down to the outlets where the water passes into field channels controlled by farmers, receive little professional attention (Wade & Chambers, 1980). They are almost totally ignored in the training of those who are to control water distribution. A major textbook on irrigation engineering devotes less than two pages out of 563 to alternatives in water scheduling, and a manual of the American Society of Civil Engineers on the operation and maintenance of irrigation and drainage systems has only some three pages on the same subject (Singh, 1979; ASCE, 1980). On many canal irrigation systems, little control is exercised over water distribution, issues at the top-ends are permissive, and tail-enders are deprived. A crop-cutting study on the Mahanadi Reservoir Project in India, which irrigates 180 000 ha, found a gradient in paddy rice yields from 1541 kg/ha at the top to only 218 kg/ha at the tail (Lenton, 1982, citing information from Water and Power Consultancy Services (India) Ltd). An examination of the tail-end deprivation on canal irrigation in Sri Lanka has found a concentration of wealth among top-enders, who harvest bigger and more reliable crops, and who can invest in tractors, businesses and education for their children; while tail-enders are poorer, with lower and less reliable yields, lower returns to labour, less access to services, and less political influence (Moore et al., forthcoming).

The need and opportunity here are to develop and use methods for the diagnostic analysis of live irrigation systems, for monitoring their performance, and for more equitable and productive scheduling of water issues. Action research is one promising approach (Early, 1980; Lenton, 1980; Bottrall, 1981b). The work of IRRI in the Philippines has shown that circumstances can exist in which main system water redistribution can be reorganised so that all farmers gain: in their pioneering work on the Penaranda River Irrigation System, Wickham and Valera (1979, p. 74) reported production increases following improved distribution of 8% at the top, 32–62% in the middle, and 137% at the tail. Flooding, waterlogging and salinity in the headreaches of canal irrigation systems are sufficiently common to suggest that 'non-zero-sum' redistribution, in which headreach farmers gain in the long run even if not in the immediate short run, may be quite a common possibility. The main beneficiaries will often be relatively deprived people – tail-enders who have suffered from an inadequate, unpredictable and untimely water supply, and who consequently have had little incentive to adopt higher-yielding practices. moreover, the production increases from water reform should be very substantial. Following his extensive study of irrigation in South, Southeast and East Asia, Anthony Bottrall concluded (1981a, p. 24) that there was 'an immense opportunity for improvements in the performance of irrigation projects through management reform', and that in the rice-growing areas of South and Southeast Asia on a very conservative assumption of 20% increases in production, this would mean production increase of 30 million tons of paddy or 20 million tons of rice. And many of those producing the rice would be farmers previously deprived of a good irrigation water supply. Unlike much of the Green Revolution, this would achieve production *and* equity goals at the same time.

(ii) Land reform when canal irrigation starts

At the time when new canal irrigation is introduced into an area, all departments are heavily engaged. Civil engineers are deeply involved in construction; land acquisition for canals and other works is a major preoccupation; and agriculturalists and agricultural extension staff are concerned with changes in cropping patterns. For those who have land which receives water, this is usually a time of dramatic increase in the value of land. The passing opportunity which this presents for the redistribution of land is often overlooked. There is a period as irrigation arrives when land could be redistributed without anyone losing from the land-reform-plus-irrigation package. The scale of this opportunity is enormous but it only comes once and must be seized when it arrives. Sites for canal irrigation development will run out. India, Mexico and Sri Lanka, for example, all propose to double their irrigated area by the end of the century. For canal irrigation in India, this means moving from the current potential said to have been created of perhaps 28–29 million hectares to close to the ultimate potential of 58.5 million hectares (Seckler, 1981, quoting IARI, 1980). Even with the shortfalls which can be expected, this will present a passing opportunity for a land-cum-irrigation reform to settle millions of landless families.

(iii) Access to common property groundwater

In South Asia, groundwater is the greatest remaining common resource which is subject to individual appropriation. Bangladesh has perhaps the finest underground aquifer in the world, but irrigates only some 18% of its potential for a second (post-monsoon or *boro*) crop. India has achieved a phenomenal explosion in lift irrigation, with electric and diesel pumpsets rising from 430 000 in 1960–61 to about 7.2 million in 1980–81 (Charlu & Dutt, 1982, p. 93). Estimates of unexploited groundwater potential in India range from a high of 70 per cent of annual renewable recharge not yet utilised in 1980 (Sangal, 1980) to a low of 39 per cent remaining in 1982 (Government sources which estimated 24.5 million hectares of land already covered out of a potential of 40 million). In either case the remaining potential is enormous.

The question usually addressed is how fast this process can take place. Perhaps more important in the long run is the other question, of who will benefit from the process (IDS, 1980). About 200 million rural people, part of the greatest concentration of rural misery in the world, live in Uttar Pradesh, Bihar and West Bengal. In Uttar Pradesh in 1976–77, 86% of all holdings, comprising almost half of the agricultural land, were reported to be less than 2 hectares in size, with a long-term trend towards even smaller holdings (Agricultural Census, 1976–77, cited in Kalra, 1981). The standard irrigation pumps are 5 horsepower, and sometimes 3 horsepower. Between these relatively large pumps on the one hand, and lift by human or animal power on the other, there lies a power gap. The issue here is whether tens of millions of very small farmers can be provided with a scale and type of lift technology which will fit their land and other resources, or whether alternatively there are feasible ways in which they can organise and combine to obtain and share larger-scale pumps.

A lift technology appropriate for very small farmers whose land lies above good groundwater has received little attention. Any such technology would have to be cheap, maintainable, and based on a renewable or easily accessible energy source. There have been numerous experiments with solar power (Halcrow, 1981), wind power, biogas, steam engines, and producer gas. Producer gas, generated by the partial combustion of carbonaceous material has the advantage of being a renewable energy source which can be obtained from agricultural wastes on the farm, and so under the farmers' direct control, unlike diesel or electricity (Pathak et al., 1981). But again and again, those developing new energy sources and pump systems think conventionally at too large a scale for the majority of farmers. An exception has been Stephen Allison who has designed photovoltaic solar systems precisely for small farmers. While the price of photovoltaic solar systems for lift irrigation are still high, reported technological breakthroughs suggest that it may be only a matter of years before there are sharp reductions in cost and solar pumping begins to spread. Producer gas or solar or both may well be major power sources of the future for lift irrigation. The question is whether very small farmers will be able to benefit. The answer to that question depends on many factors, including scale, cost and marketing. It is at least possible that power and pumping units could be so designed that they filled the power gap and met the needs of millions of small farmers in India and Bangladesh who at present cannot irrigate.

(iv) Rights to common property land and forest

Overwhelmingly, attention in India and elsewhere is directed towards agricultural lands which are private property. Statistical services, government departments, research institutes, and social scientists concentrate on the farm sector and agricultural production. In India, the impression is sometimes given that agricultural production is the only rural production that matters. Yet India has some 100 million hectares of forest and common property land (i.e. reserve forests, protected forests, panchayat land, village land, and so on – see Farmer, 1974), while the 143 million hectares of agricultural land receive almost all the attention.[2]

The potential of non-agricultural land is almost universally underestimated. Six reasons go far in explaining this. First, many of them are inaccessible and rarely visited or seen; communications are concentrated in the areas of agricultural production. Second, being subject to the tragedy of the commons, they appear more barren than they are. One estimate is that 70% of such lands in India are already degraded (pers. comm., Deep Joshi). Third, forestry has long gestation periods and so does not attract those who look for quick returns. Fourth, forest dwellers and users of common lands tend to be low status people like tribals in central India, or some nomadic pastoralists. Fifth, corrupt officials, politicians and contractors have enormous financial interests in illicit exploitation of forests and in drawing as little attention as possible to this. Finally, the management problems of communal resources are intractable and offer no easy solutions.

To take a positive view, the opportunity presented by India's non-agricultural lands is enormous. The potential value of their produce has risen sharply with growing shortages of firewood and with rising prices for timber, and can be expected to rise yet further. Their potential has also risen with the introduction of new species and new methods, of which *Leucaena* (NAS, 1977) is the most spectacular. In the early 1980s, millions of poor people who derive their livelihoods from the forest are in danger of losing out to contractors and to a custodial Forest Department. But there are also grounds for hope. Social forestry has become a widespread movement. Although it usually means growing trees on private land, once again benefitting the larger farmers, or on roadsides, canal banks and other public places without determining who shall benefit, there are examples where the intention is that the poorer should gain. In Chitrakoot (on the Uttar Pradesh–Madhya Pradesh border), landless tribal families have been allocated common property land on which they grow *Leucaena*, with the aim of their being able to support cattle subsequently. The difficulties must not, however, be underestimated. Profound hostility exists between many poor forest-users and the Forest Department. A major re-orientation of both is a precondition for any large-scale movement to enable the poor forest-users to be proprietors and partners in forest development.

(v) Priorities in agricultural research

The obvious big gains from agricultural research have been in production. The best known were the breakthroughs from changing the plant architecture of major cereals and raising their yield responses to nitrogen. But later work on pest and disease resistance and robustness has been also very important, as the successes of IR20 in Indonesia and IR36 in the Philippines have shown. For the future there may be breakthroughs through genetic engineering, tissue culture, and other techniques, perhaps leading to a nitrogen-fixing wheat or maize. Other gains may come from shifts of priority to pay more attention to crop residues (straw, bran, the roots of the plant), rooting systems, ease of processing and cooking, yield stability, and biological nitrogen-fixation, to name but some. But increased productivity is the easier problem. Increases in consumption, by the poor, must come from enhancing their command over food supplies, whether through self-provisioning or through exchange. The more difficult problem is to orient agricultural research to benefit the smaller farmers and the landless, by improving their incomes, food supplies and security through increased production and employment.

This can be done in a multiplicity of ways which require only a little imagination to see. Unfortunately this is sometimes lacking in negative social scientists and positive biological scientists alike. Examples include: effort directed towards the crops and animals of the poor rather than those of the better-off; reducing risks for small farmers, especially those in marginal environments; improving the farming systems of small farmers to produce more, and of larger farmers not only to produce more but also to require more labour over more of the year; breeding stable seeds which reproduce faithfully rather than hybrids which must be purchased again each year; biological nitrogen-fixation to reduce dependence on the market for chemical nitrogen; selecting for ease of domestic processing and cooking, reducing the work burden on women; seed-breeding of crops like sorghum for calories for the poor rather than protein to fatten the animals of the rich. The list could be lengthened. Many, many shifts of research towards the interests of the poorer rural people are possible.

Such shifts have already been made. A lead has come from the Consultative Group for International Agricultural Research which funds and oversees IRRI and the other international research centres. It has not done all that it might have done, but it has gone further than most national agricultural research systems. For over a decade it has been moving towards greater attention to marginal environments and small and poor farmers. ICRISAT (the International Crops Research Institute for the Semi-Arid Tropics) was established in 1972 to concentrate on neglected subsistence crops – sorghum, pearl millet, chickpea, and pigeon-pea. Work on cassava (manioc, tapioca), especially that of the IITA (International Institute of Tropical Agriculture) in Nigeria and of CIAT (Centro Internacional de Agricultura Tropica) in Colombia has led to sharp increases in yield and improvements in disease resistance; and cassava is the staple and fall-back food of last resort of large numbers of people in Africa, Asia and Latin America. IRRI's research priorities have been moved to give much more attention to rice which is grown under rainfed, rather than controlled irrigated, conditions. Farming systems analysis in the international centres and elsewhere, involving agricultural economists and sociologists as well as agricultural scientists, has made progress towards better understanding of small farming systems.[3] In the unirrigated semi-arid tropics ICRISAT has been unable to achieve dramatic crop-specific breakthroughs like CIMMYT's with wheat and IRRI's with rice, but it has used farming systems analysis and a farming systems approach to identify feasible synergistic combinations of improved varieties, soil and water management, and fertiliser applications with mixed cropping (see, for example, Ryan et al., 1982).

These changes of method and priority have been slow to spread in national agricultural research systems. In India, a farming systems approach is little practised outside ICRISAT. Agricultural research remains largely crop-oriented, and geared towards the resources and interests of larger and more commercial farmers. The needs and crops of the poor remain relatively neglected. Biases are stacked against them: researchers are drawn to work on commercial crops, on commercial processing, on high-input technology, on single rather than mixed cropping or farming systems, on what directly concerns men (land preparation, economic returns to cash crops) rather than women (subsistence crops, weeding, processing, storing quality, and cooking). Disciplinary specialisation, preferences for tidy research on research stations and in laboratories, departmentalism, hierarchy, and a failure to recognise small farmers as fellow professionals – all these militate against a good understanding of small farmers' needs and opportunities.

One under-researched gap is the linkages between crops, animals, fodder and trees. These fall between disciplines and between departments. Foresters are concerned mainly with trees in forests, not on farmers' fields. Agriculturalists are concerned with field crops, not tree crops. Animal specialists are concerned with animal health more than nutrition. In consequence, the potential of tree fodders such as *Leucaena* (NAS, 1977) was long to be recognised. In India, it is perhaps not surprising that it was a non-government organisation free of departmental rigidities, the Bharatiya Agro-Industries Foundation near Pune, that carried out much of the early practical research on *Leucaena*. Another under-researched gap is the potential for tree crops to act as biological pumps in areas which are waterlogged from irrigation, turning a problem (too much water) into an opportunity (to fix sunlight, gain biomass, and perhaps use it for producer gas to pump more water mechanically for irrigation).

Finally, so-called 'high' agricultural technology presents opportunities. These may be overlooked because of the fashion for appropriate technology. But however sensible appropriate technology may be, quite new approaches, if carefully designed and introduced, may also fit the needs of the poor. Nutrient film technique is one case. It has been developed in the industrialised world and it depends on a reliable year-round water supply and on the purchase of nutrients, but it has the advantage of requiring very little land. Moreover, in tropical conditions of high insolation it can produce very high yields of biomass. In Chitrakoot in India, annual fodder yields of 700 tonnes/ha (280 tons per acre) have been reported with Napier grass. Landless families have been 'settled' on 0.06 ha (one seventh of an acre) each. It is envisaged that one acre (0.4 ha) will support 20 head of cattle, provided some concentrates are added to their diet (pers. comm. R. Madhavan). Many questions have to be asked about this approach. But it is a healthy challenge to conventional thinking, opening up new possibilities for agricultural livelihoods for the landless, in which both fertile land and rainfall are of minor significance.

A professional revolution

For all the positive aspects of these opportunities, there are no easy solutions to rural poverty. In some respects, both physically and socially, it is becoming more intractable. Physically, the degradation of natural resources continues to diminish the productive base, especially of soil (see e.g. Kanwar, 1982), while populations continue to increase, with India's expected to rise from 700 million in 1982 to one billion by the year 2000. Socially, family acquisitiveness appears to have hardened. One opinion for India is that

> The socio-political situation is perhaps in some ways far less favourable to economic growth as a means of eradication of mass poverty than it was during the early years of independence . . . The newly formed, tenaciously covetous and aggressive rural middle class presents more formidable and organised resistance to the planning process than did the landed aristocracy whom it has replaced. (Joshi, 1982)

It becomes more important than ever to seek strategies which are realistic and feasible in spite of physical and social constraints.

One way forward is clearer than it was a decade ago. The modes of analysis and skills of social scientists and of physical and biological scientists are complementary. In choosing what to do, either is very limited without the other. Social scientists alone drive themselves into negative pessimism; and one suspects that those who are most negative and pessimistic have hardly ever met a physical or biological scientist who is involved in trying to change things. And physical and biological scientists on their own neglect who will gain and who will lose from their work. Some even give the impression that they have never asked themselves that question, let alone having exercised imagination to try to change the social effects of what they do. But when physical and biological scientists work together with social scientists, the outcome can be a sort of practical political economy of technological change: and analysis of power and interests, and of who stands to gain and who to lose, which can both inform and change styles and priorities in technical research, influence the way in which programmes are designed and implemented, and improve the chances that the poorer people will benefit. Destructive negativism in the social sciences, and naive optimism in the technical sciences, are luxuries which the poor rural people cannot afford.

For the 1980s and 1990s, a major focus is, therefore, professional reorientation for both social and technical scientists, and the evolution of better ways in which they can work together. One approach is for them to adopt additional, common methods of analysis. By being additional, these may not conflict unduly with their professional norms; by being common, they provide a framework for mutual learning. One example is seasonal analysis, in which the concerns of each discipline as they affect poorer people are traced and analysed through time, and inter-disciplinary linkages (between food intake, energy output, health, nutritional status, child care, migration, social relations, cash and food reserves, food prices, indebtedness, etc.) are identified, and actions designed to make the worst times of the year less bad for those who are more vulnerable (Chambers, Longhurst & Pacey, 1981). Another is to learn from rural people. Since they do not distinguish disciplinary domains, their systems of knowledge and their categories provide frames within which professionals can relate in new ways. Their knowledge of many matters which touch them closely is, moreover, often far superior to that of outsiders. Yet another is to invest the technology, crops and animals of the poor with higher professional status. This entails continuing to shift the balance from the exotic to the indigenous, from the marketed cash crop to the subsistence crop, from large animals to small, from what concerns men to what concerns women. The shifts required are not absolute, but matters of degree, and they are already occurring. For many professionals they present an opportunity. It is precisely past neglect and present ignorance of the things which are important to the poor that presents room for improvement, and that permits 'discovery' by scientists and the prestige that goes with it. If more of them recognise this, the next generation of biological technology should better fit the resources of small farmers and the needs of the landless and make things better for them than they would otherwise have been.

Social scientists will be quick to point out, correctly, that many of the broader social and political changes which are needed can only occur with more effective demand by the poor themselves. The trap here is that while poor, they cannot demand; and while they cannot demand, they remain poor. Analysed at a general level, this becomes a logic of despair. But in practice there are many points of entry. Not only in India, poor rural people are organising and being helped to organise more and more. The personal level, too, is a major starting point. Through personal changes in the values and action of professionals, many shifts are possible – in research priorities, in resource allocations, in criteria for professional advancement, in policies of journal editors, in university and training curricula; and many of these, as they affect the rural poor in the South, have changed in the past two decades, not least in the citadels of professionalism in the North.

To speak of revolutions suggests radical and often improbable change; and outside a few specially favoured geographical areas, the Green Revolution deserved the question mark which B.H. Farmer (1977) gave it. Many of the changes which can realistically benefit the rural poor are not revolutionary in the normal sense, but require small and painstaking steps taken resolutely in a consistent direction. The revolution needed for this is professional: a turning round to face the other way, to put first the resources, technology, crops and animals of the poor and give them more priority. As more and more professionals make this reversal, so more and more of their work will be directed to enable the poor better to help themselves. Nor should this reversal be dismissed lightly as an unrealistic hope. It has already been made by some and it can be made by many more. Enough professionals have already turned around to show that this may be less a naive hope than a new realism. A direct attack on rural poverty through a widespread revolution, green or red, is improbable, and would as in the past have mixed effects. A better life for disadvantaged rural people may be more feasibly sought through a different sort of change: through quiet personal revolutions in the perceptions, values and choices of processionals concerned with research, technology and action for rural development.

NOTES

1. See, for example, Frankel (1971), Byres (1972), UNRISD (1974), Palmer (1976), Dasgupta (1977), Hameed et al. (1977), Pearse (1980).
2. These figures are taken from Vohra (1980), but the statistics are unreliable. Swaminathan (1980, p. 3) points out that the forest area of India is 66 million hectares in agricultural statistics, compared with about 75 million hectares in forestry statistics. Officially there are about 16 million hectares of 'culturable waste' in India, but after an extensive review Benny Farmer (1974, p. 31) concluded that 'a large proportion of "culturable waste" is very poor land indeed, naturally infertile and often further impoverished by over-grazing and soil erosion'. Farmer considered that to make any precise estimate of the utilisable proportion of all uncultivated lands was then (1974, p. 34) impossible, in the absence of suitable land resource surveys (cf. Govt. of India, 1968).
3. See, for example, the publications of the Farming Systems Research Group, Michigan State University, and Gilbert, Norman and Winch (1980).

REFERENCES

ASCE (1981). *Operation and Maintenance of Irrigation and Drainage Systems*, ASCE Manuals and Reports on Engineering Practice No. 57, American Society of Civil Engineers, New York

Barker, R. & Pal, T.K. (1979). Barriers to increased rice production in Eastern India. *IRRI Research Paper Series* No. 25, International Rice Research Institute, Manila

Bottrall, A. (1981a). *Comparative Study of the Management and Organization of Irrigation Projects*, World Bank Staff Working Paper No. 458, World Bank, Washington DC

(1981b). Improving canal management: the role of evaluation and action research. *Water Supply and Management*, 5, 67–79

Brokensha, D.W., Warren, D.M. & Werner, O. (1980). *Indigenous Knowledge Systems and Development*, University Press of America, Lanham, Maryland

Byres, T.J. (1972). The dialectic of India's Green Revolution. *South Asian Review*, 5, 99–116

Brown, Lester R. (1970). *Seeds of Change – The Green Revolution and Development in the 1970s*. Praeger, New York

Chambers, R. & Harriss, J. (1977). Comparing twelve South Indian villages: in search of practical theory. In B.H. Farmer (ed.), *Green Revolution?* Macmillan, London, pp. 301–22

Chambers, R., Longhurst, R. & Pacey, A. (1981). *Seasonal Dimensions to Rural Poverty*. Frances Pinter, London

Charlu, T.G.K. & Dutt, D.K. (1982). *Ground Water Development in India*, Rural Electrification Corporation, New Delhi

Chinnappa, B.N. (1977). Adoption of the new technology in North Arcot District. In B.H. Farmer (ed.), *Green Revolution?* Macmillan, London, pp. 92–123

Dasgupta, Biplab (1977). *Agrarian Change and the New Technology in India*. United Nations Research Institute for Social Development, Geneva

Early, A.C. (1980). An approach to solving irrigation system management problems. In IRRI, *Report of a Planning Workshop on Irrigation Water Management*, International Rice Research Institute, Manila, pp. 83–113

Edmundson, W. (1980). Adaptation to undernutrition: how much food does Man need? *Social Science and Medicine*, 14D, 119–26

Farmer, B.H. (1974). *Agricultural Colonization in India since Independence*. Oxford University Press, London, for Royal Institute of International Affairs
  (ed.) (1977). *Green Revolution? Technology and Change in Rice-growing Areas of Tamil Nadu and Sri Lanka*. Macmillan, London
  (1979). The 'Green Revolution' in South Asian ricefields: environment and production. *Journal of Development Studies*, 15, 304–19

Frankel, F. (1971). *India's Green Revolution: Economic Gains and Political Costs*. Princeton University Press

Gilbert, E.H., Norman, D.W. & Winch, F.E. (1980). *Farming Systems Research: a critical appraisal*, MSU Rural Development Paper No. 6, Department of Agricultural Economics, Michigan State University, East Lansing

Govt. of India (1968). *Report of the Waste Land Survey (Technical) Committee*. Govt. Press, Shillong

Greeley, M. (1982). Pinpointing post-harvest losses. *Ceres*, 15 (1), no. 85, 30–7

Halcrow (1981). *Small-Scale Solar-Powered Irrigation Pumping Systems Technical and Economic Review*. Sir William Halcrow & Partners, with Intermediate Technology Development Group, London

Hameed, N.D.S. et al. (1977). *Rice Revolution in Sri Lanka*. United Nations Research Institute for Social Development, Geneva

Harriss, J. (1977). Bias in perception of agrarian change in India. In B.H. Farmer (ed.), *Green Revolution?* Macmillan, London, pp. 30–6
  (1982). *Capitalism and Peasant Farming: agrarian structure and ideology in*

Northern Tamil Nadu. Oxford University Press, Bombay, Delhi, Calcutta, Madras

IARI (1980). *Irrigation Development in India – Tasks for the Future.* Indian Agricultural Research Institute, Pusa, Delhi

IDS (1979). *Rural Development: Whose Knowledge Counts? IDS Bulletin,* 10 (2). Institute of Development Studies, University of Sussex

(1980). Who gets a last rural resource? The potential and challenge of lift irrigation for the rural poor. *IDS Discussion Paper* No. 156, by IDS Study Seminar 88, Institute of Development Studies, University of Sussex

Joshi, P.C. (1982). Institutional dimensions in agricultural planning. *Kurukshetra,* 30 (9), 16 March

Kalra, B.R. (1981). Size and distribution of operational holdings. *Kurukshetra,* 29 (23), 1–15 September

Kanwar, J.S. (1982). *Managing Soil Resources to Meet the Challenges to Mankind.* Presidential Address, 12th International Congress of Soil Science, New Delhi, 8–16 February

Lenton, R. (1980). Field experimentation and generalization in irrigation development and management. Paper presented at 17th Annual Convention of Indian Society of Agricultural Engineers, Indian Agricultural Research Institute, New Delhi

(1982). Management tools for improving irrigation performance. Ford Foundation, New Delhi

Lipton, M. (1977). *Why Poor People Stay Poor: Urban Bias in World Development.* Temple Smith, London

Mooney, P.R. (1980). *Seeds of the Earth: A Private or Public Resource?* Inter Pares, Ottawa, for Canadian Council for International Co-operation and International Coalition for Development Action, London

Moore, M.P., Abeyratne, F., Amerakoon, R. & Farrington, J. (forthcoming). Space and the generation of socio-economic inequality on Sri Lanka's irrigation schemes. *Marga* (Marga Institute, Colombo)

NAS (1977). *Leucaena: Promising Forage and Tree Crop for the Tropics.* National Academy of Sciences, Washington, DC

Palmer, I. (1976). *The New Rice in Asia: Conclusions from Four Country Studies.* United Nations Research Institute for Social Development, Geneva

Pathak, B.S., Rogers, P. & Pahoja, M.H. (1981). *Producer Gas Systems and Agricultural Applications: Proceedings of a Workshop held in New Delhi, December 5, 1981.* Indian Society of Agricultural Engineers, New Delhi

Pearse, A. (1980). *Seeds of Plenty, Seeds of Want: Social and Economic Implications of the Green Revolution.* Clarendon Press, Oxford

Poleman, T.T. (1981). A reappraisal of the extent of world hunger. *Food Policy,* 6, 4 November, 236–52

Rajaraman, Indira (1977). Growth and poverty in rural areas of the Indian State of Punjab. In *Poverty and Landlessness in Rural Asia.* International Labour Office, Geneva, pp. 61–74

Ryan, J.G., Virmani, S.M. & Swindale, L.D. (1982). Potentials and challenges from deep black soils in relatively dependable rainfall regions of India. Paper presented at the Seminar on Innovative Technologies for Integrated Rural Development, New Delhi

Sangal, S.P. (1980). Groundwater resources and development in India. Paper to Seminar on Development and Management of Ground Water Resources, Indian Association of Geohydrologists, Vigyan Bhawan, New Delhi

Seckler, D. (1980). 'Malnutrition': an intellectual odyssey. Paper presented at the Annual Meeting of the Western Agricultural Economic Association, Las Cruses, New Mexico

(1981). The new era in irrigation management in India. Ford Foundation, New Delhi (mimeo)

Sen, Amartya (1981). *Poverty and Famines: An Essay on Entitlement and Deprivation*. Clarendon Press, Oxford

Singh, Bharat (1979). *Fundamentals of Irrigation Engineering*, 6th edn. Nem Chand & Bros., Roorkee, India

Sukhatme, P.V. (1977). Malnutrition and poverty. 9th Lal Bahadur Shastri Memorial Lecture, Indian Agricultural Research Institute, New Delhi

Swaminathan, M.S. (1980). Indian forestry at the crossroads. In *Report of the Seminar on Community Forestry*, Ranchi Consortium for Community Forestry, Ranchi, Bihar, pp. 1–8

(1981). Plant breeding in preparation for the 21st century. Meghnad Saha Medal Lecture

UNRISD (1974). *The Social and Economic Implications of Large-Scale Introduction of New Varieties of Foodgrain*. United Nations Research Institute for Social Development, Geneva

Vohra, B.B. (1980). *A Policy for Land and Water*. Sardar Patel Memorial Lectures, Department of Environment, Govt. of India

Wade, R. & Chambers, R. (1980). Managing the main system: canal irrigation's blind spot. *Economic and Political Weekly*, 15, 39, Review of Agriculture, September, A-107–12

Wickham, T.H. & Valera, A. (1979). Practices and accountability for better water management. In D.C. Taylor & T.H. Wickham (eds.), *Irrigation Policy and the Management of Irrigation Systems in Southeast Asia*, The Agricultural Development Council, Inc., Bangkok, pp. 61–75

Index

Africa, *see* East Africa, Tanzania, Uganda, Zambia
agrarian reform, 18–35, 79, 274, 369
Agrarian Research and Training Institute, 321
agrarian unrest, 20, 31, 68, 78–80, 349, 362, 364
agriculture
    colonisation, 42–3, 173–4, 176, 197, 270–8, 316–36
    ecology, 113, 182, 307
    economics, 6, 24, 199, 201, 271
    enclosure, 2
    encroachment, 126, 186
    innovations, 4, 23, 24, 144, 151, 154, 198, 259, 297
    intensification, 44, 116, 147, 197, 198, 318, 364
    involution, 42, 168
    labour, and employment, 8, 104, 113, 117, 156, 162, 168, 328
    land use, 137, 141–7, 154, 161, 201–2, 274, 288
    markets, 57, 67, 71, 147, 151, 157, 163, 263–4
    output, 7, 22, 30, 146, 163, 207, 298–300, 305, 317, 353
    productivity, 6, 10, 28, 113, 117, 128, 157, 164, 204–9, 317, 333
    research, 45–6, 47, 244, 297, 371–4
    technology, 3, 43–4, 49, 146, 162, 164, 170, 298, 348, 362, 364–5, 373
    yields, 5, 11, 12, 45, 114, 146, 160, 162, 166–7, 181–3, 196, 209, 299, 302, 349–9, 362
    see also farm size, Green Revolution, irrigation, land tenure, shifting cultivation, and particular crops

Agro-Refinance Development Corporation, 60, 64
aid, *see* international aid
Alaknada river, 109, 112, 122
Almora district, 131
Andhra Pradesh, 75, 264, 265
Anuradhapura district, 296, 297, 302, 304, 305

Bangalore, 153, 257, 280, 282–6, 295
Bangalore region villages, 285
Bangladesh, 194, 206, 208, 212, 339, 342–50, 363, 366
Bangladesh Rice Research Institute, 194, 199
Barisal district, 195, 206, 207, 209, 339, 354, 355
barley, 113
beans, 29, 31, 168
Belgium, 8, 10
Bengal, 40, 43, 54, 339, 341, 351
Bhola island, 339, 353, 354
Bihar, 87, 88, 91, 96, 365, 369
Bokaro, 98, 257
Bolivia, 20, 25, 29, 33
Borlaug, N., 365
British:
    in Ceylon, 173–4, 297, 316
    in East Africa, 272, 276
    in India, 39–41, 43, 48, 89–90, 94, 99, 119–20, 133
buffaloes, 114, 156

Calcutta, 103, 256
canals, 40, 139, 154, 160, 182, 367–69, 320, 322
capital, 33, 41, 54, 56, 69, 75, 188, 192, 326–7
capitalism, 18, 24, 26, 33, 41, 154
cassava, 372
caste, 102, 118, 130, 155–6, 289–90, 364
cattle, 11, 44, 114, 222
cereals, *see* particular crops

Ceylon, ix, 173–4, 296–7
Chamoli district, 120, 126
Chayanov model, 104, 273, 327
chena, *see* shifting cultivation
Chile, 21, 22, 28, 30
chillies, 146, 148–9, 310
China, 165, 347
Chitrakoot, 371, 373
Chota Nagpur, 99, 105, 106
cities, *see* urban
Civil Supplies Corporation, 61, 73, 76
climate, *see* cyclones, drought, evapotranspiration, flood, rainfall, seasonality
Coimbatore district, 53, 66
Colombia, 21, 27
colonisation, *see* population migration
Comilla district, 195, 197, 206, 207, 209
cooperatives, 26, 32, 34, 59, 62, 66, 75, 80, 100, 331
cost/benefit analysis, 318, 319
cotton, 28, 40, 59, 64, 74, 261
Cotton Corporation of India, 59, 61, 62, 74, 78
credit, *see* capital
    crop rotations, 6, 112, 113–14, 116, 198–200;
    see also seasonality
Cuba, 20, 22, 30
cumbu, *see* millets
cyclones, 339, 350–2

Deccan, 43, 154
Delhi, 124, 130, 256, 287–93
Delhi region villages, 287–8
Denmark, 8
development, *see* agriculture, planning
Dhaka (Dacca), 195, 196
Dhaka district, 195, 197, 209
diet, *see* nutrition
diffusion, *see* agricultural innovations
Dinajpur district, 208
Doab, 40, 50

382 Index

draught animals, *see* buffaloes, cattle, horses
drought, 29, 42, 120, 188, 222, 307, 308
Dry Zone, *see* Sri Lanka
dung, 6, 114, 121, 125, 222, 292

East Africa, 270–7
ecology, *see* agriculture, forests, soils
ecosystems, 114–15, 223
Ecuador, 21, 27, 34
energy, 153, 156, 163, 301, 366, 370
    Energy Ratio, 159, 165, 170
    Gross Energy Productivity, 157
    in rice cultivation, 159–70
    Surplus Energy Income, 158
England, 2, 7, 10, 13
erosion, 113, 114–15, 155, 339, 341
evapotranspiration, 196

farm size, 23, 148–9, 155, 161, 175, 183–6, 195, 203, 324, 334
Farmer, B.H., ix–x, 50, 81, 87, 137, 153, 198, 253, 270, 296, 307, 312, 315, 318, 336, 376
fertiliser, 4, 13, 59, 125, 144, 146, 157, 165, 183, 194, 206, 222, 229, 363
finance, *see* capital
fish, 357, 358
flood, 42, 115, 188, 221, 339, 350–2, 354, 368
food, *see* nutrition and particular crops
Food and Agriculture Organisations, 6, 64
Food Corporation of India, 59, 61, 62, 64, 73
forests, 97, 114–15, 123, 125–6, 142, 197, 273, 370–1, 376; *see also* mangrove
France, 2, 3, 7, 10
fruits, 10, 25

Gal Oya Scheme, 318, 325, 326
Ganga (Ganges) river, 42, 97, 110, 112, 339
Garhwal district, 109–12, 118–33
Garhwali villages, 129–31
geomorphology, 307, 339–42
Germany, 8, 11
gingelly, 142, 147
Gini coefficient, 67, 148–9, 178, 186, 187, 191

Godaveri, 50
Green Revolution, 1, 19, 28, 33, 37, 46, 49, 87, 144, 153, 156, 165, 170, 194, 270, 298, 308, 311, 362–5, 368
    Bangladesh, 194, 363
    Bihar, 87, 104
    Garhwal, 116
    India, 37, 46–51, 362
    Karnataka, 156, 160–5
    Latin America, 19, 33–4
    Mexico, 33
    Punjab, 40, 362
    Sri Lanka, x, 175, 298, 300, 302, 308, 311
    Tamil Nadu, x, 44, 144, 148, 308
    Western Europe, 1, 13
    see also agriculture, irrigation, rice
ground water, 307–11, 355, 369–70
groundnut, 44, 261, 276, 310
Gujarat, 40, 50
Gurkhas, 118–20, 124

Hambantota district, x, 303, 315, 336
Haryana, 60, 362
high yielding varieties (HYVs), 44–5, 365, 371–2
    other crops, 31, 44, 263, 365, 371–2
    rice in Bangladesh, 194–5, 198–206, 209, 213, 216, 347–49, 354
    rice in India, 45–6, 144–6, 160, 162, 261, 363, 365
    rice in Sri Lanka, 175, 297, 303
    wheat, 261, 362, 363
    see also Green Revolution, rice
Himalaya, 109, 112, 126
horses, 10, 13
households:
    caste structure, 102–3, 149
    demographic structure, 185, 329
    incomes, 103, 170, 174, 177–81, 277
    land holdings, 102–3, 105, 148, 161, 175–83, 328, 373
    methodology of studies, 153, 177
    see also farm size

Ilsha river, 353
implements, 10, 13, 44, 114, 157, 165

income disparities, 174, 177–81, 186–9, 276
India, 37, 55, 131, 253, 280, 362, 369
industry, 74, 78, 98, 111, 169, 257–9, 284
international aid, 64, 302, 316, 349–51
International Crops Research Institute for the Semi-Arid Tropics, 138, 372, 373
International Rice Research Institute, 160, 194, 372
Ireland, 8, 10
irrigation, 45, 47, 96, 113, 138–9, 154, 162, 166–7, 174, 182, 198, 201, 205, 274, 296–312, 317–36, 355, 365, 367–70; *see also* canals, pumps, tanks, wells
Ishurdi, 221

Jamshedpur, 98, 101
Java, 168
jhangora, *see* millets
Jharkhand, 87, 88, 96
Joshi, Sharad, 71, 77, 79

Kalawewa, 297, 301
Kalpattu village, 365
Kandalama, 301
Karnataka, 75, 153, 163, 280
Kenya, 273, 274
Kerala, 42
Khunti, 101
Kilvenmanai village, 364
Kongu, 40, 43
Kotdwara, 111, 113, 121
Kotla Mubarakpur village, 287–93
Kumaon, 110, 118, 132
Kurunegala district, 302, 303, 304, 305

labour migration, *see* population
land settlement, *see* agricultural colonisation
land tenure, 20–4, 30–1, 102, 155, 161, 175, 183–6, 195, 197, 206–9, 271, 275, 278, 324, 327, 357, 369
landlords, 3, 20, 25, 42, 148, 197, 274, 364
Latin America, *see* countries
Lorenz curve, 178–9, 183
livestock, 23, 29, 114, 125; *see also* buffaloes, cattle, horses

Index

machinery, 2, 5, 10, 13, 44, 144, 157, 163, 188–9
Madhya Pradesh, 91
Madras, 40, 44, 47, 48, 54, 55, 67
Mahanadi project, 368
Maharashtra, 40, 54, 55, 68
Mahaweli project, 301–2, 306, 315–17, 319–20, 322, 324, 326, 332–5
maize, 10, 29, 31, 75
malaria, 109, 173, 297, 325
Malthusian model, 119, 342, 349
mandua, see millets
Mandya district, 153, 160, 164
mangrove, 339, 342, 355–8
Mannar district, 303
manure, *see* dung
markets, *see* agriculture
Marx, 2, 20, 38, 331
Meghna river, 341, 353, 354
merchants, 50, 54–81, 258; *see also* agricultural markets
Mexico, 18, 20, 27, 28, 29, 31, 33, 369
migration, *see* population
milk, 4, 114, 157, 163
millets, 99, 113, 116, 142, 155, 261, 372
Monergala district, x
Mussoorie, 124, 130
Mymensingh district, 206

Narayanasamy Naidu, 77, 80
Narmada valley, 40, 41, 43, 50
Nepal, 132
Netherlands, 8, 11
Nicaragua, 18, 20, 28
North Arcot district, x, 68, 146, 164, 308–10, 364
Norway, 10
nutrition, 7, 11, 25, 158–9, 244, 364, 366

Pabna district, 221
paddy, *see* rice
Pakistan, 341, 348; *see also* Bangladesh, Bengal, Punjab
Panchayati Raj programme, 261–2, 264
Panimara village, 195–209
Parakrama Samudra scheme, 176, 181
peasants, 3, 20, 24, 25, 41, 87, 155, 162, 173–4, 271, 317, 328–31, 335
Penaranda river, 368
Peru, 21, 28, 29, 30, 34

pests and pesticides, 13, 47, 165, 207, 222
Philippines, 166, 168, 347
planning:
 agrarian, 48, 87, 96, 153, 175, 212, 276
 development, 57, 194, 253–6, 265, 270–8, 362–7
 ideology and, 332, 335
 irrigation, 306–7, 315, 316, 325–6, 332–6, 355
 land colonisation, 270–8, 323–6
 national, 256–7, 262, 268, 345–7, 349
 rural, 253, 260–6
 service centre, 262–6, 325, 330
 urban, 256–7, 263–4, 280, 286, 292–4
ploughs, *see* implements
politics, 20–1, 24, 26, 70, 71, 106, 323, 337, 369; *see also* agrarian unrest, agrarian reform, cooperatives, socialism
Polonnaruwa district, 176, 302, 303, 318
Pooranur village, 138–51
population:
 control, 118, 346–7
 growth, 10, 23, 43, 96, 110, 117, 120, 125, 147, 156, 271–2, 342–7, 374
 migration, 42, 96, 109, 123–4, 127–31, 173, 185, 197, 272–4, 316, 365
 pressure, 42, 97, 112, 126, 127, 342–3
 structure, 110, 120, 147, 343–5
potatoes, 10, 12, 25
Pune, 373
Punjab, 40, 43, 44, 50, 60, 362, 364
pumps, 44, 144, 154, 162, 355, 369–70
purana villages, 175, 333, 335

Q-analysis, 213–20, 237

ragi, see millets
rainfall, 110, 139, 196, 298, 300, 307; *see also* seasonality, drought
Ramanathapuram district, 137
Ramnad district, 71, 138, 141
Ranchi and district, 96, 98, 101, 257
Randam village, 107, 146
remittances, 130–1
research, *see* agriculture

Reserve Bank of India, 63, 75, 76, 93
rice, 42, 50, 98, 142, 160, 186, 197, 304–5, 348, 354–5
 cultivation methods, 44–5, 113–14, 144–6, 155, 159–60, 164–9, 181, 183, 197–200, 222, 307, 310, 320–2, 347
 government policy towards, 29, 31, 34, 169, 311, 349
 in diet, 159, 216
 local varieties, 159, 197, 204, 216
 marketing, 59
 output, 194, 298–300, 347, 368
 soils, 141, 181–2, 196–7, 321, 351–5
 yields, 115, 146, 165, 166–9, 181–3, 209, 299, 347–9
 see also Green Revolution, high yielding varieties, irrigation, areas where grown
rice mills, 72, 180, 189

Salem district, 71
salinity, 138, 353, 354, 368
Sarawak, 165, 166
Sarbai village, 101–4
seasonality, 113–14, 120, 138, 154, 181, 190, 196–9, 202, 210, 233, 307, 308–9, 347
service centres, 262–6, 285
Shahbazpur river, 339, 341, 353
sharecropping, 175, 188, 200, 206, 208, 357
shifting cultivation, 166, 273, 304, 321, 328–9, 336
Singhbhum district, 98
social organisation, *see* caste, households, land tenure, landlords, peasants, sharecropping
socialism, 26, 78, 329, 332
soils, 46, 113, 114, 141, 154, 181–2, 191, 196, 321, 339, 353, 355
sorghum, 31, 372
South Asian Studies Centre, Cambridge, ix–x
Sri Lanka, x, 173, 296, 299, 300, 306, 311, 315, 316, 335, 348, 368, 369
 Dry Zone, ix, 173–6, 296–311, 316–36
 Wet Zone, 316
State Bank of India, 93
state trading corporations, 63, 65, 73

sugar:
  beet, 10, 12
  cane, 28, 40, 44, 155, 162, 321
Sunderbans, 339, 342, 356, 358
Surinam, 165, 167
Sweden, 8
Switzerland, 8, 11

Tamil Nadu, 42, 44, 53, 55, 68, 71, 75, 80, 136, 149, 151, 307, 309–11, 364
Tamil Nadu Civil Supplies Corporation, 59, 62
Tanganyika, 272, 276
tanks, 139, 141, 144, 296–7, 307–8, 319
Tanzania, 165, 273, 329
tea, 121, 122, 275
technology, *see* agriculture
Terai, 109, 121, 132
terracing, 113
Tetulia river, 339, 341, 353
Thaiyur village, 107
Thalpotha village, 176–89
Thanjavur district, 68, 364
Tirunelveli district, 68, 71
Tirupur, 71, 74, 75

tools, *see* implements
towns, *see* urban
tractors, *see* machinery
tribal policies, 87–96
Trichy district, 71
tubewells, *see* wells
turnip, 4, 10

Uda Walawe scheme, 315, 318, 319, 322, 326
Uganda, 272, 273, 275, 277
United States of America, 21, 167, 169
urban:
  bias, 38, 77, 253, 275
  employment, 130, 258, 288–91
  growth, 271, 280–93
  influence, 25, 54, 110, 122, 138, 151, 253, 256–60, 263
  unrest, 34
  see also service centres
Urissa, 91
Uttar Pradesh, 109, 128, 365, 369

Vaigai river, 138

Vavuniya district, 303, 310–11
vegetables, 10, 25, 29, 113, 142, 223
Venezuela, 20, 27, 29, 30, 34
village studies methodology, 136–7, 153, 329
villages, *see* Bangalore region, Delhi region, Garhwali, Kalpattu, Kilvenmanai, Kotla Mubarakpur, Panimara, Pooranur, *purana*, Randam, Sarbai, Thaiyur, Thalpotha, Wangala

Wangala village, 154–64
wells, 41, 68, 87, 197, 199, 310–11; *see also* ground water
West Bengal, 54, 68, 208, 369
Western Europe, 1–14
wheat, 4, 12, 14, 41, 59, 113, 215, 261, 362, 363

yields, *see* agriculture, rice
Yunnan, 168

Zambia, 275